Microsoft Silverlight 4 Business Application Development

Beginner's Guide

Build Enterprise-Ready Business Applications with Silverlight

Frank LaVigne

Cameron Albert

[PACKT] PUBLISHING

BIRMINGHAM - MUMBAI

Microsoft Silverlight 4 Business Application Development
Beginner's Guide

First published: April 2010

Production Reference: 1300310

Published by Packt Publishing Ltd.
32 Lincoln Road
Olton
Birmingham, B27 6PA, UK.

ISBN 978-1-847199-76-8

www.packtpub.com

Cover Image by Tina Negus (tina_manthorpe@sky.com)

Credits

Authors

Frank LaVigne

Cameron Albert

Reviewers

Joel Cochran

Laurent Duveau

Acquisition Editor

Kerry George

Technical Editor

Aditya Belpathak

Indexer

Monica Ajmera Mehta

Editorial Team Leader

Aanchal Kumar

Project Team Leader

Lata Basantani

Project Coordinator

Poorvi Nair

Proofreader

Lesley Harrison

Graphics

Geetanjali Sawant

Production Coordinator

Aparna Bhagat

Cover Work

Aparna Bhagat

About the Author

Frank LaVigne has been hooked on software development since he was 12, when he got his own Commodore 64 computer. Since then, he's worked as developer for financial firms on Wall Street and also in Europe. He has worked on various Tablet PC solutions and on building advanced user experiences in Silverlight and WPF. He lives in the suburbs of Washington, DC. He founded the CapArea.NET User Group Silverlight Special Interest Group and has been recognized by Microsoft as a Tablet PC MVP. He blogs regularly at www.FranksWorld.com.

> I would like to thank my wife Roberta for always being there for me. To my son Jacob, my world changed when I first got to hold you in my arms. Lastly, I would like to dedicate this book to my dad, who taught me the value of hard work and perseverance.

Cameron Albert is an independent software development consultant, with over ten years of experience, specializing in Microsoft technologies such as Silverlight, WPF, WCF, SQL Server, and ASP.NET. Having worked in the medical, insurance, and media/entertainment industries, he has been involved in a variety of development solutions featuring a broad range of technical issues.

Cameron also dabbles in game development, utilizing Silverlight and XNA. He maintains a blog that details his exploits in the development world at http://www.cameronalbert.com. Cameron lives with his wife in Connecticut.

> I would like to thank my wife Lisa for being the light of my life and Frank for thinking highly enough of me to include me in the writing of this book.

About the Reviewers

Joel Cochran, an AS/400 RPG programmer earlier, Joel is a former Contributing Editor for ITJungle.com (originally MidrangeServer.com) and has taught various programming languages and Internet technologies at Blue Ridge Community college. He has been developing in C# full time, since 2003 and now focuses exclusively on developing WPF and Silverlight applications with Expression Blend. A self-described "Blend Evangelist", Joel is a frequent speaker at User Groups, Code Camps, and other Community events. He enjoys teaching and writing about these and other .NET technologies, which he happily shares on his blog at `http://www.developingfor.net`. Joel has served as the Director of Operations for Stonewall Technologies, Inc., in Staunton, VA, since 2000.

> I'd like to thank Frank LaVigne and Packt Publishing for bringing me in on this project; it has been a tremendous learning experience and I had a great time to boot! I'd also like to thank all of my great friends in the Mid Atlantic .NET developer community for their constant support and interest in these fantastic new technologies. Finally, I'd like to thank my wife Kim and children Heather and Justin, without them none of this would be worthwhile.

Laurent Duveau is a Silverlight expert, the technology that fascinates him. He has followed its development since the very beginning in 2007. He has had the opportunity to give a multitude of Silverlight presentations at conferences such as TechDays, DevTeach, CodeCamp, User Group, MSDN Tour, and W3C. Laurent is a Microsoft Certified Trainer (MCT) since 2004, as well as a Silverlight MVP, Silverlight Partner, and Silverlight Insider. He is the Vice President of RunAtServer Consulting, a company based in Montreal, QC, whose focus is on Silverlight projects, coaching, and training.

Table of Contents

Preface

Welcome to the world of **Rich Internet Applications (RIA)** and Silverlight. A world in which the user experience is paramount, and easy to use yet powerful applications are what we strive to create. Silverlight brings .NET developers into the RIA space in a big way, providing the controls we know with web and Windows development and allowing us to define a custom experience to best benefit the users of our applications.

The days of plain HTML web applications are coming to end, making way for more robust and powerful applications. Already the widespread use of AJAX has helped us deliver more user friendly applications and have opened doors that were shut to plain HTML. Silverlight takes this a step further by giving .NET developers what is essentially a thin client that runs within the user's environment and can communicate with our backend servers and services. The ability to make use of the user's memory to run our application rather than sending everything to the web server for processing improves overall user experience and removes some of the traditional application wait times and general unsatisfactory behavior of web applications.

This book will bring ASP.NET and Windows developers into the Silverlight realm by showing them how to leverage their existing .NET skills with Silverlight. The transition into Silverlight should be smooth by following the contents of the chapters in order. The intent is to introduce you to the concepts of Silverlight while getting you into the code right away. We will build on each chapter while creating an application for a fictitious company that creates specialty cakes. By using the concept of the cake company we can identify some real client needs and work to provide solutions using the Silverlight platform to deliver the results.

What this book covers

Chapter 1: Getting Started introduces Silverlight development including the concept of XAML, dependency properties, and some basic controls while leveraging existing .NET skills.

Chapter 2: Enhancing a Website with Silverlight covers the use of Expression Blend, container controls, the Visual State Manager, animation, and the designer/developer workflow, while adding Silverlight to an existing web site.

Chapter 3: Adding Rich Media explains how to include media such as video and audio into a Silverlight application and how to make use of Expression Encoder to prepare video for Silverlight.

Chapter 4: Taking the RIA Experience Further with Silverlight 4 introduces Deep Zoom, the Bing Map control, and the use of the Ink Presenter control to capture ink input from a tablet or touch screen, store information in isolated storage, and communicate with a web server via HTTP.

Chapter 5: Handling Data covers collecting and handling data input from a customer, saving input on the server using Windows Communication Foundation (WCF), and making use of the powerful data binding feature of Silverlight to bind customer data to Silverlight controls.

Chapter 6: Back Office Applications covers the implementation WCF RIA Services to provide a common middle tier between our server and Silverlight application and introduction to using Silverlight in SharePoint.

Chapter 7: Customer Service Application introduces how to build a simple customer service application to allow the business to process input from customers using the Entity Framework, WCF RIA Services and the DataForm control.

Chapter 8: Executive Dashboard Application covers the topic of making use of the charting controls in Silverlight with data binding to present reports to business decision makers.

Chapter 9: Delivery Application introduces the creation of an application for delivery personnel, including a signature capture control and next level usage of the Bind Maps control and API.

Chapter 10: Where to Go From Here includes a sample of the out-of-browser mode for Silverlight, a basic introduction to Windows Presentation Foundation (WPF), and a look to toward the future of Silverlight.

What you need for this book

You will need the following tools to view the samples and run the code provided. While the Expression tools are discussed and used within the book they are not a requirement to build Silverlight applications, they simply make it easier. Visual Studio 2010 provides a design view of XAML pages so that you can visually design the interface, which saves a lot of hand coding of XAML.

- Visual Studio 2010
- Silverlight 4 Tools for Visual Studio
- WCF RIA Services
- Expression Blend

- Expression Encoder
- SQL Express
- A SharePoint VPC or development installation (for the SharePoint samples)

Who this book is for

If you are a .NET developer who wants to build business applications with Silverlight, then this is the book for you. No experience of programming Silverlight is required. A basic understanding of Visual Studio, C#, .NET development, XML, and Web development concepts (HTTP, Services) is required.

Conventions

In this book, you will find a number of styles of text that distinguish between different kinds of information. Here are some examples of these styles, and an explanation of their meaning.

Code words in text are shown as follows: "Inside the `Default.html` file, you'll see the `object` tag that actually hosts the Silverlight control."

A block of code is set as follows:

```
<UserControl.Resources>
  <Style x:Name="biggerTextStyle" TargetType="Button">
    <Setter Property="FontSize" Value="18"/>
  </Style>
</UserControl.Resources>
```

When we wish to draw your attention to a particular part of a code block, the relevant lines or items are set in bold:

```
<UserControl.Resources>
  <Style x:Name="biggerTextStyle" TargetType="Button">
    <Setter Property="FontSize" Value="18"/>
  </Style>
</UserControl.Resources>
```

New terms and **important words** are shown in bold. Words that you see on the screen, in menus or dialog boxes for example, appear in the text like this: "Start Visual Studio and open the **CakeORamaApp** solution we created in the previous chapter".

> Warnings or important notes appear in a box like this.

> Tips and tricks appear like this.

Reader feedback

Feedback from our readers is always welcome. Let us know what you think about this book—what you liked or may have disliked. Reader feedback is important for us to develop titles that you really get the most out of.

To send us general feedback, simply send an email to feedback@packtpub.com, and mention the book title via the subject of your message.

If there is a book that you need and would like to see us publish, please send us a note in the **SUGGEST A TITLE** form on www.packtpub.com or email suggest@packtpub.com.

If there is a topic that you have expertise in and you are interested in either writing or contributing to a book on, see our author guide on www.packtpub.com/authors.

Customer support

Now that you are the proud owner of a Packt book, we have a number of things to help you to get the most from your purchase.

> **Downloading the example code for the book**
>
> Visit http://www.packtpub.com/files/code/9768_Code.zip to directly download the example code.
>
> The downloadable files contain instructions on how to use them.

Errata

Although we have taken every care to ensure the accuracy of our content, mistakes do happen. If you find a mistake in one of our books—maybe a mistake in the text or the code—we would be grateful if you would report this to us. By doing so, you can save other readers from frustration, and help us to improve subsequent versions of this book. If you find any errata, please report them by visiting http://www.packtpub.com/support, selecting your book, clicking on the **let us know** link, and entering the details of your errata. Once your errata are verified, your submission will be accepted and the errata added to any list of existing errata. Any existing errata can be viewed by selecting your title from http://www.packtpub.com/support.

Piracy

Piracy of copyright material on the Internet is an ongoing problem across all media. At Packt, we take the protection of our copyright and licenses very seriously. If you come across any illegal copies of our works, in any form, on the Internet, please provide us with the location address or website name immediately so that we can pursue a remedy.

Please contact us at copyright@packtpub.com with a link to the suspected pirated material.

We appreciate your help in protecting our authors, and our ability to bring you valuable content.

Questions

You can contact us at questions@packtpub.com if you are having a problem with any aspect of the book, and we will do our best to address it.

1
Getting Started

Welcome to the wonderful world of Silverlight, Microsoft's platform for building **Rich Internet Applications (RIA)**. *The earliest versions of Silverlight focused on rich media, interactivity, and animation. Now Silverlight has gotten down to business with new features geared towards making business application development faster and easier. Of course, you still have access to all the graphics and animation tools. With the usability bar raised considerably by Web 2.0, end users are demanding more from their applications. Silverlight 4 will help you deliver steak and the sizzle to business application development.*

In this chapter, we shall:

- ◆ Leverage your existing .NET skill set to Silverlight
- ◆ Discuss the new concepts of Silverlight
- ◆ Discuss what software is needed to develop Silverlight applications
- ◆ Develop a Silverlight application

Skills needed

To get the most out of Silverlight business application development, you must be comfortable with Visual Studio, and have some knowledge of .NET development, be it ASP. NET development or Windows Forms development. As many of the core concepts of .NET development are the same across the different target platforms, the more accustomed you are to them, the easier your transition into Silverlight will be. In addition to basic .NET development skills, you should feel comfortable with XML. You need not have read the specification, but you must know your attributes from your elements, and your namespaces from your angle brackets. You should know what the CLR is and know how to tell the difference between your DLLs and your HTMLs.

As developers, we are all on a journey of learning and discovery. I was fortunate enough to have delved into the worlds of ASP.NET, Windows Forms, and WPF before encountering Silverlight. Now, let's discuss who you are and see how best to approach Silverlight.

A special note for ASP.NET developers

With web applications, the mantra for development, testing, and deployment might as well be "Write once. Run anywhere", but test everywhere in every possible configuration. The more complex your interaction code, the more you have to worry about testing your code on a myriad of browsers, platforms, and mobile devices. You know there's got to be a better way, and there is; Silverlight. It encapsulates all of the interactive features that AJAX, jQuery, and so on provide and much more. Best of all, Silverlight applications run the same way, regardless of platform or browser. Your testing burden is significantly lighter. Your applications, whether external facing or behind-the-firewall intranet applications, will benefit greatly from having Silverlight incorporated. Your users will appreciate the added interactivity and inclusion of rich media, and you, as a developer, will appreciate not having to worry about browser and platform compatibility.

A special note for Windows Forms developers

As a 'SmartClient' developer you've endured the slings and arrows of web developers who taunt you with deployment concerns and platform portability concerns. Deep down, you knew they had valid arguments about cross platform deployment, but you were frustrated at the lack of awareness of **ClickOnce**. ClickOnce has largely erased the deployment headaches normally associated with 'thick clients', a term you find both antiquated and offensive when it is applied to Windows Forms. In a very real way, you already understand the need for a declarative language for defining user interfaces on client applications, especially if you have already written code to parse out an XML file or some other data source to render Windows Forms controls to create 'forms on demand'. Microsoft has not deprecated the technology, but it is also not releasing new versions. The time for this technology is coming to an end.

The direct successor to Windows Forms is **WPF(Windows Presentation Foundation)**, which shares many traits in common with Silverlight. Despite the initial learning curve, the journey to Silverlight will be well worth it, as you will have learned quite a bit about WPF as well. Two technologies for the 'price' of one!

A special note for WPF developers

If you are already comfortable with WPF, then you are well prepared to enter the world of Silverlight. You are already familiar with many of the key concepts such as XAML, Storyboards, and dependency properties. However, your journey is not without its challenges. WPF and Silverlight do share a common language and philosophy, but there are numerous differences between the two platforms. Silverlight has been built from the ground up, to be cross-platform and web centric, whereas WPF has been designed to develop applications only on Windows.

> Silverlight's original 'codename' was WPF/E, or WPF Everywhere.

WPF has access to the whole .NET Framework and all the resources on a user's machine. However, due to security concerns, Silverlight runs in a 'sandbox' mode. This means that the Silverlight runtime has certain security restrictions, even with full trust mode enabled. For example, Silverlight applications do not have direct access to the full file system.

A special note for Flash/FLEX developers

Flash developers have been at the forefront of RIA development for nearly as long as there has been a World Wide Web to host Rich Applications on. However, times are changing, competition is coming to this space and Silverlight will add more tools to the tool belts of web designers and developers everywhere. Silverlight and Flash come from different perspectives on RIA, and if you know both, you can pick the platform that is best for the needs of your projects.

New concepts of Silverlight

If you haven't developed WPF applications before, there will be quite a few things in Silverlight that may be new to you at first. However, even if you have experience with developing WPF applications, there are still a few surprises in store for you.

Separation of presentation and Logic

A good developer works hard to separate logical elements and presentation code. In web development terms, this means specifying your logical elements in HTML and styling those logical elements with CSS. HTML and CSS use different syntaxes and switching between the two can test one's patience. Fortunately for us, separation of logic and presentation is a key design principle in Silverlight, not an afterthought like CSS was to HTML. **XAML(eXtensible Application Markup Language)** is the vehicle for providing this separation by splitting the concerns of logic and presentation, while providing a basis for a smoother workflow between developers and designers. Fortunately, Karsten Januszewski and Jaime Rodriguez have written an excellent white paper on that very subject and much more. It is available online at: http://windowsclient.net/wpf/white-papers/thenewiteration.aspx.

XAML: Relax it's just XML

XAML is just XML, that's it! There's no magic or hocus pocus behind it. It's simply a common way to serialize object graphs into XML. In other words, the elements and attributes that you see in XAML will ultimately manifest themselves as objects in memory. It's not a language per se, but it does have a common set of rules, patterns, and behaviors much like a language. In many ways XAML resembles HTML as both define an interface declaratively.

Consider the following example: a button on a web page. The code to implement this in ASP. NET is fairly straightforward:

```
<form id="form1" runat="server">
  <div>
    <asp:Button ID="Button1" runat="server" Text="Button" />
  </div>
</form>
```

The above code yields the following result:

The code to create a similar button in XAML is also quite straightforward:

```
<Grid x:Name="LayoutRoot" Background="White">
  <Button Width="100" Height="50" Content="Button"></Button>
</Grid>
```

And you get a very similar result, as you can see in the following screenshot:

You are also free to define elements in code, as well as in XAML. To create the same button in code, here is the equivalent of writing it out in C#:

```
Button b = new Button();
b.Width = 100;
b.Height = 50;
b.Content = "Button";

LayoutRoot.Children.Add(b);
LayoutRoot.Background = new SolidColorBrush(Colors.White);
```

You'll see that, in both code and XAML, you are defining a button, setting attributes, adding it to a grid, and setting the grid's background to white. If all that seems a little confusing right now, don't worry, pretty soon XAML will be second nature to you.

Astute readers will notice that I included `Width` and `Height` attributes in my **Button** declaration. In the *Have a go hero* section, you'll have the opportunity to remove the parameters and see what happens.

Dependency properties

Dependency properties are a 'new wrinkle on the old reliable property' system of the **CLR**. On the surface, you may not even notice anything different about them. However, upon closer inspection you will see that dependency properties provide a means to compute a property's value, based on other inputs as well as adding a notification system for when a dependency property's value has changed. For now, think of a dependency property as a regular property that Silverlight has a little more control over managing. We'll learn much more about dependency properties as the book progresses.

Bumps along the road to Silverlight bliss

Nearly every developer who starts off in Silverlight has hit the following snags. To save you the trouble, I have pointed them out below, to avoid frustration.

GIF files need not apply

Silverlight can do a lot of things, but one thing it will not do is load a `GIF` file. Many developers are surprised to learn this, but the `GIF` file format is somewhat antiquated. It supports only 8 bits of color and one bit of transparency. In the 21st century our video cards have evolved, with 24-bit color and 8-bits of transparency supported by the `PNG` file format. If you have image assets that are only available to you in `GIF` format, you can easily convert them to `PNG` or `JPG` using your favorite image editing software. If you're starting to get anxious about other popular web image formats such as, `JPG`, then don't. `JPG`s are supported in Silverlight.

Visibility != Boolean

Another point of confusion for many .NET developers is the `Visibility` property. It has always been a Boolean. After all, a visual element is either visible or it's not. What could be simpler?

In Silverlight, you will find that the Visibility property is no longer a Boolean but is now an enumeration of two values: Collapsed and Visible. Why complicate such a simple concept? Why use an enumeration when a Boolean has worked fine for all these years? The answer lies in WPF.

In WPF, an element's visibility consists of three states: Visible, Collapsed, and Hidden. Collapsed tells the layout engine to rearrange elements on the screen, whereas Hidden does not. In order to facilitate compatibility between WPF and Silverlight, the Silverlight team decided to stick with this model. However, Silverlight does not support the Hidden state.

> Remember: Silverlight has only two visibility states: **Visible** and **Collapsed.**

It's Button.Content, not Button.Text

If you looked at my earlier XAML sample, you may have noticed that the Button object used a property called Content. Many seasoned developers would have expected the property to be Button.Text. Why would Silverlight do this differently? The answer will change the way you think about Silverlight, control layout, and maybe even life in general.

Consider the following XAML:

```
<Grid x:Name="LayoutRoot" Background="White">
  <Button Height="50" Width="100" >
    <Button.Content>
      <CheckBox Content="CheckBox"></CheckBox>
    </Button.Content>
  </Button>
</Grid>
```

The Content property has now been expanded into an XML element which contains a **CheckBox** control. The rendered XAML can be seen in the following screenshot:

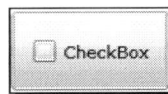

But wait, there's more!

The **CheckBox** also has a Content property, which means that we could place yet another control inside it! We can do this by inputting the following code:

```
<Grid x:Name="LayoutRoot" Background="White">
  <Button Height="50" Width="100">
```

```
    <Button.Content>
      <CheckBox>
        <CheckBox.Content>
          <Button Content="Button"></Button>
        </CheckBox.Content>
      </CheckBox>
    </Button.Content>
  </Button>
</Grid>
```

If we did that, we'd have the following screenshot:

The Content property of both the **Button** here and the **CheckBox** controls shows previously is a ContentPresenter, a special kind of container that can contain just about anything, including other ContentPresenters. The end result is a control that can contain other controls, which in turn can contain other controls, and so on. Whether or not this particular example provides for improved usability, is another matter entirely. However, it is nice to know that you can easily build something so strange and complex.

Imagine doing this in HTML or Windows Forms!

Tools needed

Now that we've covered the skills that are required to effectively use Silverlight, and saw the concepts which are new to Silverlight, let's go over what tools you will need to start developing in Silverlight.

At a bare minimum, you will need the following software installed on your Windows powered computer:

◆ Visual Studio 2010 or Visual Studio 2008 SP1 with Visual Studio Tools for Silverlight
◆ The Silverlight runtime
◆ Silverlight Toolkit
◆ Expression Blend 3

> The **Get Started** section on the official Silverlight site: http://silverlight.net/GetStarted/ will have the most up to date links and installation instructions.

Visual Studio 2008 or Visual Studio 2010

Visual Studio is the **Integrated Development Environment (IDE)** for developers working on Microsoft's .NET platform. You can use either Visual Studio 2008 or Visual Studio 2010. If you're already a .NET developer, then Visual Studio will feel very familiar to you. The following screenshot should look recognizable to you, even if you've never opened up a Silverlight project before. You can readily identify the **Solution Explorer, Toolbox** and all the usual suspects. ASP.NET developers will instantly recognize the split window pane of the rendered view and the markup view:

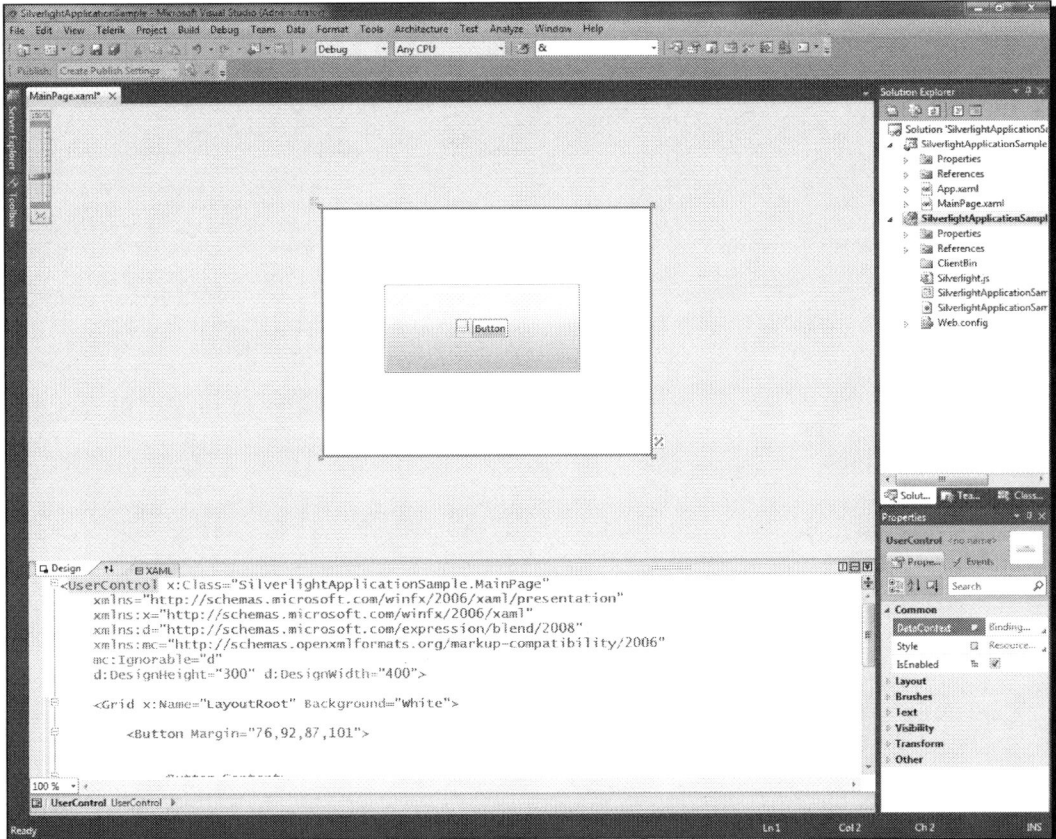

Silverlight runtime

To develop applications in Silverlight, you will need to have the Silverlight plugin installed. If you come across a page that uses Silverlight and you do not have it installed, you will likely see an image like the one in the following screenshot:

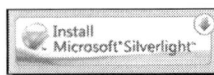

Silverlight toolkit

The Silverlight toolkit contains Silverlight controls, components, and utilities built by the Microsoft Silverlight product team. The toolkit adds extra functionality quickly for designers and developers outside of the regular Silverlight product development cycle. It includes full source code, unit tests, sample code, and documentation for the over two dozen controls in the toolkit. You can download the Silverlight Toolkit for free at: `http://www.codeplex.com/Silverlight`.

Expression Blend

Developers often find Expression Blend's stark interface somewhat confusing at first. Gone are the familiar layout of tools and properties from the last several versions of Visual Studio. Expression Blend is primarily aimed at designers, whereas Visual Studio is aimed at developers. Accordingly, Blend's interface more closely resembles essential design tools such as Adobe Illustrator or Adobe Photoshop, as you can see in the following screenshot:

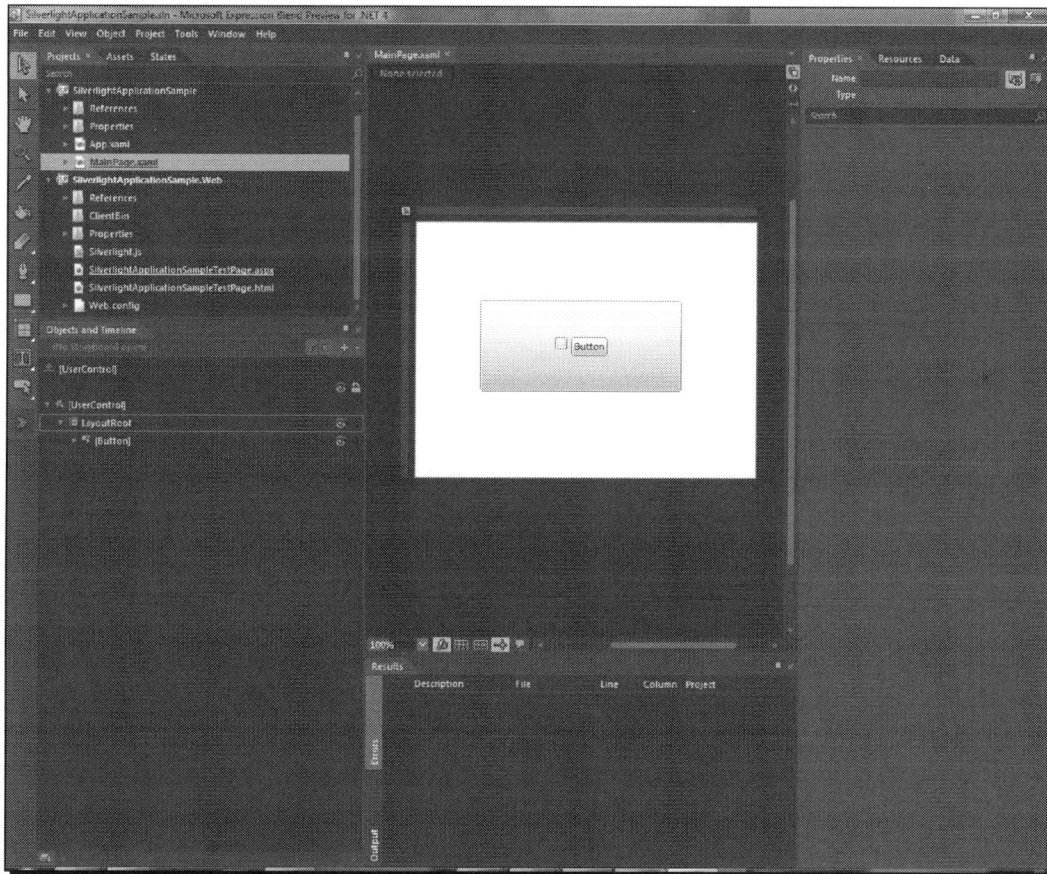

I know what you're thinking: "I'm a developer so why would I care about a silly design tool?" In this instance, you should resist the temptation to dismiss Expression Blend as nonessential.

Blend will make your work in Silverlight easier and maybe even more fun. If you are still not sure about the place of Expression Blend within your development toolkit, think of it as a really large XAML generator. While Visual Studio 2010 made incredible advances in the Silverlight developer experience, Blend still adds considerable value. Blend has a much better tool for creating animations and you can import assets directly from Adobe Photoshop and Adobe Illustrator into your Silverlight projects. You can certainly develop Silverlight applications without Blend, but once you see its power and elegance, Blend will become an essential part of your development toolkit.

Throughout the course of this book, we will be using Blend as well as Visual Studio. By the time you reach the end, you'll feel right at home with this great new tool.

Other useful tools

In many business application development situations, the bare minimum software tools will rarely get the development job done. While Visual Studio and Blend are fully-featured development and design tools, there are a few other essential tools that you should have in your Silverlight development toolkit.

Deep Zoom Composer

One of the coolest features of Silverlight is **Deep Zoom**, where your users can browse high resolution images, without having to wait for the files to download. A great example of Deep Zoom put to good use is Hard Rock's Memorabilia web site at: `http://memorabilia.hardrock.com`, where you can browse gigabytes of images instantly. If you want to create your own Deep Zoom experiences, you will need to download **Deep Zoom Composer**, which as of this writing is a free download from: `http://www.microsoft.com/downloads/details.aspx?FamilyID=457B17B7-52BF-4BDA-87A3-FA8A4673F8BF&displaylang=en`.

Silverlight Spy

Silverlight Spy is a utility that lets you peek into a running Silverlight application, enabling you to break down, analyze, and even alter the XAML or code of any Silverlight application. If you ever wondered "How they did it" or like to learn by reverse engineering, then this is the tool for you. Just remember to respect other's intellectual property.

> Silverlight Spy is available as a free trial download and will automatically install locally on your machine. You can download the Silverlight Spy trial at: `http://firstfloorsoftware.com/silverlightspy/download-silverlight-spy`.

When running, Silverlight Spy looks like this:

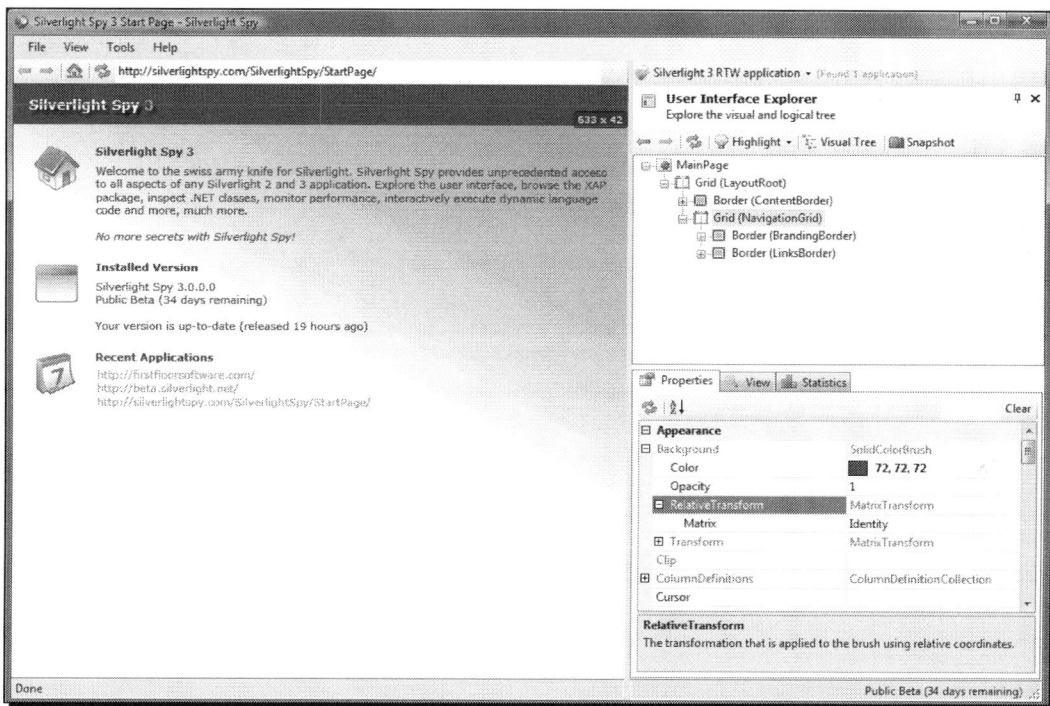

Expression Design

Expression Design is a vector graphics tool, and the ideal companion application to Expression Blend. If you're familiar with other vector drawing tools, Design, illustrated in the following screenshot, will look familiar to you:

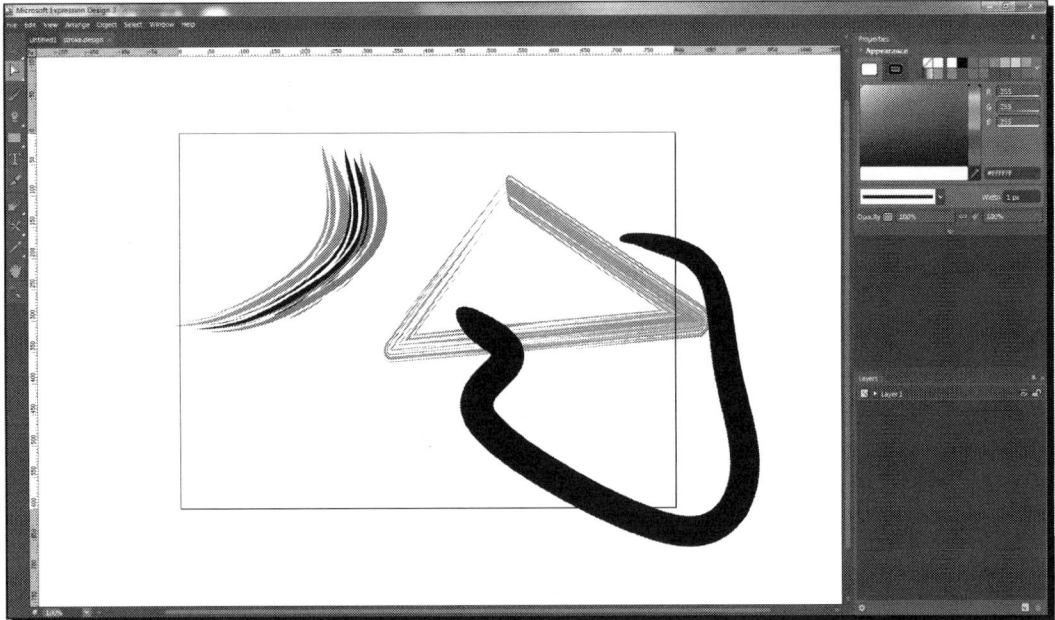

Indeed, Expression Design bears many similarities to other vector graphic tools, but its tight integration with XAML sets it apart. With Design, you can create graphics to use in your Silverlight applications, either by exporting the artwork to XAML, or by selecting elements and choosing **Copy XAML** from the **Edit** menu.

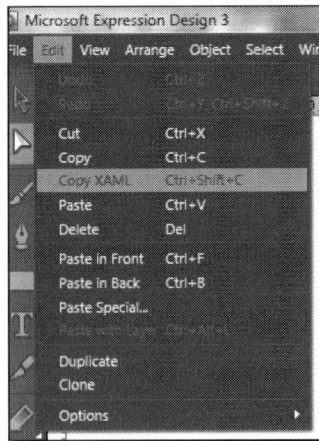

Expression Studio 3, includes Blend and Design, as well as Encoder, and Web. This suite package is available for purchase by MSDN subscribers with Visual Studio Professional MSDN Premium, and higher. For details, check out: `https://msdn.microsoft.com/en-us/subscriptions/securedownloads/default.aspx`.

Expression Encoder

Expression Encoder is a multimedia conversion and rudimentary editing tool. Silverlight supports certain media formats natively, and encoders can convert a wide array of video file formats into file formats that Silverlight supports.

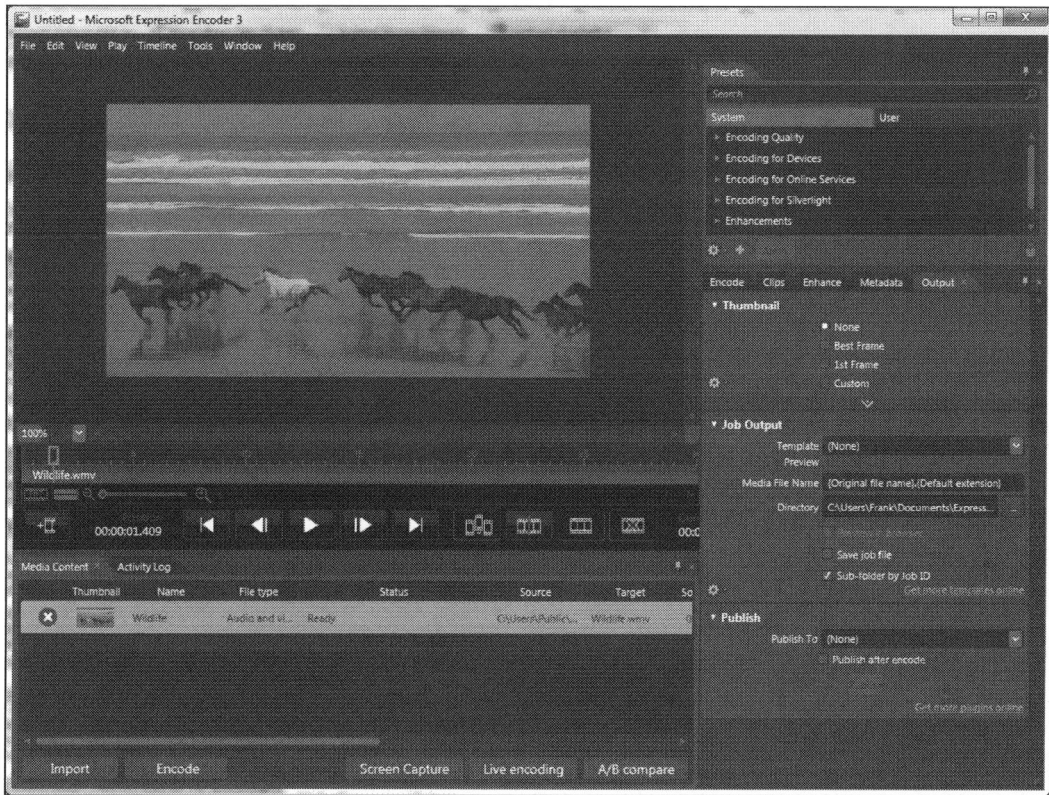

You can also enhance your media with overlays and advertising with Encoder. While this may sound daunting at first, Encoder's user interface is friendly and approachable. We'll focus on Expression Encoder and integrating rich media into your Silverlight solutions in Chapter 3.

InkScape

InkScape is an open source vector graphics editing application. If you do not have access to Adobe Illustrator or Expression Design, you can use InkScape for all your vector graphics needs.

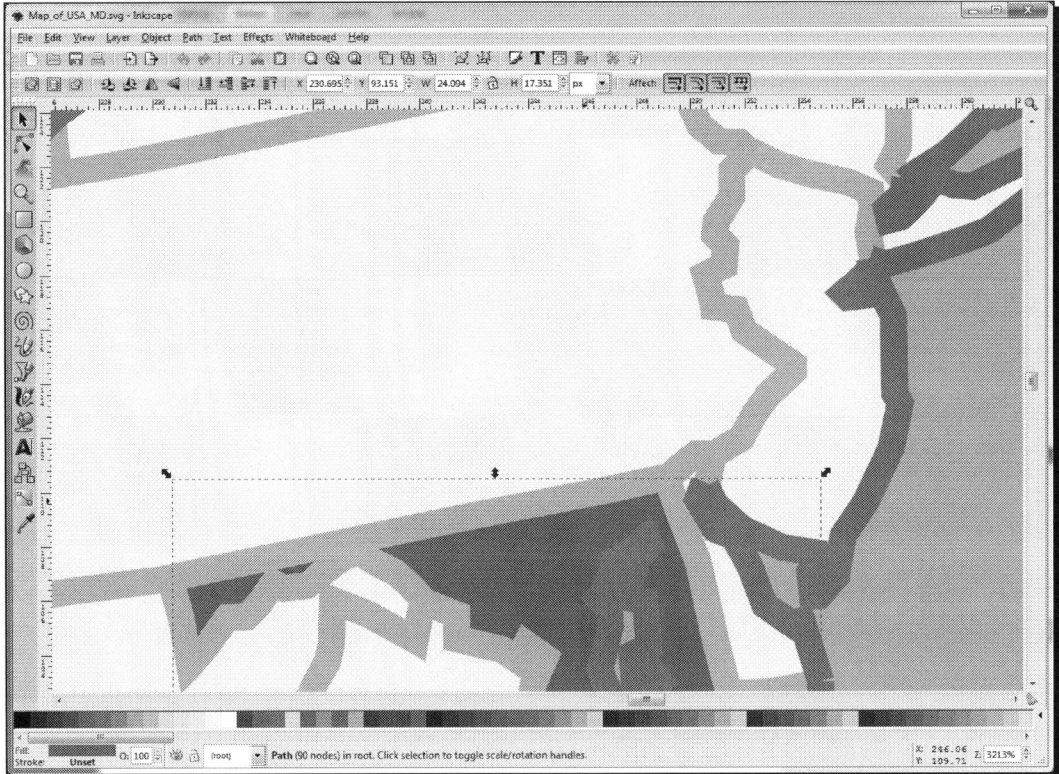

Even if you have other vector tools at your disposal, InkScape still has its benefits. It supports importing and exporting XAML files, tracing bitmaps images to vector graphics, and a myriad of other features. You can download InkScape for free at: http://www.inkscape.org/.

Time for action – creating a Silverlight project

Enough of the theory, let's create a Silverlight project and play around a bit. To do this you will need to do the following:

1. Launch Visual Studio and click on **File | New Project**.

2. Choose to create a new **Silverlight Application** as shown below, then click **OK**.

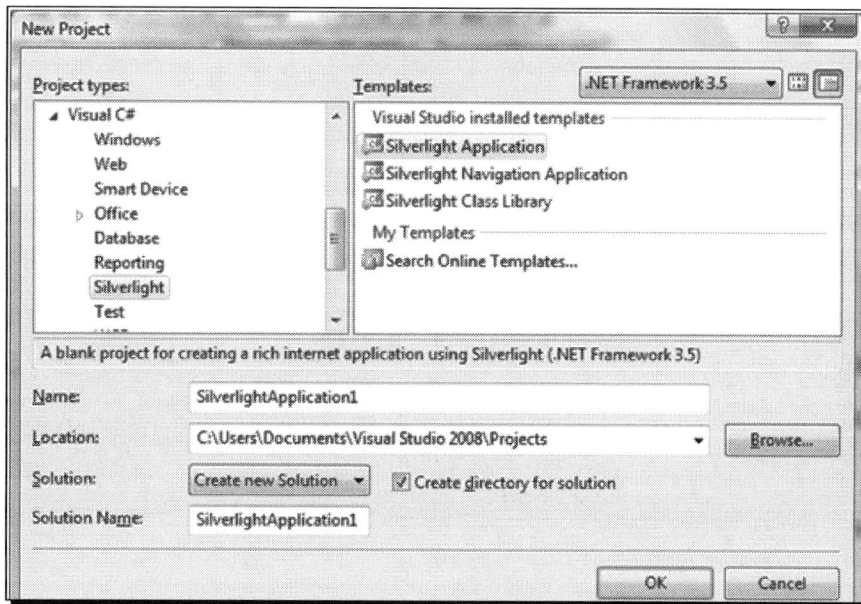

3. When the following dialog box comes up asking you to optionally create a new ASP.NET web project, accept the default settings and click **OK**:

4. The `MainPage.XAML` will open up automatically.

5. Between the `Grid` elements in the XAML file, add the following line of code:

```
<Button Width="100" Height="50" Content="Button"></Button>
```

6. Hit *F5* or choose **Start Debugging** from the **Debug** menu.

7. Make sure that the radio button enabling debugging is checked and click **OK** on the dialog box below. This dialog will only appear the first time you run a new Silverlight application.

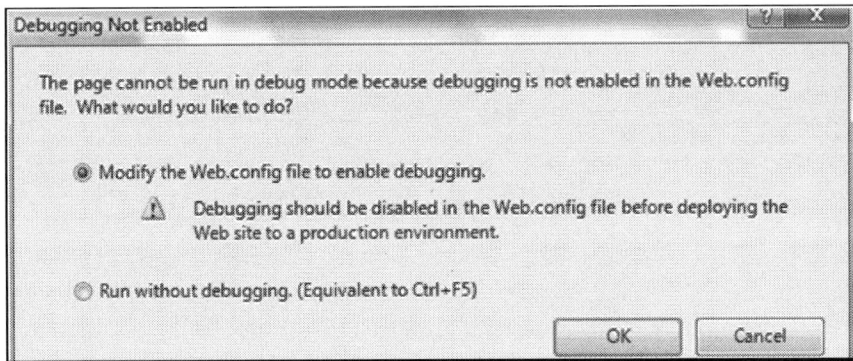

8. You will see a button in your default browser as follows:

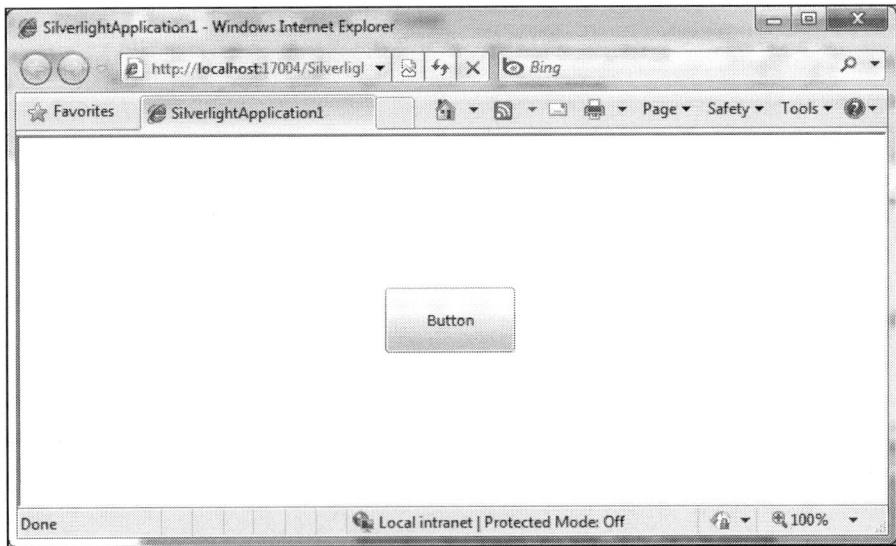

9. Congratulations! You've just created your first Silverlight application.

> We could have just as easily done this exercise in Expression Blend. However, since you are already an ace .NET developer, I thought it best if we started out in familiar territory like Visual Studio. In Chapter 2, we'll learn about developing in Blend.

Have a go hero

Now that we have a Silverlight application up and running, try removing the `Height` and `Width` attributes from the **Button** element and run the solution again. See how the button changes to take up the entire grid. That's not very useful in most circumstances:

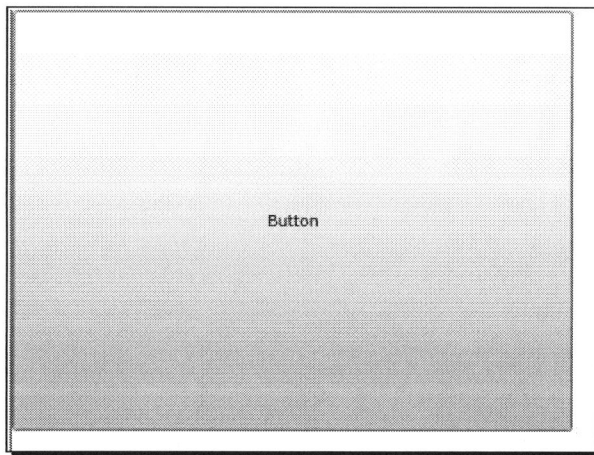

The real power of the `Grid` layout panel is the ability to add rows and columns to define a layout similar to a HTML table.

In our test application, let's define two columns of equal size and place the button in the right-hand column. To do this, we'll change the XAML using the following code:

```
<Grid x:Name="LayoutRoot" Background="White">
    <Grid.ColumnDefinitions>
      <ColumnDefinition Width=".5*"></ColumnDefinition>
      <ColumnDefinition Width=".5*"></ColumnDefinition>
    </Grid.ColumnDefinitions>
  <Button Grid.Column="1" Content="Button"></Button>
</Grid>
```

And our Silverlight application will look like this:

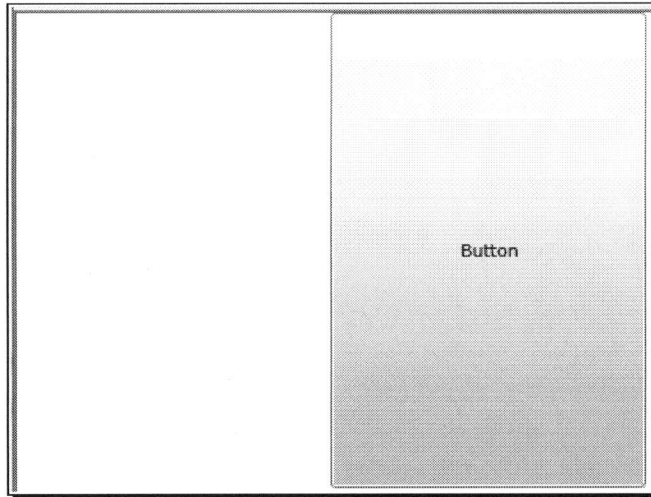

In the XAML, we defined two columns by adding two ColumnDefinitions inside the Grid. ColumnDefinition element. To place the button in the right-hand column, we added an attribute to the **Button** tag. The Grid.Column="1" tells the Grid to place the button in the second column in the ColumnDefinition list. The ColumnDefinition list is a zero based array and 1 points to the second item. Had we not defined the Grid.Column attribute, the Grid would have assumed that we meant zero and the button would appear in the left-hand column.

> You can define as many rows and columns as you like, just remember the simpler the better.

Let's try a completely different layout panel: the Canvas. Change the outer Grid container to Canvas and remove the Grid Column definitions until the XAML looks like this:

```
<Canvas x:Name="LayoutRoot" Background="White">
  <Button Content="Button"></Button>
</Canvas>
```

Look at the design surface or run the solution again and you'll see that the button's placement has changed yet again. It's now at the top left of the application:

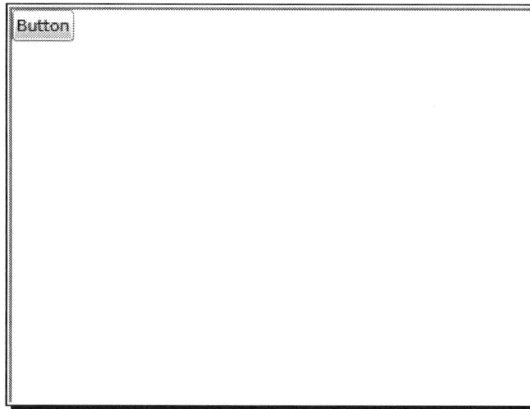

Button

What if you wanted the button to not be so close to the edge? Let's change the XAML for the Button to this:

```
<Button Canvas.Left="100" Canvas.Top="50" Content="Button"></Button>
```

Our application now looks similar to the following screenshot:

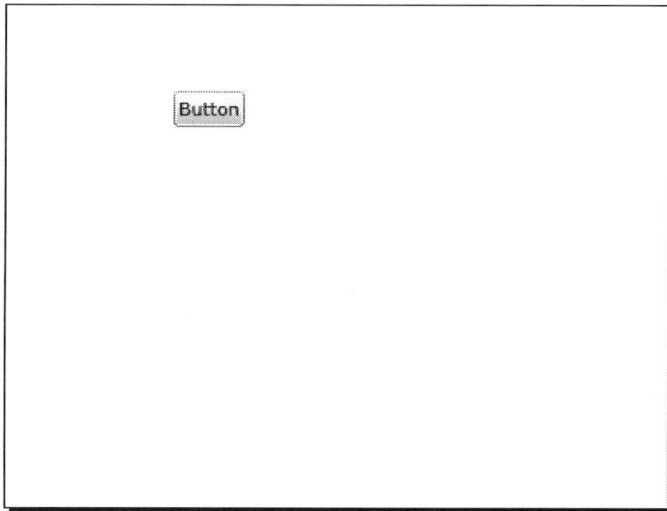

Button

Feel free to explore the solution; you'll notice it has two projects: one Silverlight project and one ASP.NET project.

What just happened

Not only did you just create your first Silverlight Application, you also modified the XAML, ran the application to see the changes that you made, and did some XAML debugging. Additionally, you experimented with two different types of layout panel; the **Grid** and the **Canvas.** Depending on the specific needs of your user interface, you'll want to use different container objects to lay out your controls. If you want to lay out your controls in a manner similar to a HTML table, then you'd want to use a Grid. If you need absolute positioning, then use a Canvas. There are a few other layout panel options, such as **StackPanel** that 'stack' the controls next to or on top of one another. This would come in handy if you wanted to create a toolbar, for example. We'll talk about the different types of containers in the next chapter.

Summary

In this chapter, we discussed how prior experience with .NET development will help you in your move to Silverlight application development. We also looked at some of the new concepts to Silverlight, such as dependency properties, XAML, and the ContentPresenter, the tools needed to develop Silverlight applications, and how to create a Silverlight application.

Specifically, we learnt the following:

- ◆ Previous .NET experience will help you in your grasp of Silverlight
- ◆ XAML is a declarative language based on XML
- ◆ Controls can contain other controls, which can contain other controls
- ◆ Expression Blend is an amazing tool that is well worth the initial learning curve
- ◆ How to create a Silverlight application, experimenting with different layout panels

Now that we've discussed the basics of Silverlight, we're ready to move on to spicing up our business application using Silverlight, which will be explored in the next chapter.

2

Enhancing a Website with Silverlight

Imagine that you have been contacted by a small company that makes custom cakes for various occasions. Like many businesses, they already have a public facing website. The client would like to upgrade to the Web 2.0 era and have chosen to use Silverlight in order to do so. They would also like to integrate their back end systems into the website. This is the scenario we will be working with throughout the course of this book.

In this chapter, we shall:

- Create a navigation widget in Silverlight to add to the current website
- Understand Expression Blend and how to use it in conjunction with Visual Studio.
- Use control templates to enhance the look and feel of the navigation widget.
- Add the navigation widget to an existing website
- Create an interactive logo using Silverlight and incorporate it into the website

Retrofitting a website

The first thing the client would like to do to their website is spice it up with a new navigation control and a playful, interactive logo for the top of the page.

First, we'll work on a navigation control to replace the text links on the left hand side of the page of the current website. As you will notice in the following image, the current website navigation mechanism isn't fancy, but it's simple. However, the client would like the website to be more modern, while preserving ease of use.

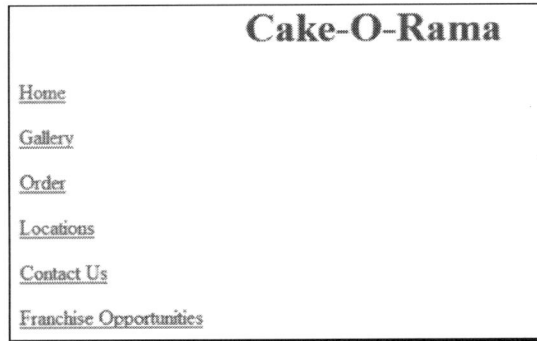

Adding pizzazz with Silverlight

Cake-O-Rama would like to add a fancy navigation widget to their site. They've commissioned a graphic artist to create the following look for the widget.

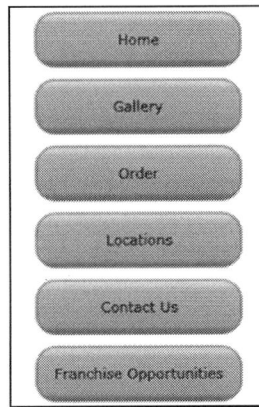

A few words on search engine optimization

We could easily create a Silverlight application that would encompass all the content and functionality of a whole website. However, doing so would severely limit the website's visibility to search engines. Search engines have programs called spiders, or robots, that 'crawl' the internet scanning for content. Generally, these programs can only see text exposed in the HTML. Search results are ranked based on this text-only content. Placing all our content inside a rich internet application platform like Silverlight would effectively hide all of our content. The net result would be reduced visibility on search engines.

> All Rich Internet Application (RIA) platforms have this issue with search engine visibility.

Until this problem is resolved, the best approach is to augment the page's HTML content on sites that you want to be found more easily by search engines.

Building a navigation control from the ground up

In the previous chapter, we looked at two different layout panels: the `Grid` and the `Canvas`. In addition, Silverlight 4 also has `StackPanel`, `Border`, `WrapPanel`, `ViewBox`, and `ScrollViewer`. Why are there so many? Well, each one serves a unique purpose.

Picking the right kind of container

You wouldn't fill a cardboard box with water or drink milk out of a gasoline can, would you? The same could be said of the various layout containers in Silverlight, each one serves a unique purpose and some are better at certain tasks than others.

For instance, when you want to create a toolbar, you would probably use a `StackPanel` or `WrapPanel`, and not a `Canvas`. Why? While you could manually code the layout logic to place all the child controls, there's no good reason to. After all, there are already controls to do the heavy lifting for you.

Below are the most common layout containers in Silverlight 4:

Container	Layout Behavior
Canvas	Manual positioning of items using X and Y coordinates
Grid	Lays out items using a defined grid of rows and columns
InkPresenter	Canvas that can handle digital ink
StackPanel	Stacks items on top of or next to one another
WrapPanel	Lines up items and wraps them around
Border	Draws a border around an item
Viewbox	Scales an item up to take up all the available space
ScrollViewer	Places a scroll bar around the control

Silverlight also provides the means to write your own layout code. While there may be situations where this is warranted, first think about how you can achieve the desired result with a combination of the existing containers.

Stack it up: Using the StackPanel

Based on the website's current navigation links, `StackPanel` seems like the best choice. As the name implies, it lays out child controls in a stack, which seems like a good fit for our list of links.

Time for action – building navigation buttons in Silverlight

Now, let's make a `StackPanel` of button controls to navigate around the site. In order to do this, we will need to do the following:

1. Launch Visual Studio 2010 and click on **File|New Project**.

2. Choose to create a new **Silverlight Application** as shown in the next screen:

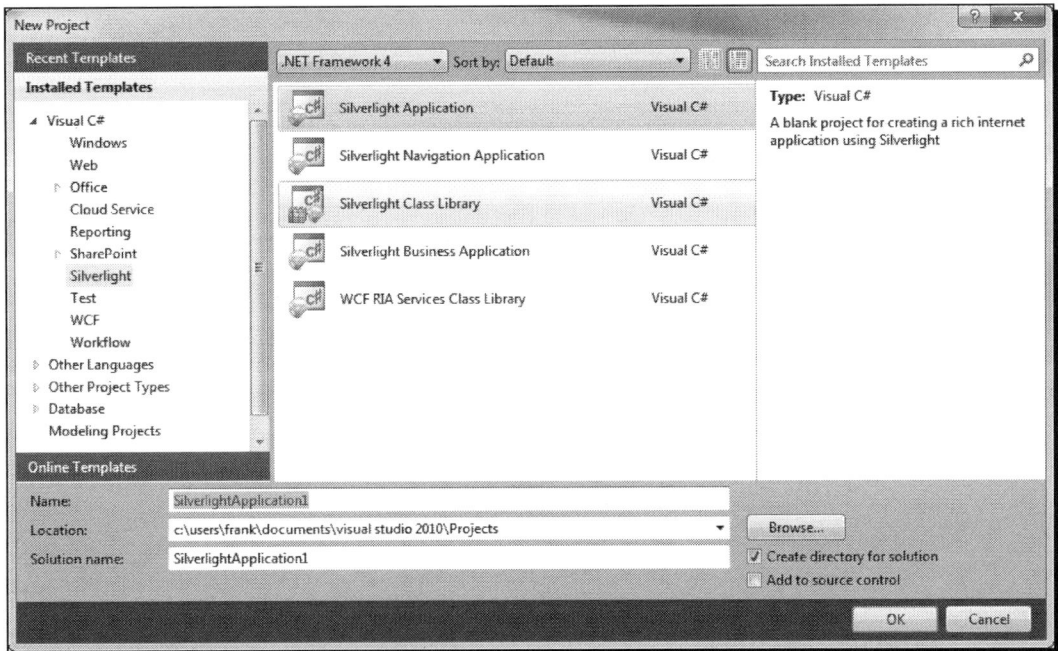

3. Name the project **CakeNavigationButtons** and click **OK** to accept the default settings.

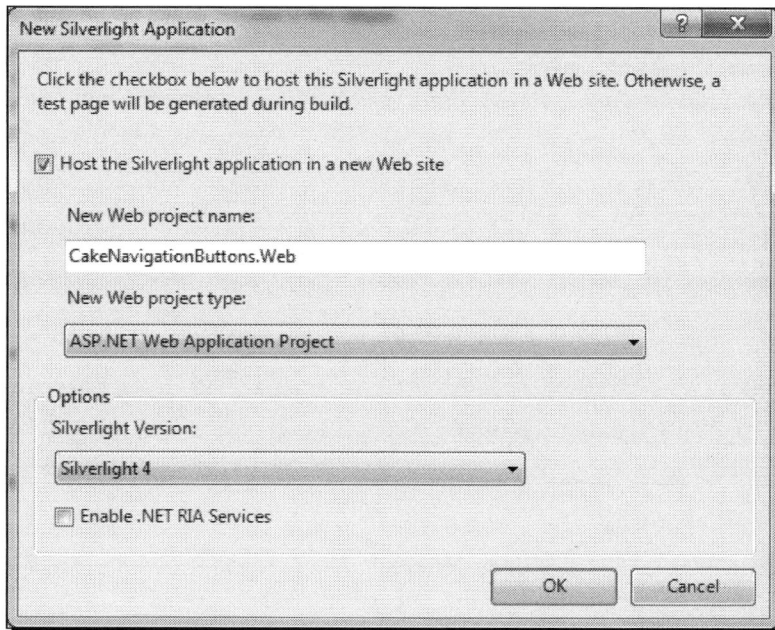

4. In the `MainPage.xaml` file, write the following lines of XAML inside the `Grid` tag:

```
<StackPanel>
    <Button Content="Home" />
    <Button Content="Gallery"/>
    <Button Content="Order"/>
    <Button Content="Locations"/>
    <Button Content="Contact Us"/>
    <Button Content="Franchise Opportunities"/>
</StackPanel>
```

5. Return to Visual Studio 2010 and click on **Debug -> Start Debugging** or press *F5* to launch the application.

6. On the following screen, click **OK** to enable debugging.

7. Your application should look something like this:

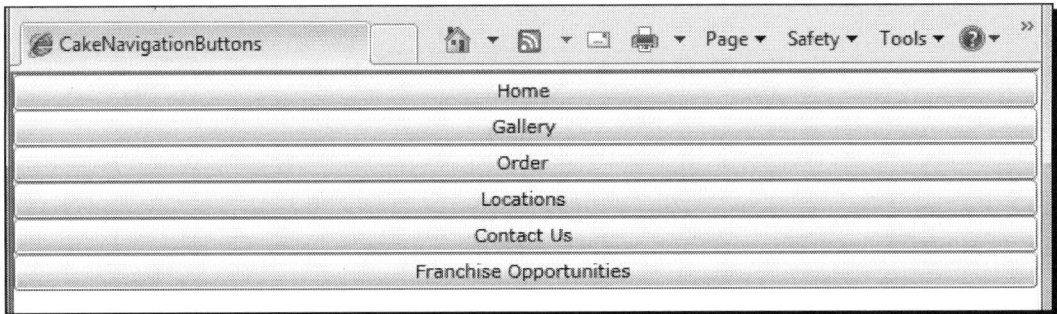

We have now created a `StackPanel` of button controls to navigate around the website using Silverlight, but the application is not exactly visually appealing, not to mention, the buttons don't do anything. What we need them to do is reflect the design we've been provided with and navigate to a given page when the user clicks on them.

What just happened?

What we created here is the foundation for what will eventually become a dynamic navigation control. You have created a new Silverlight application, added a `StackPanel`, and then added button controls to it. Now, let's move on to make this little navigation bar sparkle.

Adding a little style with Styles

Many people refer to Silverlight controls as being "lookless", which may sound strange at first as they clearly have a "look." The term refers to the fact that the logic in a control defines its behavior rather than its appearance. That means that all the controls you've seen in Silverlight so far have no presentation logic in them. Their look comes from a default resource file. The good news is that we can create our own resources to customize the look of any control. You can re-style a control in Silverlight in much the same way as you can in **Cascading Style Sheets (CSS).**

Styles

For instance, what if we wanted the text in the buttons to be larger? We could add a `FontSize` attribute to every button control, so that our XAML code would look like this:

```
<StackPanel>
    <Button Content="Home" FontSize="18" />
    <Button Content="Gallery" FontSize="18"/>
    <Button Content="Order" FontSize="18"/>
```

```
<Button Content="Locations" FontSize="18"/>
<Button Content="Contact Us" FontSize="18"/>
<Button Content="Franchise Opportunities" FontSize="18"/>
</StackPanel>
```

While this would give us the desired effect, it also bloats the XAML and, should we change our minds about the font size later, forces us into a situation where we'll have to do a lot of typing. A **Style** would provide a more elegant solution to this problem. For example, I can define a style that bumps up the FontSize to 18 as shown below:

```
<Style x:Name="biggerTextStyle" TargetType="Button">
  <Setter Property="FontSize" Value="18"/>
</Style>
```

The above snippet of XAML actually defines a style named biggerTextStyle and declares that it is for button controls. Inside the style, there can be any number of Setter nodes. In this style, there is only one and it sets the FontSize property to 18. To use this style, we're going to need to do two things: place it into our application and tell our buttons to reference the style.

In Silverlight, styles are considered a **Resource**, which are any kind of data stored inside an object. Accordingly, we'll place the Style inside the Resources collection of our UserControl, which is the root element of the MainPage.XAML file. This would be analogous to the HEAD section of an HTML document, where document-wide resources reside:

```
<UserControl.Resources>
  <Style x:Name="biggerTextStyle" TargetType="Button">
    <Setter Property="FontSize" Value="18"/>
  </Style>
</UserControl.Resources>
```

We have several options for storing resources in Silverlight. Many controls have a Resources collection and we can store resources in App.xaml, where it is accessible to the entire application. Alternatively, we can even define a **Resource Dictionary**, which is a separate file that contains resources. A resource dictionary is analogous to an external CSS file in HTML. Resource dictionaries can be shared across applications.

Once the style is in place, we need to tell the Button to use it by adding a reference to it in the Style attribute to the button, so the XAML for the buttons now looks like this:

```
<Button Content="Home" Style="{StaticResource biggerTextStyle}" />
<Button Content="Gallery" Style="{StaticResource biggerTextStyle}" />
<Button Content="Order" Style="{StaticResource biggerTextStyle}" />
<Button Content="Locations" Style="{StaticResource biggerTextStyle}"
/>
```

```
<Button Content="Contact Us" Style="{StaticResource biggerTextStyle}"
/>
<Button Content="Franchise Opportunities" Style="{StaticResource
biggerTextStyle}" />
```

You may be wondering what those curly braces are doing inside of an XAML document. They are a special cue for the XAML processing engine to execute certain commands, called a **Markup Extension**. The markup extension above tells the Silverlight runtime to set the style property to the resource named biggerTextStyle.

In each Button we reference the same biggerTextStyle Style resource for all of our buttons. This is to make sure they all use the same Style resource. This bloats our code somewhat. Wouldn't it be great if there were a way to create a default style that would apply to all the buttons in our application? Fortunately, for us this feature was added in Silverlight 4. We now have the option to define a default style for a particular type of control. Simply remove the x:Name="biggerTextStyle" attribute from the Style declaration, so that the XAML looks like this:

```
<Style TargetType="Button">
  <Setter Property="FontSize" Value="18"/>
</Style>
```

By removing the x:Name attribute, we create an **anonymous style**, or a default style, that applies to all the Button controls in our application. Now, our XAML markup looks nice and tidy:

```
<Button Content="Home" />
<Button Content="Gallery" />
<Button Content="Order"/>
<Button Content="Locations"/>
<Button Content="Contact Us"/>
<Button Content="Franchise Opportunities"/>
```

> **Overriding an anonymous style**
>
> If you want to override an anonymous style and revert to the control's default appearance, set the Style attribute to null using this code:
> Style="{x:Null}"

Enough of the theory, let's create a default style now!

Time for action – adding the style

Now it's time to create a **Style** in XAML and tell all the buttons in our project to use that style. This will make all of the buttons have a common text size. You will need to do the following:

1. Go back to the **CakeNavigationButtons** project in Visual Studio.

2. Open the `MainPage.XAML` file.

3. Edit the XAML so that it looks like this:

```
<UserControl x:Class="CakeNavigationButtons.MainPage"
    xmlns="http://schemas.microsoft.com/winfx/2006/xaml/
presentation"
    xmlns:x="http://schemas.microsoft.com/winfx/2006/xaml"
    xmlns:d="http://schemas.microsoft.com/expression/blend/2008"
    xmlns:mc="http://schemas.openxmlformats.org/markup-
compatibility/2006"
    mc:Ignorable="d"
    d:DesignHeight="300" d:DesignWidth="400">
    <UserControl.Resources>
        <Style TargetType="Button">
            <Setter Property="FontSize" Value="18"/>
        </Style>
    </UserControl.Resources>
    <Grid x:Name="LayoutRoot" Background="White">
        <StackPanel>
            <Button Content="Home" />
            <Button Content="Gallery" />
            <Button Content="Order"/>
            <Button Content="Locations"/>
            <Button Content="Contact Us"/>
            <Button Content="Franchise Opportunities"/>
        </StackPanel>
    </Grid>
</UserControl>
```

4. Run the solution and you'll notice that the text on every button is larger.

5. Stop the project and return to the `MainPage.XAML` file.

6. Change the `FontSize` to 9.

7. Add another `Setter` node to the style:

```
<Setter Property="Background" Value="Red"/>
```

8. Run the project again and you'll see that the font is much smaller and the buttons have taken on a red tone:

What just happened?

We just created a Style and added it to our navigation application. Then we referenced the Style using a Markup Extension in the `Style` property of the button. We then modified the Style, which changed all the controls that referenced it. This should give you a little taste of the power of using Styles in Silverlight.

You may be thinking that editing styles "by hand" can get tedious if we try to do anything more complex, and you're right! Hand editing XAML can only get you so far. Now we'll take our design to the next level by using Expression Blend.

Creating applications in Expression Blend

What we've done so far falls short of some of the things you may have already seen and done in Silverlight. Hand editing XAML, assisted by Intellisense, works just fine to a point, but to create anything complex requires another tool to assist with turning our vision into code.

> Intellisense is a feature of Visual Studio and Blend that auto-completes text when you start typing a keyword, method, or variable name.

Expression Blend may scare off developers at first with its radically different interface, but if you look more closely, you'll see that Blend has a lot in common with Visual Studio. For starters, both tools use the same Solution and Project file format. That means it's 100% compatible and enables tighter integration between developers and designers. You could even have the same project open in both Visual Studio and in Blend at the same time. Just be prepared to see the **File Modified** dialog box like the one below when switching between the two applications:

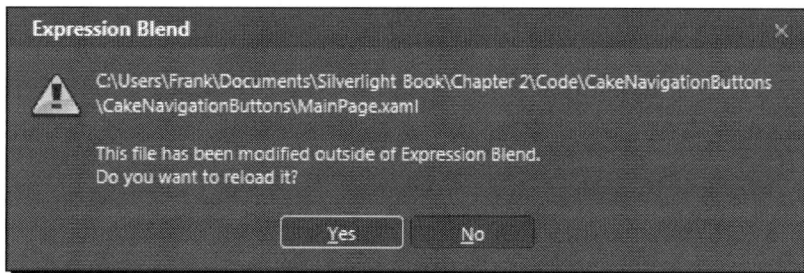

If you've worked with designers on a project before, they typically mock up an interface in a graphics program and ship it off to the development team. Many times, a simple graphic embellishment can cause us developers to develop heartburn. Anyone who's ever had to implement a rounded corner in HTML knows the special kind of frustration that it brings along. Here's the good news: those days are over with Silverlight.

A crash course in Expression Blend

In the following screenshot, our **CakeNavigationButton** project is loaded into Expression Blend. Blend can be a bit daunting at first for developers that are used to Visual Studio as Blend's interface is dense with a lot of subtle cues. Solutions and projects are opened in Blend in the same manner as you would in Visual Studio.

Just like in Visual Studio, you can customize Expression Blend's interface to suit your preference. You can move tabs around, dock, and undock them to create a workspace that works best for you as the following screenshot demonstrates:

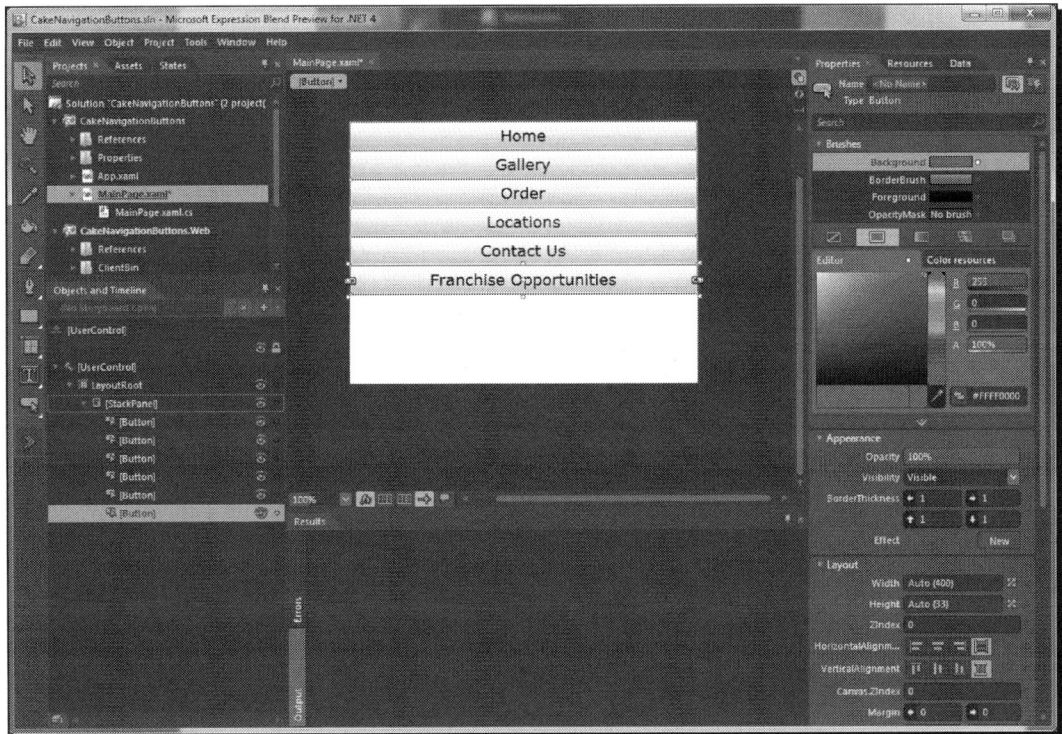

An artsy Visual Studio?

If you look at the **CakeNavigationButton** project, on the left hand side of the application window, you have the toolbar, which is substantially different from the toolbox in Visual Studio.

The toolbar in Blend more closely resembles the toolbar in graphics editing software such as Adobe Photoshop or Adobe Illustrator. If you move the mouse over each button, you will see a tooltip that tells you what that button does, as well as the button's keyboard shortcut. In the upper-left corner, you'll notice a tab labeled **Projects**. This is functionally equivalent to the **Solution Explorer** in Visual Studio. The asterisk next to MainPage.XAML indicates that the file has not been saved. Examine the next screenshot to see Blend's equivalent to Visual Studio's Solution Explorer:

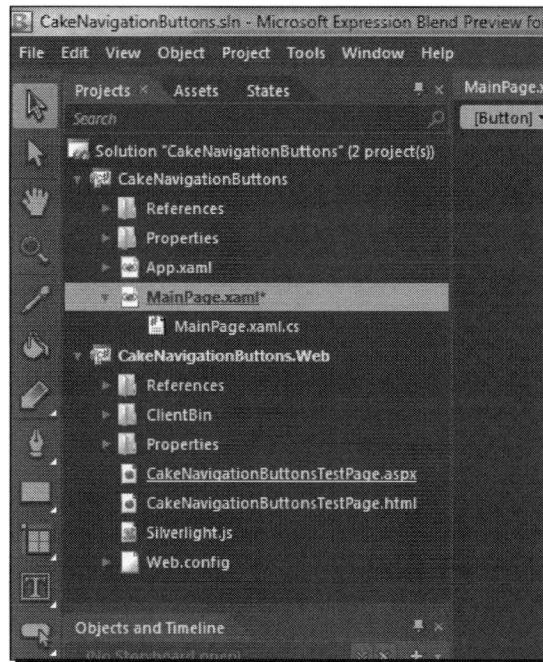

If we look at the following screenshot, we find the **Document** tab control and the design surface, which Blend calls the **art board**. On the upper-right of the art board, there are three small buttons to control the switch between **Design view**, **XAML view**, or **Split view**.

On the lower edge of the art board, there are controls to modify the view of the design surface. You can zoom in to take a closer look, turn on snap grid visibility, and turn on or off the snapping to snap lines.

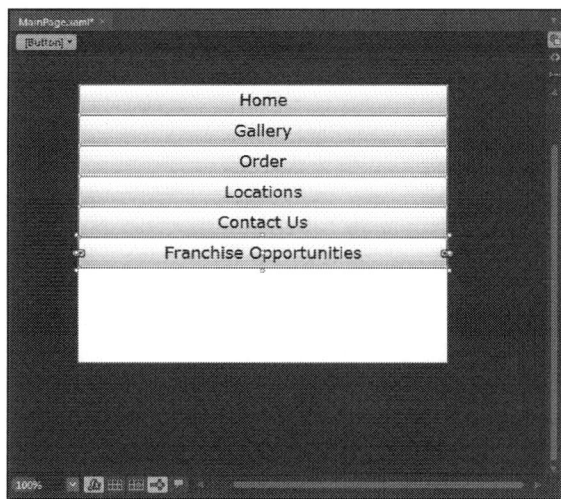

If we then move to the upper-right corner of the next screen, we will see the **Properties** tab, which is a much more evolved version of the **Properties** tab in Visual Studio. As you can see in this screenshot, the color picker has a lot more to offer. There's also a search feature that narrows down the items in the tab based on the property name you type in.

At the lower left side of the next screen, there is the **Objects and Timeline** view, which shows the object hierarchy of the open document. Since we have the MainPage.XAML of our **CakeNavigationButtons** project, the view has **StackPanel** with six **Buttons** all inside a grid named **LayoutRoot** inside of a **UserControl**. Clicking on an item in this view selects the item on the art board and vice versa.

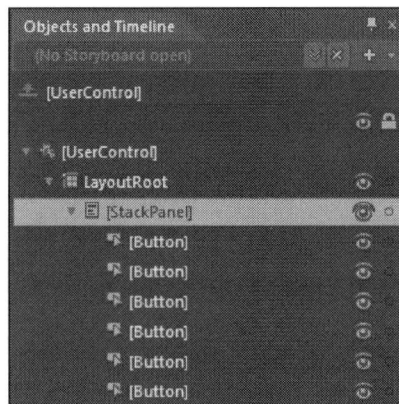

Expression Blend is an intricate and rich application; we'll be learning more about Blend throughout the course of this book.

Time for action – styles revisited in Blend

Earlier in this chapter, we created and referenced a style directly in the XAML in Visual Studio. Let's modify the style we made in Blend to see how to do it graphically. To do this, we will need to:

1. Open up the **CakeNavigationButtons** solution in Expression Blend.

2. In the upper right corner, there are three tabs (**Properties**, **Resources**, and **Data**).

3. On the **Resources** tab, expand the tree node marked **[UserControl]** and click on the button highlighted below to edit the **[Button default]** resource.

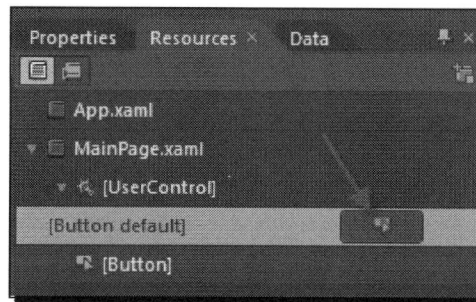

4. Your art board should look something like this:

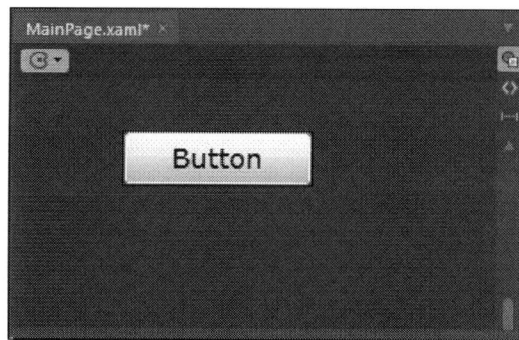

5. Click on the **Properties** tab and scroll down to the `Text` section:

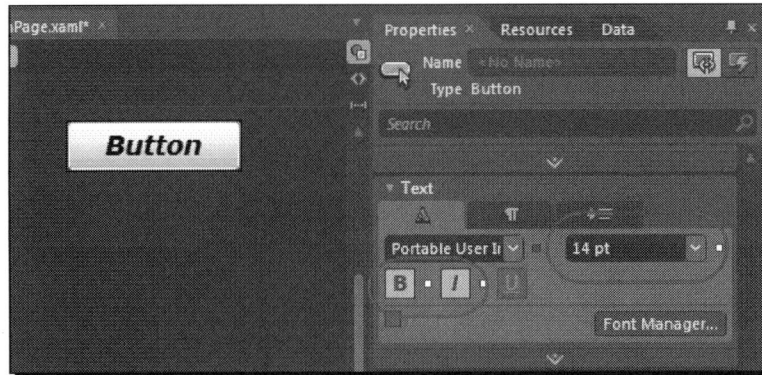

6. Change the Font size to **14** and click on the **B** and the **I** buttons to toggle on `Bold` and `Italic`.

7. Type **cursor** into the **Search** box. Notice how the **Properties** tab displays only the **Cursor** property.

8. Next, change the value in the drop down list to **Hand**:

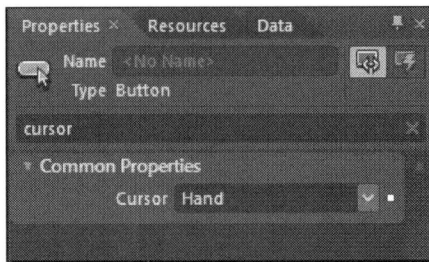

9. Type **margin** into the search box and put **5** into each of the text boxes as shown in the following screenshot:

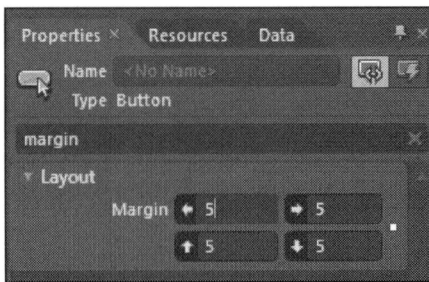

10. Look over to the left hand side of the screen; you'll see a tab named **Objects and Timeline.** Click on the button with the up arrow that I've highlighted in the following screenshot. This will get you out of **Style** editing mode and back into the main level of our application:

11. Choose **Run Project** from the **Project** menu or hit *F5* to run the project.

12. Notice what's changed. There is now a space around each button, the font's appearance has changed and the cursor changes to a hand when you mouse over each of the buttons. Your application will now look similar to the following screenshot:

13. The buttons have a red tint to them, but there is still some way to go.

What just happened?

We have just edited a style in Expression Blend and the software did all the heavy lifting for us. If you take a peek at the XAML markup, you will see that the Style has been expanded to include a few more Setter nodes. Each one corresponds to the changes that we made:

```
<Style TargetType="Button">
    <Setter Property="FontSize" Value="14"/>
    <Setter Property="Background" Value="Red"/>
    <Setter Property="Cursor" Value="Hand"/>
    <Setter Property="FontStyle" Value="Italic"/>
    <Setter Property="FontWeight" Value="Bold"/>
    <Setter Property="Margin" Value="5,5,5,5"/>
</Style>
```

You most certainly *could have* created this XAML by hand, but as you've just seen, it's often faster to use Blend for this. In many real world scenarios, you will have to get your hands dirty in the XAML from time to time to tweak a value.

Have a go hero

So, we have a style that defines the way we would like our buttons to look. What if we wanted to override certain properties? For example, if you wanted the font size on the **Home** button to be different than the others, you could specify a smaller or larger value. Once again, you can do this in Blend via the **Properties** tab or in the XAML using the following code:

```
<Button Content="Home" FontSize="9" />
```

By using this code, you will be presented with this screenshot:

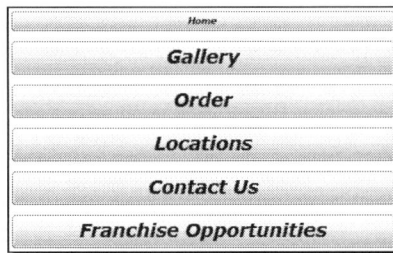

Alternatively, you could define another style; one that specifies a smaller font size. We've seen that done in XAML, but not in Blend yet.

Let's do that now. Make sure that the **UserControl** element is selected, then click on the **Object** menu, and then **Edit Style|Create Empty...** You will then see the following dialog box:

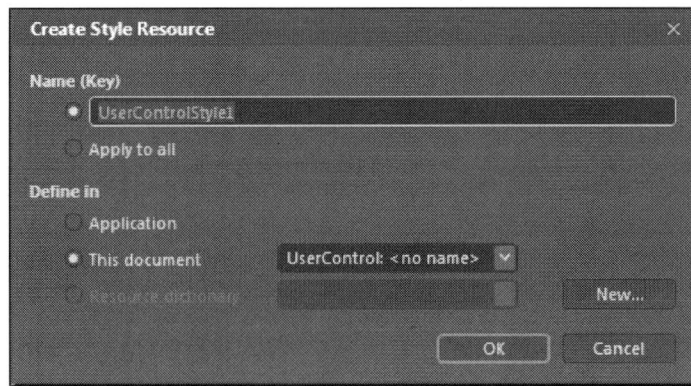

Next, change the **Name** to **smallerTextStyle** then click **OK.** Use the **Properties** tab to change the font size to **9.** Feel free to change some other properties too.

When you are finished, click the up button on the **Objects and Timeline** tab to exit style editing mode. Once you are back in the main view, select the **Home** button. Type **style** into the search box on the **Properties** tab. You will find the **Properties** tab on the right-hand side of Blend's window. Under **Miscellaneous**, you will see a **Style** property with a little square next to it as in the screenshot below. In Blend, this means that there are more properties for you to edit. Click the square to bring up the **Advanced Property Options** context menu.

Once you click on the square, the following context menu appears. Choose **Local Resource|smallerTextStyle** from the sub-menu just as you see it in the following screenshot:

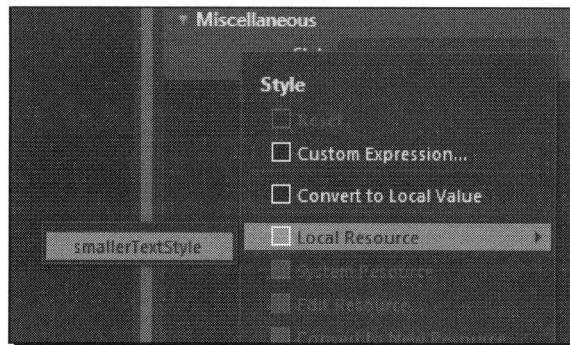

Run the solution again or look at the art board to see how the button has changed. You can experiment with assigning this style to some of the other buttons, editing the existing styles, or creating new styles. On buttons where the `smallerTextStyle` is applied, the button text will be smaller. On buttons where the default style is applied, the button text will be larger.

Skinning a control

So far, you've seen that while styles can change the look of a control, they can only go so far. No matter how many changes we make, the buttons still look like old-fashioned buttons. Surely, there must be a way to customize a control further to match our creative vision. There is a way, its called **skinning**.

Controls in Silverlight are extremely flexible and customizable. This flexibility stems from the fact that controls have both a **VisualTree** and a **LogicalTree**. The **Visual Tree** deals with all the visual elements in a control, while the Logical tree deals with all the logical elements. All controls in Silverlight come with a default template, which defines what a control should look like. You can easily override this default template by redefining a control's visual tree with a custom one.

> Designers can either work directly with XAML in Blend or use a design tool that supports exporting to XAML. Expression Design is one such tool. You can also import artwork from Adobe Illustrator and Adobe Photoshop from within Blend.

In our scenario, let us pretend that there is a team of graphic designers. From time to time graphic designers will provide us with visual elements and, if we're lucky, snippets of XAML. In this case, the designers have sent us the XAML for a rectangle and gradient for us to base our control on:

```
<Rectangle Stroke="#7F646464" Height="43" Width="150"
StrokeThickness="2" RadiusX="15" RadiusY="15" VerticalAlignment="Top"
>
  <Rectangle.Fill>
    <LinearGradientBrush EndPoint="0.5,1" StartPoint="0.5,0">
      <GradientStop Color="#FFEE9D9D" Offset="0.197"/>
      <GradientStop Color="#FFFF7D7D" Offset="0.847"/>
      <GradientStop Color="#FFF2DADA" Offset="0.066"/>
      <GradientStop Color="#FF7E4F4F" Offset="1"/>
    </LinearGradientBrush>
  </Rectangle.Fill>
</Rectangle>
```

After inputting the above XAML, you will be presented with this image:

We need to make this rectangle the template for our buttons.

Time for action – Skinning a control

We're going to take the XAML snippet above and skin our buttons with it. In order to achieve this we will need to do the following:

1. Open up the **CakeNavigationButtons** project in Blend.

2. In the `MainPage.XAML` file, switch to **XAML View**, either by clicking the **XAML** button on the upper-right corner of the art board or choosing **View|Active Document View|XAML** from the menu bar.

3. Type in the following XAML after the closing tag for the `StackPanel`:

```
(</StackPanel>)
<Rectangle Stroke="#7F646464" Height="43" Width="150"
StrokeThickness="2" RadiusX="15" RadiusY="15"
VerticalAlignment="Top" >
  <Rectangle.Fill>
    <LinearGradientBrush EndPoint="0.5,1" StartPoint="0.5,0">
      <GradientStop Color="#FFEE9D9D" Offset="0.197"/>
      <GradientStop Color="#FFFF7D7D" Offset="0.847"/>
      <GradientStop Color="#FFF2DADA" Offset="0.066"/>
      <GradientStop Color="#FF7E4F4F" Offset="1"/>
    </LinearGradientBrush>
  </Rectangle.Fill>
</Rectangle>
```

4. Switch back to **Design View**, either by clicking on the appropriate button on the upper right corner of the art board or choosing **View|Active Document View|Design View** from the menu bar.

5. Right-click on the rectangle and click on **Make Into Control**.

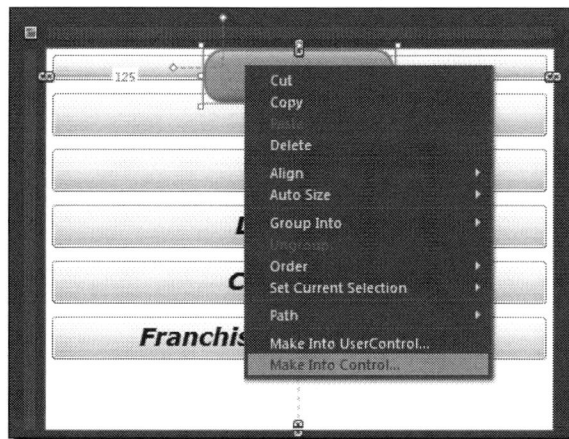

6. In the dialog box, choose **Button**, change the **Name (Key)** field to **navButtonStyle** and click **OK**.

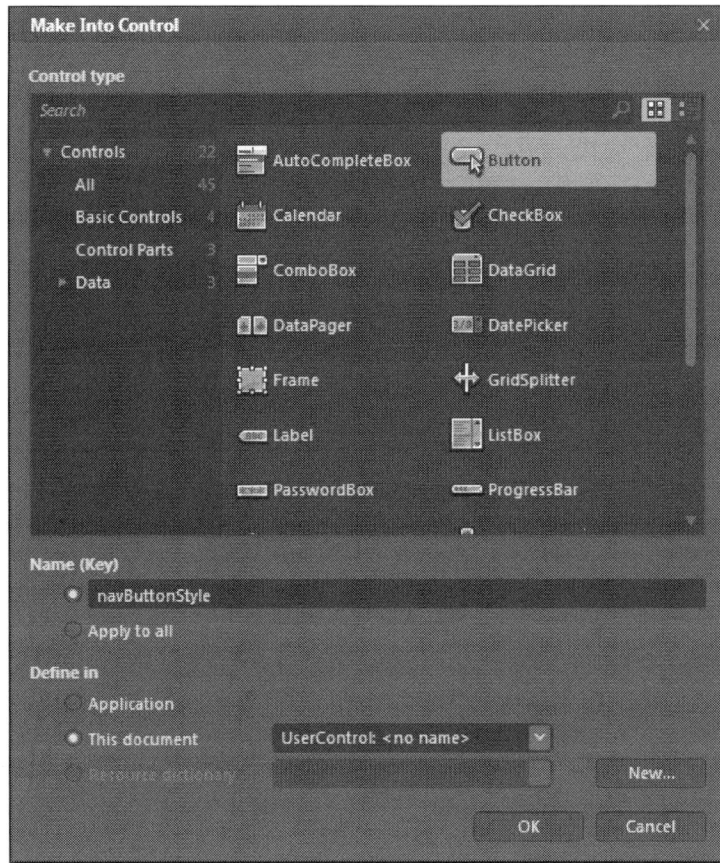

7. You are now in template editing mode. There are two on-screen indicators that you are in this mode: one is the **Objects and Timeline** tab:

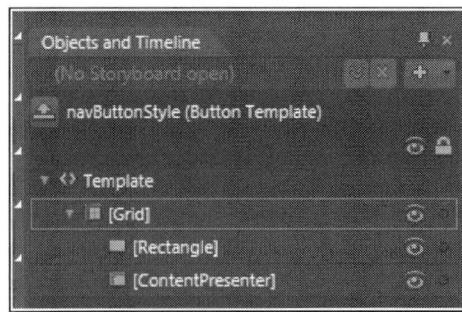

8. And one is the `MainControl.xaml` at the top of the art board:

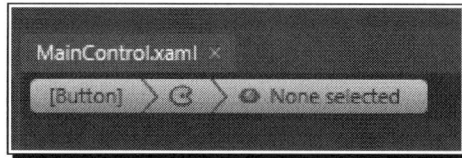

9. Click on the up button to exit template editing mode.

10. Delete the button that our **Rectangle** was converted into.

11. Select all the buttons in the `StackPanel` by clicking on the first one and then *Shift*+clicking on the last one.

12. With all the buttons selected, go to the **Properties** tab, type **Style** into the search box.

13. Using the techniques you've learned in this chapter, change the style to **navButtonStyle**, so that your screen now looks like this:

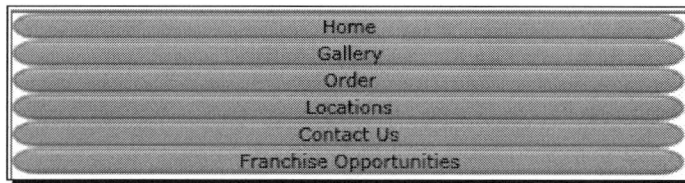

The result is still not quite what we're looking for, but it's close. We need to increase the font size again; fortunately, we know how easy that is in Blend.

14. Click on one of the buttons and choose **Object|Edit Style|Edit Current** from the menu bar to get into style editing mode.

15. Make note of all the visual indicators. In the **Properties** tab, change the **Font Size** to **18**, the **Cursor** to **Hand**, the **Height** to **45**, and the **Width** to **200**. You should see the changes immediately. The cursor change will only be noticeable at run time.

16. Exit the template editing mode.

17. There is a slight problem with the last button; the font is a little too large. Click on the button and use the **Properties** tab to change the **Font Size** to **12**.

18. Run the project and your application will look something like this:

19. Run your mouse over the buttons. The button no longer reacts when you mouse over it, we'll fix that next.

What just happened?

We just took a plain old button and turned it into something a little more in line with the graphic designers' vision but how did we do it?

> **When in doubt, look at the XAML**
>
> The nice thing about Silverlight is that you can always take a look at the XAML to get a better understanding of what's going on. There are many places where things can "hide" in a tool like Blend or even Visual Studio. The raw naked XAML, however, bares all.

For starters, we took a chunk of XAML and, using Blend, told Silverlight that we wanted to "take control" over how this button looks. This data was encapsulated into a `Style` and we told all our buttons to use our new style. When the new style was created, we lost some of our formatting data. We then inserted it back in and added a few more properties.

If you're really curious to see what's going on, let's take a closer look at the XAML that Blend just generated for us:

```
<Style TargetType="Button">
    <Setter Property="FontSize" Value="18.667"/>
    <Setter Property="Background" Value="Red"/>
    <Setter Property="FontStyle" Value="Italic"/>
    <Setter Property="FontWeight" Value="Bold"/>
    <Setter Property="Cursor" Value="Hand"/>
    <Setter Property="Margin" Value="5"/>
</Style>
```

```xml
<Style x:Key="smallerTextStyle" TargetType="Button">
    <Setter Property="FontSize" Value="9"/>
    </Style>
<Style x:Key="navButtonStyle" TargetType="Button">
  <Setter Property="Template">
    <Setter.Value>
      <ControlTemplate TargetType="Button">
        <Grid>
          <Rectangle RadiusY="15" RadiusX="15" Stroke="#7F646464"
StrokeThickness="2">
            <Rectangle.Fill>
              <LinearGradientBrush EndPoint="0.5,1"
StartPoint="0.5,0">
                <GradientStop Color="#FFEE9D9D" Offset="0.197"/>
                <GradientStop Color="#FFFF7D7D" Offset="0.847"/>
                <GradientStop Color="#FFF2DADA" Offset="0.066"/>
                <GradientStop Color="#FF7E4F4F" Offset="1"/>
              </LinearGradientBrush>
            </Rectangle.Fill>
          </Rectangle>
          <ContentPresenter HorizontalAlignment="{TemplateBinding
HorizontalContentAlignment}" VerticalAlignment="{TemplateBinding
VerticalContentAlignment}"/>
        </Grid>
      </ControlTemplate>
    </Setter.Value>
  </Setter>
  <Setter Property="FontSize" Value="24"/>
  <Setter Property="Cursor" Value="Hand"/>
  <Setter Property="Height" Value="45"/>
  <Setter Property="Width" Value="200"/>
</Style>
```

You'll immediately notice how verbose XAML can be. We've not done a great deal of work, yet we've generated a lot of XAML. This is where a tool like Blend really saves us all those keystrokes. The next thing you'll see is that we're actually setting the Template property inside of a Setter node of a Style definition. It's not until toward the end of the Style definition that we see the Rectangle which we started with. There's also a lot of code here devoted to something called the Visual State Manager.

Prior to us changing the control's template, you'll remember that when you moved your mouse over any of the buttons, they reacted by changing color. This was nice, subtle feedback for the user. Now that it's gone, we really miss it and so will our users. If you carefully study the XAML, it should come as no surprise to you that the button doesn't do anything other than just sit there: we've not defined anything for any of the states listed here. The nodes are blank. Let's do that now.

States of mind

The **Visual State Manager**, as its name implies, helps you manage the visual states of controls. It is a simple and powerful means to provide state transitions to controls, while hiding a lot of the animation mechanisms behind them.

Time for action – learning the Visual State Manager

In this exercise, we are going to use the Visual State Manager to add visual cues to our control template. While we could type out all this XAML, let's have Blend generate all the XAML for us. In order to do this, we will need to complete the following steps:

1. In the `MainPage.XAML` file of the **CakeNavigationButtons** project, right-click on any of the buttons that use the `navButtonStyle`.

2. Click **Edit Template|Edit Current** from the context menu as in this screenshot:

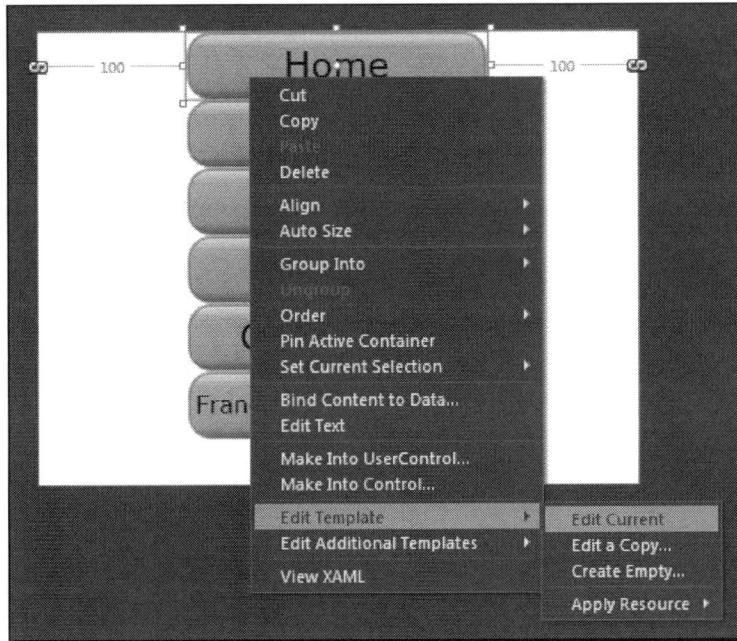

3. Click on the **States** tab in the upper-left part of the Blend window as shown below:

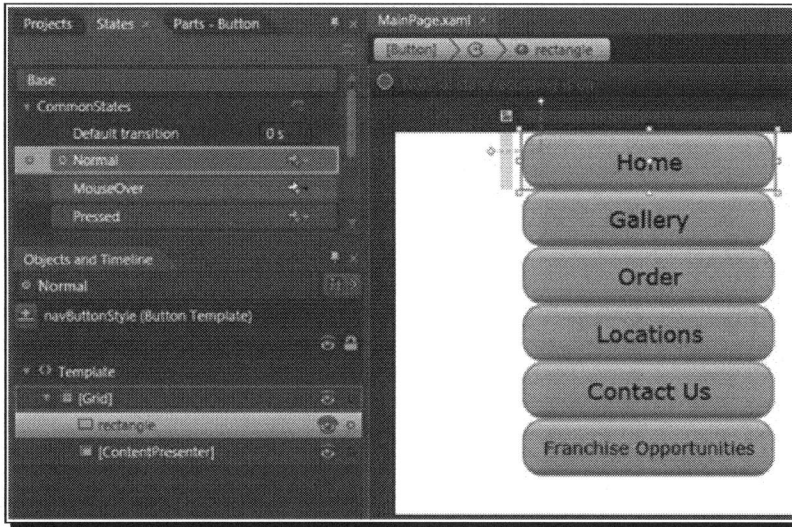

4. Click on **Normal**. Note how the art board gets a red border and tells you that **Normal state recording is on.**

5. Click on **MouseOver** and then click on **Rectangle** in the **Objects and Timeline** tab.

6. Use the **Properties** tab to change the background of the rectangle by changing the colors of the gradient. You can do this by clicking each one of the "stops" along the gradient line as seen in the following screenshot:

7. First click on stop, then use the color picker to choose a new color. You can pick your own colors. Repeat for each of the four gradient stops.

8. Click the up button on the **Objects and Timeline** tab to exit the template editing mode.

9. Run the solution and each button changes color when you mouse over it :

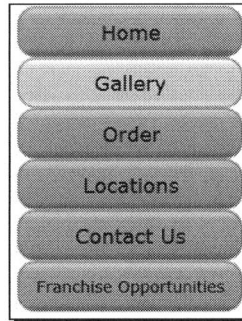

10. Then, close the browser and go back to Blend. While that worked, it doesn't quite have that same natural feel that the default button template had.

11. We can quickly remedy that by going back into the template editing mode and changing the **Default Transition** property in the **States** tab to **0.2s** as shown in the following screenshot:

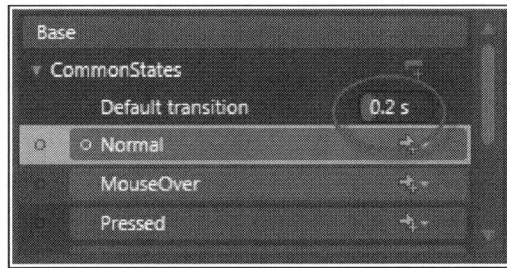

12. Run the solution again and notice how "natural" that feels. Experiment with different timings to see how it changes the feel of your application. You can use any time in the range of 0 to 1 second.

What just happened?

We restored the natural "feel" of our navigation button by modifying how it transitions from one state to another. Because we used the `Button` control as a basis, several states were already defined and we got a lot of functionality "for free."

If you take a closer look at the XAML, it is starting to get really bloated at this point. Yet, our button code is still simple and humble. It's largely remains unchanged from when we started this chapter:

```
<Button Content="Home" Style="{StaticResource navButtonStyle}" />
<Button Content="Gallery" Style="{StaticResource navButtonStyle}" />
<Button Content="Order" Style="{StaticResource navButtonStyle}" />
<Button Content="Locations" Style="{StaticResource navButtonStyle}" />
<Button Content="Contact Us" Style="{StaticResource navButtonStyle}"
/>
<Button Content="Franchise Opportunities" Style="{StaticResource
navButtonStyle}" FontSize="14" />
```

Obviously, all of the work is being done inside the `Style` and the `Control Template`. The XAML code for that is quite long winded. I will just show a snippet for brevity. Here is the definition for the `MouseOver` state:

```
<vsm:VisualState x:Name="MouseOver">
  <Storyboard>
    <ColorAnimationUsingKeyFrames BeginTime="00:00:00"
Duration="00:00:00.0010000" Storyboard.TargetName="rectangle"
Storyboard.TargetProperty="(Shape.Fill).(GradientBrush.GradientStops)[
3].(GradientStop.Color)">
      <EasingColorKeyFrame KeyTime="00:00:00" Value="#FFFFFFFF"/>
    </ColorAnimationUsingKeyFrames>
    <ColorAnimationUsingKeyFrames BeginTime="00:00:00"
Duration="00:00:00.0010000" Storyboard.TargetName="rectangle"
Storyboard.TargetProperty="(Shape.Fill).(GradientBrush.GradientStops)[
1].(GradientStop.Color)">
      <EasingColorKeyFrame KeyTime="00:00:00" Value="#FFB1DCF4"/>
    </ColorAnimationUsingKeyFrames>
    <ColorAnimationUsingKeyFrames BeginTime="00:00:00"
Duration="00:00:00.0010000" Storyboard.TargetName="rectangle"
Storyboard.TargetProperty="(Shape.Fill).(GradientBrush.GradientStops)[
0].(GradientStop.Color)">
      <EasingColorKeyFrame KeyTime="00:00:00" Value="#FFE2E2E2"/>
    </ColorAnimationUsingKeyFrames>
    <ColorAnimationUsingKeyFrames BeginTime="00:00:00"
Duration="00:00:00.0010000" Storyboard.TargetName="rectangle"
Storyboard.TargetProperty="(Shape.Fill).(GradientBrush.GradientStops)[
2].(GradientStop.Color)">
```

```
        <EasingColorKeyFrame KeyTime="00:00:00" Value="#FFFDFDFD"/>
      </ColorAnimationUsingKeyFrames>
    </Storyboard>
  </vsm:VisualState>
```

You have to admire the way the Visual State Manager hid a lot of the animation XAML mark-up from us. Don't worry if it doesn't quite make sense yet. There's a lot going on here that relates to animation, but first let's get back to slinging code.

Adding event handlers

That's right, code, good old fashioned code. We are more than halfway through this chapter and we have not written one single line of procedural code. Sure, we've created plenty of XAML, but not one single line of C# or Visual Basic.NET code. How is this possible?

Sharp-eyed readers may have already noticed that our `MainPage.xaml` file has a code behind it named `MainPage.xaml.cs` (`MainPage.xaml.vb`, if you're using Visual Basic. NET). Curious readers may have already taken a peek at the code behind the file.

Here is the complete listing of code that powers our buttons:

```
using System.Windows.Controls;
using System.Windows.Documents;
using System.Windows.Input;
using System.Windows.Media;
using System.Windows.Media.Animation;
using System.Windows.Shapes;
namespace CakeNavigationButtons
{
    public partial class MainPage : UserControl
    {
        public MainPage()
        {
            InitializeComponent();
        }
    }
}
```

Could that be all there is? Let's fire up Visual Studio now and take a closer look at what's going on.

Time for action – back to coding

Let's take a peek at all the code and files automatically generated for us to see what makes a typical Silverlight project tick. Let's also wire up a few event handlers to make the navigation control interactive. In order to this, we will need to do the following:

1. Open up the **CakeNavigationButtons** project in Visual Studio.

2. Open up the `MainPage.xaml.cs` file.

3. Right-click on the `InitializeComponent` method call and select **Go to Definition** from the context menu.

4. Notice that we are now in a file called `mainpage.g.cs`, a file that is automatically generated.

5. Close this file and go back to the `MainPage.xaml.cs` file and comment out the call to `InitializeComponent`.

6. Run the solution and watch what happens, absolutely nothing.

7. Stop the solution either in Visual Studio or closing the host browser window.

8. Uncomment the call to `InitializeComponent`.

9. Open the `MainPage.xaml` file and inside the **Home** button XAML node, type **Click=** at which point Intellisense will offer to create a new event handler for you:

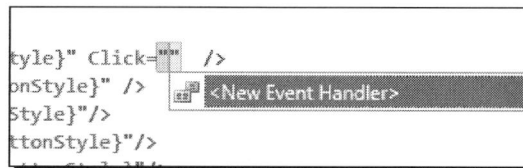

10. Click **<New Event Handler>**.

11. Your button node now has a binding to an event handler.

12. Right mouse click on `Click="Button_Click"` and click on **Navigate to Event Handler** from the context menu.

13. Inside the event handler, add the following line of code and run the solution:

    ```
    MessageBox.Show("Hello from Silverlight");
    ```

14. Click on the **Home** button and you will see this:

15. Click **OK** and then close the host browser window.

16. Remove the following line of code we just added that showed the `Alert` dialog box:

```
MessageBox.Show("Hello from Silverlight");
```

17. Replace it with this line of code:

```
System.Windows.Browser.HtmlPage.Window.Navigate(new Uri("http://www.packtpub.com/"));
```

18. Run the project and click on the **Home** button once more to be taken to the Packt Publishing home page.

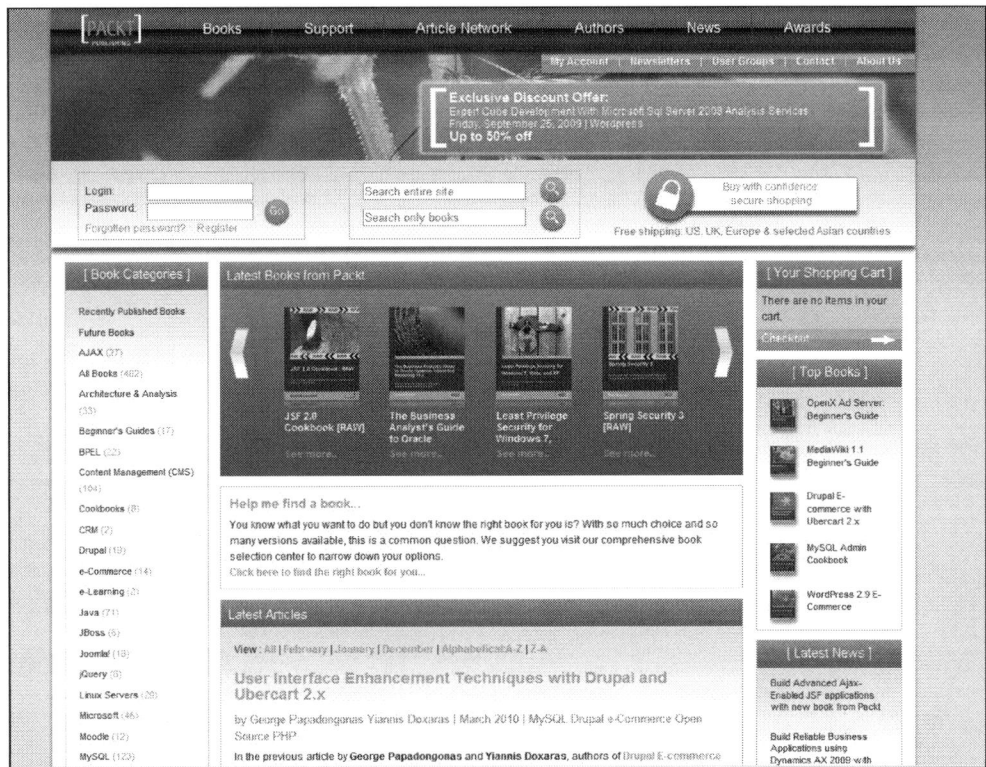

What just happened?

This should look awfully familiar to ASP.NET developers: you have a mark-up file that wires up event handlers defined in an associated code behind file. We also wrote code that popped up an alert window in the browser. This is the same kind of popup as you would see if you had coded a call to `Alert` in Javascript. You may not have realized it yet, but you spoke JavaScript to the host browser. The `System.Windows` namespace has all sorts of ways to talk to the browser and it handles all the differences between platforms and host browsers for you. Silverlight provides an **HTML Bridge** which allows you to interact with the host browser, and hosting HTML document.

We also could have defined the event handler and written the code in Blend, but we hadn't used Visual Studio in a while. I was beginning to worry that it may have been feeling neglected with all the work we've been doing in Blend.

Where are we really?

Now is a good time to remind ourselves where our code will run. Yes, we all know that Silverlight is cross-browser and cross-platform and can run on Windows, Macintoshes, Linux, and even on mobile devices. That means that your application runs on the Silverlight runtime, which resides in an HTML **Document Object Model (DOM)** hosted in a browser on the end user's operating system.

As you can see from this diagram, there are a lot of layers between your code and the actual silicon it's running on:

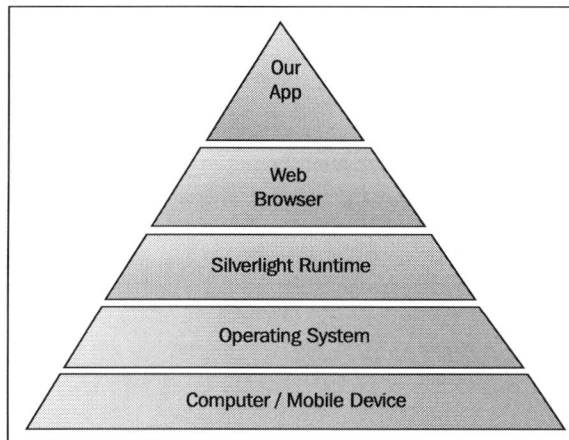

Silverlight 4 has out-of-browser functionality. Despite the name, you are actually running in a browser via some clever sleight of hand.

Animation in Silverlight

Silverlight sports a rich animation system that is surprisingly easy to use. The animation model in Silverlight is time based, meaning that movements occur based on a set timeline. At the heart of every animation is a **StoryBoard**, which contains all the animation data and independent timeline. Silverlight controls can contain any number of Storyboards.

StoryBoards contain one or more **Key frame** elements, which are responsible for making objects on screen change position, color, or any number of properties. There are four general types of Key frames in Silverlight 4: **Linear**, **Discrete**, **Spline**, and **Easing**. The table below illustrates what each one does:

Key frame type	Description
Linear	Moves from the starting state to the end state in a smooth, linear fashion.
Discrete	Jumps from the starting state to the end state instantaneously.
Spline	Moves from the starting state to the end state varying speed based on mathematically defined curve..
Easing	A more evolved version of the Spine, this type of key frame moves from the starting state to the end state based on an Easing function.

Very different than Flash

The animation model in Silverlight is markedly different than the one found in Adobe Flash. Animations in Flash are frame-based, whereas in Silverlight they are time-based.

The term **StoryBoard** comes from the motion picture industry, where scenes are drawn out before they are filmed.

Time for action – animation time

The client would like to transform their text-only logo into something a little more elaborate. The designers have once again given us a XAML snippet of code exported from their graphic design tool. We will need to do the following:

1. Open up the **CakeORama** logo project from the Chapter 2 directory in Blend.

2. Blend should have automatically loaded the `MainControl.xaml` file and your screen should look like this:

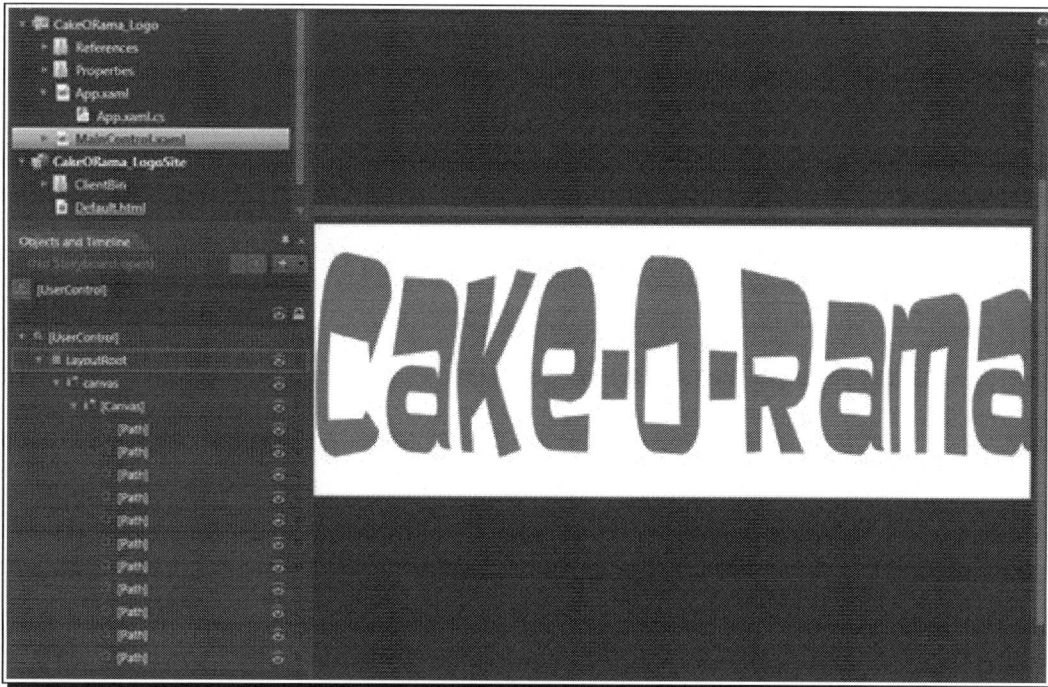

3. In the **Objects and Timeline** tab, you'll see a list of objects that make up this vector drawing. There is `Path` object for every character.

4. Let's add an animation. On the **Object and Timeline** tab, click the plus sign (**+**) to create a new **StoryBoard**.

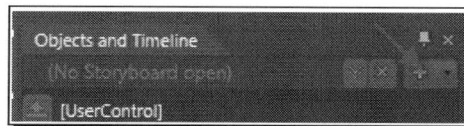

5. In the **Create Storyboard Resource** dialog, type **introAnimationStoryboard** into the text box and click **OK**.

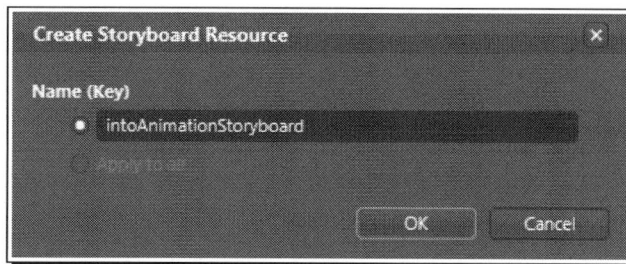

6. You'll notice a couple of changes to your screen. For one, the art board is surrounded by a red border and a notification that: **intoAnimationStoryboard timeline recording is on** just like in this screenshot:

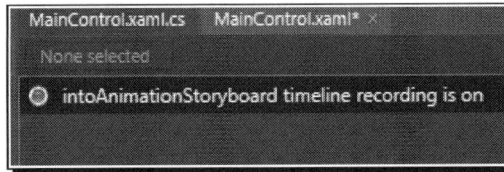

7. If you take a look at the **Objects and Timeline** tab, you'll see the timeline for our newly created **introAnimationStoryboard**:

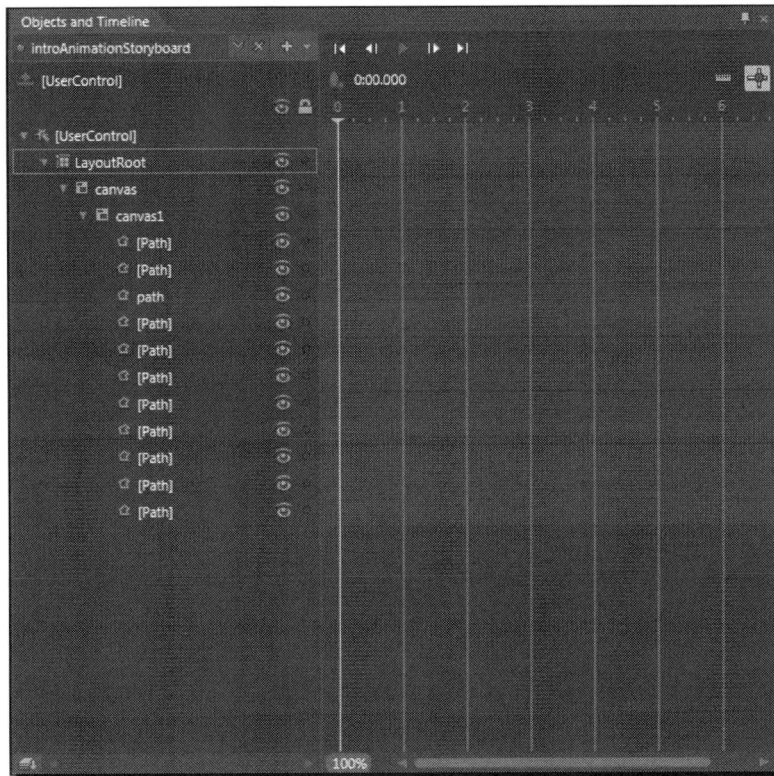

8. Let's add a key frame at the very beginning. The vertical yellow line is the play head, which marks where you currently are in the timeline. Select the **canvas1** object.

> You can switch to the Animation Workspace in Blend by pressing *F6*.

9. Click on the square icon with a green plus sign to create a new Key frame here at position **0**. A white oval appears representing the Key frame that you just created. It should look similar to the following screenshot:

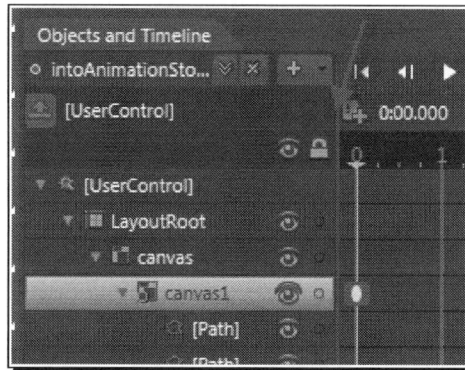

10. Move the play head to 0.7 seconds, by clicking on the tick mark to the immediate left of the number 1.

11. Click the same button you did in step 9 to create a new key frame here so that your timeline looks like this:

12. Move the play head back to zero.

13. Make sure the **canvas1** object is still selected, click and drag the logo graphic up, so that all of it is in the grey area. This moves the logo "off stage".

14. Hit the play button highlighted in the below screenshot, to preview the animation and enjoy the show!

15. Now all we need to do is tell Silverlight to run the animation when our control loads, but first we need to get out of recording mode. To do this, click the **x** button on the **Objects and Timeline** tab.

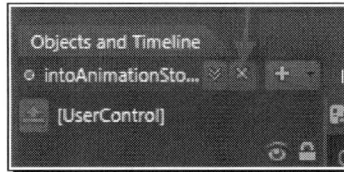

16. Click on **[UserControl]** in the **Objects and Timeline** tab.

17. On the **Properties** tab, you'll see an icon with a lightning bolt on it. Click on it to see the events associated with a **UserControl** object:

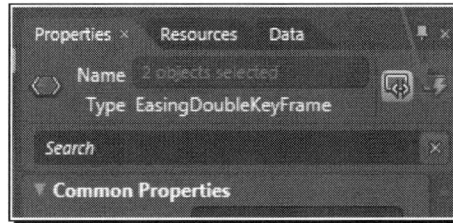

18. To wire up an event handler for the **Loaded** event, type **UserControl_Loaded** in the text box next to **Loaded**, as shown in the next screenshot:

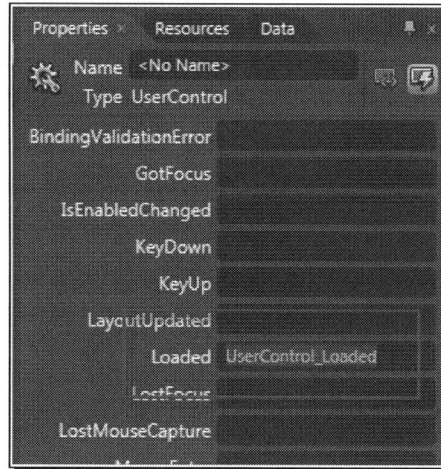

19. Once you hit *Enter*, the code behind will immediately pop up with your cursor inside the event handler method.

20. Add this line of code to the method:

```
introAnimationStoryboard.Begin();
```

Run the solution via the menu bar or by pressing *F5.* You should see the logo graphic smoothly and evenly animate into view. If for some reason the animation doesn't get displayed, refresh the page in your browser. You should see it now.

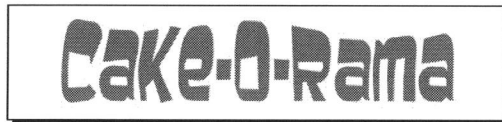

What just happened?

You just created your first animation in Silverlight. First you created a Storyboard and then added a couple of Key frames. You changed the properties of the canvas on one key frame and Silverlight automatically interpolated them in between points to create a nice smooth animation. If your animation didn't show up on the initial page load but did when you reloaded the page, then you've just experienced how seriously the Silverlight animation engine respects time. Since our animation length is relatively short (0.7 seconds) it's possible that more than that amount of time elapsed from the call of the `Begin` method, to the amount of time it took for your computer to render it. Silverlight noticed that and "jumped" ahead to that part of the timeline to keep everything on schedule.

Just like we did before, let's take a look at the XAML to get a better feel of what's really going on. You'll find the Storyboard XAML in the `UserControl.Resources` section towards the top of the document. Don't worry if the values are slightly different in your project:

```
<Storyboard x:Name="introAnimationStoryboard">
  <DoubleAnimationUsingKeyFrames BeginTime="00:00:00" Storyboard.
TargetName="canvas1" Storyboard.TargetProperty="(UIElement.RenderTrans
form).(TransformGroup.Children)[3].(TranslateTransform.Y)">
<EasingDoubleKeyFrame KeyTime="00:00:00" Value="-229"/>
<EasingDoubleKeyFrame KeyTime="00:00:00.7000000" Value="0"/>
  </DoubleAnimationUsingKeyFrames>
<DoubleAnimationUsingKeyFrames BeginTime="00:00:00" Storyboard.
TargetName="canvas1" Storyboard.TargetProperty="(UIElement.RenderTrans
form).(TransformGroup.Children)[3].(TranslateTransform.X)">
<EasingDoubleKeyFrame KeyTime="00:00:00" Value="1"/>
<EasingDoubleKeyFrame KeyTime="00:00:00.7000000" Value="0"/>
  </DoubleAnimationUsingKeyFrames>
</Storyboard>
```

There are a couple of things going on here, so let's dissect the animation XAML starting with the Storyboard declaration which creates a Storyboard and assigns the name we gave it in the dialog box:

```
<Storyboard x:Name="introAnimationStoryboard">
```

That's easy enough, but what about the next node? This line tells the Storyboard that we will be modifying a `Double` value starting at 0 seconds. It also further specifies a target for our animation: `canvas1` and a `property` on our target:

```
<DoubleAnimationUsingKeyFrames BeginTime="00:00:00" Storyboard.
TargetName="canvas1" Storyboard.TargetProperty="(UIElement.RenderTrans
form).(TransformGroup.Children)[3].(TranslateTransform.Y)">
```

Clear enough, but what does the `TargetProperty` value mean? Here is that value highlight below.

```
(UIElement.RenderTransform).(TransformGroup.Children)[3].(TranslateTr
ansform.Y)
```

We know that the net effect of the animation is that the logo moves from above the visible area back to its original position. If we're familiar with X, Y coordinates, where X represents a horizontal coordinate and Y a vertical coordinate, then the `TranslateTransform.Y` part makes sense. We are changing or, in Silverlight terms, transforming the Y property of the canvas. But what's all this `TransformGroup` about?

Take a look at our `canvas1` node further down in the XAML. You should see the following lines of XAML that weren't there earlier:

```
<Canvas.RenderTransform>
  <TransformGroup>
    <ScaleTransform />
    <SkewTransform/>
    <RotateTransform/>
    <TranslateTransform/>
  </TransformGroup>
</Canvas.RenderTransform>
```

Blend automatically inserted them into the `Canvas` when we created the animation. They have no properties. Think of them as stubbed declarations of these objects. If you remove them, Silverlight will throw an exception at runtime like the one below complaining about not being able to resolve `TargetProperty`:

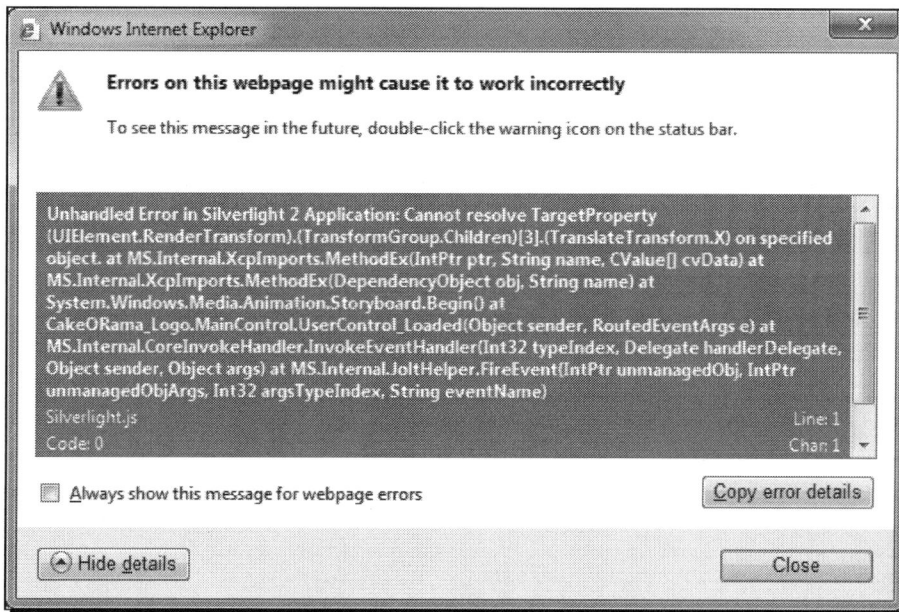

Clearly this code is important, but what's really going on here? The `TranslateTransform` object is a type of `Transform` object which determines how an object can change in Silverlight. They are packaged in a `TransformGroup`, which can be set in the `RenderTransform` property on any object descending from **UIElement**. UIElement is the base class for any kind of visual element.

With that bit of knowledge, we now see that `(TransformGroup.Children)[3]` refers to the fourth element in a zero-based collection. Not so coincidentally, the `TranslateTransform` node is the fourth item inside the `TransformGroup` in our XAML. Changing the order of the transforms in the XAML will also cause an exception at runtime.

That line of XAML just tells the Silverlight runtime that we're going to animation, now we tell it how and when with our two `EasingDoubleKeyFrame` nodes:

```
<EasingDoubleKeyFrame KeyTime="00:00:00" Value="-229"/>
<EasingDoubleKeyFrame KeyTime="00:00:00.7000000" Value="0"/>
```

The first `EasingDoubleKeyFrame` node tells Silverlight that, at zero seconds, we want the value to be `-229`. This corresponds to when the logo was above the visible area. The second `EasingDoubleKeyFrame` node tells Silverlight that at 0.7 seconds, we want the value of the property to be `0`. This corresponds to the initial state of the logo, where it was before any transformations were applied.

Silverlight handles all changes to the value in between the start and the end point. Silverlight's default frame rate is 60 frames per second, but Silverlight will adjust its frame rate based on the hardware that it is running on. Silverlight can adjust the amount by which it changes the values to keep the animation on schedule. If you had to reload the web page to see the animation run, then you've already experienced this. Once again, notice how few lines (technically only one line) of procedural code you had to write.

Have a go hero – exploring animation options

The animation we just created worked, but it feels too mechanical. What if there was a way, we could change the rate at which it "fell down" onto the screen.

In the real world, objects typically bounce when they hit a hard surface. Let's replicate that here by using a built in Easing function. To do this, we will need to do the following:

1. Go back to Expression Blend and click on the drop down button highlighted here:

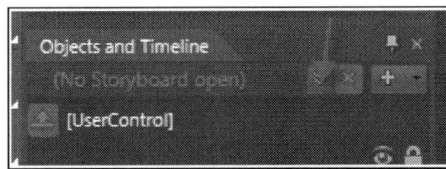

2. Click on **introAnimationStoryboard** to edit that timeline.
3. Click on the key frame oval at 0.7 seconds.

4. You'll notice that the **Properties** tab on the right has a combo box that has an angled straight line next to the word **None** like this:

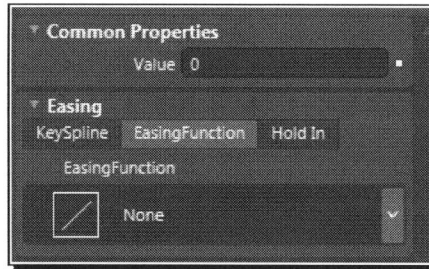

5. Click on the items marked **Bounce** in the **Out** Column and the text in the combo box should read **Bounce Out** like this:

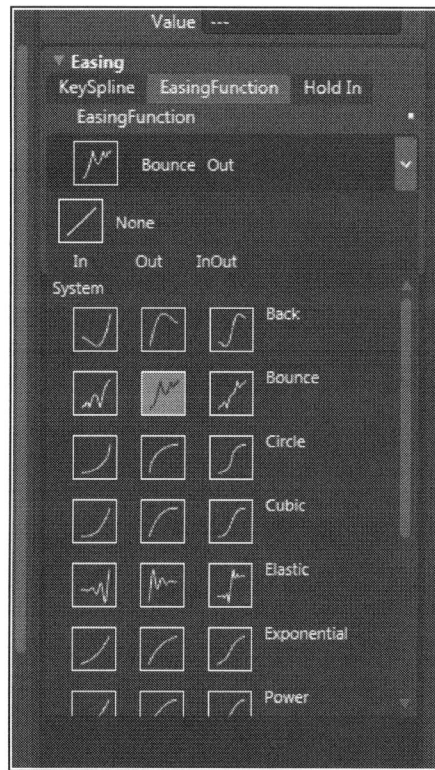

6. Run the solution via the menu bar or pressing *F5,*.and notice how the logo bounces onto the screen.

7. You can also tweak the parameters of the bounce effect by changing the **Bounces** and **Bounciness** values.

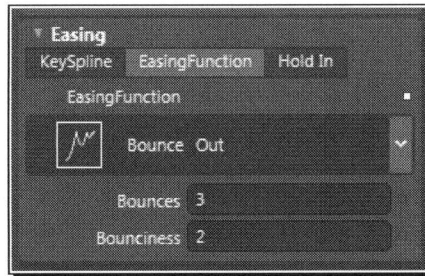

8. To further experiment, you could click on **KeySpline** where the graph appears, representing the rate of animation. By default, it starts out as a straight line:

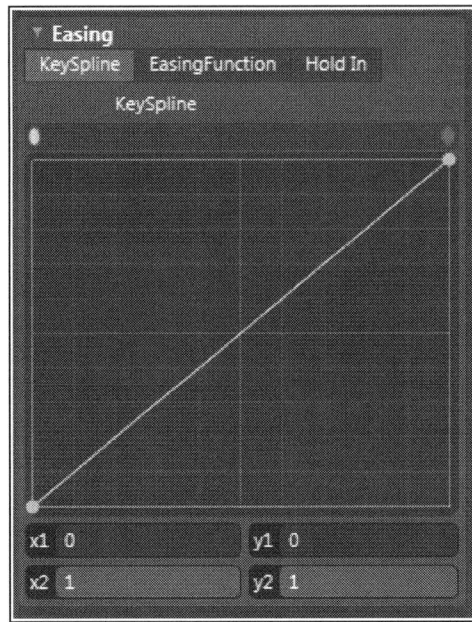

9. Hit the play button to preview the animation.

10. You can change the line by clicking and dragging the yellow circles around or by inserting values into the **x1,x2, y1,y2** text boxes, so that your graph looks something like this:

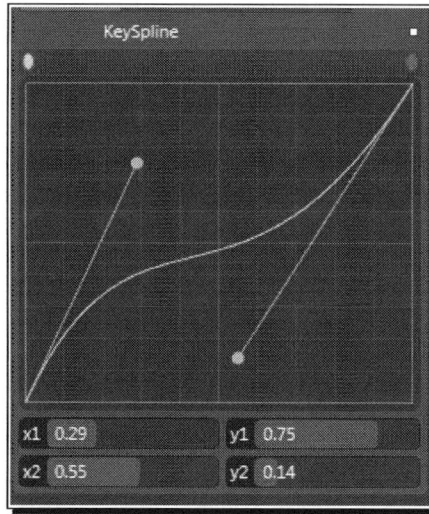

11. Preview the animation again and note the changes.

12. Click on the **Hold In** button highlighted here:

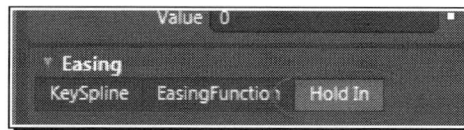

Preview the animation once more to see how it just simply "jumps" from one value to the other. Feel free to experiment with different options for animating this logo.

Getting on the same page

So far, we've created two different Silverlight projects; one for the navigation buttons and one for the animated logo. Each resided in their own projects, on their own page. How can we integrate the two projects onto the HTML that we already have for our client's home page?

To do that we should take a look at the test page Blend and Visual Studio automatically created for us and see how to embed a Silverlight application onto a web page.

Time for action – getting Silverlight onto a web page

We need to get both the logo and the navigation buttons on the same page. In this exercise, we're going to bring some new life to our old page:

1. Open up the **CakeNavigationButtons** solution in Visual Studio.

2. Let's take a closer look at the `CakeNavigationButtons.Web` project.

3. The project looks much like any other ASP.NET project, except for the **ClientBin** directory.

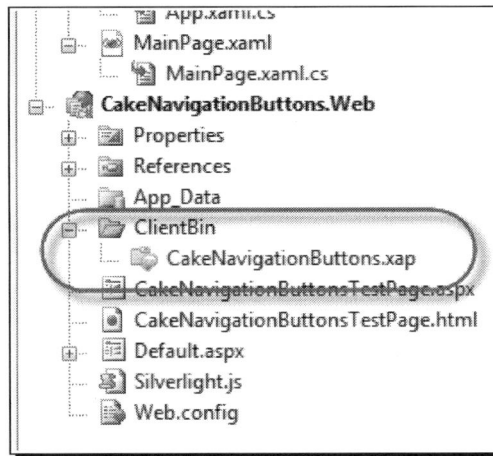

4. Double-click on the `CakeNavigationButtonsTestPage.html` to open it in our editor and scroll down the page until you see the following code:

```
<div id="silverlightControlHost">
    <object data="data:application/x-silverlight-2,"
type="application/x-silverlight-2" width="100%" height="100%">
      <param name="source" value="ClientBin/CakeNavigationButtons.
xap"/>
      <param name="onerror" value="onSilverlightError" />
      <param name="background" value="white" />
      <param name="minRuntimeVersion" value="4.0.41108.0" />
      <param name="autoUpgrade" value="true" />
      <a href="http://go.microsoft.com/fwlink/?LinkID=141205"
style="text-decoration: none;">
      <img src="http://go.microsoft.com/fwlink/?LinkId=108181"
alt="Get Microsoft Silverlight" style="border-style: none"/>
      </a>
```

```
     </object>
     <iframe style='visibility:hidden;height:0;width:0;border:0px'>
</iframe>
</div>
```

Seasoned web developers will instantly recognize a plugin object wrapped inside a `DIV` tag. The `object` tag contains a number of `param` tags, which pass along parameters to the object. By default, the height and width are set to `100%`, which fills up all the space available. Combined with the CSS rule `#silverlightControlHost`, both are Silverlight applications and will be much larger than they need to be. The `source` parameter points to the `CakeNavigationButtons.xap` file in the `ClientBin` directory. The XAP file contains the compiled content of our Silverlight control.

The `minRuntimeVersion` parameter indicates that the user must have at least Silverlight 4 in order to run the embedded Silverlight content.

The HTML inside the object tag is what displays if the user does not have Silverlight installed on their computer. Further up on the page, you'll see a reference to a `Silverlight.js` file. This contains all the plugin detection code.

5. Let's go back to our original HTML document, to see where the new code would best fit:

```
<html xmlns="http://www.w3.org/1999/xhtml">
<head>
<title>Cake-O-Rama</title>
<style type="text/css">
<!--
.Headline {
  color: #039;
}
-->
</style>
</head>
<body>
<h1 align="center" class="Headline">Cake-O-Rama</h1>
<p align="left"><a href="#">Home</a></p>
<p align="left"><a href="#">Gallery</a></p>
<p align="left"><a href="#">Order</a></p>
<p align="left"><a href="#">Locations</a></p>
<p align="left"><a href="#">Contact Us</a></p>
<p align="left"><a href="#">Franchise Opportunities</a></p>
</body>
</html>
```

6. In the same folder as the Cake-O-Rama HTML file, we will need to create a directory called ClientBin. We could name this directory anything we wanted, but for now, let's stick to the naming convention.

7. Copy the CakeNavigationButtons.xap and CakeORama_Logo.xap files to the ClientBin directory we just created.

8. Change the HTML, so that the contents of the body tag are now:

```
<div align="center">
<object data="data:application/x-silverlight-2,"
type="application/x-silverlight-2" width="908" height="258">
        <param name="source" value="ClientBin/CakeORama_Logo.xap"/>
        <param name="background" value="white" />
        <param name="minRuntimeVersion" value="4.0.41108.0" />
        <param name="autoUpgrade" value="true" />
            <H1 align="center" class="Headline">Cake-O-Rama</H1>
        <a href="http://go.microsoft.com/fwlink/?LinkID=141205"
style="text-decoration: none;">Get Silverlight</a> to experience
this site's interactive features.
   </object>
</div>
<object data="data:application/x-silverlight-2,"
type="application/x-silverlight-2" width="214" height="281">
        <param name="source" value="ClientBin/CakeNavigationButtons.
xap"/>
        <param name="background" value="white" />
        <param name="minRuntimeVersion" value="4.0.41108.0" />
        <param name="autoUpgrade" value="true" />
<p align="left"><a href="#">Home</a></p>
<p align="left"><a href="#">Gallery</a></p>
<p align="left"><a href="#">Order</a></p>
<p align="left"><a href="#">Locations</a></p>
<p align="left"><a href="#">Contact Us</a></p>
<p align="left"><a href="#">Franchise Opportunities</a></p>
        <a href="http://go.microsoft.com/fwlink/?LinkID=141205"
style="text-decoration: none;">Get Silverlight</a> to experience
this site's interactive features.
</object>
```

Load up the page in your browser. If you're running locally on your file system, you may get an error like this:

To help protect your security, Internet Explorer has restricted this webpage from running scripts or ActiveX controls that could access your computer. Click here for options... ✕

Or, if you are a user who hasn't installed Silverlight, you may see the following when you load the page:

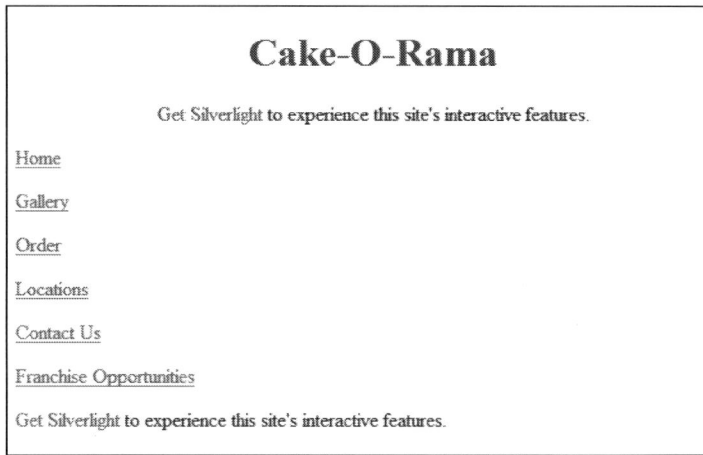

Cake-O-Rama

Get Silverlight to experience this site's interactive features.

Home

Gallery

Order

Locations

Contact Us

Franchise Opportunities

Get Silverlight to experience this site's interactive features.

9. Right-click on the security warning bar on the top of the browser window and choose **Allow Blocked Content**.

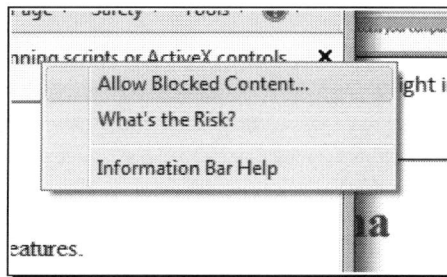

Allow Blocked Content...

What's the Risk?

Information Bar Help

10. The page will reload and you will now see the client's home page in all its Silverlight glory.

What just happened?

We took the output of our two Silverlight projects and combined them onto one page. In the process, we saw how Silverlight is embedded onto a static web page.

The client's home page right now is just static HTML, but it can get quite dynamic once you add Silverlight to it. The important thing to remember is that Silverlight is a client-side technology and the backend server could run on any platform.

Summary

In this chapter, we learnt about Expression Blend, Container controls, Visual State Manager, Animation, and Designer/Developer workflow. We covered a lot of ground in this chapter and it lays the foundation for the work ahead of us. We took a drab website and turned it into something a little more modern. Certainly, the websites you will be migrating to Silverlight will not be this plain. I wanted to demonstrate with something as simple as possible, so that the concepts stood out.

Specifically, we looked at:

- ◆ Using container controls
- ◆ Using styles to customize the look of a control
- ◆ Working in Expression Blend
- ◆ Changing the look and feel of a control using Control Templates
- ◆ Using the Visual State Manager to add subtle transitions to controls
- ◆ Creating animations in Silverlight and making them natural by using Easing Key frames
- ◆ Embedding Silverlight controls onto a static web page
- ◆ The power of declarative programming

Most of all, we learned how to use the power of XAML to create a rich experience with hardly any procedural code. Think about it: we really have only written two lines of C# code (three if you count the one that we deleted). Most of the work was done in XAML, and most of the XAML was actually generated by Blend.

In the next chapter, we will look at kicking our website up a notch by incorporating sound and video.

3
Adding Rich Media

Sites such as YouTube and Hulu have pushed the boundaries of web video. Once thought to be impossible or impractical, watching everything from movie trailers to entire movies online is now commonplace.

Silverlight provides great support for rich media content. Media can enrich any application. Whether it's a sound to indicate that you've received a new email, help in the form of a video tutorial, or a greeting message from your company's CEO, incorporating multimedia into your application can give it extra depth and an edge over the competition.

One of the key features of Silverlight is the integration of multimedia. A full discourse on delivering rich media over the internet could fill an entire book. However, for all but the most sophisticated applications, a little knowledge will go a long way. Silverlight hides a lot of the complicated parts of deploying media over the web.

In this chapter, we shall:

- ◆ Add sound and video to our website
- ◆ Learn how to fill shapes with video, using video as a brush
- ◆ Enhance the navigation control with sound
- ◆ Use Expression Media Encoder to encode our own video clips

Adding media to a Silverlight project

Silverlight provides built-in support for playing a variety of media formats, both movie and sound files. The process for adding media to Silverlight projects is relatively easy to do; you may find yourself dreaming up all kinds of ways to enhance all your projects with rich media. You could add background music to create ambience or add sounds to provide feedback that a button has been clicked or a process completed, the options are endless.

Tread carefully

Just because you can add media to your Silverlight applications doesn't mean you should. There are a number of factors to consider, such as additional bandwidth usage, media rights, and the patience of your users. Add media when it adds value, not just to show off your Silverlight skills!

Time for action – adding background music

Let's see how we can add some background music to the animated logo application that we created in the previous chapter. By doing this, we will add a little bit of atmosphere to our homepage. In order to get started, we will need to complete the following steps:

1. Open up the **CakeORama Logo** solution (that we worked on in Chapter 2) in Expression Blend. We're going to enhance that solution with sound and video.

   Right-click on the **CakeoRama Logo** project in the **Solution** and choose **Add Existing Item...**

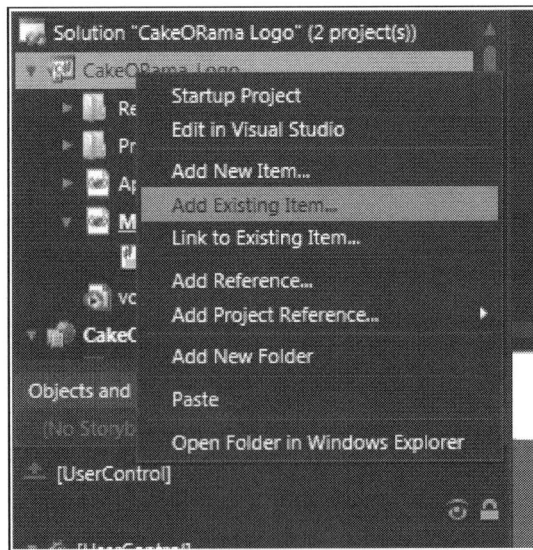

2. Browse to the mp3 or WAV audio file that you'd like to use and place it in our project. You can use the one included in the downloadable content for this book (**vocals.mp3**) or another file on your hard drive. Now we need to add a MediaElement control to play our sound file. Click on the **Assets** button on the toolbar. It has chevrons pointing to the right:

3. When the dialog appears, type **Media** to limit the list to controls that contain the word 'media'. Click on **MediaElement**:

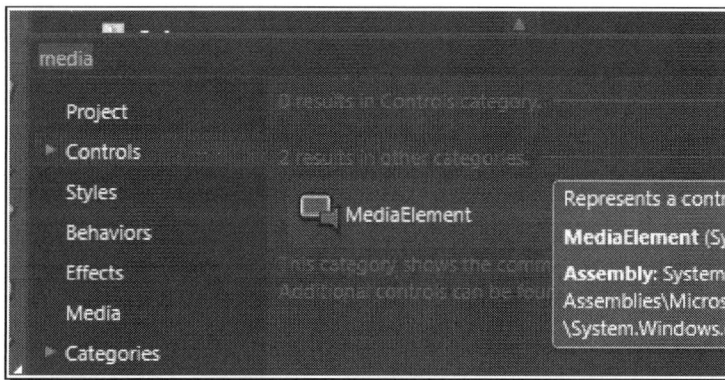

4. Double-click anywhere on the art board to insert the MediaElement control. Since we're only playing audio, the control can be invisible.

5. By default, the newly created MediaElement control will be selected. Use the **Properties** tab to name it **mediaMusic**.

6. Further down in the **Properties** tab are the **Media** properties. Choose **/vocals.mp3** from the drop down menu next to the **Source** property.

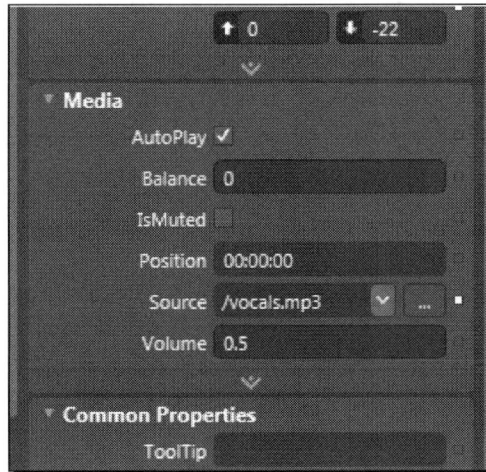

7. Make sure that **AutoPlay** is checked.

8. Run the solution. The animation will work as it did before, and you will hear the music in the background.

What just happened?

We just added some music to our logo application to add a fun atmosphere to our site. As you can see, it didn't take a single line of procedural code. We simply added a music file to our project, created a `MediaElement` control and set the source of the control to our music file. That's all there was to it.

However, behind the scenes a few things happened here. When Blend added the audio file to the solution, it set the file's **Build Action** to **Content**:

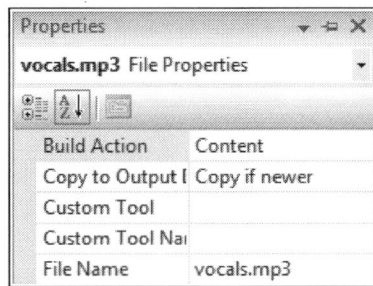

If you open up the solution in Visual Studio, you can verify this for yourself. This tells the compiler to embed the sound file into the XAP deployment file. If you were to add the same file in Visual Studio, the default **Build Action** would be **None**. Blend did the extra step for you.

Embedding files versus referencing files

Embedding a media file is generally a bad idea as it can bloat the size of your XAP file. The **CakeORama Logo** XAP file was 11k before adding the music loop. Now it's over 350k! Generally, this is not a good idea. However, for smaller sound effects, embedding the sound file makes more sense.

For larger media files, the best approach would be to place the media file in the web project or on a web server and then tell Silverlight to load it from there. This keeps the size of your XAP file smaller, so that it downloads and starts executing faster. Your application is still going to need time to download the larger media file, but you'll be able to control the experience. When it comes to the time to deploy your solution, make sure you copy over all your media files as well as your XAP file.

Have a go hero – improving the experience

Currently, the sound on our **CakeORama Logo** solution isn't interactive and plays only once. To keep up the atmospheric effect, we may wish to have the sound repeat indefinitely. Users should also have the ability to mute the sound. Additionally, the music file is contained within the XAP file. We want to display the logo as quickly as possible. The best way to do this is to take the music file of the Silverlight solution and place it into our web project. Let's make both of these improvements now:

1. Firstly, we will need to open up the **CakeORama Logo** solution in Expression Blend.

2. In the **CakeORama_LogoSite** project, expand the **ClientBin** directory and right-click on that directory then choose **Add Existing Item...** from the context menu:

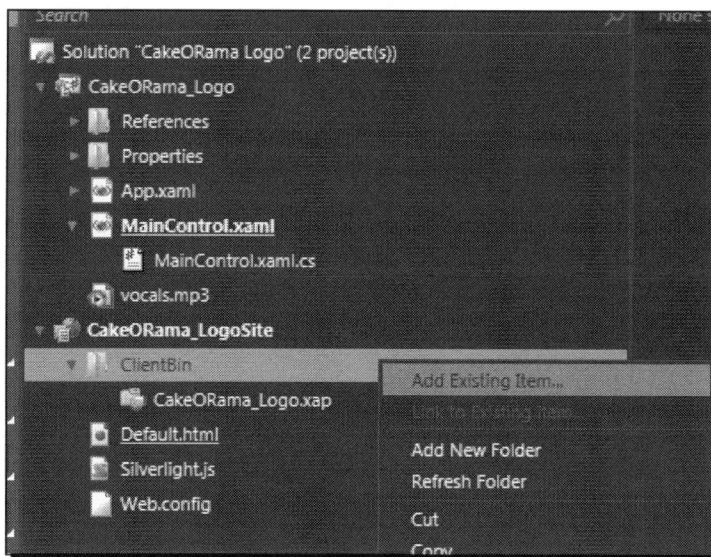

3. Browse to a location which contains the **vocals.mp3** file and click on **Open** to add it to the **CakeORama_LogoSite** web site project.

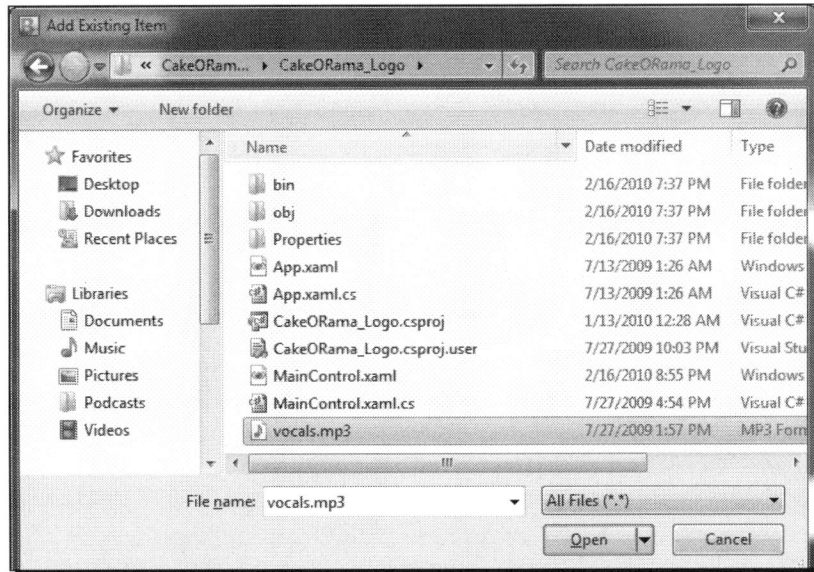

4. Next, let's remove the **vocals.mp3** file from the **CakeORama_Logo** Silverlight project, so that it won't be embedded in the compiled XAP file. Right-click on the **vocals.mp3** file in the **CakeORama_Logo** project and click **Delete**.

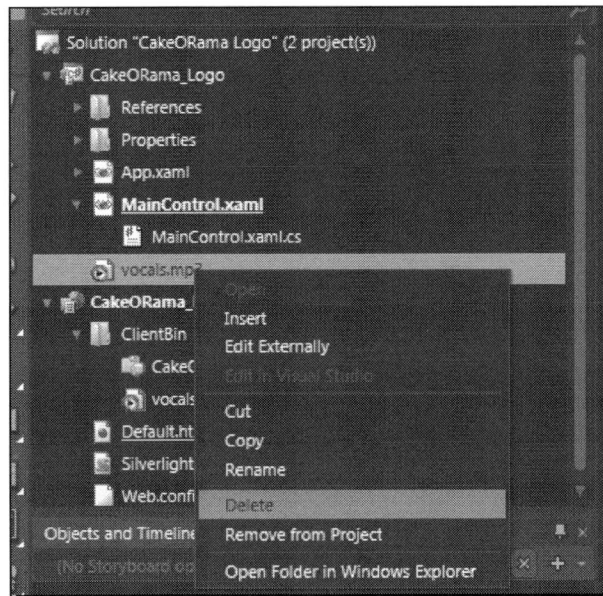

5. Click **Yes** in the confirmation dialog box.

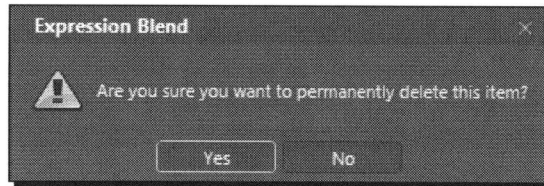

6. Build the project by choosing **Build Project** from the **Project** menu or by pressing *Ctrl+Shift+B*.

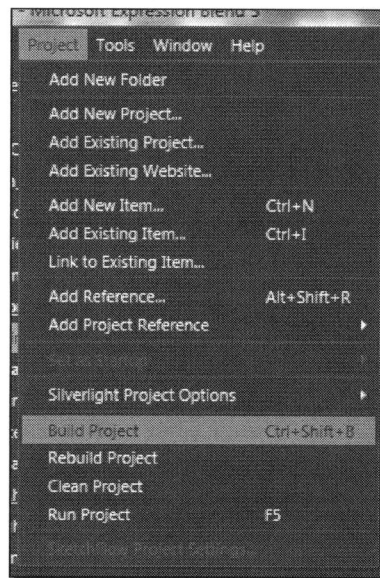

7. Right-click on the **ClientBin** folder in the **CakeORama_LogoSite** project and click **Open Folder** in **Windows Explorer** on the context menu.

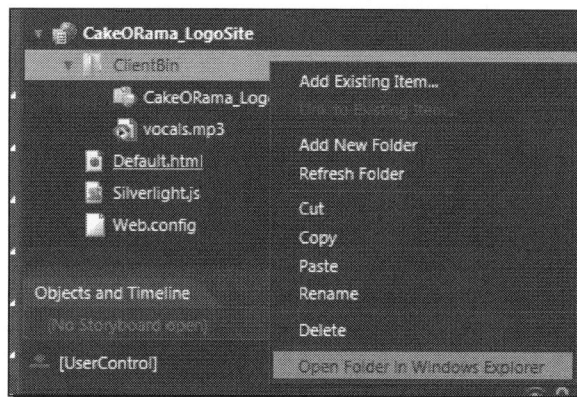

8. The **ClientBin** folder will open in Windows Explorer, and you'll see that our XAP file is back down to its original size.

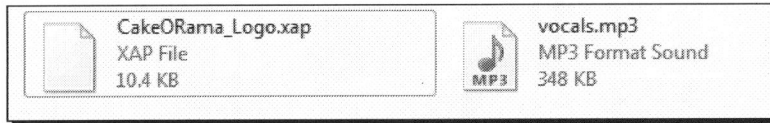

> CakeORama_Logo.xap
> XAP File
> 10.4 KB
>
> vocals.mp3
> MP3 Format Sound
> 348 KB

9. Go back to Expression Blend and select the **mediaMusic, MediaElement**.

10. Click the **Events** button in the **Properties** tab to show all the events the **MediaElement** control exposes:

> Properties × Resources Data
> Name mediaMusic
> Type MediaElement
> Search

11. Among the events listed is the **MediaEnded** event. It fires when the media reaches the end.

    Type **mediaMusic_MediaEnded** into the textbox next to **MediaEnded** and press *Enter*, as shown in the next screenshot:

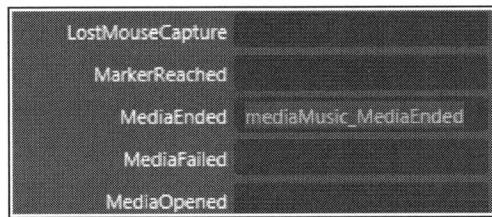

> LostMouseCapture
> MarkerReached
> MediaEnded   mediaMusic_MediaEnded
> MediaFailed
> MediaOpened

12. Add the following lines of code into the event handler that Blend automatically created:

```
mediaMusic.Stop();
mediaMusic.Play();
```

13. Run the solution again. The original clip is 22 seconds long. You'll notice that after it finishes playing, it starts over again.

14. Close the browser window and go back into Blend. Select the **LayoutRoot** grid object from the **Objects and Timeline** tab:

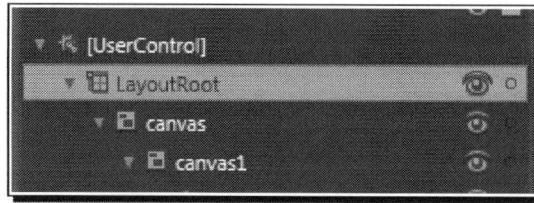

15. The **Properties** tab should still be in **Events** mode, type **LayoutRoot_MouseLeftButtonUp** into the text box next to **MouseLeftButtonUp** and press *Enter* to create the event handler:

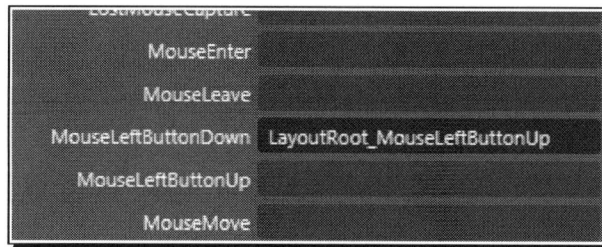

16. In the event handler, add the following line of code:

```
mediaMusic.Volume = 0;
```

17. Run the solution. You will be able to click anywhere on the logo to mute the music.

Before we put this into production, we should probably make this feature more obvious, perhaps by adding a mute button. We could simply add a button with an event handler that contained the line of code in step 13 then set the **Volume** property to **0**.

Adding video to a Silverlight project

The process of adding video to a Silverlight project is very similar to that of adding sound to a page. In the previous section where we added sound to a project, we didn't care that much about where we placed the MediaElement control or what it looked like. The sound we played didn't have a visual element. Therefore, the placement and appearance simply didn't matter. However, adding video requires us to have a visual element.

Time for action – adding video

We're going to add a short video clip to the animated logo project. We will place the media player element inside the **O** in **Cake-O-Rama**. This is the same project to which we just added the background music. To get started, we will need to do the following:

1. Open up the **CakeORama Logo** solution in Expression Blend.

   In the `Cakeorama_LogoSite` project, right-click on the `ClientBin` folder.

2. Click **Add Existing Item** in the context menu. Browse for a `WMV` file, in the sample videos directory:

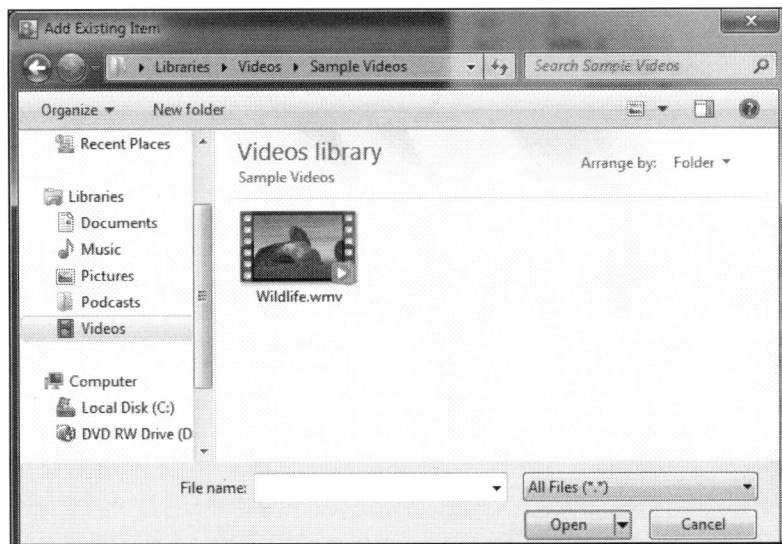

3. Choose `Butterfly.wmv`. Your `ClientBin` folder should look like this:

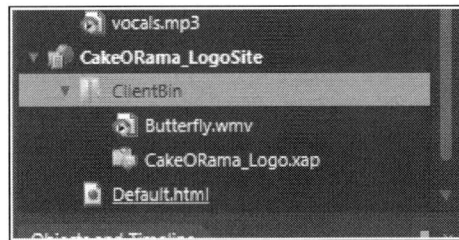

4. Then, go to the `MainPage.XAML` file in the **CakeORama Logo** project and add a new `MediaElement` control.

5. Make sure that the newly created `MediaElement` control is selected, and look for the **Source** property in the **Properties** tab.

6. Click the drop down and choose `Butterfly.wmv`:

7. Run the solution and we should have something that looks like this:

8. That's a start, but let's move the image of the flower so that it fits inside the **O** in **Cake-O-Rama**. Close the browser window and go back to Blend.

9. Use the mouse to re-size and position the `MediaElement` control. You'll notice that the movie thumbnail keeps its aspect ratio.

10. To change the `MediaElement` control's resizing behavior, change its **Stretch** property to **Fill**:

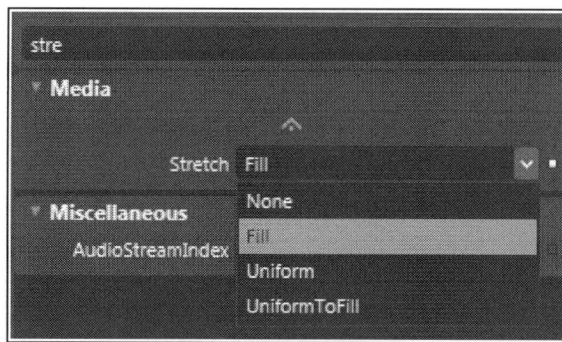

11. The `MediaElement` control should look like this:

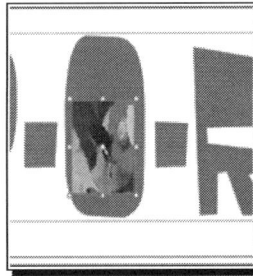

12. Run the solution once more. It looks nice, but what if we wanted the movie to animate along with the logo?

13. To do this, we would need to close the browser window and go back into Blend. In the **Objects and Timeline** tab, click on the **[MediaElement]** control, and drag it onto **canvas1**:

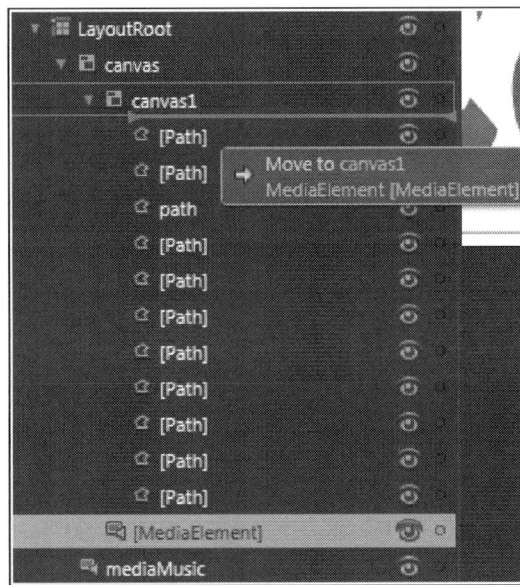

14. You'll immediately notice that the `MediaElement` control with our movie clip in it has changed locations on screen. Its placement on screen is relative to its parent and we just changed its parent.

15. Move the `MediaElement` again with the mouse to re-position it. Run the solution and you'll see that the movie plays with the animation.

What just happened?

We just added video to our Silverlight application and we saw that it's just as easy to add video as it is to add sound. We also learned how to add media resources that exist *outside* of our Silverlight XAP file. Lastly, we saw how a MediaElement control is just like any other control: it can be moved around, re-sized, and animated. We're going to have a lot of fun with that shortly.

Using video as a brush

What if we wanted the video to fill every letter in the logo? Or what if we wanted to have the video fill any kind of shape, text, or control? How would we go about that?

The answer lies in making a **VideoBrush**, or a brush that renders a video stream. To create a VideoBrush in XAML, all you need to do is declare it and get its content from a MediaElement control. The code to declare a VideoBrush is as easy as this:

```
<VideoBrush x:Key="brushName" SourceName="mediaElementControlName"/>
```

To use the VideoBrush, we simply reference it from where we want to use it:

```
Fill="{StaticResource brushName }"
```

The curly braces indicate that we are using markup extensions. The StaticResource keyword tells the Silverlight runtime to refer to resources available to the control. In plain English, the above XAML snippet tells the object to fill the object with the VideoBrush named brushName.

Time for action – creating and using a VideoBrush

We're going to fill the entire **Cake-O-Rama** logo with video by using a VideoBrush to fill up the shapes from a MediaElement control. So, let's get started.

1. Open up the **CakeORama Logo** solution in Expression Blend.

2. In the previous section, we didn't name the MediaElement control; let's do that now. Find the [MediaElement] control in the **Objects and Timeline** panel.

3. Right-click on the control and choose **Rename.** Rename the control to **meButterfly**.

4. With the **meButterfly** MediaElement selected, choose **Make Brush Resource|Make Brush Resource...** from the **Tools** menu.

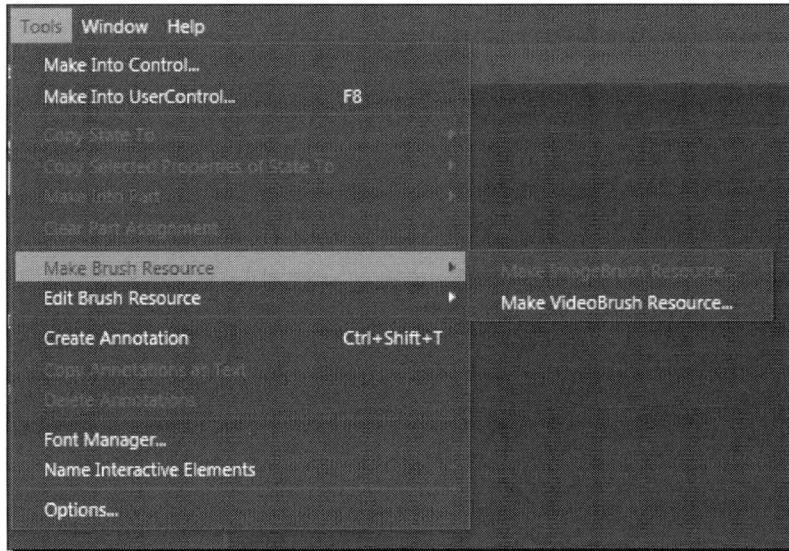

5. When the **Create VideoBrush Resource** dialog appears, enter butterFlyVideoBrush in to the **Name (Key)** textbox and click **OK**.

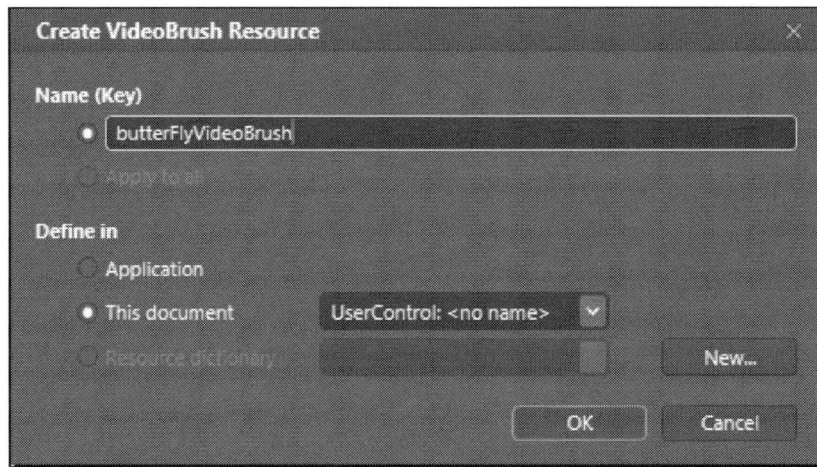

6. Go back to **Design** view and in the **Objects and Timeline** tab, select all the **Path** objects inside **canvas1**:

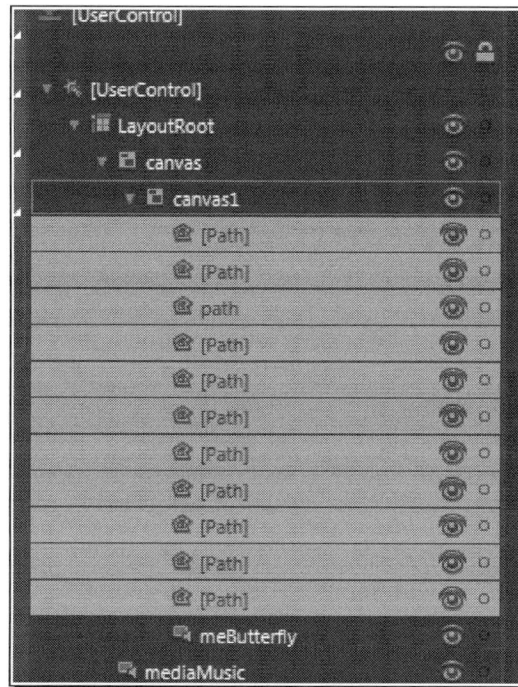

7. While all the **Path** objects are selected, go to the **Properties** tab and click on the **Brush Resource** button (it's the one on the far right side of the screen).

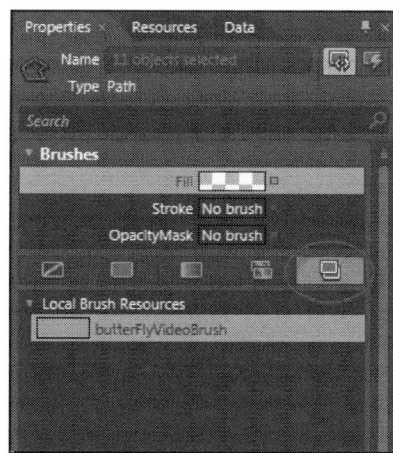

8. We should have one item in the list named **butterFlyVideoBrush**:

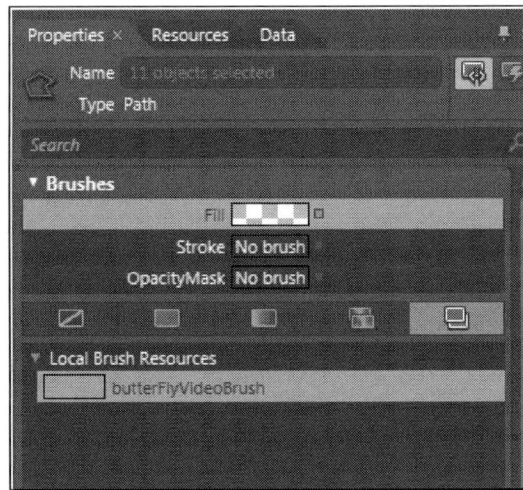

9. Click on **butterFlyVideoBrush** to select it and run the solution. You'll see that the entire logo is filled with the video image:

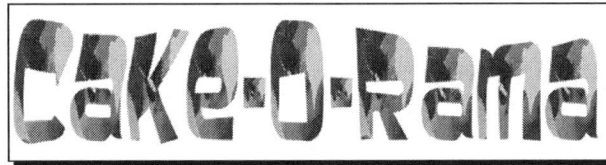

10. However, there is one small problem. Our MediaElement control is still there, filling in the middle of the **O**. We will need to close the browser, go back into Blend and delete the meButterfly control.

11. Run the solution again, and you will see that everything is blank!

12. Close the browser and go back into Blend. Press *Ctrl+Z* to undo that last change.

13. Select the meButterfly control and in the **Properties** tab, set its **Visibility** to **Collapsed**.

14. Run the solution again to see that everything is right with the logo now:

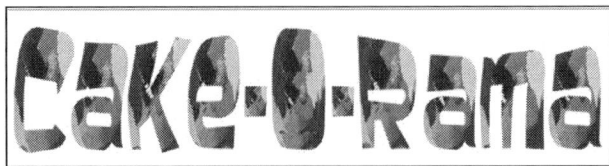

What just happened?

We just experienced the flexibility of the Silverlight rendering engine. Not only can you play video in Silverlight, you can play with it! We also saw that any given `VideoBrush` relies on the `MediaElement` control referenced in the **SourceName** property. Delete that and everything goes haywire! This is because each `VideoBrush` references a `MediaElement` control. If you want the source `MediaElement` control to be visible, simply set its `Visibility` property to `Collapsed`. This hides the control from view, but still keeps it available to any dependent `VideoBrush` elements.

Enriching an application with audio cues

So far we've seen how to add sounds and videos to our Silverlight project, that are passive. They don't really interact with the user. Consider our navigation buttons application from Chapter 2. Wouldn't it be nice to have a sound play, when the user moves the mouse over each button? It would make the navigation buttons feel a little more tangible.

Time for action – adding interactive sounds

Let's add subtle audio cues to our site navigation project to provide a slightly more engaging experience for the user. We're going to add a short sound effect that plays when the user moves their mouse over any of the buttons, by completing the following steps:

1. Open up the **CakeNavigationButtons** solution in Expression Blend that we created in Chapter 2.

2. Let's add a sound to the project by right mouse clicking in the **CakeNavigationButtons** project and choosing **Add Existing Item...** as in the screen shot below:

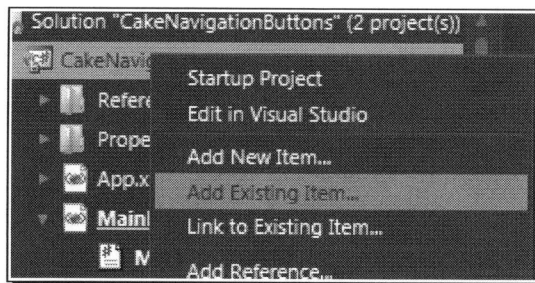

3. Browse to the `twang.mp3` file and add it to the project.

4. Expand the items in the **Objects and Timeline** panel, so that all the buttons are visible. Right-click on any one of the buttons.

5. Choose **Edit Template|Edit Current** from the context menu to edit the control template just like in this screenshot:

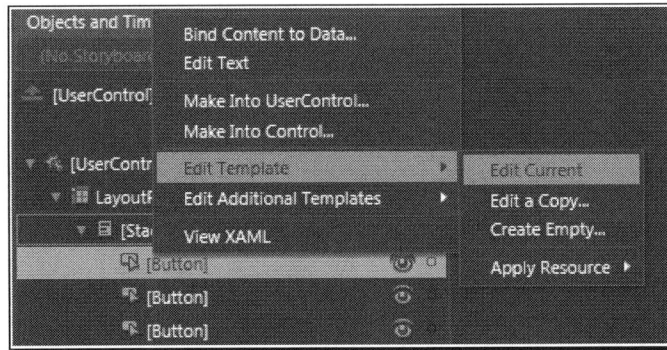

6. Now that we are in template editing mode, click on the **[Grid]** object in the **Objects and Timeline** tab to select it as you can see below:

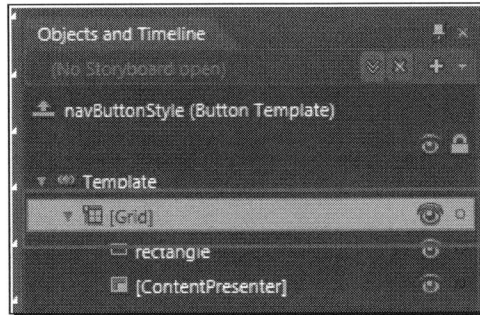

7. In the upper left corner, next to the **Projects** tab, is a tab labeled **Assets**, click on it.

8. Next , click on **Behaviors** to see all the Behavior objects available to you. Double-click on the **PlaySoundAction** behavior:

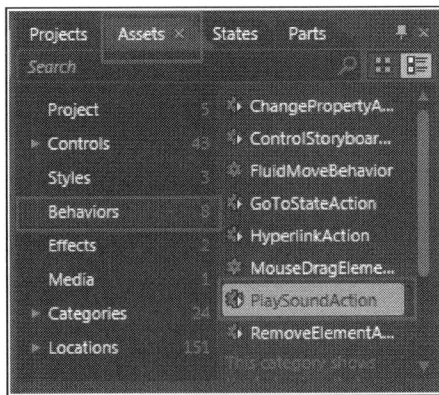

9. The **Objects and Timeline** list should now contain a new item labeled **[PlaySoundAction]:**

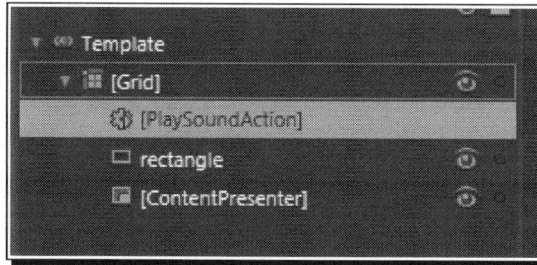

10. With the **[PlaySoundAction]** item selected, look at the **Properties** tab. Let's change it so that the event is triggered by the **MouseEnter** event. Choose that event from the drop down list next to **EventName**.

11. Then, use the drop down list to choose **/Twang.mp3**, as shown in the following screenshot:

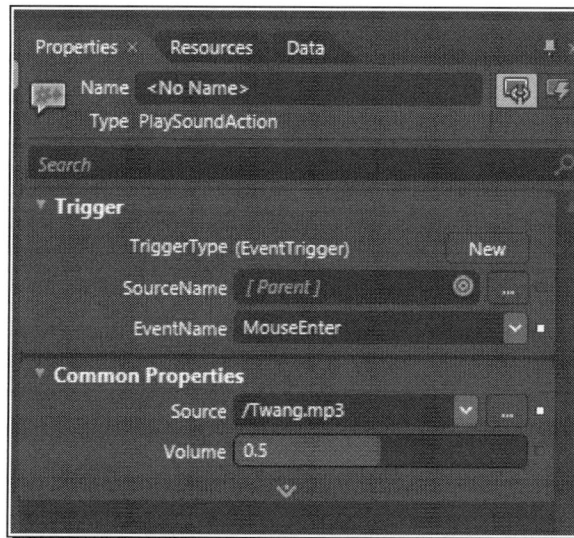

12. Run the solution. When you move the mouse over each button, the `Twang.mp3` sound plays.

What just happened?

We just added an MP3 file to our solution and edited the control template to insert a `Behavior` that plays a sound when a `MouseEnter` event is triggered. We didn't write a single line of procedural code. If you open up the XAML and examine the control template, you'll see that the following lines have been inserted into the control template:

```
<i:Interaction.Triggers>
  <i:EventTrigger EventName="MouseEnter">
    <im:PlaySoundAction Source="/Twang.mp3"/>
  </i:EventTrigger>
</i:Interaction.Triggers>
```

We could have just as easily assigned a `Behavior` to each button that did the same thing. However by adding it to the template, we only need to do it once. In the future, if we decide to change the sound or any other property, we'd only have to change the code in one location.

Have a go hero – adding a few more sounds

Our client likes the new and improved navigation buttons. In fact, they like them so much that they've requested two changes: add another sound when the user clicks on a button and lower the volume on the mouse over sound. Let's do this now:

1. Go back to the **CakeNavigationButtons** solution in Expression Blend.

2. Right-click in the **CakeNavigationButtons** project and choose **Add Existing Item...**

3. Browse to where the project resources are and choose **/thump.mp3**. If you're not already in template editing mode, right-click on any of the buttons and choose **Edit Template|Edit Current** from the context menu.

4. Click on the **[PlaySoundAction]** item in the **Objects and Timeline** tab. Next, in the **Properties** tab, change the **Volume** property to **0.25** to cut the volume in half on this sound:

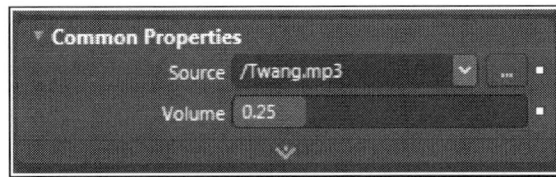

5. Select the **[Grid]** again in the **Objects and Timeline** tab. Add another **PlaySoundAction** behavior and select the newly created **[PlaySoundAction]**.

6. In the **Properties** tab, choose **MouseLeftButtonDown** from the **EventName** drop down list and `thump.mp3` from the **Source** dropdown list:

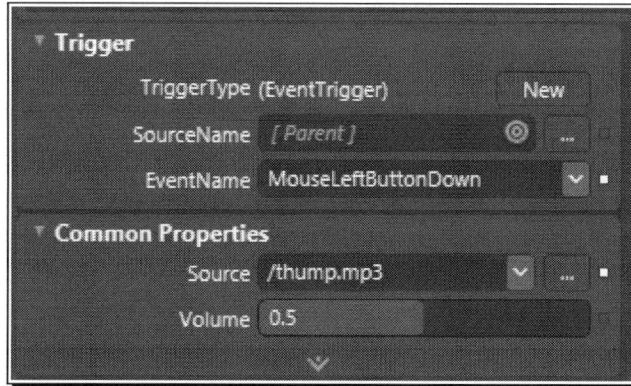

7. Run the solution again. The mouse over sound should be a little more subtle and you'll hear the thump sound when you click on any of the buttons. You can add as many **PlaySoundAction** behaviors as you like. However, consider that your users may get tired of hearing too many clicks, pops or thumps. A little subtlety goes a long way.

Coding videos with Expression Media Encoder

If you would like to use your own media content and need to convert it into a format that Silverlight supports, then **Expression Media Encoder** will do the job. When you first launch Expression Media Encoder, you may think for a moment that you are back in Blend. Its resemblance to Blend is not a coincidence. Media Encoder is in the same product family as Blend, and all products in the Expression line have a similar look and feel.

A tour of the workspace

The Expression Media Encoder user interface can be broken down into four areas which I've marked in the following screenshot:

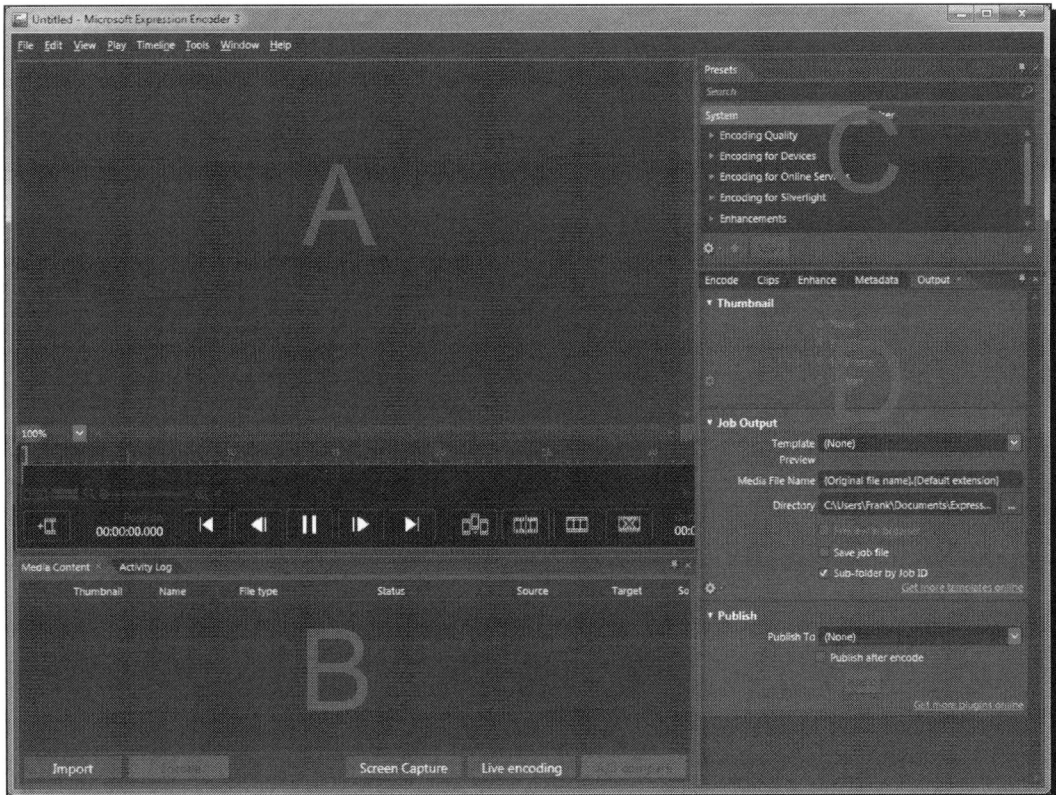

The upper left portion of the screen, marked in the above image as area **A**, contains the video preview. This is where you will be able to view the video to be encoded as well as perform some basic editing functions. Think of this section as similar to the art board in Blend. Area **B** is where you will see all the movie files you have queued up for processing. This is similar to the **Solution** tab in Blend or **Solution Explorer** in Visual Studio. Areas **C** and **D** contain all the settings and parameters for encoding the video. This is where you will be able to control video quality, sound and video compression settings, editing metadata, as well as exporting options.

Encoding video

The primary purpose of Expression Media Encoder is encoding media files into a video format that Silverlight can understand. You also have the option of tweaking the settings to fit your needs. If bandwidth is a concern, you can use compression to shrink down the size of the file. If your users demand high quality video, you can adjust to a higher quality at the cost of file size. Most often, you'll want to have a happy medium between video quality and file size.

> If you want to use QuickTime movie files in your Silverlight application, you'll need to have QuickTime installed on your system to encode the Media Encoder. Once encoded, the video will work with Silverlight on any machine that support Silverlight. You can download Quicktime for free at: http://www.apple.com/quicktime/download/.

A quick word on video formats

Silverlight supports various audio and video formats in a variety of deployment scenarios. When used in conjunction with **IIS7 Smooth Streaming**, you can pretty much guarantee a stutter-free media experience to the end user. You will rarely need to worry about which software; media players or codecs are installed on your end user's computers. Silverlight encapsulates a large number of formats. If you ever have any doubts about a media source's compatibility, you could always run the file through Expression Media Encoder to ensure compatibility with Silverlight.

> IIS7 Smooth Streaming provides a high-quality viewing experience that scales quite well. Smooth Streaming works by adapting the video stream sent to Silverlight clients based on network speed. When conditions are optimal, the client gets the highest quality feed. If network conditions degrade, the server will automatically adjust the video stream to play smoothly on the client.

Codec stands for 'coder-decoder' and refers to the encoding and decoding of a digital data. The term usually refers to the compression mechanism of digital media files. The bottom line for now, is that Silverlight natively supports WMV, WMA, MP3, and MPEG-4-based H.264/ AAC audio. If you're a High Definition individual, then you'll be happy to learn that Silverlight supports full HD (720p+) playback and the H.264 codec. If this sounds like alphabet soup to you, then don't worry. The chances are that unless you work for a media company you will never have to concern yourself with such minute details.

> **Hey, where's my favourite codec?**
>
> If you are stuck on the fact that your favourite codec isn't listed among the supported formats, then don't worry. The **Raw AV pipeline** opens up a wider variety of third-party codec support. You could decode audio and video outside the runtime and render them in Silverlight.

Time for action – let's encode a video!

Expression Media Encoder 3 encodes video into formats that Silverlight can natively understand. Additionally, the software will also resize media files by adjusting resolution and compression. You can tweak your source files to meet the specific needs of your projects. We're going to take a high definition video and shrink it down to a more manageable size and along the way get a feel for how Expression Media encoder works.

Firstly, we will need to download and install Expression Media Encoder 3. If you've not already done so, you can download the program from: `http://www.microsoft.com/expression/products/Encoder_Overview.aspx`. Expression Media Encoder is also bundled with Expression Studio 3.

1. Launch Expression Media Encoder 3.

2. Click on the **Import** button at the bottom of the screen:

3. Browse to a video file on your hard drive and click **open**. The video will load into your main work area.

4. Expand **Encoding for Silverlight | VC-1 | Constant bitrate | VC-1 512k DSL CBR** in the **Presets** panel on the right hand side of the window as the following screenshot shows:

   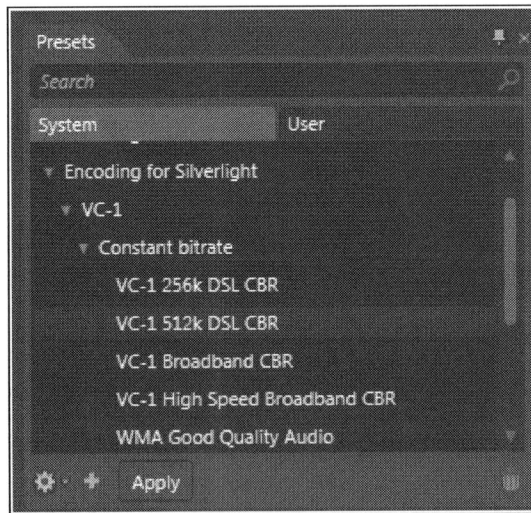

5. Click **Apply**. Below the **Presets** tab, you'll find a tab named **Output**, click on it to reveal the **Job Output** options.

6. Choose **Clean** from the **Template** dropdown list, as the following screenshot shows:

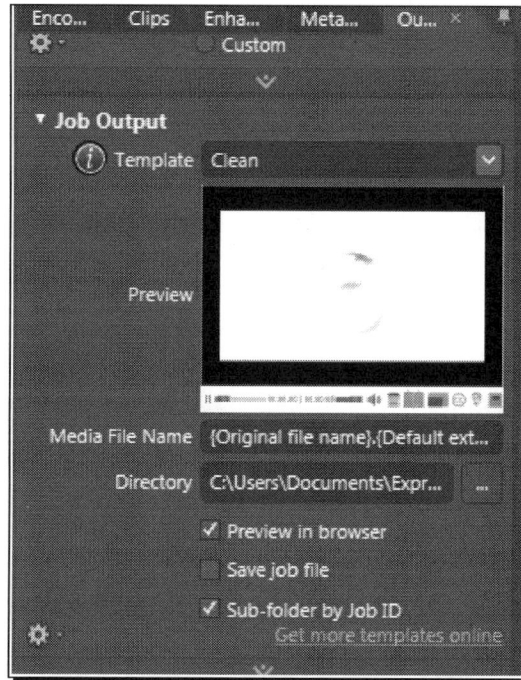

7. In the area below the video preview window, find the **Encode** button and click on it:

8. You'll see a progress bar like the one in the following screenshot, indicating that the encoding has begun:

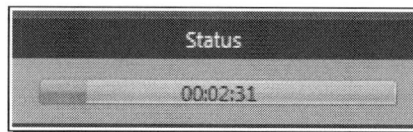

9. When completed, Expression Media Encoder will launch the video and the template video player in your default browser:

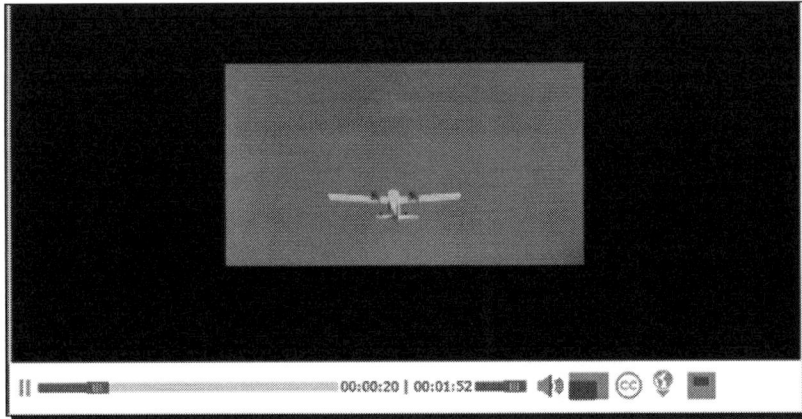

10. Test out the video player. Be sure to examine all the features that the templated player comes with: full screen, pause/play, the progress slider and volume controls.

11. Close the browser window and go back into Expression Media Encoder. On the **Output** panel, there's a little button that looks like the gear in this screenshot:

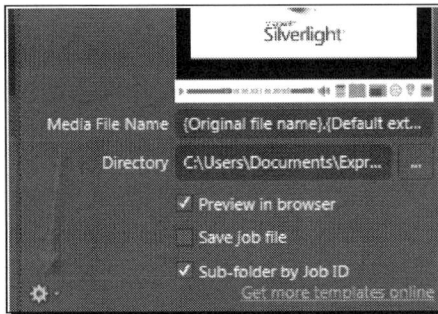

12. Clicking on the gear reveals a popup menu as shown in the next screenshot:

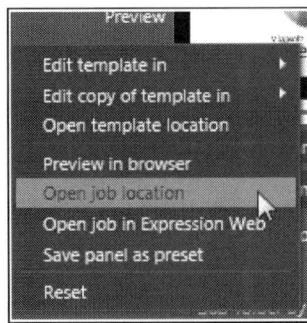

13. Click **Open Job Location** and you will see a list of files in Windows Explorer:

Name	Type	Size
AdrenalineRush.wmv	Windows Media A...	6,037 KB
Default.html	HTML Document	7 KB
MediaPlayerTemplate....	XAP File	140 KB
Preview.png	Adobe Fireworks ...	5 KB
Settings.dat	DAT File	26 KB
SmoothStreaming.xap	XAP File	67 KB

14. Here you can see what Media Encoder has just created for you: a video file, the HTML test page, and a XAP file containing the default player.

What just happened?

We told Media Encoder to take a video file and compress it to a smaller size. We also told it to use a template video player reminiscent of YouTube. You could easily upload this to your web server. We didn't have to write any code here, at least not yet, as Media Encoder did all the work. If you want to use the exported video in your own projects, independent of the provided media player, simply place the video onto a web server. Then you will need to add a `MediaElement` control to your application and set its `Source` property to the video file's URL.

Have a go hero – explore the other templates

You can explore the other templates that Media Encoder comes with or click the **Get more templates online** link to see what other templates are available:

Summary

In this chapter, we added a little bit of multimedia magic to make our web site really stand out. The navigation control now responds with visual and auditory cues which usability experts recommend to engage users. We saw that a `MediaElement` control is just like any other control, it can be resized and animated. We also learned how to encode video with Expression Media Encoder.

Specifically, we learnt how to do the following:

- Add audio to our Silverlight project
- Use the `MediaElement` control to play media
- Control media playback via code
- Insert a movie file into our projects
- Use the **PlaySoundAction** behavior to play a sound clip based on user initiated events
- Understand the video and audio formats natively supported by Silverlight
- Understand Expression Media Encoder
- Encode a movie file in Expression Media Encoder
- Use the video player templates in Expression Media Encoder

Once again, we saw that XAML does a lot of the work that we developers are usually used to doing in procedural code. Thus far, we've not written a lot of procedural code. That is all going to change in the next chapter when we combine the power of XAML with code to build incredible experiences with Silverlight.

4

Taking the RIA Experience Further with Silverlight

So far we've explored the power of declarative programming to build our interfaces. While everything we've done so far will certainly spice up any website or online application, let's kick it up a notch. With Silverlight 4, we can take the web to the next level by adding advanced interactivity. Silverlight provides inbuilt support for adding impressive user interactions.

In this chapter we shall:

- Create a Deep Zoom experience
- Add a map of business locations with the Bing Map control
- Use digital ink to sketch out ideas
- Learn about Isolated Storage

Deep Zoom

First publicly demonstrated at the MIX08 trade show in March 2008, Deep Zoom introduces a novel way to display image collections on the web that challenges all pre-conceived notions about putting high resolution imagery online. Users can browse through hundreds of images without any noticeable lag time. The technology automatically shows the images at the resolution required at any given moment. The end result is a smooth experience for the end user. To anyone who remembers dial-up access to the internet, it appears almost magical.

MIX is an annual conference showcasing Microsoft's technologies in the design, user experience, and web space.

The magic lies in how larger images are broken down into smaller ones. At design time, you can use the Deep Zoom Composer to break down larger images into smaller versions. At runtime, the `MultiScaleImage` control automatically downloads only what is needed. There may be gigabytes of images on the server, but the user can only view a very small fraction of that at any given moment.

Deep Zoom works by breaking down each image into tiles. For example, a 1024 x 1024 pixel image will be resized to 512 x 512 and 256 x 256 pixel versions. Each of these images will be further broken down into tiles. The entire process is shown in the following screenshot:

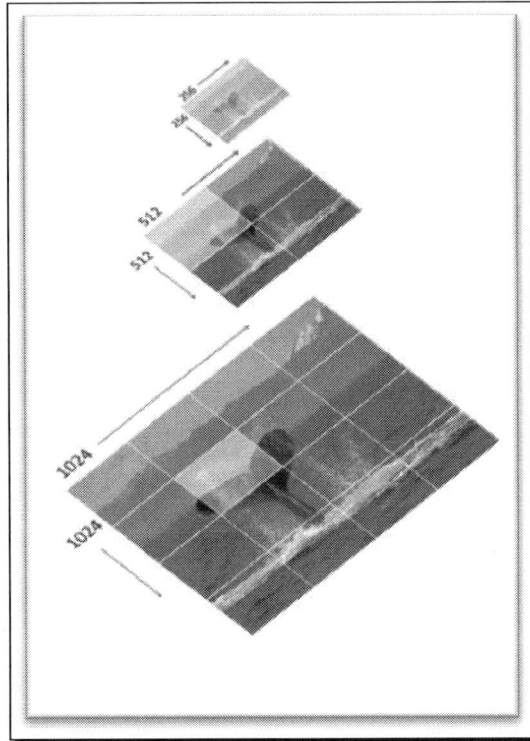

Best of all, as a developer, you don't need to consider the implementation details.

> If you're wondering how much extra storage you'll need to handle all the files at different resolutions, the overhead Deep Zoom introduces is roughly 30%. This means that if you have 1GB of images to convert to display via Deep Zoom, plan on using about 1.3GB of disk space, give or take a hundred megabytes or so.

Deep Zoom in action

The best way to understand Deep Zoom and its implications is to see it in action. The canonical example of Deep Zoom technology is the Hard Rock Cafe's **Memorabilia** website at: `http://memo.hardrock.com`. If you've ever been to a Hard Rock Cafe, then you have undoubtedly seen some of the items that they have in their collection of music-related articles. When you first load the **Hard Rock Memorabilia** website, it looks like the screenshot below:

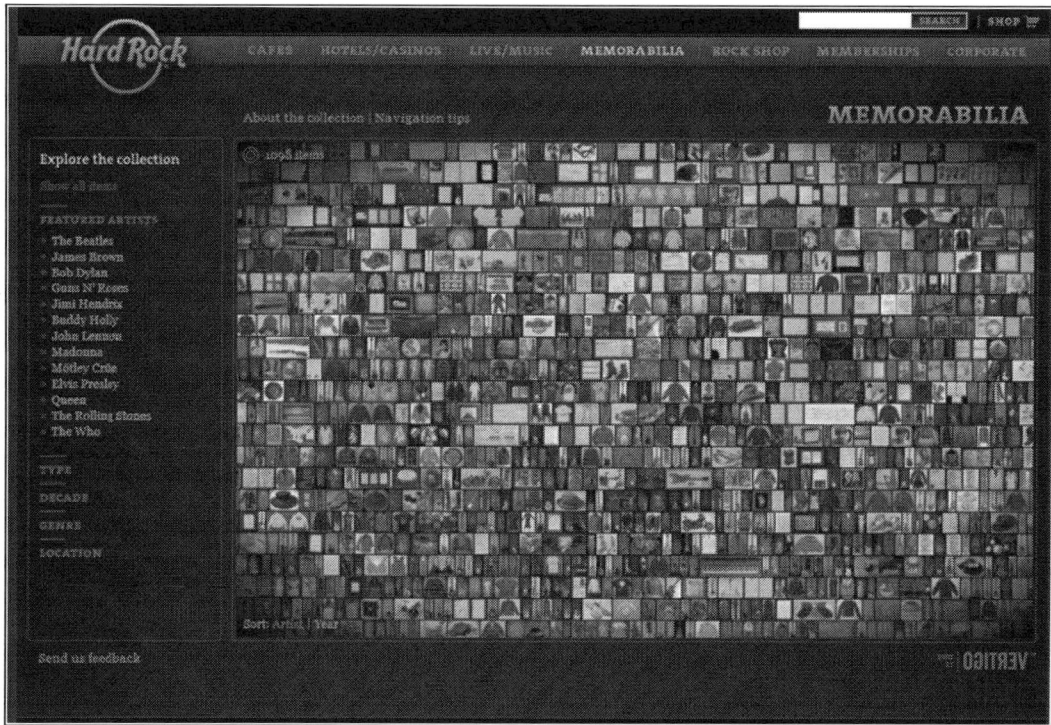

Using the mouse wheel, you can zoom in to individual images to an amazing level of detail. In fact, you can zoom close enough in to a picture of Bo Diddley's guitar to see fingerprints on it:

Notice that while you zoom and pan around, the images start out fuzzy or pixelated and then suddenly 'pop' into clearer detail. This is Deep Zoom loading the higher resolution images over the lower resolution ones. You may also notice the subtle 'springiness' added to the animation. This is built-in to the MultiScaleImage control. If you don't happen to like it, this feature can be turned off.

> While on the **Hard Rock Memorabilia** site, type **V** into the **Search** text box and press *Enter* to activate an Easter Egg. You'll be zoomed 'deep' into the image collection. Zoom out to see where you started from to get a better appreciation of Deep Zoom.

With Deep Zoom, the Hard Rock Cafe showcased a collection that spans six continents on one web page. We're going to do something similar. Instead of guitars and autographed photos, we're going to show off the cakes that our client, Cake-O-Rama, has created.

Time for action – creating a Deep Zoom photo montage

We're going to see just how easy it is to create a Deep Zoom photo montage application using Deep Zoom Composer.

1. Assuming that you already have Deep Zoom Composer installed, launch **Deep Zoom Composer**. If you don't have the application installed, you can download it from: `http://www.microsoft.com/downloads/details.aspx?FamilyID=457B17B7-52BF-4BDA-87A3-FA8A4673F8BF&displaylang=en`.

2. After the splash screen disappears, you will see the **Welcome** Screen:

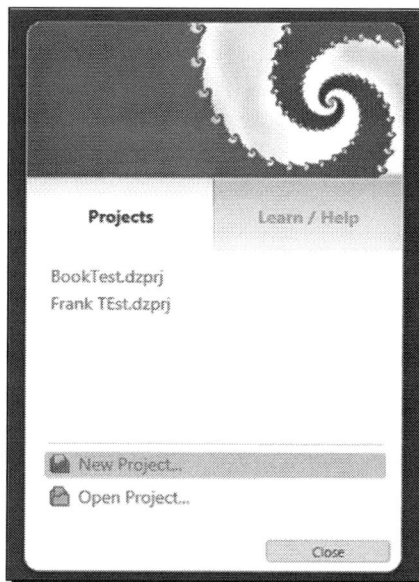

3. To create a new project, click on **New Project**. After which, the **New Project** dialog box appears.

4. Enter **CakeShowCase** in the **Name** field. The **Location** can be any valid path on your computer:

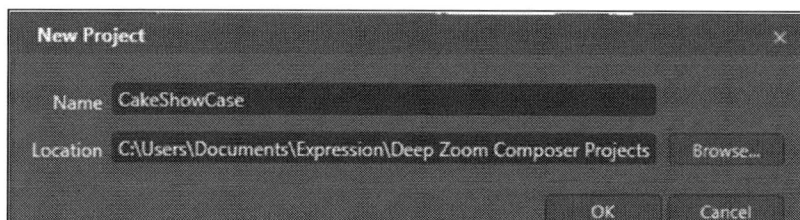

5. Click **OK** to create the project.

6. You will then be presented with an empty screen, reminiscent of Expression Blend:

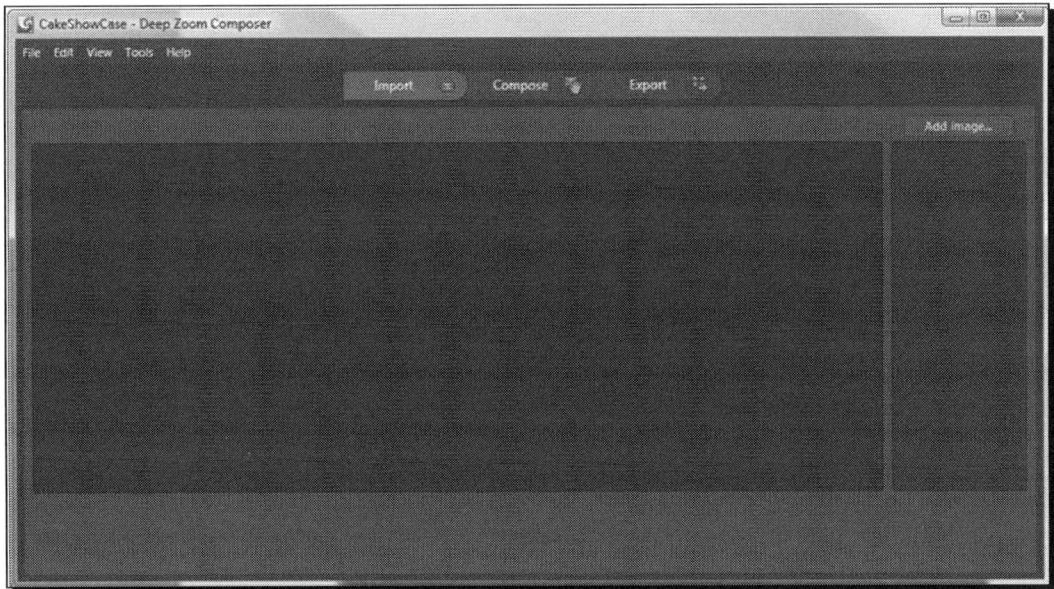

7. In the top part of the screen you'll notice three buttons: **Import**, **Compose**, and **Export**. **Import** should be highlighted by default. If not, click on it now to go into **Import** mode:

8. When in **Import** mode, you will be able to add images to your collage by clicking on the **Add image...** button, as in the following screenshot:

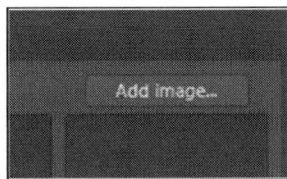

9. Click on **Add image** now and browse for files. You can choose to use the sample image files or your own.

10. As you add images to your project, they will appear as thumbnails in the list box on the right hand side of the screen. After you've added enough files, your screen will resemble the screenshot below:

11. Once you've added enough images, we can move on to composing our montage by clicking **Compose**.

12. Initially, your composition area will appear blank with the images you added lined up at the bottom:

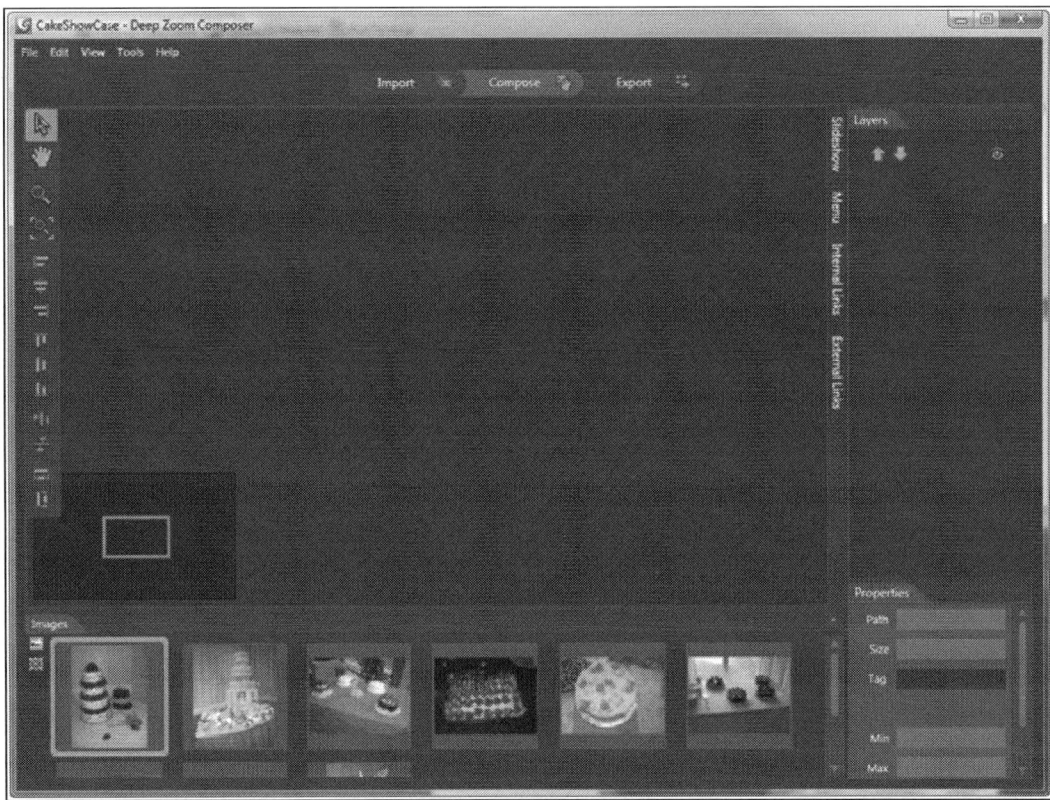

13. To add an image to our composition, simply click and drag an image from the bottom of the composition area:

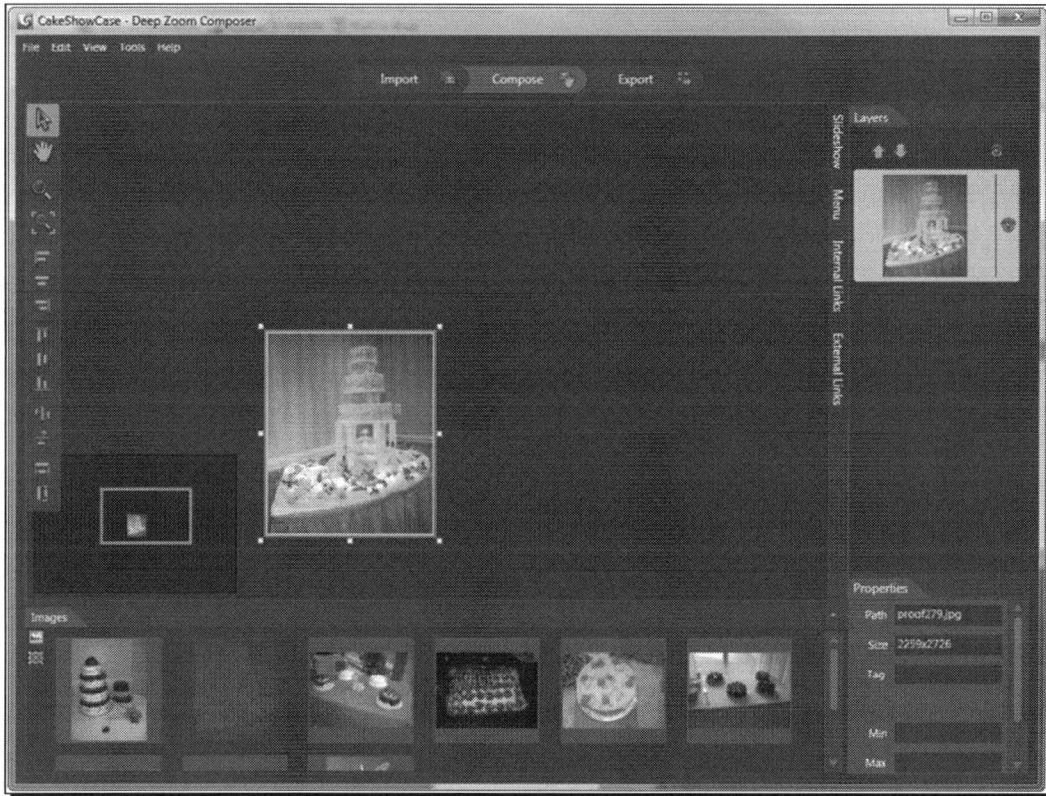

14. Add as many images as you like. Deep Zoom Composer will even assist you in aligning images with one another with snap lines like so:

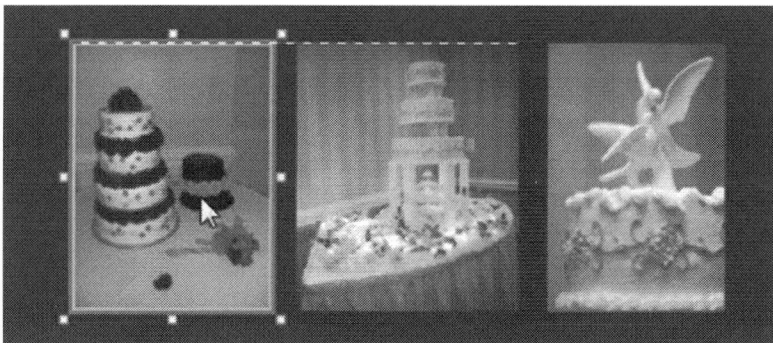

15. Once you've added a few images, or more, if you are industrious, click on the **Export** button at the top of the screen to see how to get our creation out of Deep Zoom Composer and into a Silverlight project.

16. There are a number of options in the **Export** menu. For our purposes, we'll want to click on the **Custom** tab as in the following screenshot:

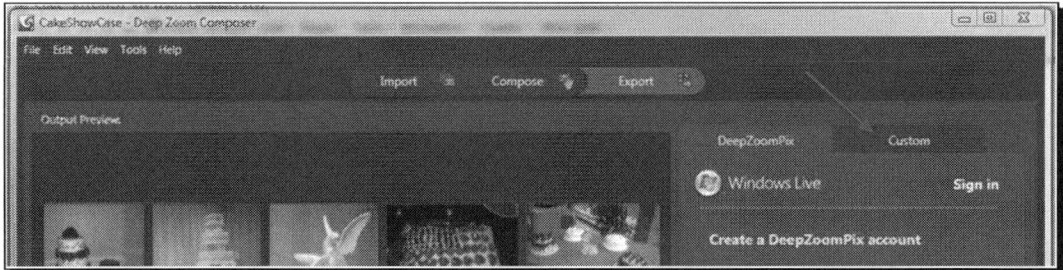

17. The **Custom** tab presents us with a large number of export options. For now, we are going to keep things simple. Enter **CakeShowCase** in the **Name** field. Make sure all the other field entries and settings match the following screen shot:

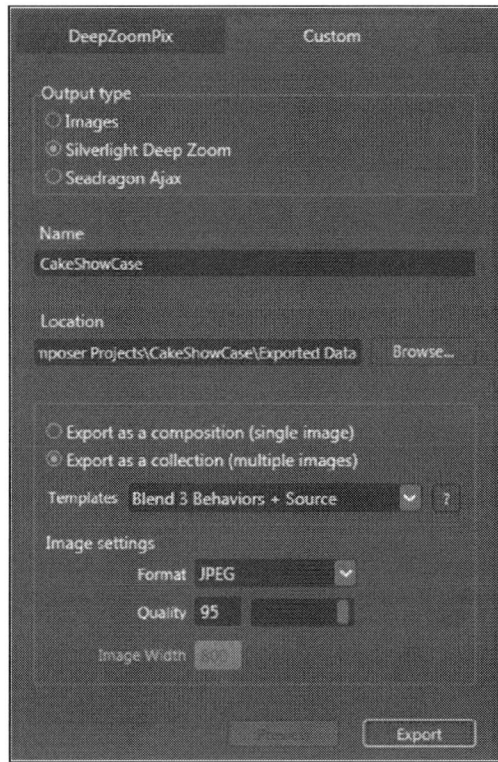

18. When you are ready, click on **Export** to export the project. The export process will take a few moments. How long it will take depends on the number of images in the composition, the resolution of the images, and the speed of your computer.

19. When the export process is complete you will see the following dialog:

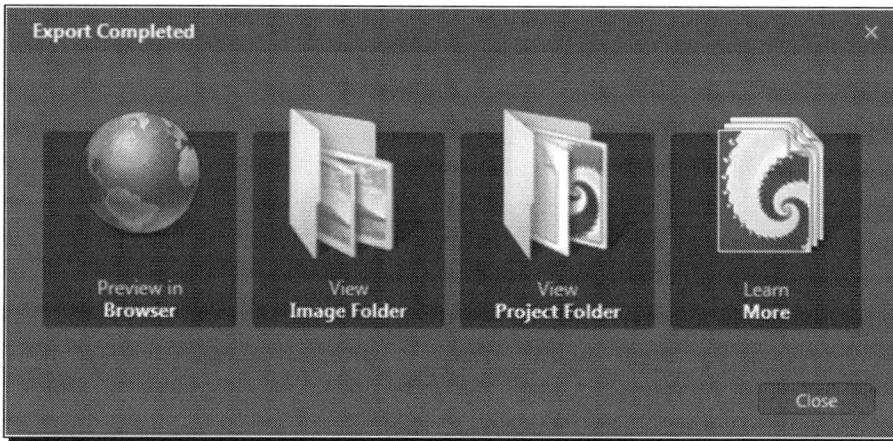

20. Click on **Preview in Browser**, to see that we've actually created a Silverlight project with Deep Zoom content. You should see the web page load up with the following content:

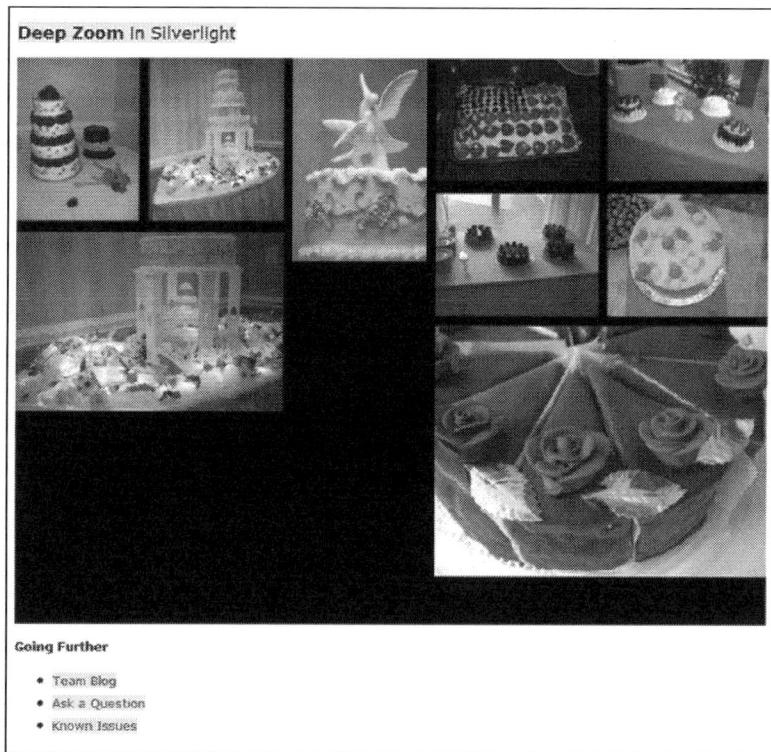

21. Click around to explore the montage. Use the mouse wheel to zoom in and out. If you do not have a mouse wheel, click to zoom in on an image and *Shift*+click to zoom out.

22. Close your browser window and go back to Deep Zoom Composer.

23. The previous dialog box should still be on screen. Click on **View Project Folder** to see the Silverlight project Deep Zoom Composer just generated for you.

What just happened?

The Deep Zoom Composer just did a lot of work for us. Not only did the program process our images, it also created a solution with everything set up for us. The program built more or less everything we need to deliver a nice DeepZoom montage to our client. Naturally, we'll want to take a closer look at what the program built for us.

If you were to open the `DeepZoomProject.sln` that we just created, in Blend 3, you would see the two project solutions that we've become familiar with over the last few chapters: one project for the Silverlight project and another for the web project.

First, let's take a look at the `Default.html` file that hosts our Silverlight control. We can open the file, by double-clicking the `Default.html` file in the **Projects** tab in Blend:

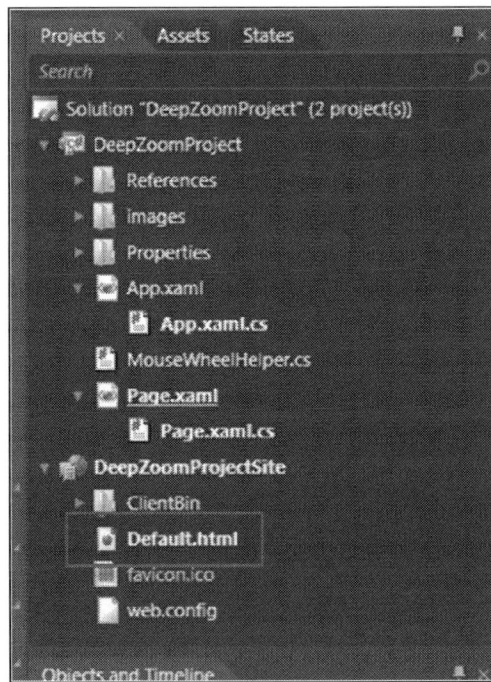

Inside the `Default.html` file, you'll see the `object` tag that actually hosts the Silverlight control. Inside the object tag, you'll notice a series of `param` tags. Take special note of the `param` tag with the name attribute of `initparams`. It is highlighted in the code snippet below:

```
<object data="data:application/x-silverlight-2," type="application/x-
silverlight-2" width="800px" height="600px">
<param name="source" value="ClientBin/DeepZoomProject.xap"/>
  <param name="onerror" value="onSilverlightError" />
  <param name="background" value="white" />
  <param name="initparams" value="path=GeneratedImages/dzc_output.
xml,zoomIn=3" />
    <param name="minRuntimeVersion" value="3.0.40624.0" />
    <param name="autoUpgrade" value="true" />
    <a href="http://go.microsoft.com/fwlink/
?LinkID=149156&v=3.0.40624.0" style="text-decoration:none">
    <img src="http://go.microsoft.com/fwlink/?LinkId=108181" alt="Get
Microsoft Silverlight" style="border-style:none"/>
    </a>
</object>
```

The value attribute contains a name/value list of parameter names and values that get read by the Silverlight runtime into a Dictionary object. If you open the Silverlight project and open up the `App.xaml.cs` file, you'll find this code inside the `Application_Startup` method. The `Application_Startup` method is actually an event handler that fires when our Silverlight application starts up. The highlighted code reads all items in the `InitParams` property into the application resources object. This means we can access the value from anywhere in our Silverlight application:

```
private void Application_Startup(object sender, StartupEventArgs
e)
{
    this.RootVisual = new Page();

    if (e.InitParams != null)
    {
    foreach (var data in e.InitParams)
    {
        this.Resources.Add(data.Key, data.Value);
    }
    }
}
```

Next, open the `Page.xaml` file in the same Silverlight project. In design view you will see a `MultiScaleImage` control named `msi` in the **Objects and Timeline** tab as in the following screenshot:

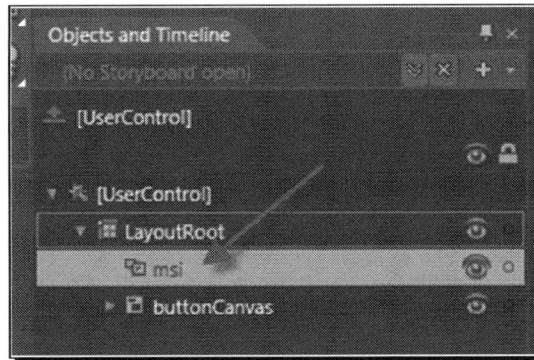

Or, if you prefer looking at the XAML:

```
<MultiScaleImage x:Name="msi"/>
```

The source value for the `MultiScaleImage` control is actually set in the `Page_Loaded` event handler. The code below sets the Source attribute based on the value in the application Resource dictionary, which was populated by contents of the param tag in the hosting HTML file:

```
string path = App.Current.Resources["path"].ToString();

this.msi.Source = new DeepZoomImageTileSource(new Uri(path, UriKind.
Relative));
```

Why go through all this trouble? Why not just set the source URI property of the MultiScaleImage control in XAML or in the code-behind? Simply put, this approach provides a greater deal of flexibility. We can easily change the `Source` property of `MultiScaleImage` by simply changing the content of the hosting HTML page. And we don't need to recompile a new XAP file to do that.

Have a go hero – exploring the tiles

Now that we've explored the code that Deep Zoom Composer automatically generated for us, let's see how it broke apart the images into tiles. In the web project of the solution Deep Zoom Composer created, expand the **ClientBin** directory and the **GeneratedImages** directory. Right mouse click the `dzc_output.xml` file and choose **Open Folder in Windows Explorer**, as the following screenshot demonstrates:

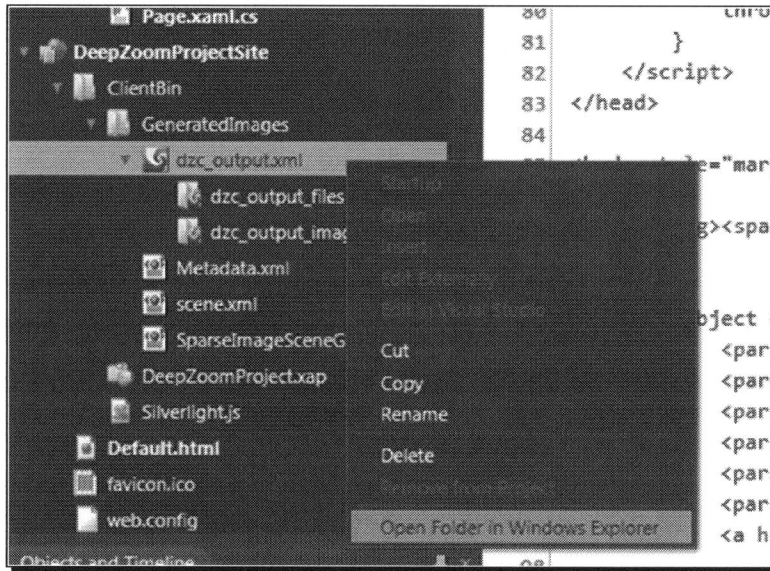

A Windows Explorer window will open and display a series of files and directories. We are most interested in the contents of the dzc_output.xml file and the dzc_output_images directory. The dzc_output.xml acts as an index linking all the image meta data files. The MultiScaleImage control uses the data in these files to stitch the image tiles back together. The dzc_output_images directory contains all the image tiles, that Deep Zoom Composer created. Each one of the directories here contains subdirectories with image tiles in them.

Feel free to explore them to see how Deep Zoom breaks apart larger images. An example of the image tiles in thumbnail view is shown in the following screenshot:

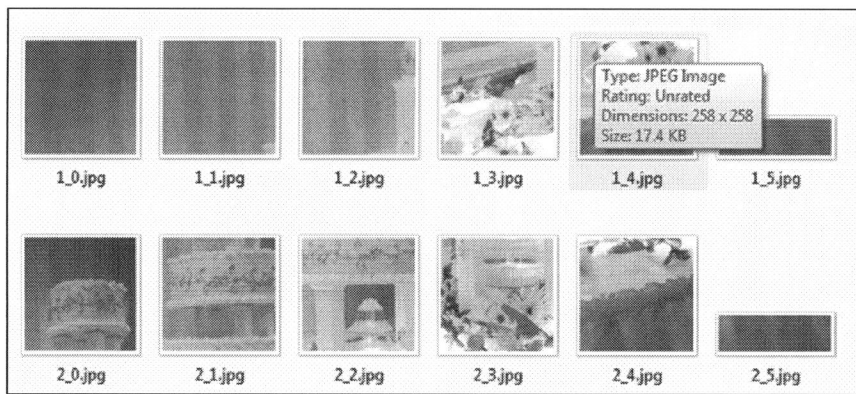

> **Renaming and moving Deep Zoom image collections**
>
> If you decide to rename or move files around, remember to update the XML files accordingly!

Using the Bing Maps Silverlight Control

Mapping was one of the first great applications on the web. Customers could search for store locations, print directions from their house to just about anywhere and even check traffic; all from their computer.

Every major search engine has some kind of mapping feature. While all the major search engines offer publicly accessible **APIs (application programming interfaces)**, only Bing Maps integrates tightly with Silverlight with a custom Silverlight control. You can use this control to easily add mapping functionality to any Silverlight project. What makes the Bing Maps Silverlight Map Control so great is that it leverages the power of Deep Zoom to seamlessly blend different aerial photos together for a much smoother map viewing experience.

Integrating mapping solutions into your website keeps your users on your site, and not off to a third party site where they could easily get distracted or click on a competitor's ad.

> At the time of writing this, Microsoft was in the middle of re-branding Live Maps and Virtual Earth to Bing Maps. As a result, you may see both names used in the documentation, sample code, and namespaces.

In November 2009, Microsoft released version 1 of the Bing Maps Silverlight Map Control and made the control available as a free download from Microsoft. Browse to: `http://www.microsoft.com/downloads/details.aspx?displaylang=en&familyid=beb29d27-6f0c-494f-b028-1e0e3187e830` and you'll see the **Bing Maps Silverlight Control SDK** download page. Click the **Download** button (highlighted in the following screenshot) to start the download.

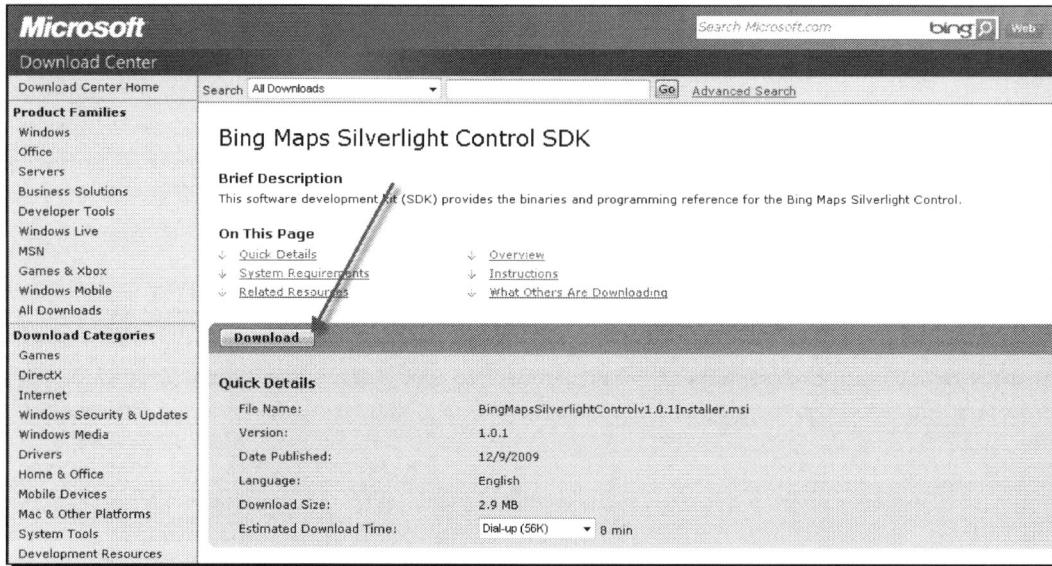

Once the download completes, run the install program and follow the onscreen directions in the installation wizard. The final screen (shown in the following screenshot) will give you the option to launch the **Bing Maps Silverlight Control SDK** help file after the install completes.

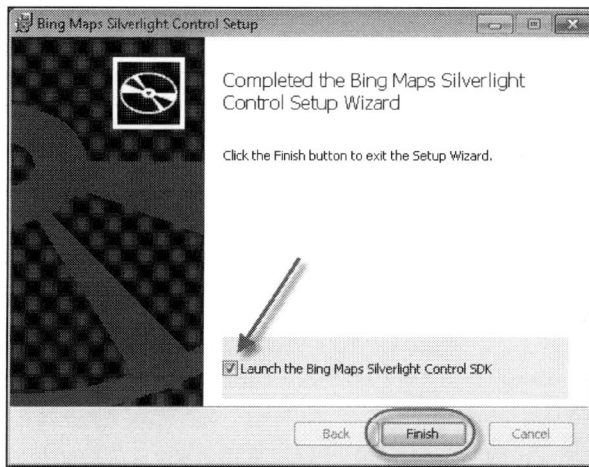

Leaving the checkbox checked will automatically launch the Windows **Help** file: `BingMapsSilverlightControlSDK.chm` which you can use to read more about the control's features, methods, and properties. This file contains a great deal of information about the control:

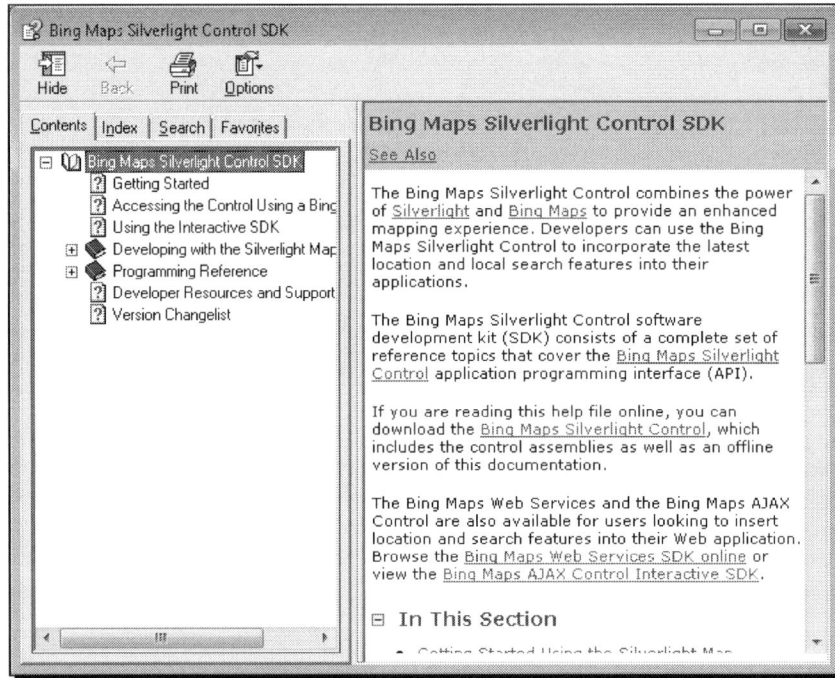

The installer places all the relevant files in the `C:\Program Files\Microsoft Virtual Earth Silverlight Map Control\v1` directory. This directory contains a license file and two subdirectories: one for documentation and the other for a DLL that contains the actual control.

> If you changed the destination folder when you ran the installer, then all of these components will be in the location that you specified.

If the Microsoft Help file documentation isn't helpful enough for you, then you can consult the **Interactive SDK** which is available at: `http://www.microsoft.com/maps/isdk/silverlight/`.

The **Interactive SDK** is a real time example of the control in use as well as how to use its many features. The following screenshot demonstrates the interactive SDK in action. Simply click on what you would like to do on the left-hand side and click on the **Source Code** tab to see the XAML code that made it work:

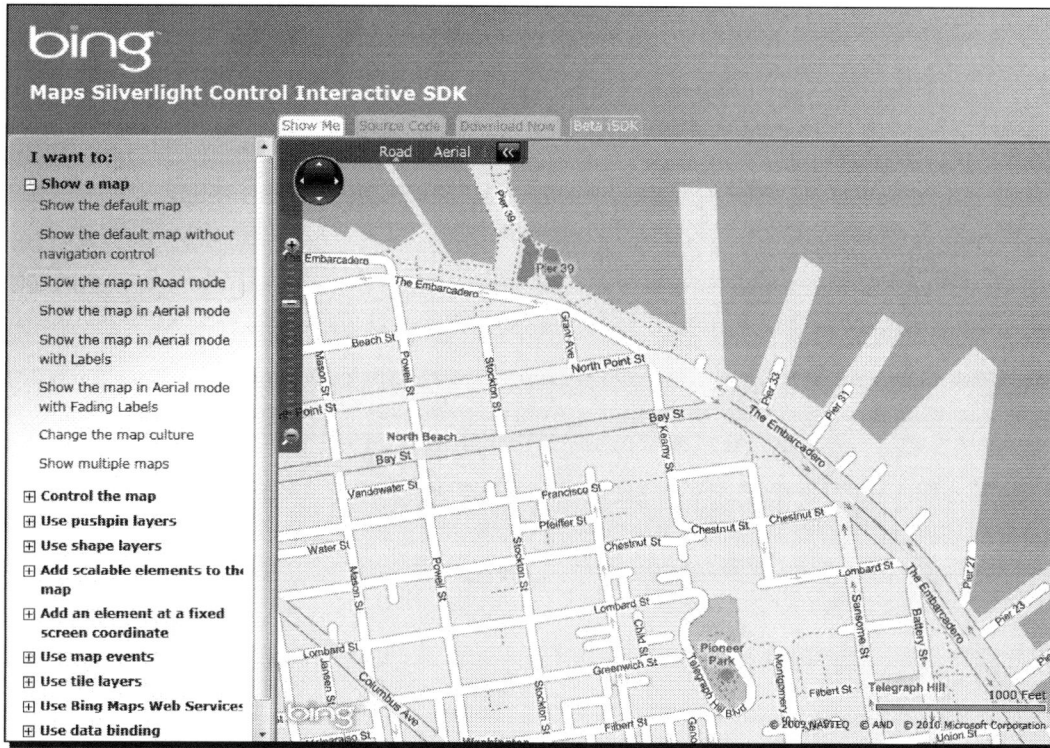

Using the Map Control

Once you have the `Bing Maps Silverlight Map Control` installed on your development machine, you'll need to add a reference to the DLL in order to use the control in your projects.

Time for action – getting started with mapping

Let's get started and create a Silverlight application that shows a map.

1. Launch Visual Studio and create a new Silverlight application by choosing **File|New|Project** and then selecting **Silverlight Application** from the application templates.

2. Name the solution `CakeORamaLocations`. Once its loads, go to the **Solution Explorer**, expand the **References** directory in the `CakeORamaLocations` project. Right-click on the **References** directory and click on the **Add Reference...** context menu, as the following screenshot demonstrates:

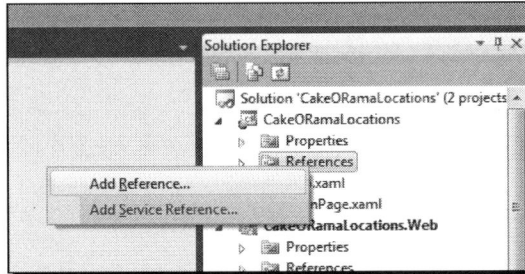

3. This will bring up a dialog box, so click on the **Browse** tab. Using the file browser on this tab, browse to the `C:\Program Files\Microsoft Virtual Earth Silverlight Map Control\CTP\Libraries\` directory. (If you changed the install path, then you will need to use that directory instead.)

4. Once in the proper directory, you will see the `Microsoft.Maps.MapControl.dll` and `Microsoft.Maps.MapControl.Common.dll` files. Select both these files and then click **OK**:

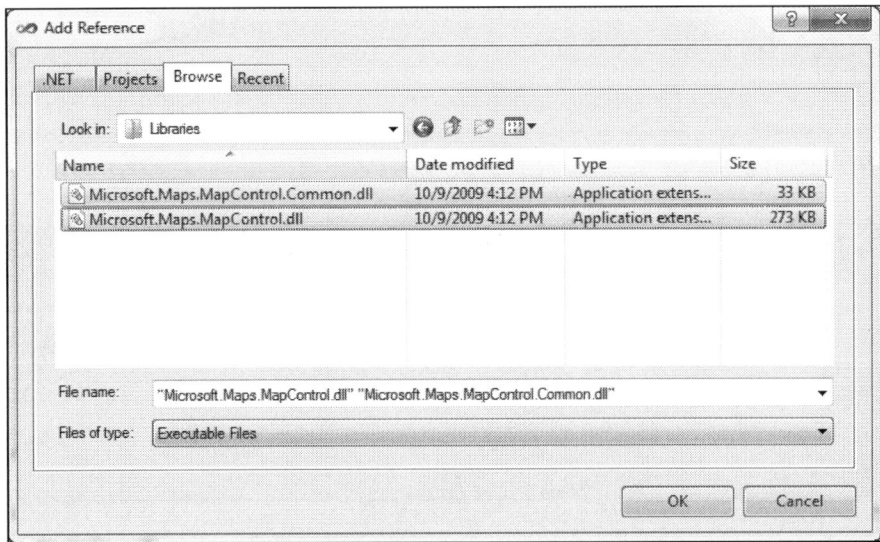

5. We'll need to reference the namespace of the map control in the `MainPage.xaml` file in order to use it. Add the two highlighted lines, our XAML now looks like this:

```
<UserControl x:Class="CakeORamaLocations.MainPage"
    xmlns="http://schemas.microsoft.com/winfx/2006/xaml/
presentation"
    xmlns:x="http://schemas.microsoft.com/winfx/2006/xaml"
    xmlns:d="http://schemas.microsoft.com/expression/blend/2008"
    xmlns:mc="http://schemas.openxmlformats.org/markup-
compatibility/2006"
    mc:Ignorable="d"
    xmlns:map="clr-namespace:Microsoft.Maps.MapControl;assembly=Mi
crosoft.Maps.MapControl"
    d:DesignHeight="300" d:DesignWidth="400">
    <Grid x:Name="LayoutRoot" Background="White">
        <map:Map />
    </Grid>
</UserControl>
```

6. Run the solution. If prompted, choose to allow debugging. Your application should now appear:

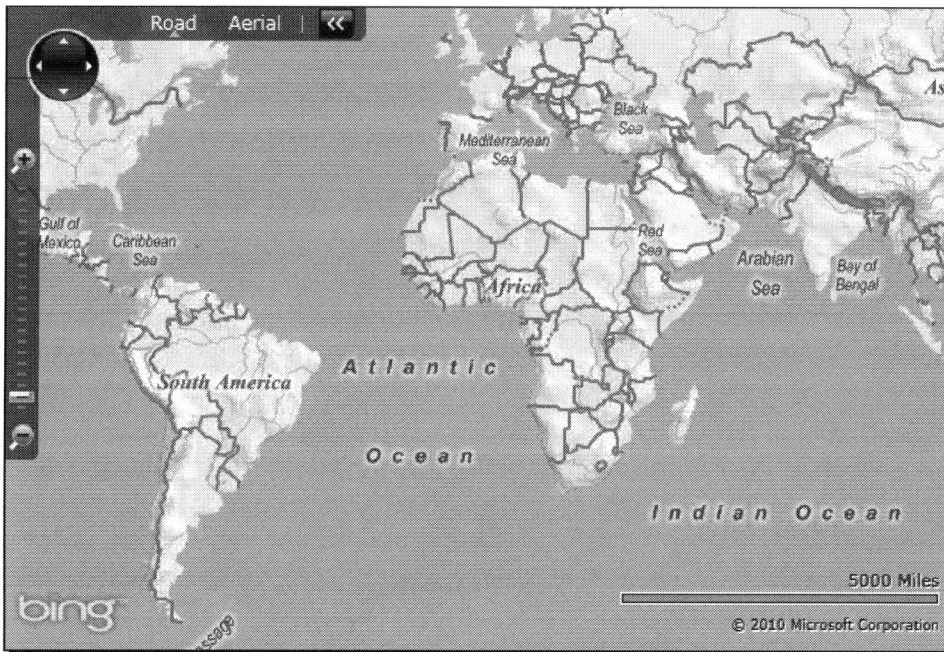

7. Click to explore and zoom around.

8. After a moment, you may notice an error message appear saying you have **Invalid Credentials**:

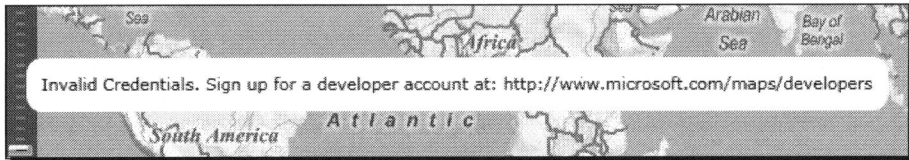

9. Close the host browser window. We'll fix this shortly.

What just happened?

We just created our first map using the `Bing Maps Silverlight Map Control`! Since the map control is not part of the normal DLLs referenced by a Silverlight application, we had to add the reference to the project. The XAML file needs to have a way to address the assembly in which the map control resides. We did this by assigning an XML namespace that references that assembly:

```
xmlns:map="clr-namespace:Microsoft.Maps.MapControl;assembly=Microsoft.
Maps.MapControl"
```

Once referenced, Visual Studio probably even provided you with Intellisense to assist you in typing out the XAML as follows:

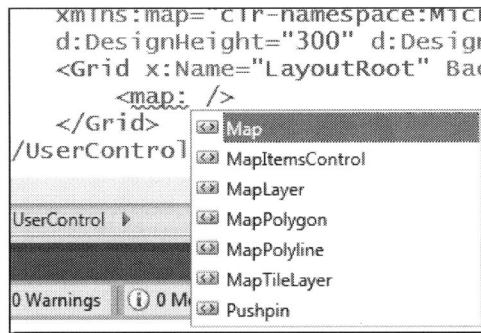

Getting credentials

In the previous section, we added a fully functional map control that worked quite well aside from a message about Invalid Credentials. In order to use the `Bing Silverlight Maps` control, we will need to sign up for a **Bing Maps Account**. Signing up for a developer account is free and is quite easy to do. To start the process, open up `http://www.microsoft. com/maps/developers/` in your browser. This is the developer home page for Bing Maps and contains a lot of information about developing mapping solutions with Bing. Click on the **Get a Bing Maps Account** button (highlighted in the following screenshot) to go to the **Bing Maps Account** page.

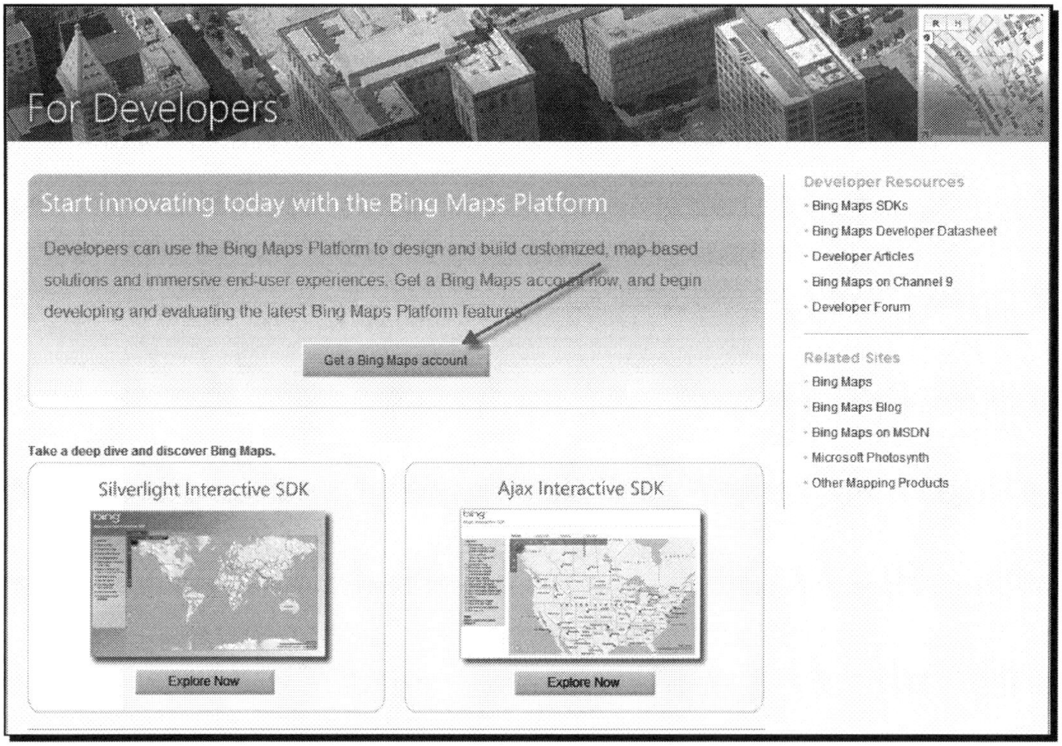

At the **Bing Maps Account Center** home page (shown below), you'll need to login with your **Windows Live ID** to proceed further.

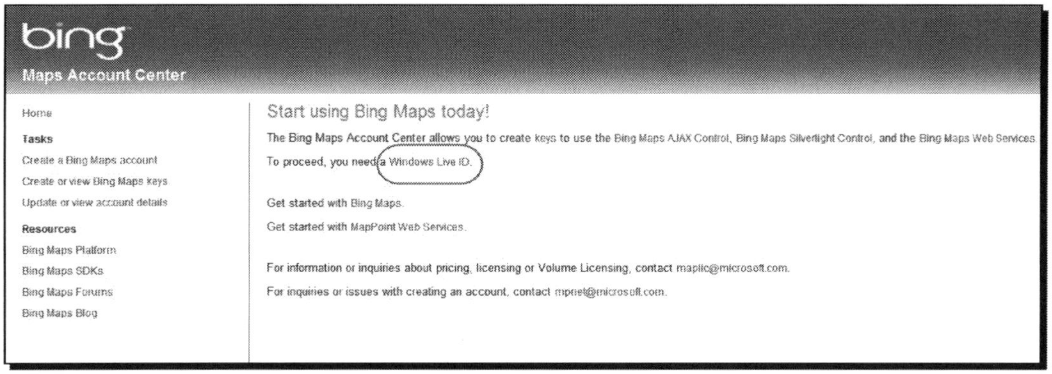

You most likely have a **Windows Live ID** if you use Hotmail or Windows Live Messenger. If you do not have one, you can create one by clicking on the link highlighted below and then clicking the **Sign Up** button.

Once you've logged in to Windows Live, your browser will take you back to the **Bing Maps Account Center** homepage. The page will prompt you to create a Bing Maps key. Enter an application name and the domain name of your site and then click **Create Key**.

You will now see a key on the screen uniquely assigned to you. (I've blocked it out in the screenshot below).

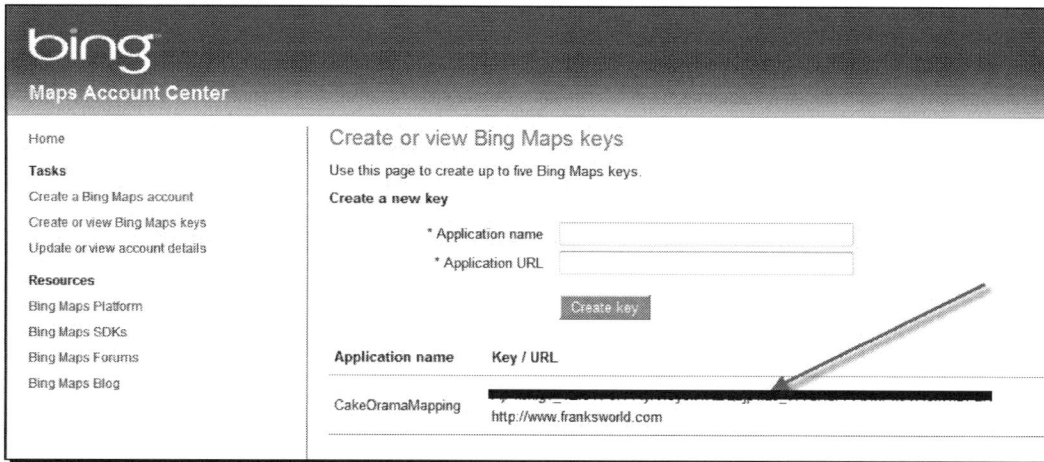

Store this key in a safe location and don't share it. We will use this key in our applications in order to remove the onscreen warning.

Time for action – adding our credentials

Let's add the Bing Maps key we just created to our XAML to remove the Invalid Credentials warning.

1. Go back into the CakeORamaLocations solution from the previous section.

2. Open the MainPage.xaml file and modify the code `<map:Map/>` to look like this:

   `<map:Map CredentialsProvider="[Bing Maps Account Key]">`

3. Replace the [Bing Maps Account Key] with the key that we just created in the **Bing Maps Account Center**. For instance, if the key were 12345678, then we would type: CredentialsProvider="12345678"

4. Run the solution once again, and you'll notice that the invalid credentials warning is gone.

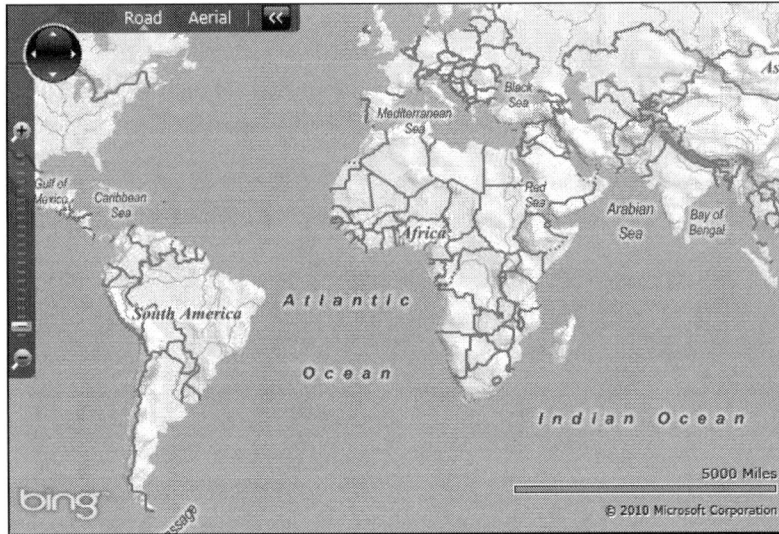

5. Close the host browser window to end the debugging session.

While the control is sufficient by itself, it doesn't do much of anything for our client. As they do not have any locations in Africa or South America (yet), centering the map on that part of the world will do Cake-O-Rama no good.

Taking control of the Map control

In the previous section, we supplied the map control with no parameters. We simply defined a map. In the absence of a latitude and longitude, the control will use 0 degrees West and 0 degrees North (a location just off the west coast of Africa on the equator). If you have a GPS system in your car or mobile phone, then you are at least casually familiar with latitude and longitude. Your car or phone ties the map data it has with the data received from the GPS satellite system using latitude and longitude, sometimes abbreviated to **LatLong,**

Latitude (usually shown as a horizontal line) is the angular distance of a point north or south of the Equator. **Longitude** (usually shown as a vertical line) is the angular distance of a point east or west of the Prime (Greenwich) Meridian. For reference, the Prime Meridian is near London, UK.

What we need to do is center the map nearer to an area that Cake-O-Rama cares about. Since most of their locations lie in Maryland between the cities of Washington, DC and Baltimore, we should probably place the map's initial location in that region of the world.

Time for action – taking control of the Map control

Let's change the map so that it starts out somewhere more relevant to our client.

1. Return to the `CakeORamaLocations` solution in Visual Studio.

2. Add a `Center` attribute to the `Map` node, so that it now looks like this:

```
<map:Map Center="39.04801,-76.84817" CredentialsProvider="[Bing
Maps Account Key]" />
```

3. Run the solution and you'll see that we've changed the initial location of the map, but we're still zoomed out:

4. Close the browser window and return to the `MainPage.xaml` file in Visual Studio.

5. We can also set the initial zoom level on the map control by adding a `ZoomLevel` attribute to out map like so:

```
<map:Map Center="39.04801,-76.84817" ZoomLevel="10" CredentialsPro
vider="[Bing Maps Account Key]" />
```

6. Run the solution again and you'll see we're at a more reasonable zoom level:

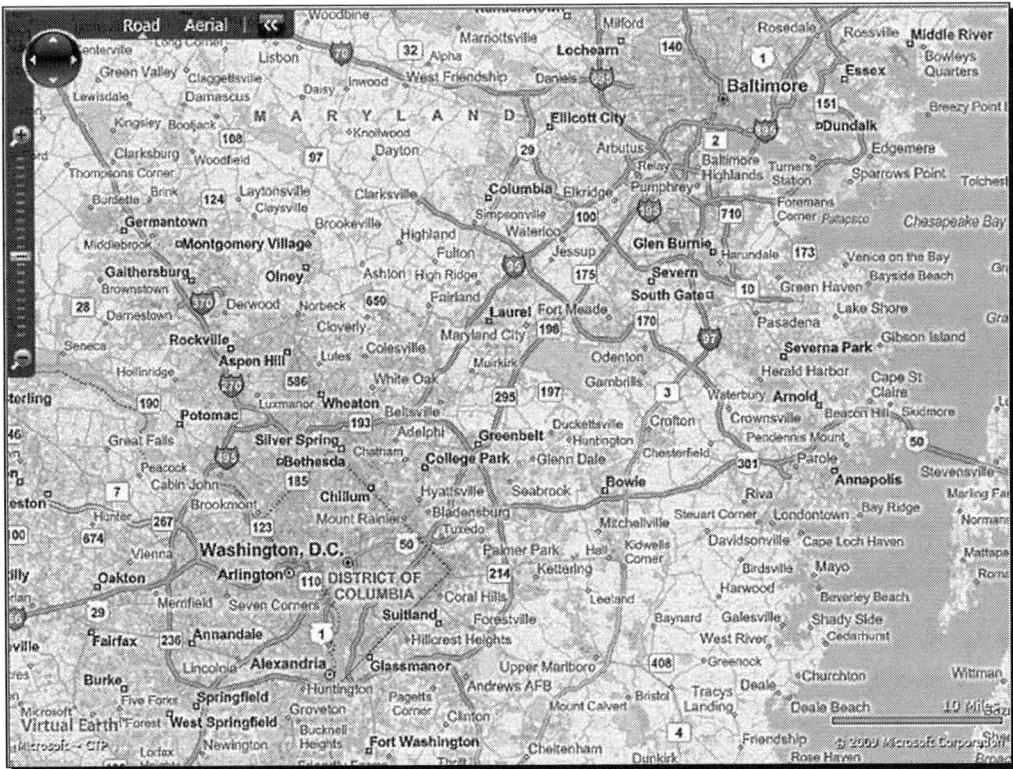

7. Close the solution and go back to the `MainPage.xaml` file in Visual Studio.

8. What the client would really like to see is a map that has the aerial view with map data overlaid. Fortunately, that's an easy modification. Change the `Map` control node to:

```
<map:Map Center="39.04801,-76.84817" ZoomLevel="10"
Mode="AerialWithLabels" CredentialsProvider="[Bing Maps Account
Key]" />
```

9. Run the solution again and you'll see that the map has changed.

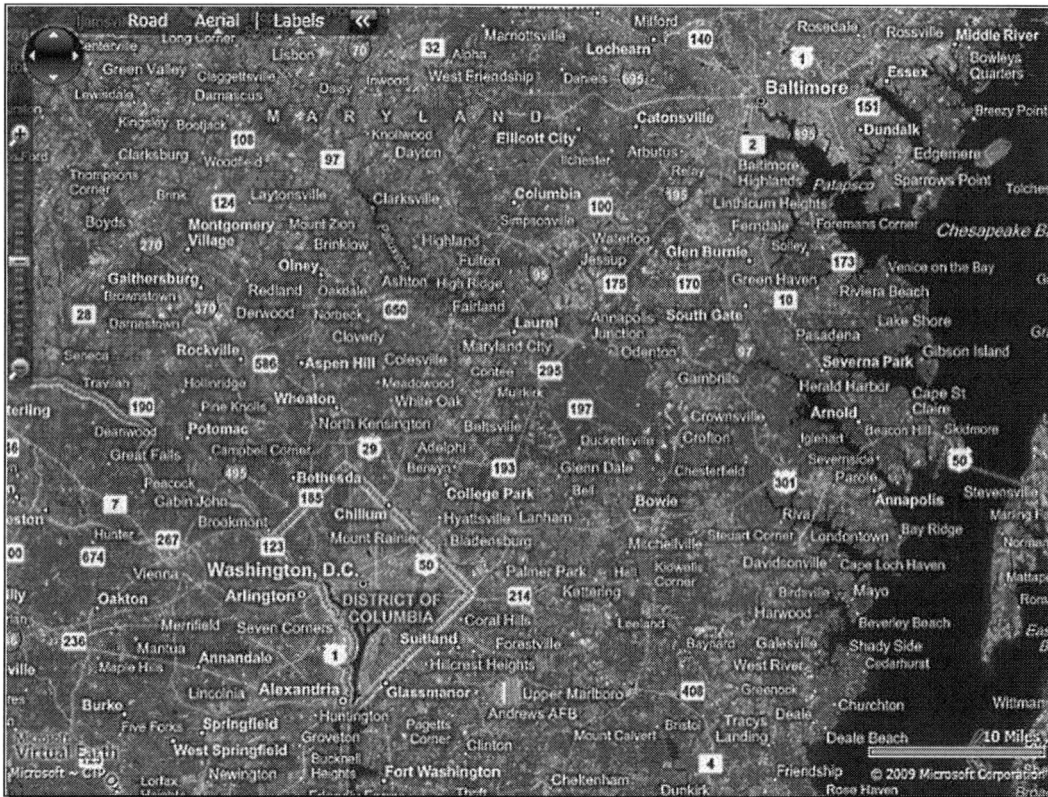

10. Now close the host browser window.

What just happened?

The `Bing Maps Silverlight Map` control has a lot of built in properties for changing the location, zoom level, and view mode. We changed where the map is initially centered on, its zoom level and the type of map that we would like to see. We've not written a single line of procedural code so far, yet we've got a fully functional professional-looking map.

The map has three modes: **Road**, **Aerial** and **AerialWithLabels**. We've already seen Road and AerialWithLabels. Aerial is the aerial view without any labels for roads, towns, or geographic features superimposed on it.

For now, let's pretend we know the LatLongs coordinates of all the places that we are interested in. In Chapter 9, we'll discuss converting street addresses, place names, and postal codes into latitude and longitude coordinates for use in our mapping solutions in a process called Geo-Coding.

Have a go hero – changing the map programmatically

Right now, Cake-O-Rama is small, but they have global ambitions. In fact, they are launching their franchise program and hope to have stores all over the world. They would like to have a map that is able to move to different areas. Therefore, they would like to have buttons to move the map view to various markets that they are in. There will likely be franchisees added in New York City and London. Let's add that feature now:

1. Return to the `CakeORamaLocations` solution in Visual Studio.

2. Edit the `MainPage.xaml` so that the contents of the `Grid` control contains the following:

```
<Grid x:Name="LayoutRoot" Background="White">
<Grid.RowDefinitions>
    <RowDefinition Height="40" />
    <RowDefinition Height="*" />
</Grid.RowDefinitions>
    <StackPanel Orientation="Horizontal">
        <Button x:Name="btnDC"
                Content="US-DC Area Locations"
                Click="btnDC_Click" />
        <Button x:Name="btnNY"
                Content="US-NY Area Locations"
                Click="btnNY_Click" />
        <Button x:Name="btnUK"
                Content="UK-LON Area Locations"
                Click="btnEurope_Click" />
    </StackPanel>
    <map:Map x:Name="map"
             Center="39.04801,-76.84817"
             ZoomLevel="10"
             Mode="AerialWithLabels"
             Grid.Row="1"
             CredentialsProvider="[Bing Maps Account Key]" />
</Grid>
```

3. Add the following code to the `MainPage.xaml.cs`:

```
private void btnDC_Click(object sender, RoutedEventArgs e)
{
    this.map.Center = new Location(39.04801, -76.84817);
}

private void btnEurope_Click(object sender, RoutedEventArgs e)
{
    this.map.Center = new Location(51.51228, -0.12286);
```

```
}

private void btnNY_Click(object sender, RoutedEventArgs e)
{
    this.map.Center = new Location(40.73647, -73.98190);
}
```

4. Run the solution. Click on the **UK-London Area Locations** button and you'll see the map move from DC to New York City. Now click on the **US-NY Area Locations** button to see New York:

5. Close the host browser window.

6. If you don't like the animation that the map control automatically generated, you can turn it off by adding `AnimationLevel="None"` to the `map` control.

7. Run the solution again. You will now see that the animation effect is gone.

Adding store locations to the map

So far, we have a Silverlight application that shows a map of various metropolitan areas. To make the map more useful, we should add markers where Cake-O-Rama has locations so prospective customers can find a Cake-O-Rama location easily. Let's add those markers now.

Time for action – adding store locations

Let's add markers to the map where Cake-O-Rama currently has shops.

1. Return to the `CakeORamaLocations` solution in Visual Studio.

2. Let's change the `Map` control node in the `MainPage.xaml` file so that it contains the following:

```
<map:Map x:Name="map"
         Center="39.04801,-76.84817"
         ZoomLevel="10"
         Mode="Road"
         Grid.Row="1"
         CredentialsProvider="[Bing Maps Account Key]" >
    <map:Pushpin Location="39.28345, -76.61714" />
    <map:Pushpin Location="39.21485, -76.86082" />
    <map:Pushpin Location="38.95981, -77.08540" />
    <map:Pushpin Location="38.89153, -77.0850" />
    <map:Pushpin Location="39.12242, -77.23495" />
    <map:Pushpin Location="38.92415, -77.22659" />
    <map:Pushpin Location="39.09325, -76.85680" />
    <map:Pushpin Location="38.97804, -76.48695" />
    <map:Pushpin Location="38.9589,-77.3623" />
</map:Map>
```

3. Run the solution and you'll see markers (known as pushpins) scattered across the map; each marker represents a Cake-O-Rama location:

4. Zoom in and you will notice how the pushpin stays the same size:

5. Zoom out and you will notice how the pushpin remains the same size:

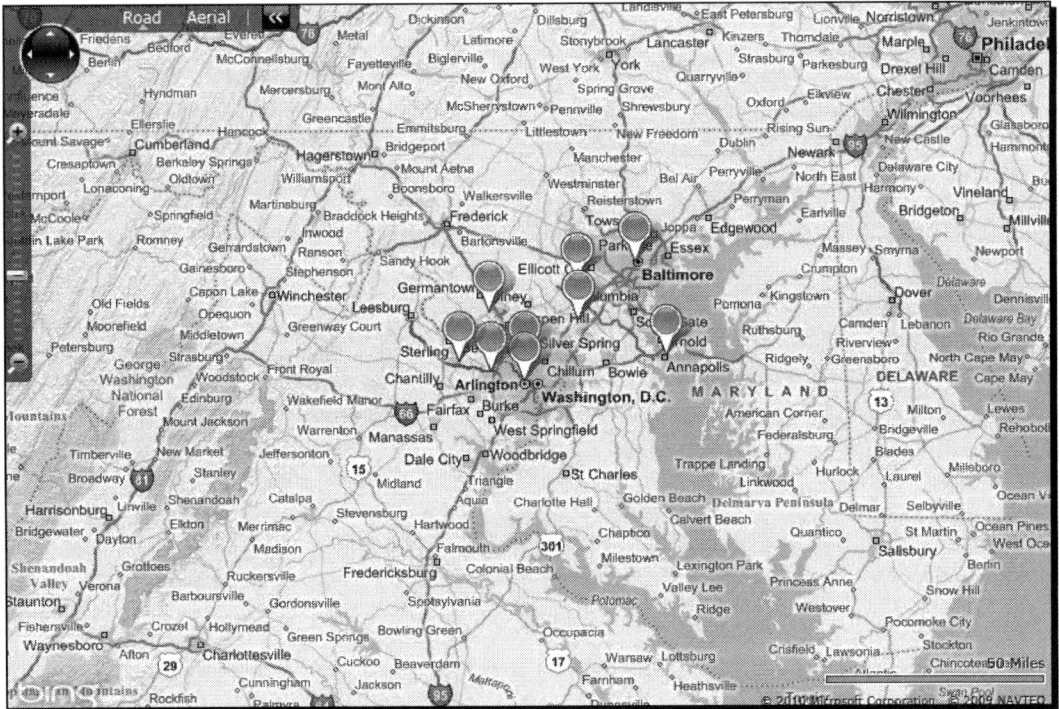

6. Close the host browser window.

What just happened?

We just added pushpin markers to the map by placing them 'inside' the beginning and end tags of the map control. Let's examine the XAML of one of these Pushpin controls more closely to learn more:

```
<map:Pushpin Location="38.95981, -77.08540" />
```

The Pushpin object has a Location property which accept a LatLong property. This tells the map control where to place the PushPin on the map. By default, they look rather unremarkable, as shown in the next screenshot:

Let's see how we can use the power of Silverlight to re-style the marker.

Have a go hero – re-styling a Pushpin

Right now, Cake-O-Rama is small, but they have global ambitions. In fact, they are launching their franchise program and hope to have stores all over the world. They would like to have a map that is able to move to different areas. Therefore, they would like to have buttons to move the map view to various markets that they are in. There will likely be franchisees added in New York City and London. Let's add that feature now:

1. Return to the `CakeORamaLocations` solution in Visual Studio.

2. Edit the `MainPage.xaml` and modify the XAML to that it looks like this: (I've highlighted the new and modified lines of code.)

```xml
<UserControl x:Class="CakeORamaLocations.MainPage"
    xmlns="http://schemas.microsoft.com/winfx/2006/xaml/
presentation"
    xmlns:x="http://schemas.microsoft.com/winfx/2006/xaml"
    xmlns:d="http://schemas.microsoft.com/expression/blend/2008"
    xmlns:mc="http://schemas.openxmlformats.org/markup-
compatibility/2006"
    mc:Ignorable="d"
    xmlns:map="clr-namespace:Microsoft.Maps.MapControl;assembly=Mi
crosoft.Maps.MapControl"
    d:DesignHeight="300" d:DesignWidth="400">
  <UserControl.Resources>
    <ControlTemplate x:Key="FancyMarker" TargetType="map:
Pushpin">
        <Canvas Width="50"
                Height="80"
                Opacity="0.8"
                map:MapLayer.PositionOrigin="BottomCenter">
          <Path Data="M 0,0 L 50,0 50,50 25,80 0,50 0,0"
                Fill="LightBlue"
                StrokeEndLineCap="Round"
                Stroke="DarkRed"
                StrokeThickness="2" />
          <TextBlock FontSize="10"
                Width="50"
                Foreground="Black"
                Margin="1"
                TextAlignment="Center"
                Text="{TemplateBinding Content}" />
        </Canvas>
    </ControlTemplate>
```

```xml
    </UserControl.Resources>
<Grid x:Name="LayoutRoot" Background="White">
    <Grid.RowDefinitions>
        <RowDefinition Height="40"></RowDefinition>
        <RowDefinition Height="*"></RowDefinition>
    </Grid.RowDefinitions>

    <StackPanel Orientation="Horizontal">
        <Button x:Name="btnDC"
                Content="US-DC Area Locations"
                Click="btnDC_Click" />
        <Button x:Name="btnNY"
                Content="US-NY Area Locations"
                Click="btnNY_Click" />
        <Button x:Name="btnUK"
                Content="UK-LON Area Locations"
                Click="btnEurope_Click" />
    </StackPanel>

    <map:Map x:Name="map"
            Center="39.04801,-76.84817"
            ZoomLevel="10"
            Mode="Road"
            Grid.Row="1"
            CredentialsProvider="[Bing Maps Account Key]" >
        <map:Pushpin Location="39.28345, -76.61714"

                    Template="{StaticResource FancyMarker}"
                    Content="Baltimore" />
        <map:Pushpin Location="39.21485, -76.86082"
                    Template="{StaticResource FancyMarker}"
                    Content="Columbia" />
        <map:Pushpin Location="38.95981, -77.08540"
                    Template="{StaticResource FancyMarker}"
                    Content="DC" />
        <map:Pushpin Location="38.89153, -77.0850"
                    Template="{StaticResource FancyMarker}"
                    Content="Arlington" />
        <map:Pushpin Location="39.12242, -77.23495"
                    Template="{StaticResource FancyMarker}"
                    Content="Kentlands" />
```

```
            <map:Pushpin Location="38.92415, -77.22659"
                         Template="{StaticResource FancyMarker}"
                         Content="Tysons" />
            <map:Pushpin Location="39.09325, -76.85680"
                         Template="{StaticResource FancyMarker}"
                         Content="Laurel" />
            <map:Pushpin Location="38.97804, -76.48695"
                         Template="{StaticResource FancyMarker}"
                         Content="Annapolis" />
            <map:Pushpin Location="38.9589,-77.3623"
                         Template="{StaticResource FancyMarker}"
                         Content="Reston" />
        </map:Map>
    </Grid>
</UserControl>
```

3. Run the solution now and you'll see that the Pushpins look quite different:

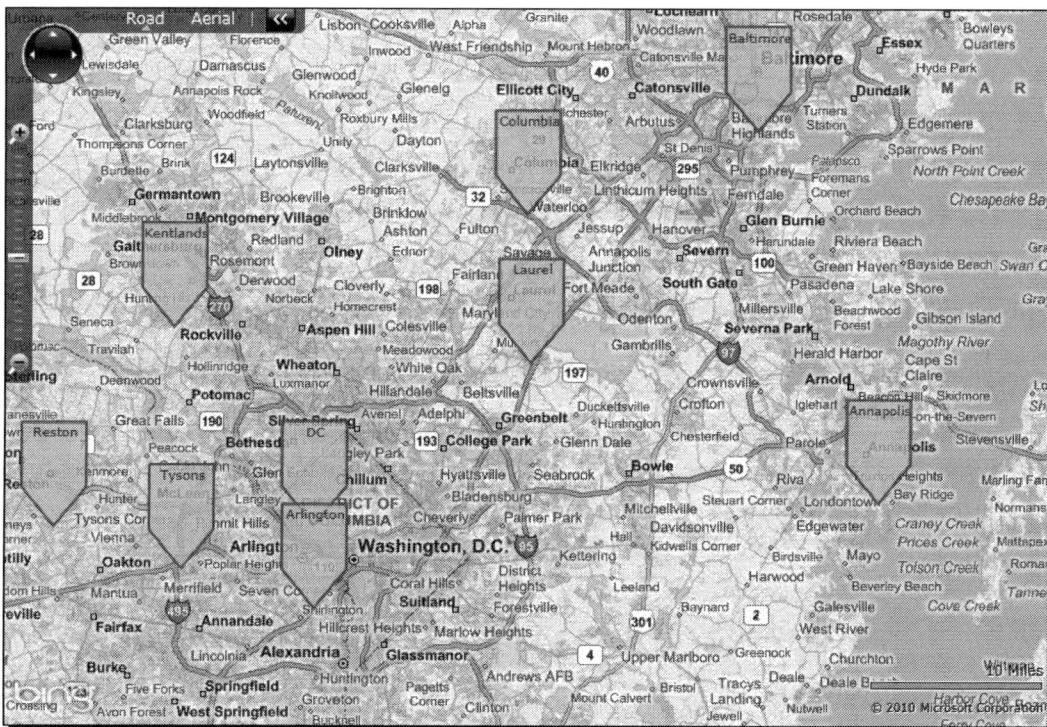

4. Close the browser window to end the debugging session.

Yet again, we see how powerful and flexible Silverlight can be in terms of re-styling controls.

What just happened?

We created a new `ControlTemplate` to override the appearance of a `PushPin` using some of the techniques we've used before. However, we simply created a `ControlTemplate`, instead of defining a `Style` which contains one. Here is the new `ControlTemplate` with some of the more interesting lines highlighted:

```
<UserControl.Resources>
  <ControlTemplate x:Key="FancyMarker" TargetType="map:Pushpin">
    <Canvas Width="50"
            Height="80"
            Opacity="0.8"
            map:MapLayer.PositionOrigin="BottomCenter">
      <Path Data="M 0,0 L 50,0 50,50 25,80 0,50 0,0"
            Fill="LightBlue"
            StrokeEndLineCap="Round"
            Stroke="DarkRed"
            StrokeThickness="2" />
      <TextBlock FontSize="10"
                 Width="50"
                 Foreground="Black"
                 Margin="1"
                 TextAlignment="Center"
                 Text="{TemplateBinding Content}" />
    </Canvas>
  </ControlTemplate>
</UserControl.Resources>
```

Our new `ControlTemplate` contains a `Canvas` panel with a `Path` and a `TextBlock` inside it. We're already familiar with the `TextBlock` control, but the `Path` object may be unfamiliar to you. Paths define geometric shapes in Silverlight. You may be looking at the contents of the `Data` attribute and wonder what all that gibberish means. It is a form of shorthand called the **Path Mini-Language** to define geometric paths in XAML.

> You can read more about the **Path Mini-Language** on MSDN at: `http://msdn.microsoft.com/en-us/library/cc189041(VS.95).aspx`.

The `Path` defines a shape that creates with a sharp point focused at the bottom center. We want to make sure that the bottom center of our custom marker is aligned with the LatLong given to the Pushpin.

We need to tell the `map` control how to align the `PushPin` control. We want the bottom center to line up with the Location and that's exactly what this attribute does:

`map:MapLayer.PositionOrigin="BottomCenter"`

As an added touch, the custom template also adds a TextBlock, which displays the name of the town in which a given store is located. Looking closely at the code, you'll notice that the `Text` property of the `TextBlock` is set to {`TemplateBinding Content`}. This markup extension binds the value of the Pushpin's `Content` property to the TextBlock in our control template.

There's one last step: tell our Pushpins to use our new control template. It has a `Key` property of `FancyMarker`. Now all we have to do is set each Pushpin's `Template` property to {`StaticResource FancyMarker`} and set a value for the `Content` property to populate the textbox in our control template.

```
<map:Pushpin Location="39.28345, -76.61714" Template="{StaticResource
FancyMarker}" Content="Baltimore" />
```

Naturally, hard coding the store nodes in the XAML may not be a great long term strategy as Cake-O-Rama adds more stores. We will revisit the map control in the Chapter 9 to learn how to include directions routing and more.

To learn more about the Bing Maps Silverlight control, watch the **Deep Dive on Bing Maps Silverlight Control** session from the Professional Developers Conference 2009 (PDC09) at: `http://microsoftpdc.com/Sessions/CL36`.

Drawing out ideas

Designing a custom cake sometimes requires creative input from the customer. Cake-O-Rama would like to put this process on the web by allowing the end user to draw out their ideas on a virtual sketchpad. Potential customers can submit this sketch along with other data when they request more information. A couple looking for a wedding cake, for example, could sketch out what they would like to have made. The following sketch conveys the customer's wishes much better than mere words could:

The InkPresenter control

In 2001, Microsoft introduced the Tablet PC and with it an SDK, software development kit, for handling digital ink. Much of the same code that powers Tablet PC development resides in Silverlight as well. This means that, among other things, we can quickly create a simple drawing system with just a little bit of code.

The control that renders and allows us to edit and render **Ink** is the `InkPresenter` control. Ink is a data type that stores a series of X and Y coordinates in containers called Strokes. A **Stroke** is analogous to the stroke of pen. A stroke starts when you place your pen down on a piece of paper (or a Tablet PC screen) and release. It contains one or more `Points` in a `StylusPointCollection`. In the absence of a stylus, the mouse acts as a substitute. Clicking and holding the mouse button down simulates the pressing down on the screen with a stylus.

> A stylus is another word for pen, usually reserved for dealing with computerized pen input devices.

Creating an `InkPresenter` control is quite easy. The XAML is simply:

```
<InkPresenter />
```

However, this alone would do nothing. Unlike many Silverlight controls, which have built in functionality, the `InkPresenter` control needs a little bit of help from us to capture strokes. The `InkPresenter` contains only the bits necessary to render the ink, not collect it. We'll have to attach some code to make it work like a drawing canvas.

> `InkPresenter` has none of the built in amenities of WPF's `InkCanvas` control, which both renders and collects ink.

Capturing strokes

Fortunately, capturing strokes isn't all that difficult. What we really need to do is make note of when the user presses the mouse button, moves the mouse around, and releases the mouse button. We can do all of this by attaching event handlers to the appropriate events: `MouseLeftButtonDown`, `MouseLeftButtonUp` and `MouseMove` events. Doing this in XAML is fairly straightforward as the following code snippet demonstrates:

```
<InkPresenter MouseLeftButtonDown="inkPresenter_MouseLeftButtonDown"
              MouseLeftButtonUp="inkPresenter_MouseLeftButtonUp"
              MouseMove="inkPresenter_MouseMove"
              />
```

Naturally, the event handlers have to actually have code in them to be of any use. By adding code that collects the movement of the user's mouse (or stylus) we can build a nice drawing application fairly easily. Let's build our sketching application now.

Time for action – building a basic sketching application

Let's build out a sketching application in Silverlight using the `InkPresenter` control and a little bit of code.

1. Launch Visual Studio and create a new Silverlight application by choosing **File|New|Project** from the file menu and choosing **Silverlight Application** in the dialog box that follows.

2. Name the solution **SilverInk**.

3. Once the solution is created, we'll want to add the following line of XAML inside the Grid element already in our `MainPage.xaml`:

```
<InkPresenter x:Name="inkPresenter" Background="LightBlue" MouseLe
ftButtonDown="inkPresenter_MouseLeftButtonDown"
               MouseLeftButtonUp="inkPresenter_MouseLeftButtonUp"
               MouseMove="inkPresenter_MouseMove"
               />
```

4. The fastest and easiest way to create event handlers is to let Visual Studio do it for us. Right-click on the `MouseLeftButtonDown` event handler attribute to get the following context menu:

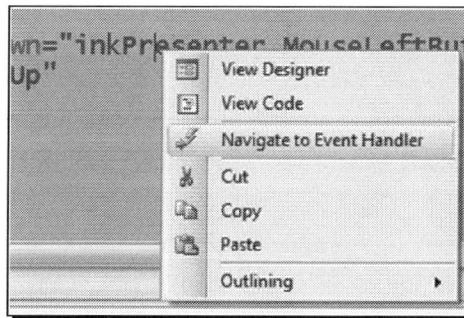

5. Click on **Navigate to Event Handler**.

6. Visual Studio will automatically create an empty event handler method for you and transfer you to the `MainPage.xaml.cs` code behind file:

```
private void inkPresenter_MouseLeftButtonDown(object sender,
MouseButtonEventArgs e)
{

}
```

7. Repeat steps 2 through 4 for the `MouseLeftButtonUp` and `MouseMove` events to create empty handler methods for both of these events as well.

8. Next, we'll want to add a reference to the namespace where all the Ink related objects are. Towards the top of the `MainPage.xaml.cs` file add the following statement:

```
using System.Windows.Ink;
```

9. Let's create a Stroke object member in our `MainPage` class:

```
Stroke _stroke;
```

10. In the `MouseLeftButtonDown` event handler, we'll need to add code to create a new `Stroke` object and assign the `_stroke` variable to it and add this to the `Stroke` property of the `InkPresenter` like so:

```
this._stroke = new Stroke();
this.inkPresenter.Strokes.Add(this._stroke);
```

11. Next, we'll need to capture any mouse or stylus movements that occur over our `InkPresenter` control as we move the mouse or stylus. Add these lines of code to the `inkPresenter_MouseMove` method:

```
if (this._stroke != null)
{
  this._stroke.StylusPoints.Add(
       e.StylusDevice.GetStylusPoints(this.inkPresenter)
       );
}
```

12. Finally, we'll need to stop collecting strokes when the `MouseLeftButtonUp` event occurs. We'll also need to set the `_stroke` variable to null to indicate that we are no longer adding strokes to the `InkPresenter`. In the `inkPresenter_MouseLeftButtonUp` method, add the following lines of code:

```
if (this._stroke != null)
{
   this._stroke = null;
}
```

13. Your entire code file should look like this:

```
using System;
using System.Collections.Generic;
using System.Linq;
using System.Net;
using System.Windows;
using System.Windows.Controls;
using System.Windows.Documents;
using System.Windows.Input;
using System.Windows.Media;
using System.Windows.Media.Animation;
using System.Windows.Shapes;
using System.Windows.Ink;
namespace SilverInk
{
    public partial class MainPage : UserControl
  {
      Stroke _stroke;
      public MainPage()
      {
          InitializeComponent();
      }
      private void inkPresenter_MouseLeftButtonDown(object sender,
MouseButtonEventArgs e)
      {
          this._stroke = new Stroke();
          this.inkPresenter.Strokes.Add(this._stroke);
      }
      private void inkPresenter_MouseLeftButtonUp(object sender,
MouseButtonEventArgs e)
      {
          if (this._stroke != null)
          {
            this._stroke = null;
          }
      }
      private void inkPresenter_MouseMove(object sender,
MouseEventArgs e)
      {
          if (this._stroke != null)
          {
              this._stroke.StylusPoints.Add(
                e.StylusDevice.GetStylusPoints(this.inkPresenter)
```

```
            );
         }
      }
   }
}
```

14. Run the solution now by choosing **Start Debugging** from the **Debug** menu or pressing the *F5* key.

15. If prompted, choose to enable debugging.

16. Use the mouse to draw inside the light blue area. Hold the left mouse button down while you move the mouse around to draw. Release the left mouse button to stop drawing. Depending on your artistic skill set, your screen will look something like this:

17. Next, close down the host browser and return to Visual Studio.

What just happened?

We just created a simple drawing application leveraging an existing control in Silverlight: the InkPresenter. Notice that we didn't write any code to handle rendering our drawing. All our code was focused on creating a Stroke object and adding StylusPoints points to it.

> A **Point** is a structure that has two members: an X and Y coordinate.

A **StylusPoint** is a typical point object with an added property of **PressureFactor** to track the relative amount of pressure applied by the stylus. Its value is between 0 and 1. Many Tablet and touch screen devices also record the amount of pressure applied to the stylus or screen. If you're using a device that does not track applied pressure, like a mouse, then the value of `PressureFactor` is always set to $.5$.

> The topic of developing for Tablet PCs and touch devices is a passion of mine. There is enough content to write a book about it. Perhaps, one day I will.

Changing drawing attributes

It may be cool to us developers to create a simple sketching program with hardly any code, but our end users may expect a little more. Our application still lacks many features that any drawing program worth its salt should have. For instance, what if you wanted to write with a wider stroke or draw in a different color? Fortunately for us, this is actually quite easy.

The `Stroke` object contains a property called **DrawingAttribute**, which lets us alter the height, width and color of any given `Stroke` object. For instance, if we wanted to make a Stroke red we would write the following line of code:

```
_stroke.DrawingAttributes.Color = Colors.Red;
```

What if we wanted to create a highlighter effect, like the one demonstrated below:

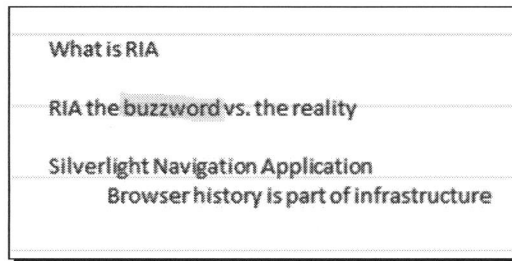

What is RIA

RIA the buzzword vs. the reality

Silverlight Navigation Application
        Browser history is part of infrastructure

We would need to use a semi-transparent yellow. Yellow in the RGB color space is 255, 255, 0. A semi-transparent yellow in the ARGB color space would be represented as 127, 255, 255, 0. To set a Stroke's `DrawingAttribute` to a semi-transparent yellow requires the following code:

```
_stroke.DrawingAttributes.Color = Color.FromArgb(127, 255, 255, 0);
```

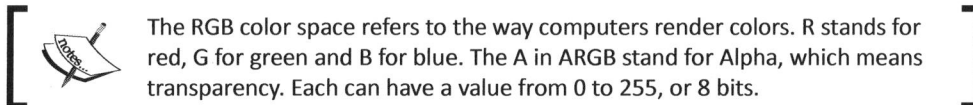

> The RGB color space refers to the way computers render colors. R stands for red, G for green and B for blue. The A in ARGB stand for Alpha, which means transparency. Each can have a value from 0 to 255, or 8 bits.

Highlighter pen tips also tend to be taller than they are wide. To create an accurate highlighter, we would also need to mimic that. To do this, we'll set the height to a larger number like so:

```
this._stroke.DrawingAttributes.Height = 10;
```

Time for action – controlling the appearance of Ink

Let's add the ability to highlight our drawing. We'll need to add a few interface elements to switch back and forth between highlighter mode and regular pen mode. We will do this now as follows:

1. Firstly, load up the project we created in the `SilverInk` solution just created in Launch Visual Studio.

2. Let's add some space for a miniature toolbar in our application to hold buttons.

3. To do this, we'll need to split the Grid named `LayoutRoot` into two rows. In `MainPage.xaml`, add the following XAML code belongs right below the line of code `<Grid x:Name="LayoutRoot" Background="White">`:

```
<Grid.RowDefinitions>
    <RowDefinition Height="40" />
    <RowDefinition Height="*" />
</Grid.RowDefinitions>
```

4. The above line creates two rows or space for controls to reside. The top space is 40 units high and the bottom space takes up the remaining space.

5. We'll need to add an attribute to our `InkPresenter` control to tell it to reside inside the second row. Add the following attribute to the `InkPresenter` XAML node:

```
Grid.Row="1"
```

6. If you look at the **Preview** pane in Visual Studio, you should see the following screenshot:

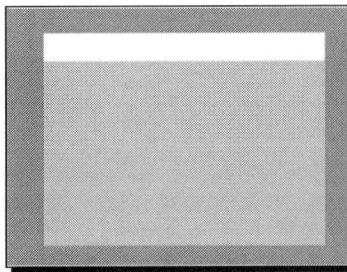

7. Now, we need to make a toolbar of buttons in the top row. We'll need to add a `StackPanel` and fill it with buttons. To do this, add the following XAML code to our Grid node:

```
<StackPanel Orientation="Horizontal">
    <Button x:Name="btnPen"
            Content="Pen"
            Click="btnPen_Click" />
    <Button x:Name="btnHighlighter"
            Content="Highlighter"
            Click="btnHighlighter_Click" />
</StackPanel>
```

8. Right-click on both the button nodes and choose **Navigate to Event Handler** to have Visual Studio generate both the `btnHighlighter_Click` and `btnHighlighter_Click` event handlers.

9. Go to the code behind file (`MainPage.xaml.cs`) and add the two following members to the class file:

```
Color _strokeColor = Colors.Black;
double _strokeHeight = 3;
```

10. Next, add the following two lines of code to the `inkPresenter_MouseLeftButtonDown` method:

```
this._stroke.DrawingAttributes.Color = this._strokeColor;
this._stroke.DrawingAttributes.Height = this._strokeHeight;
```

11. Change the button event handlers so they look like this:

```
private void btnPen_Click(object sender, RoutedEventArgs e)
{
    this._strokeColor = Colors.Black;
    this._strokeHeight = 3;
}
private void btnHighlighter_Click(object sender, RoutedEventArgs
e)
{
    this._strokeHeight = 10;
    this._strokeColor = Color.FromArgb(192, 255, 255, 0);
}
```

12. The `MainPage.XAML.cs` code behind should contain the following code:

```
using System;
using System.Collections.Generic;
using System.Linq;
using System.Net;
```

```csharp
using System.Windows;
using System.Windows.Controls;
using System.Windows.Documents;
using System.Windows.Input;
using System.Windows.Media;
using System.Windows.Media.Animation;
using System.Windows.Shapes;
using System.Windows.Ink;

namespace SilverInk
{
  public partial class MainPage : UserControl
  {
    Stroke _stroke;
    Color _strokeColor = Colors.Black;
    double _strokeHeight = 3;

    public MainPage()
    {
        InitializeComponent();
    }

    private void inkPresenter_MouseLeftButtonDown(object sender,
MouseButtonEventArgs e)
    {
        this._stroke = new Stroke();
        this._stroke.DrawingAttributes.Color = this._strokeColor;
        this._stroke.DrawingAttributes.Height = this._
strokeHeight;

        this.inkPresenter.Strokes.Add(this._stroke);

    }

  private void inkPresenter_MouseLeftButtonUp(object sender,
MouseButtonEventArgs e)
  {
    if (this._stroke != null)
    {
       this._stroke = null;
    }
  }

  }
```

```
private void inkPresenter_MouseMove(object sender, MouseEventArgs
e)
  {
      if (this._stroke != null)
      {
          this._stroke.StylusPoints.Add(
              e.StylusDevice.GetStylusPoints(this.inkPresenter)
          );
      }
  }

 private void btnPen_Click(object sender, RoutedEventArgs e)
  {
      this._strokeColor = Colors.Black;
      this._strokeHeight = 3;
  }

 private void btnHighlighter_Click(object sender, RoutedEventArgs
e)
  {
      this._strokeHeight = 10;
      this._strokeColor = Color.FromArgb(192, 255, 255, 0);
  }
 }
}
```

13. Run the solution and draw! You should be presented with the following:

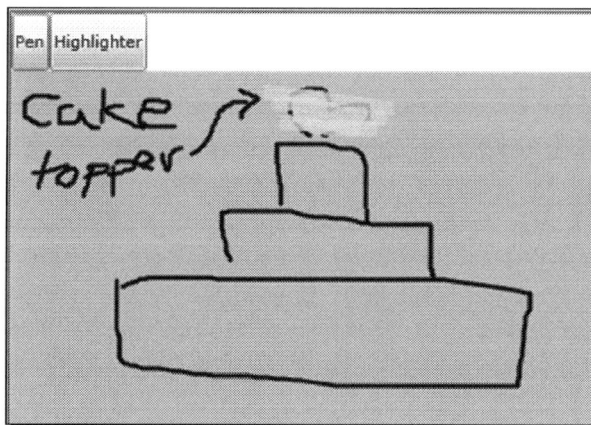

14. Close the host browser window.

What just happened?

We just enhanced our drawing application by giving the user a choice in what brush to paint with. We're certainly a long way off from giving Microsoft Paint or Adobe Photoshop any competition, but our users will appreciate the added functionality.

Erasing Strokes

If you've played with the sample application enough, you're probably wishing there was an option to delete what you've drawn. There are actually two ways to erase ink.

One option is to delete the stroke or strokes from the `Strokes` collection of an `InkPresenter`. To clear an `InkPresenter` entirely, simply clear its `Strokes` collection. The code to do this is a simple one liner:

```
inkPresenter.Strokes.Clear();
```

With a little bit of logic to narrow down the Stroke that we wish to remove from the `Stroke` collection of an `InkPresenter`, we can be a bit more selective in what we remove. The code to determine which stroke, can take on many forms, but it could be as simple as this:

```
inkPresenter.Strokes.Remove(strokeToDelete);
```

Removing the last stroke comes in handy when you want to provide an undo function to your drawing application. To remove the last stroke added to an `InkPresenter`, we could get the last item in the Strokes collection of an `InkPresenter`:

```
inkPresenter.Strokes.Remove(this.inkPresenter.Strokes.Last());
```

> The **Last** method used in the above line of code is an **Extension Method**. Extension methods form the basis of **LINQ**, which is something we'll be seeing a lot of in forthcoming chapters.

So far all the approaches to deleting ink strokes involve removing the entire stroke, which doesn't feel natural to an end user. What we'd really like to do is erase only what the user moves the mouse over. Think about moving an eraser across a piece of paper: only the pencil strokes that the eraser touches are erased. To duplicate this, we'll need to capture the stroke that the user makes when intending to erase strokes and then use the `HitTest` method to determine if there are any intersections. Both `Stroke` and `StrokeCollection` have a `HitTest` method that accepts a `StylusPointCollection`. This method comes in handy when you want to add delete functionality.

For example, the following code removes strokes from the `inkPresenter` using a `StylusPointCollection` named, `_erasePoints`:

```
StrokeCollection hitStrokes = this.inkPresenter.Strokes.HitTest(_
erasePoints);
if (hitStrokes.Count > 0)
{
    foreach (Stroke hitStroke in hitStrokes)
    {
        this.inkPresenter.Strokes.Remove(hitStroke);
    }
}
```

Time for action – adding an erase feature

Let's improve our sketching application in Silverlight by adding an erase feature.

1. Open the `SilverInk` application in Visual Studio.

2. We're going to add three new buttons: one to switch to eraser mode, the second to delete the last stroke added, and the third one to clear the entire `inkPresenter`.

3. Add the following XAML to the `StackPanel` where all the other buttons reside:

```
<Button x:Name="btnErase"
        Content="Eraser"
        Click="btnErase_Click" />
<Button x:Name="btnDeleteLastStroke"
        Content="Delete Last Stroke"
        Click="btnDeleteLastStroke_Click" />
<Button x:Name="btnClear"
        Content="Clear All"
        Click="btnClear_Click" />
```

4. Right-click on each of the `Button` nodes and select **Navigate to Event Handler** to have Visual Studio create the event handlers in code.

5. Right now, our application should look like this in design preview mode:

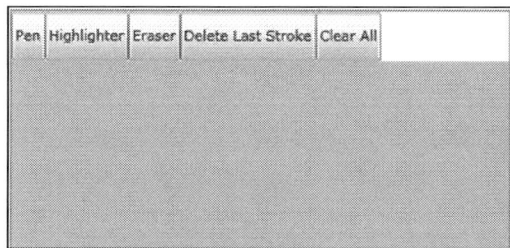

6. In order to support erasing, we'll need to add two new members to our class file. Add the following two lines of code to our class:

```
StylusPointCollection _erasePoints;
bool _erase = false;
```

7. We'll need to modify the MouseLeftDown, MouseLeftUp, and MouseMove event handlers to support erasing. We'll use the _erase Boolean to store the erase state. Here are the modifications to these methods:

```
private void inkPresenter_MouseLeftButtonDown(object sender,
MouseButtonEventArgs e)
{
  if (this._erase == false)
  {
    this._stroke = new Stroke();
    this.inkPresenter.Strokes.Add(this._stroke);

    this._stroke.DrawingAttributes.Color = this._strokeColor;
    this._stroke.DrawingAttributes.Height = this._strokeHeight;

  }
  else
  {
    _erasePoints = e.StylusDevice.GetStylusPoints(this.
inkPresenter);
  }
}

private void inkPresenter_MouseLeftButtonUp(object sender,
MouseButtonEventArgs e)
{
    if (this._stroke != null)
    {
      this._stroke = null;
    }

}
private void inkPresenter_MouseMove(object sender, MouseEventArgs
e)
{
  if (this._erase == false)
  {
    if (this._stroke != null)
    {
      this._stroke.StylusPoints.Add(
```

```
                    e.StylusDevice.GetStylusPoints(this.inkPresenter));
            }
        }
        else
        {
            if (this._erasePoints != null)
            {
                _erasePoints.Add(
                    e.StylusDevice.GetStylusPoints(this.inkPresenter));

                StrokeCollection hitStrokes =
                    this.inkPresenter.Strokes.HitTest(_erasePoints);

                if (hitStrokes.Count > 0)
                {
                    foreach (Stroke hitStroke in hitStrokes)
                    {
                        this.inkPresenter.Strokes.Remove(hitStroke);
                    }
                }
            }
        }
    }
}
```

8. We'll need to turn erase mode off when we click on Pen or Highlighter and on when we click Eraser. Accordingly, we'll modify the event handlers like so:

```
private void btnPen_Click(object sender, RoutedEventArgs e)
{
    this._erase = false;
    this.inkPresenter.Cursor = Cursors.Stylus;

    this._strokeColor = Colors.Black;
    this._strokeHeight = 3;
}

private void btnHighlighter_Click(object sender, RoutedEventArgs
e)
{
    this._erase = false;
    this.inkPresenter.Cursor = Cursors.Stylus;

    this._strokeHeight = 10;
    this._strokeColor = Color.FromArgb(192, 255, 255, 0);
}
```

```
private void btnErase_Click(object sender, RoutedEventArgs e)
{
    this._erase = true;
    this.inkPresenter.Cursor = Cursors.Eraser;
}
```

9. Finally, we'll want to add some code to delete the last stroke and to clear all the ink from the `inkPresenter`:

```
private void btnDeleteLastStroke_Click(object sender,
RoutedEventArgs e)
{
    if (inkPresenter.Strokes.Count > 0)
    {
        this.inkPresenter.Strokes.Remove(
            this.inkPresenter.Strokes.Last());
    }
}

private void btnClear_Click(object sender, RoutedEventArgs e)
{
    this.inkPresenter.Strokes.Clear();
}
```

10. Run the solution, you should notice that the cursor changes to an eraser when in eraser mode:

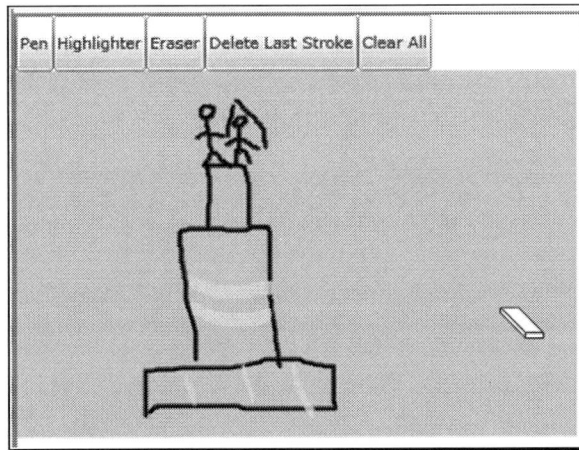

What just happened?

My artwork aside, you can see that we've built a relatively functional drawing program that customers can use to sketch out their ideas. However, before we can call this finished we'll need to find a way to preserve our artwork and then submit it to Cake-O-Rama.

Storing Strokes in Isolated Storage

With the sample sketching application we created earlier in this chapter, we could easily lose our artwork if we were to close our browser window, reboot our computer or do anything that would reload the page. This may not be a big deal for our development time doodles, but customers who put a lot of time and effort into getting their ideas down on the computer, might feel otherwise.

Isolated Storage

You may have heard that Silverlight does not have access to the local file system, but it does support something known as **Isolated Storage**. Isolated storage can be treated like a file system or persist like application settings in key/value pairs. Isolated Storage allows your Silverlight applications to store data locally on the end users' computers. Isolated storage is per user storage, per computer, and per application (technically, per application URI). This means that one Silverlight application cannot access the file store of another directly. The same goes for different users on the same computer. This is a security feature. You wouldn't want anyone to write malware that could snoop around the hard drive or access other users' data.

> In full trust mode, Silverlight has more access to the local file system.

Another interesting feature of isolated storage is that it is browser independent. If your Silverlight application saves data to isolated storage in FireFox, you will be able to access that data from Internet Explorer on the same machine.

You can see a list of all the Silverlight applications that store data on your computer by right-clicking on any Silverlight application and selecting on **Silverlight** from the context menu. Click on the **Application Storage** tab to see what is being stored on your computer:

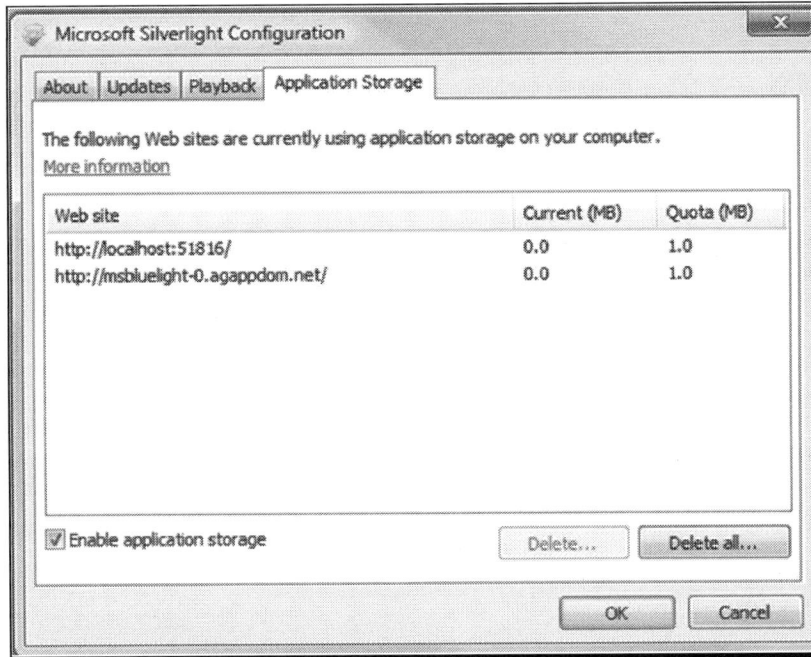

Silverlight applications receive a quota of 1MB of disk space. In order to receive more space, an application must request more space and the user must accept the request. Silverlight Out-of-Browser applications automatically get 25MB of space and must get permission from the user to use more. You'll also notice that users have the ability to turn application storage off as well as delete the local application store. They will be asked to confirm their decision with another dialog box like this:

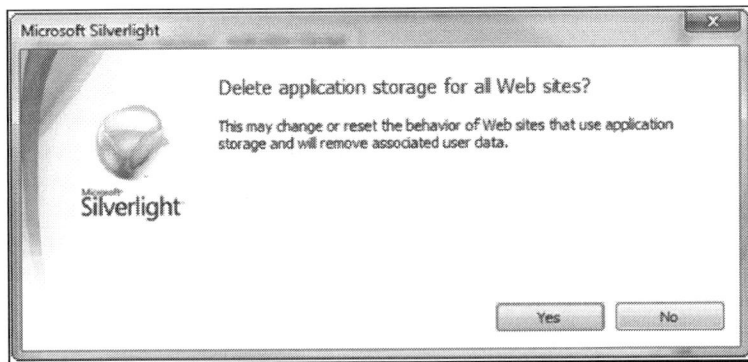

> Always treat data in isolation storage as volatile, as you never know when it could be deleted.

Also remember that the data in isolated storage is stored on the local computer, not the web server. This means that if your application stores data on one computer, the content in isolated storage will not automatically appear on another computer even if it's the same user. Typically, you'll want to treat isolated storage as a temporary caching mechanism and post the changes to some kind of server-side service. Naturally, you'll want to minimize the number of roundtrips to the server.

Time for action– adding persistence

Let's make sure that no sketches are lost when the user reloads the page. The best way to approach this is to save the stroke data as they draw. When the user reloads our application, we should add code that checks to see if there is already ink data in the local store.

> We could also write files to isolated storage.

We will now save the Strokes collection to isolated storage every time a stroke is added to the inkPresenter control. We will do this by completing the following steps:

1. Firstly, open the SilverInk application in Launch Visual Studio.

2. In the MainPage.xaml.cs file, add the following using statements:

```
using System.IO.IsolatedStorage;
using System.Text;
using System.Xml;
using System.Windows.Markup;
```

3. Add a method that will take the Strokes in the inkPresenter control and convert them into a XAML string:

```
private string ConvertStrokesToXaml()
{
  StringBuilder stringBuilder = new StringBuilder();
  XmlWriter xmlWriter = XmlWriter.Create(stringBuilder);

  xmlWriter.WriteStartElement("StrokeCollection",
    "http://schemas.microsoft.com/winfx/2006/xaml/presentation");
```

```
foreach (Stroke stroke in this.inkPresenter.Strokes)
{
  xmlWriter.WriteStartElement("Stroke");
  xmlWriter.WriteStartElement("Stroke.DrawingAttributes");
  xmlWriter.WriteStartElement("DrawingAttributes");
  xmlWriter.WriteAttributeString("Width",
    stroke.DrawingAttributes.Width.ToString());
  xmlWriter.WriteAttributeString("Height",
    stroke.DrawingAttributes.Height.ToString());

  xmlWriter.WriteAttributeString("Color",
    string.Format("#{0:X2}{1:X2}{2:X2}{3:X2}",
    stroke.DrawingAttributes.Color.A,
    stroke.DrawingAttributes.Color.R,
    stroke.DrawingAttributes.Color.G,
    stroke.DrawingAttributes.Color.B));

  xmlWriter.WriteAttributeString("OutlineColor",
    string.Format("#{0:X2}{1:X2}{2:X2}{3:X2}",
    stroke.DrawingAttributes.OutlineColor.A,
    stroke.DrawingAttributes.OutlineColor.R,
    stroke.DrawingAttributes.OutlineColor.G,
    stroke.DrawingAttributes.OutlineColor.B));

  xmlWriter.WriteEndElement();
  xmlWriter.WriteEndElement();

  xmlWriter.WriteStartElement("Stroke.StylusPoints");
  xmlWriter.WriteStartElement("StylusPointCollection");

  foreach (StylusPoint sp in stroke.StylusPoints)
  {
      xmlWriter.WriteStartElement("StylusPoint");
      xmlWriter.WriteAttributeString("X", sp.X.ToString());
      xmlWriter.WriteAttributeString("Y", sp.Y.ToString());
      xmlWriter.WriteEndElement();
  }

  xmlWriter.WriteEndElement();
  xmlWriter.WriteEndElement();
  xmlWriter.WriteEndElement();

}
```

```
    xmlWriter.WriteEndElement();
    xmlWriter.Flush();

    return stringBuilder.ToString();
}
```

4. Create a method called `PersistInk` that will write the ink to isolated storage:

```
private void PersistInk()
{
   IsolatedStorageSettings settings =
    IsolatedStorageSettings.ApplicationSettings;

   string strokesXaml = ConvertStrokesToXaml();

   if (settings.Contains("sketchData"))
   {
      settings["sketchData"] = strokesXaml;
   }
   else
   {
      settings.Add("sketchData", strokesXaml);
   }
}
```

5. Next we'll add a call to `PersistInk` to any method that modifies the Stroke collection of the `inkPresenter`. Specifically, these methods: `inkPresenter_MouseLeftButtonUp`, `btnDeleteLastStroke_Click`, and `btnClear_Click`.

6. In the `MainPage.xaml` file, add an event handler for the `Loaded` event:

```
Loaded="UserControl_Loaded"
```

7. In the `MainPage.xaml.cs` file, add the following code which will look inside the isolated storage for stored data. If it finds data, it will de-serialize the XAML code describing the strokes and load it into the `InkPresenter` control:

```
private void UserControl_Loaded(object sender, RoutedEventArgs e)
{
    IsolatedStorageSettings settings =
      IsolatedStorageSettings.ApplicationSettings;

    if (settings.Contains("sketchData"))
    {
      string sketchXAML = settings["sketchData"] as string;
      this.inkPresenter.Strokes = XamlReader.Load(sketchXAML) as
        StrokeCollection;
    }
}
```

8. Next, run the solution and draw anything!

9. Reload the page and it should re-appear.

10. Close the browser window and return back to Visual Studio. Run the solution again and your sketch should reappear.

11. Copy the location in the browser's address bar. Then, launch another browser.

12. Paste the address into the address bar and you'll see your sketch re-appear. Close the browser window again.

What just happened?

You created some strokes and saved them into isolated storage as an application setting. There was a lot of code inside the `ConvertStrokesToXaml` method. The important thing to take away is that it took the `StrokesCollection` of the `InkPresenter` and converted it to a fragment of XAML code as demonstrated below:

```
<?xml version="1.0" encoding="utf16" ?>
<StrokeCollection
  xmlns="http://schemas.microsoft.com/winfx/2006/xaml/presentation" >
  <Stroke>
  <Stroke.DrawingAttributes>
    <DrawingAttributes Width="3" Height="3" Color="#FF000000"
        OutlineColor="#00000000" />
  </Stroke.DrawingAttributes>
  <Stroke.StylusPoints>
    <StylusPointCollection>
        <StylusPoint X="127" Y="28" />
      <StylusPoint X="125" Y="33" />
      <StylusPoint X="123" Y="40" />
      <StylusPoint X="118" Y="48" />
      <StylusPoint X="114" Y="57" />
    </StylusPointCollection>
    </Stroke.StylusPoints>
  </Stroke>
</StrokeCollection>
```

The `PersistInk` method uses this XAML and places it inside the `ApplicationSettings`, which is essentially a Dictionary, with key and value pairs. The code fragment below checks to see if a given key already exists. If it does, it overwrites the value. Otherwise, it adds a new key/value pair and sets its initial value:

```
IsolatedStorageSettings settings =
 IsolatedStorageSettings.ApplicationSettings;

string strokesXaml = ConvertStrokesToXaml();
```

```
if (settings.Contains("sketchData"))
{
    settings["sketchData"] = strokesXaml;
}
else
{
    settings.Add("sketchData", strokesXaml);
}
```

The following line of code de-serializes the XAML in the application store and uses the as keyword in C# to cast it as a `StrokeCollection` and sets the `Strokes` property of our `inkPresenter`:

```
this.inkPresenter.Strokes = XamlReader.Load(sketchXAML) as
    StrokeCollection;
```

What we did in this last step should be familiar to any seasoned developer: we serialized data, stored it and de-serialized it.

Have a go hero – where is isolated storage?

You may be a little curious about where the data you place into isolated storage ends up. Well, that all depends on what operating system your application runs on.

In the table below, you will see where the isolated storage files actually resides on disk.

Platform	Path
Windows 7 and Windows Vista	`%userprofile%\AppData\LocalLow\Microsoft\Silverlight\is`
Windows XP	`%userprofile%\Local Settings\Application Data\Microsoft\Silverlight\is`
MacOS	`/Users/<user>/Library/Application/Support/Microsoft/Silverlight/is`

For security reasons, the file and directory names are randomly generated, but if you dig around enough you'll eventually see a file named `__LocalSettings`, which contains the application settings data for a given Silverlight application. The file in the image below happens to be the settings file for our `SilverInk` application:

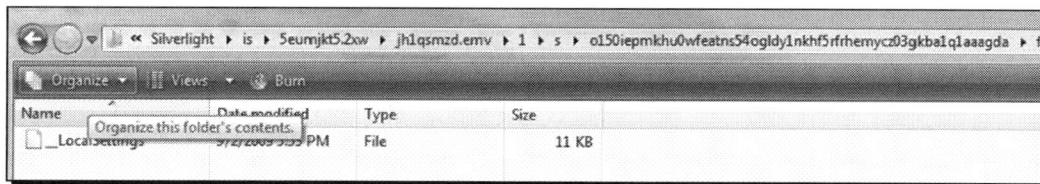

> Never store sensitive data unencrypted in isolated storage. You never know who will be snooping for what!

You can open this file in notepad:

```
ArrayOfKeyValueOfstringanyType xmlns:i="http://www.w3.org/2001/
XMLSchema-instance" xmlns="http://schemas.microsoft.com/2003/10/
Serialization/Arrays"><KeyValueOfstringanyType><Key>sketchData</
Key><Value xmlns:d3p1="http://www.w3.org/2001/XMLSchema" i:type="d3p1:
string">&lt;?xml version="1.0" encoding="utf-16"?&gt;&lt;StrokeCollec
tion
```

Note that this information is not encrypted or automatically protected. Security by obscurity is a terrible policy that is sure to get you hacked. Never store sensitive data such as passwords or credit card numbers unencrypted in isolated storage.

One more important warning: be careful what you store in your code as well. Any code in your Silverlight application can be decompiled and examined. SilverlightSpy, a tool I recommend for all Silverlight developers in Chapter 1, does exactly that. Keep in mind that your code executes on the client computer and, as such, the client computer has access to it. This means that malicious persons can snoop around your code and look for sensitive data.

> We've barely just scratched the surface of the feature set of `inkPresenter`. To learn more about using the `inkPresenter` in Silverlight, Stefan Wick's blog is a superb resource for a more in depth look at using Ink in Silverlight: `http://blogs.msdn.com/swick/`.
>
> The code in the `ConvertStrokesToXaml` came from one of his blog posts.

Uploading sketches

In order for our application to be of use to Cake-O-Rama, we'll need to take the stored sketches and send them up to the server. The process of uploading to the server involves serializing our data, then making a connection to the receiving server and sending the serialized data up. We should probably also inform the user whether or not the process succeeded.

Asynchronous calls

All network operations take time. Anyone who has ever waited for a web page to load knows this. The amount of time a network operation takes varies based on a wide number of factors, including but not limited to network traffic, volume of data to transfer, and server load. Why does this matter? Silverlight runs network operations asynchronously, meaning that while we wait for a network operation to complete, we can move on to doing other things. The network operations run on a separate thread from the user interface. This will become important in the next section.

Time for action – submitting sketches

Thus far, we've built a simple drawing application that stores its data locally. Now, it's time to share our artwork with the world, or at least the server at Cake-O-Rama. Once there, the receiving computer can do anything with the ink data. Let's add that ability now.

1. Open the `SilverInk` solution in Launch Visual Studio.

2. In the `MainPage.xaml` file, let's add another button. In the same `StackPanel` as all the other buttons, add this line of XAML:

    ```
    <Button x:Name="btnSend"
            Content="Send Sketch"
            Click="btnSend_Click"
            Margin="20,0,0,0" />
    ```

3. Right-click on each of the Button nodes and select **Navigate to Event Handler** to have Visual Studio create the event handlers in code.

4. In the `MainPage.xaml.cs` file, we'll need to add two more members. Their meaning and purpose will become clear shortly:

    ```
    public delegate void UpdateUI(HttpStatusCode httpStatusCode);
    static string _postData;
    ```

5. Next, we need to put some code into the event handler we had Visual Studio create for us in step 3:

    ```
    private void btnSend_Click(object sender, RoutedEventArgs e)
    {
        _postData = ConvertStrokesToXaml();

        SendData();
    }
    ```

6. Now, we'll need to define the `SendData` method, add the following code:

```
private void SendData()
{
    HttpWebRequest httpRequest =
        (HttpWebRequest)WebRequest.Create(new
            Uri("http://www.franksworld.com/"));
    httpRequest.Method = "POST";
    httpRequest.ContentType = "application/x-www-form-urlencoded";
    httpRequest.BeginGetRequestStream(new
        AsyncCallback(ResponseActive), httpRequest);
}
```

7. In the above snippet of code, I've highlighted a line that creates an asynchronous callback delegate. If you're not familiar with the concept, this is a way of telling Silverlight to call the `ResponseActive` method. We'll need to add that method now by adding the following code:

```
private void ResponseActive(IAsyncResult asyncRes)
{

    // Continue getting response
    HttpWebRequest httpRequest =
        (System.Net.HttpWebRequest)asyncRes.AsyncState;

    System.IO.StreamWriter postStreamWriter = new System.IO.Stre
amWriter(httpRequest.EndGetRequestStream(asyncRes), System.Text.
Encoding.Unicode);

    postStreamWriter.Write("XAML=" +    System.Windows.Browser.
HttpUtility.UrlEncode(_postData));
            postStreamWriter.Close();

    httpRequest.BeginGetResponse(new
        AsyncCallback(ResponseCompleteAsync), httpRequest);
}
```

8. Here is another snippet of code and another asynchronous callback delegate. You guessed it, we need to define the `ResponseCompleteAsync` method now by writing the following code:

```
private void ResponseCompleteAsync(IAsyncResult asyncRes)
{

    System.Net.HttpWebRequest httpRequest =
        (System.Net.HttpWebRequest)asyncRes.AsyncState;
    System.Net.HttpWebResponse httpResponse =
```

```
(System.Net.HttpWebResponse)httpRequest.EndGetResponse(async
Res);

    this.Dispatcher.BeginInvoke(new UpdateUI(ReportUploadStatus),
      httpResponse.StatusCode);
}
```

9. We will need to add another method. This one notifies the user whether or not the upload was successful:

```
private void ReportUploadStatus(HttpStatusCode httpStatusCode)
{
    if (httpStatusCode == HttpStatusCode.OK)
    {
      MessageBox.Show("Sketch successfully sent!");
    }
    else
    {
      MessageBox.Show("An error has occurred. Please try again.");
    }
}
```

10. Next, run the solution. After you draw something, your screen should look similar to the following screenshot:

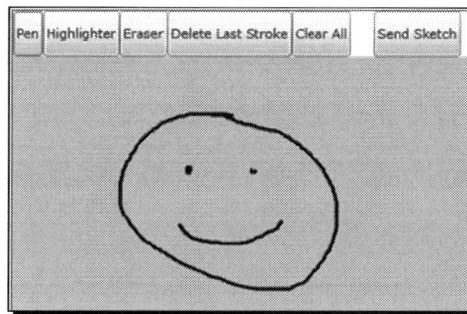

11. Click on the **Send Sketch Button.** After a moment, you should see a dialog box pop up to tell you that the result was successful.

12. Click **OK** and then close the browser host window.

What just happened?

We just added the ability for our drawing application to send drawings back to a web server. Along the way, we got a glimpse of networking programming and making asynchronous calls in Silverlight. We used the `HttpWebRequest` class to make an HTTP POST call to a URI on the internet.

Veteran ASP.NET developers ought to know what I mean when I say HTTP POST. For all others, it means I sent our serialized stroke data to a web page using a protocol built in to HTTP. But let's not get too caught up in the particulars of our implementation. We'll talk a lot more about making network calls in the next chapter.

Summary

In this chapter, we covered some of the wow factors of Silverlight that will give your RIA projects an added edge over the competition. You may be thinking that you'll never need to browse images via Deep Zoom, but you may be wrong.

You may not be working with cakes or rock star memorabilia, but imagine allowing users to browse through terabytes of scanned documents with a minimum drain on your company's network resources. Remember, only the bits being viewed get sent across the wire. Deep Zoom can save time and money.

You may also think you'll never need to use mapping, but consider that you can leverage **GIS (Geographic Information Systems)** data consider changing to "to" quickly populate a map in your applications.

Lastly, adding the power of digital ink to your solutions could allow you to electronically sign documents with a stylus or create a white board application, where multiple users could share ideas. You are only limited by your imagination. In this chapter, we discussed the following:

- How to create a Deep Zoom photo montage in Deep Zoom Composer
- How to work with the Bing Map control
- How to sign up for a Bing Maps developer account
- How to add a reference to other DLLs in our Silverlight projects
- The wonders of the inkPresenter
- How to use Isolated Storage
- How to communicate over HTTP
- How to make asynchronous calls in Silverlight

Although, we only briefly covered the last two points in this chapter, it does make for a great cliff-hanger to keep you on the edge of your seats for the next chapter.

5
Handling Data

Business applications are all about data; input received from clients, metrics regarding performance or sales, inventory, assets, and so on. Silverlight provides a robust and easy way to handle, bind, and validate this data.

In addition to data handling capabilities, Silverlight can also communicate via Windows Communication Foundation (WCF) services, providing an extensible means of communication with backend servers and data stores.

In this chapter, we shall:

- ◆ Create a WCF service and business object for receiving data
- ◆ Create a form for allowing users to submit information
- ◆ Bind the data from a data object to Silverlight controls
- ◆ Validate data and display feedback to the user

Data applications

When building applications that utilize data, it is important to start with defining what data you are going to collect and how it will be stored once collected. In the last chapter, we created a Silverlight application to post a collection of ink strokes to the server. We are going to expand the `inkPresenter` control to allow a user to submit additional information.

Most developers would have had experience building business object layers, and with Silverlight we can still make use of these objects, either by using referenced class projects/libraries or by consuming WCF services and utilizing the associated data contracts.

Time for action – creating a business object

We'll create a business object that can be used by both Silverlight and our ASP.NET application. To accomplish this, we'll create the business object in our ASP.NET application, define it as a data contract, and expose it to Silverlight via our WCF service.

Start Visual Studio and open the **CakeORamaData** solution. When we created the solution, we originally created a Silverlight application and an ASP.NET web project.

1. In the web project, add a reference to the `System.Runtime.Serialization` assembly.

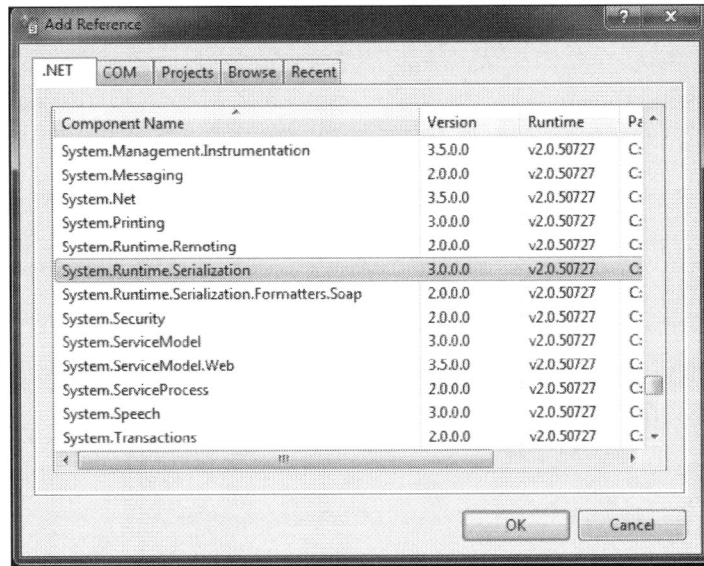

2. Right-click on the web project and choose to add a new class. Name this class `ServiceObjects` and click **OK**.

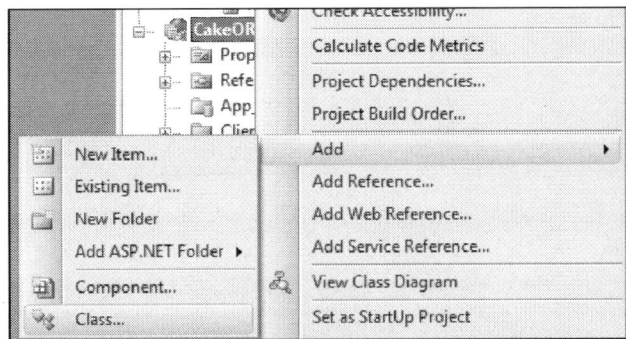

3. In the `ServiceObjects` class file, replace the existing code with the following code:

```
using System;
using System.Runtime.Serialization;

namespace CakeORamaData.Web
{
  [DataContract]
  public class CustomerCakeIdea
  {
    [DataMember]
    public string CustomerName { get; set; }
    [DataMember]
    public string PhoneNumber { get; set; }
    [DataMember]
    public string Email { get; set; }
    [DataMember]
    public DateTime EventDate { get; set; }
    [DataMember]
    public StrokeInfo[] Strokes { get; set; }
  }

  [DataContract]
  public class StrokeInfo
  {
    [DataMember]
    public double Width { get; set; }
    [DataMember]
    public double Height { get; set; }
    [DataMember]
    public byte[] Color { get; set; }
    [DataMember]
    public byte[] OutlineColor { get; set; }
    [DataMember]
  public StylusPointInfo[] Points { get; set; }
  }

  [DataContract]
  public class StylusPointInfo
  {
    [DataMember]
    public double X { get; set; }
    [DataMember]
    public double Y { get; set; }
  }
}
```

4. What we are doing here is defining the data that we'll be collecting from the customer.

What just happened?

We just added a business object that will be used by our WCF service and our Silverlight application. We added serialization attributes to our class, so that it can be serialized with WCF and consumed by Silverlight.

The [DataContract] and [DataMember] attributes are the serialization attributes that WCF will use when serializing our business object for transmission. WCF provides an opt-in model, meaning that types used with WCF must include these attributes in order to participate in serialization. The [DataContract] attribute is required, however if you wish to, you can use the [DataMember] attribute on any of the properties of the class.

By default, WCF will use the System.Runtime.Serialization. DataContractSerialzer to serialize the DataContract classes into XML. The .NET Framework also provides a NetDataContractSerializer which includes CLR information in the XML or the JsonDataContractSerializer that will convert the object into **JavaScript Object Notation (JSON)**. The WebGet attribute provides an easy way to define which serializer is used.

> For more information on these serializers and the WebGet attribute visit the following MSDN web sites:
>
> http://msdn.microsoft.com/en-us/library/system.runtime.serialization.datacontractserializer.aspx.
>
> http://msdn.microsoft.com/en-us/library/system.runtime.serialization.netdatacontractserializer.aspx.
>
> http://msdn.microsoft.com/en-us/library/system.runtime.serialization.json.datacontractjsonserializer.aspx.
>
> http://msdn.microsoft.com/en-us/library/system.servicemodel.web.webgetattribute.aspx.

Windows Communication Foundation (WCF)

Windows Communication Foundation (WCF) provides a simplified development experience for connected applications using the service oriented programming model. WCF builds upon and improves the web service model by providing flexible channels in which to connect and communicate with a web service. By utilizing these channels developers can expose their services to a wide variety of client applications such as Silverlight, Windows Presentation Foundation and Windows Forms.

Service oriented applications provide a scalable and reusable programming model, allowing applications to expose limited and controlled functionality to a variety of consuming clients such as web sites, enterprise applications, smart clients, and Silverlight applications.

When building WCF applications the service contract is typically defined by an interface decorated with attributes that declare the service and the operations. Using an interface allows the contract to be separated from the implementation and is the standard practice with WCF.

> You can read more about Windows Communication Foundation on the MSDN website at: `http://msdn.microsoft.com/en-us/netframework/aa663324.aspx`.

Time for action – creating a Silverlight-enabled WCF service

Now that we have our business object, we need to define a WCF service that can accept the business object and save the data to an XML file.

1. With the **CakeORamaData** solution open, right-click on the web project and choose to add a new folder, rename it to `Services`.

2. Right-click on the web project again and choose to add a new item. Add a new **WCF Service** named `CakeService.svc` to the `Services` folder. This will create an interface and implementation files for our WCF service. Avoid adding the Silverlight-enabled WCF service, as this adds a service that goes against the standard design patterns used with WCF:

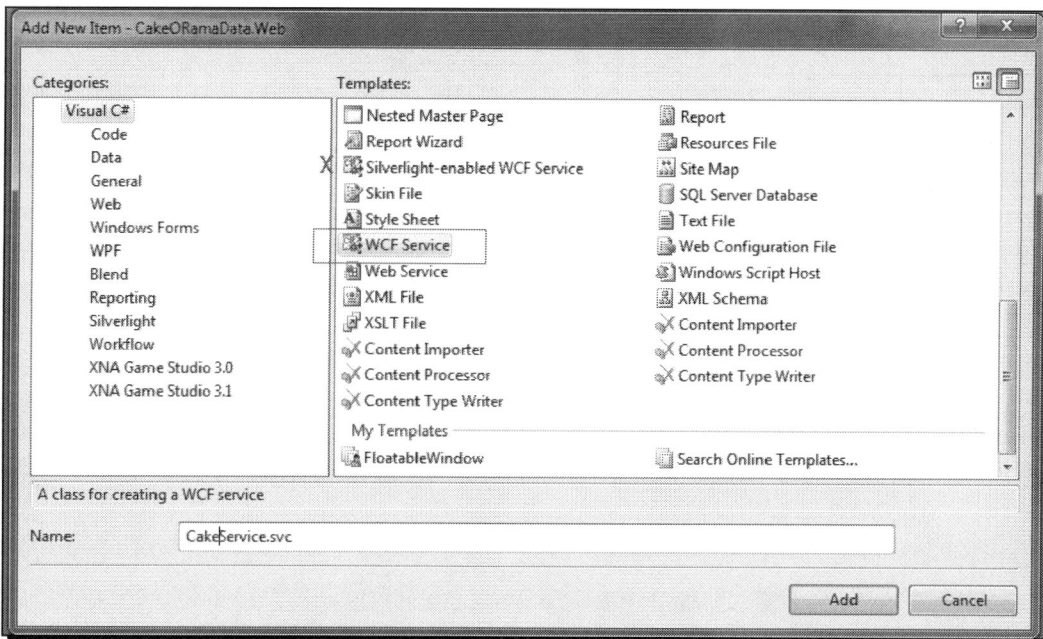

The standard design practice with WCF is to create an interface that defines the `ServiceContract` and `OperationContracts` of the service. The interface is then provided, a default implementation on the server. When the service is exposed through metadata, the interface will be used to define the operations of the service and generate the client classes. The Silverlight-enabled WCF service does not create an interface, just an implementation, it is there as a quick entry point into WCF for developers new to the technology.

3. Replace the code in the `ICakeService.cs` file with the definition below. We are defining a contract with one operation that allows a client application to submit a `CustomerCakeIdea` instance:

```
using System;
using System.Collections.Generic;
using System.Linq;
using System.Runtime.Serialization;
using System.ServiceModel;
using System.Text;

namespace CakeORamaData.Web.Services
{
  // NOTE: If you change the interface name "ICakeService" here,
  you must also update the reference to "ICakeService" in Web.
  config.
  [ServiceContract]
  public interface ICakeService
  {
    [OperationContract]
    void SubmitCakeIdea(CustomerCakeIdea idea);
  }
}
```

4. The `CakeService.svc.cs` file will contain the implementation of our service interface. Add the following code to the body of the `CakeService.svc.cs` file to save the customer information to an XML file:

```
using System;
using System.ServiceModel.Activation;
using System.Xml;

namespace CakeORamaData.Web.Services
{
  // NOTE: If you change the class name "CakeService" here, you
  must also update the reference to "CakeService" in Web.config.
```

```
[AspNetCompatibilityRequirements(RequirementsMode =
AspNetCompatibilityRequirementsMode.Allowed)]
  public class CakeService : ICakeService
  {
    public void SubmitCakeIdea(CustomerCakeIdea idea)
    {
      if (idea == null) return;

      using (var writer = XmlWriter.Create(String.Format(@"C:\
Projects\CakeORama\Customer\Data\{0}.xml", idea.CustomerName)))
      {
        writer.WriteStartDocument();

        //<customer>
        writer.WriteStartElement("customer");
        writer.WriteAttributeString("name", idea.CustomerName);
        writer.WriteAttributeString("phone", idea.PhoneNumber);
        writer.WriteAttributeString("email", idea.Email);

        // <eventDate></eventDate>
        writer.WriteStartElement("eventDate");
        writer.WriteValue(idea.EventDate);
        writer.WriteEndElement();

        // <strokes>
        writer.WriteStartElement("strokes");

        if (idea.Strokes != null && idea.Strokes.Length > 0)
        {
          foreach (var stroke in idea.Strokes)
          {
            // <stroke>
            writer.WriteStartElement("stroke");

            writer.WriteAttributeString("width", stroke.Width.
            ToString());
            writer.WriteAttributeString("height", stroke.Height.
            ToString());

            writer.WriteStartElement("color");
            writer.WriteAttributeString("a", stroke.Color[0].
            ToString());
            writer.WriteAttributeString("r", stroke.Color[1].
            ToString());
            writer.WriteAttributeString("g", stroke.Color[2].
            ToString());
```

```csharp
            writer.WriteAttributeString("b", stroke.Color[3].
            ToString());
            writer.WriteEndElement();

            writer.WriteStartElement("outlineColor");
            writer.WriteAttributeString("a", stroke.
            OutlineColor[0].ToString());
            writer.WriteAttributeString("r", stroke.
            OutlineColor[1].ToString());
            writer.WriteAttributeString("g", stroke.
            OutlineColor[2].ToString());
            writer.WriteAttributeString("b", stroke.
            OutlineColor[3].ToString());
            writer.WriteEndElement();

            if (stroke.Points != null && stroke.Points.Length > 0)
            {
              writer.WriteStartElement("points");
              foreach (var point in stroke.Points)
              {
                    writer.WriteStartElement("point");
                    writer.WriteAttributeString("x", point.
                    X.ToString());
                    writer.WriteAttributeString("y", point.
                    Y.ToString());
                    writer.WriteEndElement();
              }
              writer.WriteEndElement();
            }

            // </stroke>
            writer.WriteEndElement();
          }
        }

        // </strokes>
        writer.WriteEndElement();

        //</customer>
        writer.WriteEndElement();

        writer.WriteEndDocument();
      }
     }
    }
   }
```

> *[notes]* We added the `AspNetCompatibilityRequirements` attribute to our `CakeService` implementation. This attribute is required in order to use a WCF service from within ASP.NET.

5. Open **Windows Explorer** and create the path `C:\Projects\CakeORama\Customer\Data` on your hard drive to store the customer XML files.

> *[tip]* One thing to note is that you will need to grant `write` permission to this directory for the ASP.NET user account when in a production environment.

6. When adding a WCF service through Visual Studio, binding information is added to the `web.config` file. The default binding for WCF is **wsHttpBinding**, which is not a valid binding for Silverlight. The valid bindings for Silverlight are **basicHttpBinding**, **binaryHttpBinding** (implemented with a **customBinding**), and **netTcpBinding**. We need to modify the `web.config`, so that Silverlight can consume the service. Open the `web.config` file and add this `customBinding` section to the `<system.serviceModel>` node:

```
<bindings>
  <customBinding>
    <binding name="customBinding0">
      <binaryMessageEncoding />
      <httpTransport>
        <extendedProtectionPolicy policyEnforcement="Never" />
      </httpTransport>
    </binding>
  </customBinding>
</bindings>
```

7. We'll need to change the `<service>` node in the `web.config` to use our new `customBinding`, (we use the `customBinding` to implement binary HTTP which sends the information as a binary stream to the service), rather than the `wsHttpbinding` from:

```
<service behaviorConfiguration="CakeORamaData.Web.Services.
CakeServiceBehavior"
 name="CakeORamaData.Web.Services.CakeService">
  <endpoint address="" binding="wsHttpBinding"
contract="CakeORamaData.Web.Services.ICakeService">
    <identity>
      <dns value="localhost" />
```

```
        </identity>
      </endpoint>
      <endpoint address="mex" binding="mexHttpBinding" contract="IM
etadataExchange" />
    </service>
```

To the following:

```
<service behaviorConfiguration="CakeORamaData.Web.Services.
CakeServiceBehavior"
  name="CakeORamaData.Web.Services.CakeService">
    <endpoint address="" binding="customBinding" bindingConfiguratio
n="customBinding0"
      contract="CakeORamaData.Web.Services.ICakeService" />
    <endpoint address="mex" binding="mexHttpBinding" contract="IMeta
dataExchange" />
  </service>
```

8. Set the start page to the `CakeService.svc` file, then build and run the solution. We will be presented with the following screen, which lets us know that the service and bindings are set up correctly:

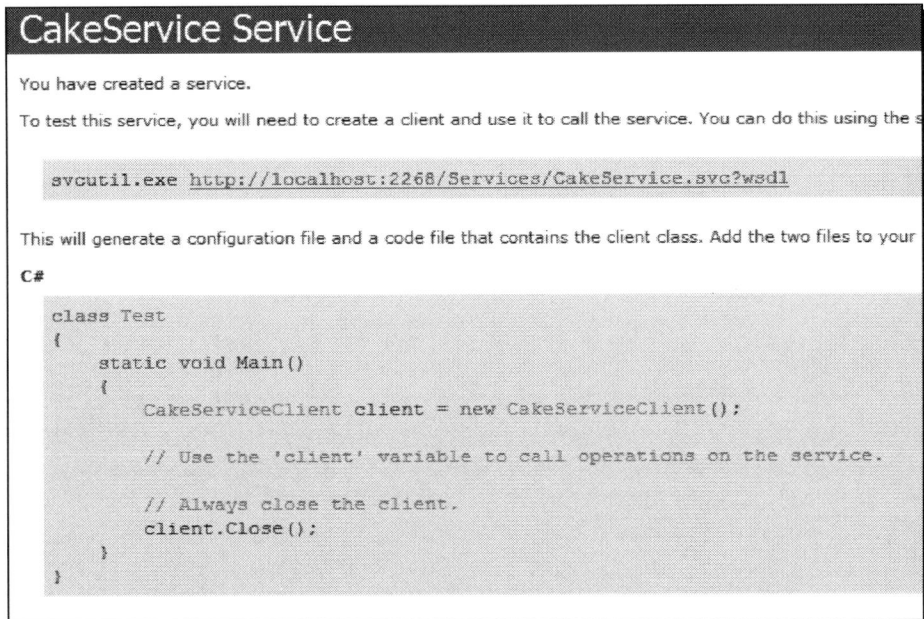

9. Our next step is to add the service reference to Silverlight. On the Silverlight project, right-click on the **References** node and choose to **Add a Service Reference:**

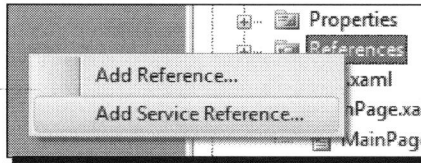

10. On the dialog that opens, click the **Discover** button and choose the **Services in Solution** option. Visual Studio will search the current solution for any services:

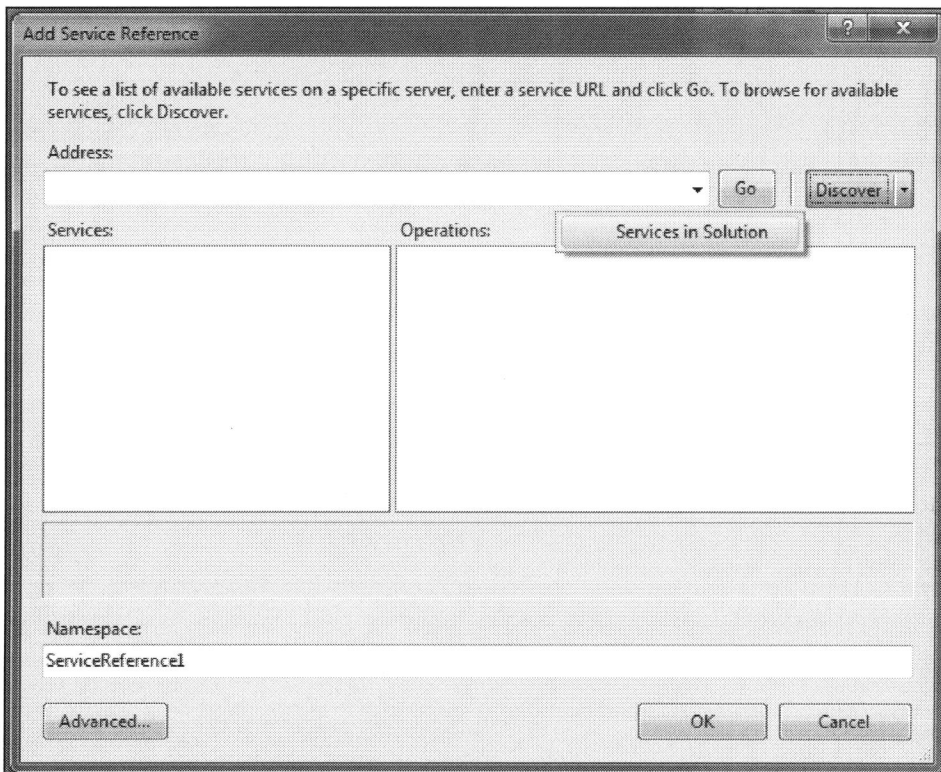

11. Visual Studio will find our **CakeService** and all we have to do is change the **Namespace** to something that makes sense such as **Services** and click the **OK** button:

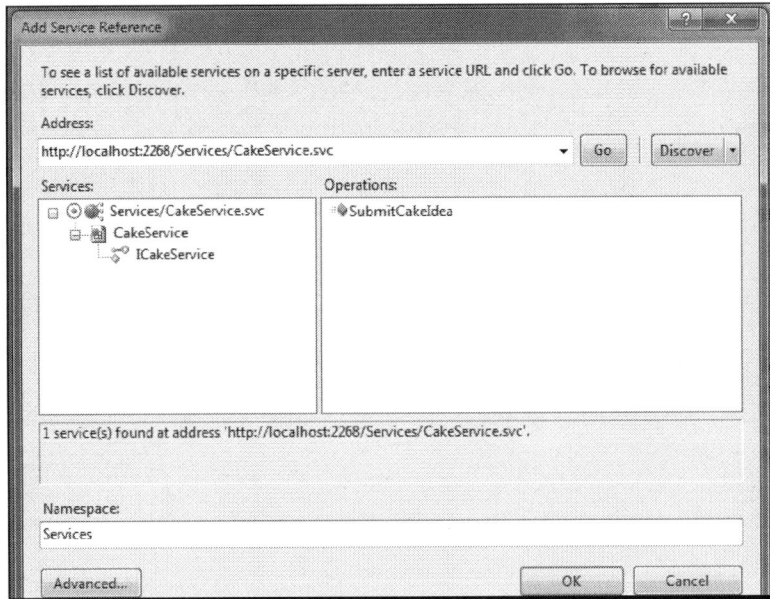

12. We can see that Visual Studio has added some additional references and files to our project. Developers used to WCF or Web Services will notice the assembly references and the **Service References** folder:

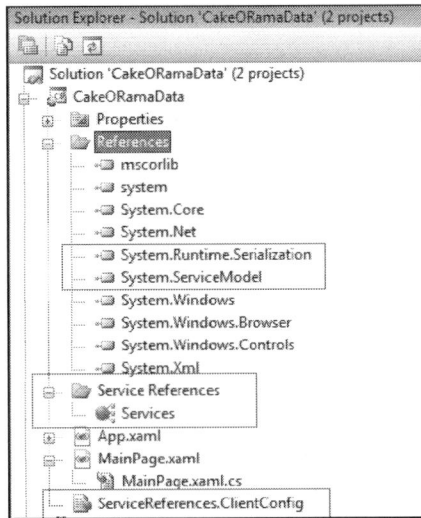

13. Silverlight creates a `ServiceReferences.ClientConfig` file that stores the configuration for the service bindings. If we open this file, we can take a look at the client side bindings to our WCF service. These bindings tell our Silverlight application how to connect to the WCF service and the URL where it is located:

```
<configuration>
    <system.serviceModel>
        <bindings>
            <customBinding>
                <binding name="CustomBinding_ICakeService">
                    <binaryMessageEncoding />
                    <httpTransport
maxReceivedMessageSize="2147483647" maxBufferSize="2147483647">
                        <extendedProtectionPolicy policyEnforcemen
t="Never" />
                    </httpTransport>
                </binding>
            </customBinding>
        </bindings>
        <client>
            <endpoint address="http://localhost:2268/Services/
CakeService.svc"
                binding="customBinding" bindingConfiguration="Cust
omBinding_ICakeService"
                contract="Services.ICakeService"
name="CustomBinding_ICakeService" />
        </client>
    </system.serviceModel>
</configuration>
```

What just happened?

We created a Windows Communication Foundation service that is Silverlight ready. In the process, we also followed the best practice guidelines by defining a service interface and a separate implementation. The service accepts a complex data object and writes the data to an XML file.

We included the `AspNetCompatibilityRequirements` attribute to the `CakeService.svc.cs` class which is required in order to host a WCF service from within ASP.NET. We added to the class declaration rather than the interface, because it is implementation-specific and is only valid on class declarations.

We saw how easy it is to create a WCF service and add a service reference to a Silverlight application.

Collecting data

Now that we have created a business object and a WCF service, we are ready to collect data from the customer through our Silverlight application. Silverlight provides all of the standard input controls that .NET developers have come to know with Windows and ASP.NET development, and of course the controls are customizable through styles.

Time for action – creating a form to collect data

We will begin by creating a form in Silverlight for collecting the data from the client. In the last chapter, we created an `Ink` control to allow clients to draw their cake ideas and submit them. We are going to modify this page to include a submission form to collect the name, phone number, email address, and the date of event for the person submitting the sketch. This will allow the client (Cake O Rama) to contact this individual and follow up on a potential sale.

We'll change the layout of `MainPage.xaml` to include a form for user input. We will need to open the **CakeORama** project in Expression Blend and then open `MainPage.xaml` for editing in the Blend art board.

> **1.** Our `Ink` capture controls are contained within a `Grid`, so we will just add a column to the `Grid` and place our input form right next to the `Ink` surface. To add columns in Blend, select the `Grid` from the **Objects and Timeline** panel, position your mouse in the highlighted area above the `Grid` and click to add a column:

2. Blend will add a `<Grid.ColumnDefinitions>` node to our XAML:

```
<Grid.ColumnDefinitions>
<ColumnDefinition Width="0.94*"/>
<ColumnDefinition Width="0.06*"/>
</Grid.ColumnDefinitions>
```

3. Blend also added a `Grid.ColumnSpan="2"` attribute to both the `StackPanel` and `InkPresenter` controls that were already on the page.

4. We need to modify the **StackPanel** and **inkPresenter**, so that they do not span both columns and thereby forcing us to increase the size of our second column. In Blend, select the `StackPanel` from the **Objects and Timeline** panel:

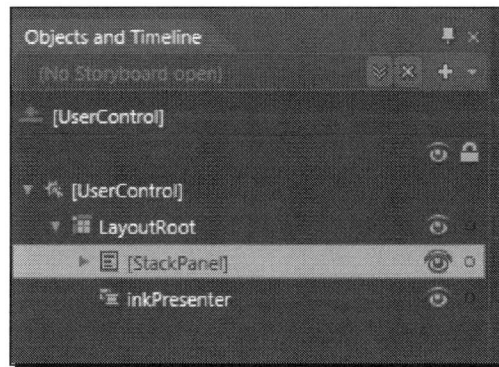

5. In the **Properties** panel, you will see a property called **ColumnSpan** with a value of **2**. Change this value to **1** and press the *Enter* key.

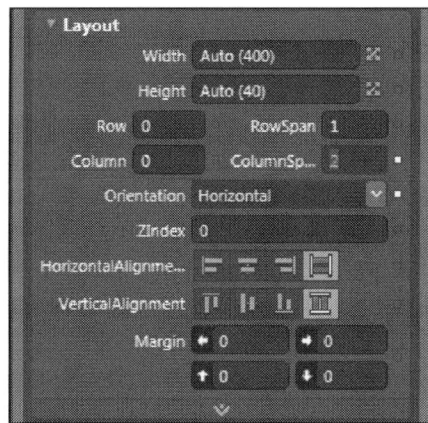

6. We can see that Blend moved the `StackPanel` into the first column, and we now have a little space next to the buttons.

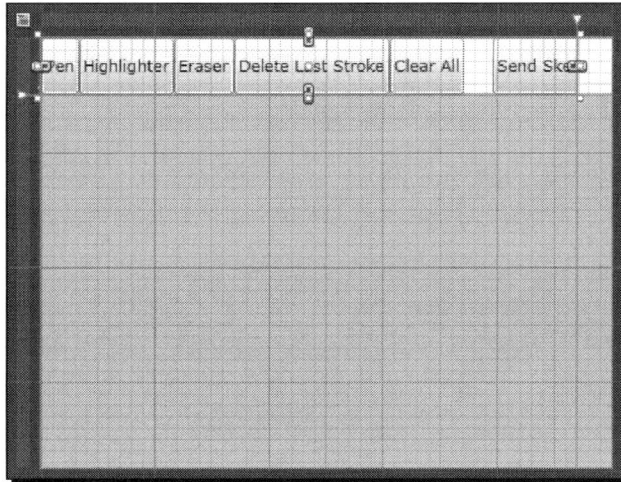

7. We need to do the same thing to the **inkPresenter** control, so that it is also within the first column. Select the **inkPresenter** control from the **Objects and Timeline** panel:

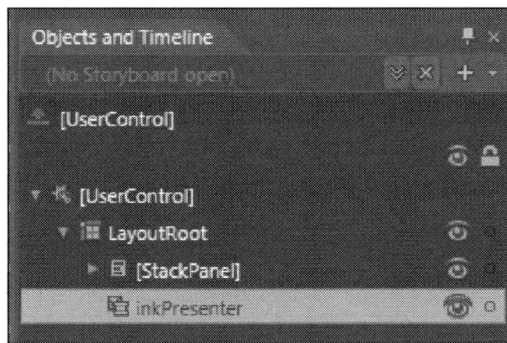

8. Change the **ColumnSpan** from **2** to **1** to reposition the **inkPresenter** into the left column:

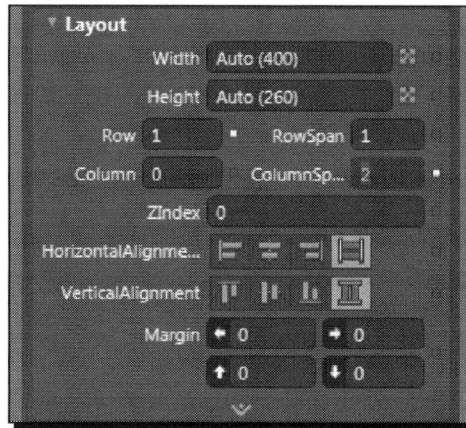

9. The **inkPresenter** control should be positioned in the left column and aligned with the `StackPanel` containing our ink sketch buttons:

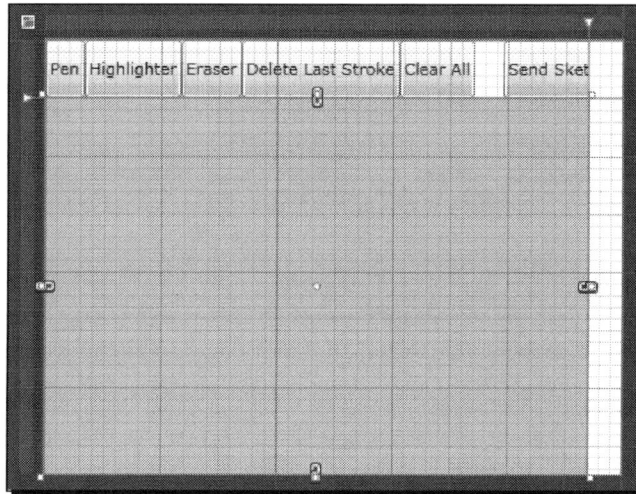

10. Now that we have moved the existing controls into the first column, we will change the size of the second column, so that we can start adding our input controls. We also need to change the overall size of the `MainPage.xaml` control to fit more information on the right side of the `ink` control.

11. Click on the `[UserControl]` in the **Objects and Timeline** panel, and then in the **Properties** panel change the **Width** to **800**:

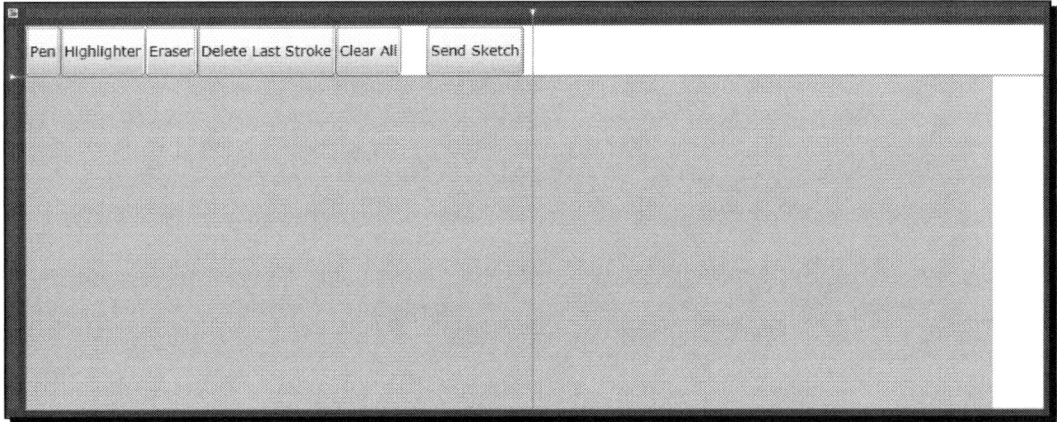

12. Now we need to change the size of our grid columns. We can do this very easily in XAML, so switch to the XAML view in Blend by clicking on the XAML icon:

13. In the XAML view, change the grid column settings to give both columns an equal width:

```
<Grid.ColumnDefinitions>
<ColumnDefinition Width="0.5*"/>
<ColumnDefinition Width="0.5*"/>
</Grid.ColumnDefinitions>
```

14. Switch back to the design view by clicking on the design button:

15. Our `StackPanel` and `inkPresenter` controls are now positioned to the left of the page and we have some empty space to the right for our input controls:

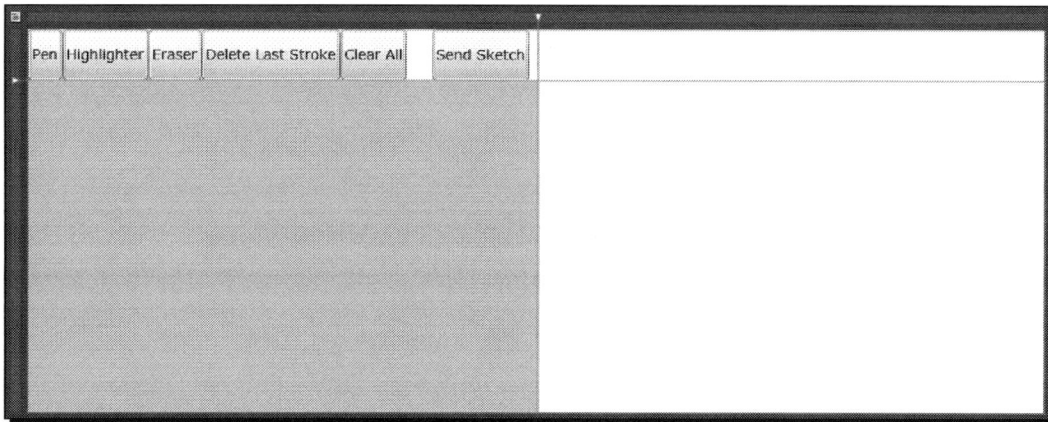

16. Select the `LayoutRoot` control in the **Objects and Timeline** panel and then double-click on the **TextBlock** control in the Blend toolbox to add a new `TextBlock` control:

17. Drag the control to the top and right side of the page:

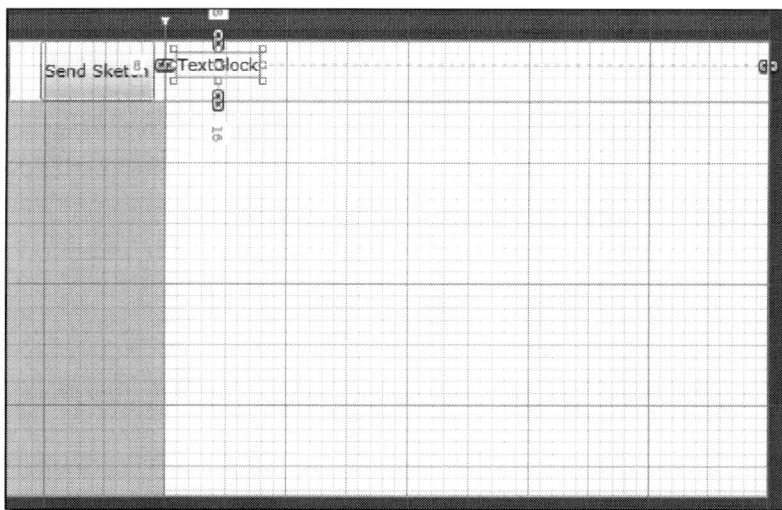

18. On the **Properties** panel, change the **Text** of the `TextBlock` to **Customer Information**, change the `FontSize` to **12pt** and click on the **Bold** indicator:

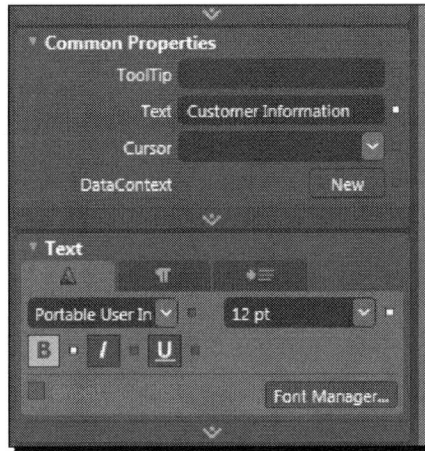

19. The `MainPage.xaml` should look like the following:

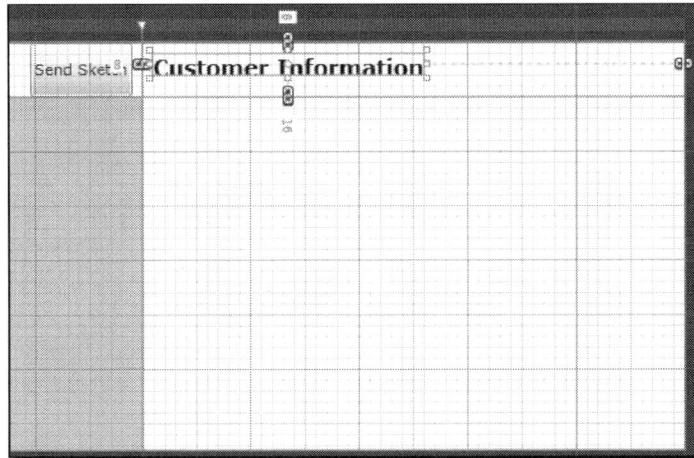

20. Double-click the **TextBlock** icon on the toolbox again and drop this into the top-left of column 2, row 2.

21. On the **Properties** panel, change the text of the `TextBlock` to **Name**. This will serve as the label for our `Name` textbox control:

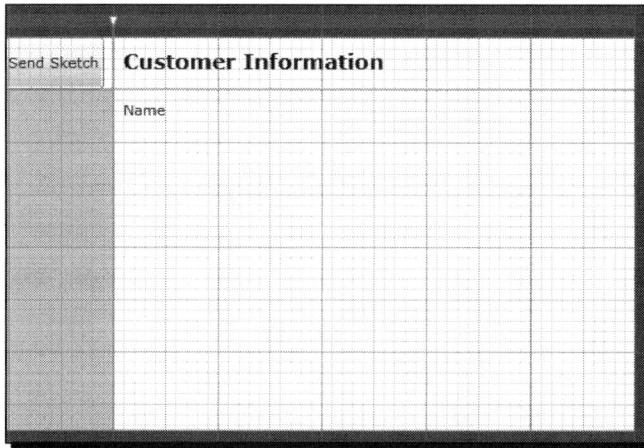

22. Repeat this process, adding **Phone Number**, **Email Address**, and **Date of Event** labels, and rearranging them on the page as illustrated.

Duplicating Controls

If you click on a control in the **Objects and Timeline** panel, you can make a copy of the control by holding down the *Alt* key, left-click the mouse, and drag the copy into the new position.

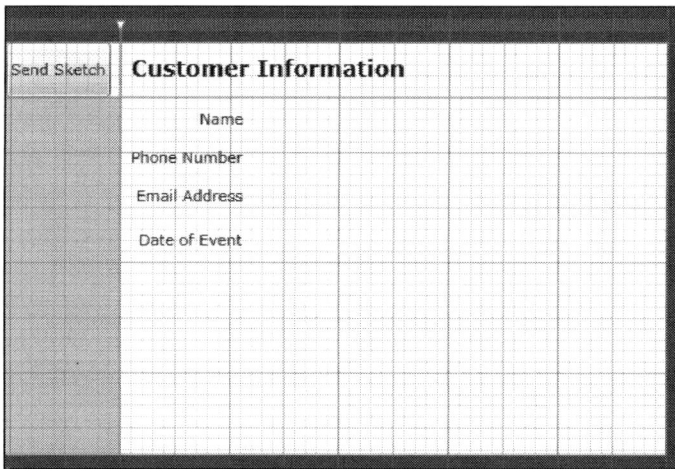

23. Right-click the **TextBlock** icon in the toolbox again and choose the **TextBox** control:

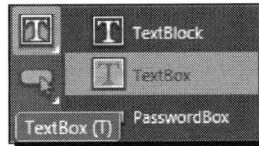

24. Double click the **TextBox** control, which adds a new textbox to the page. Drag this control next to our **Name** label and resize it to maximize the available space:

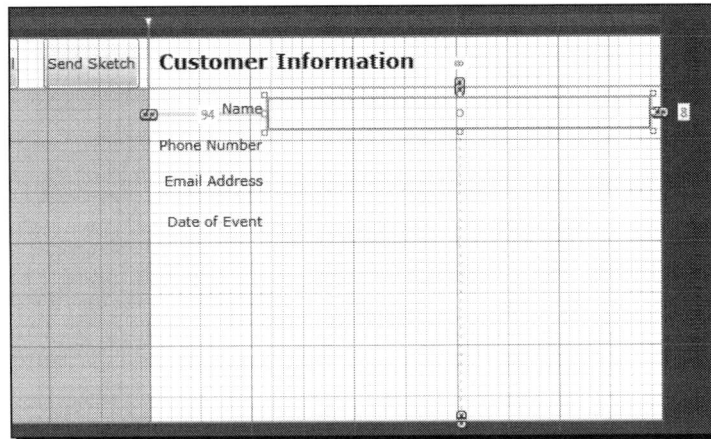

25. Name the textbox **customerName** in the **Properties** panel, and set its **MaxLength** to **40**. The **MaxLength** can be found by typing **MaxLength** in the search field of the **Properties** panel:

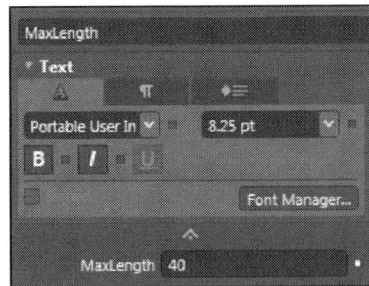

26. Create textbox controls for both the **Phone Number** and **Email Address** fields and name them **phoneNumber** and **emailAddress** respectively; position them on the page next to the appropriate labels. Set the **MaxLength** of the phoneNumber field to **15** and the **MaxLength** of the **emailAddress** field to **120**:

27. To make date entry easier for our users, we will add a **DatePicker** control to our page to allow the user to page through a calendar and select the date of their event. To add a DatePicker control, click the **Assets** button, type the word **date** into the search field and select the DatePicker control:

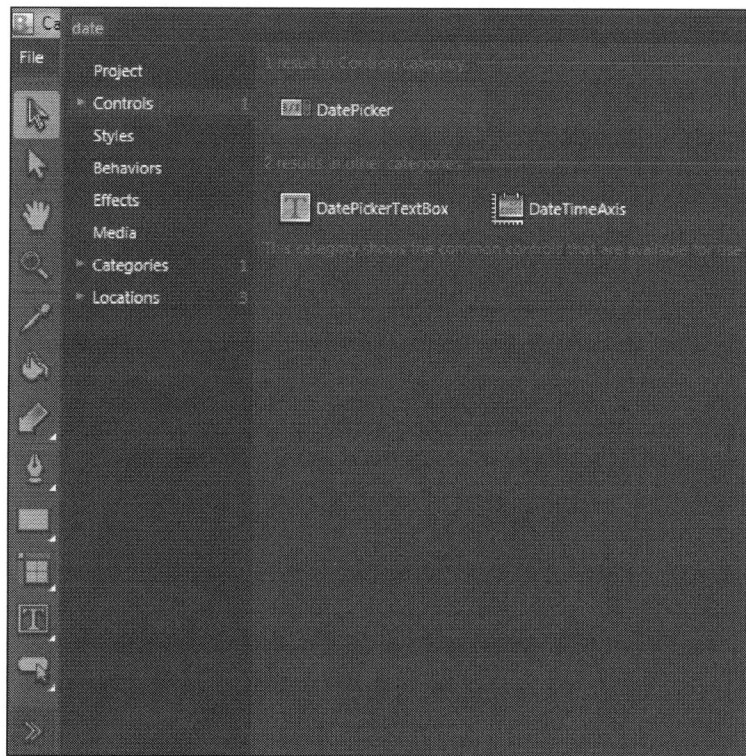

28. Double-click on the `DatePicker` in the toolbox to add it to the page, drag the `DatePicker` next to the `TextBlock` label for **Date of Event** and name the control **eventDate**:

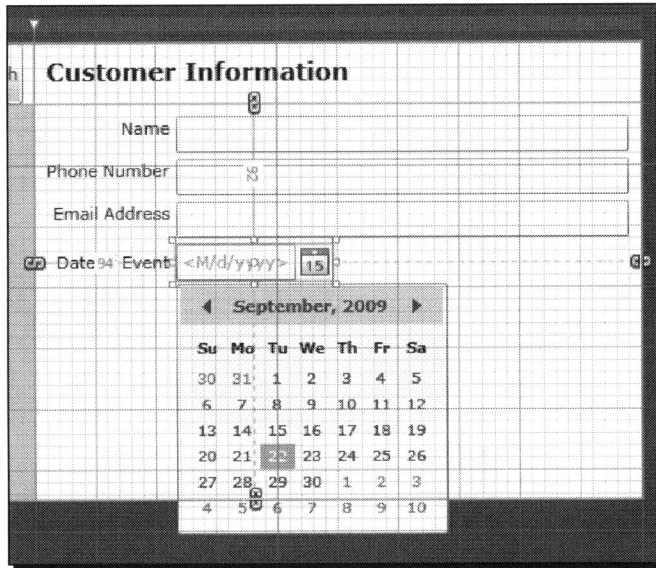

29. Add a button control to the page, drag down below the input controls, name the button `submitButton` and change the `Content` of the control to **Submit**:

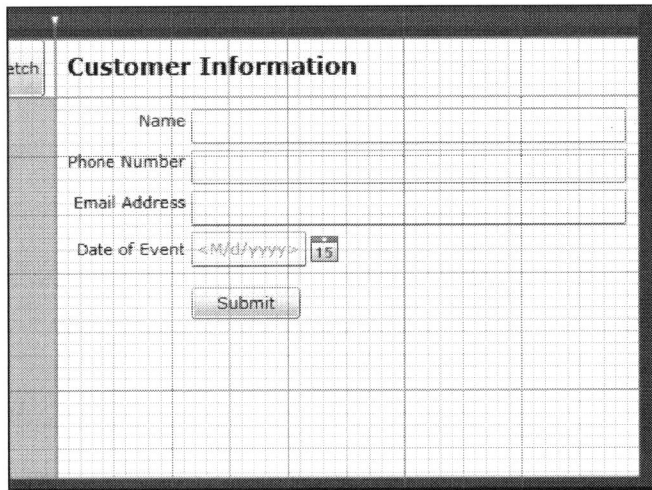

30. Select our **Submit** button and in the **Properties** panel click on the **Events** icon:

31. Double-click inside of the `Click` event field to have Blend auto create the event handler for the button click event:

32. We added a new **Submit** button, so now we need to hide the **Send Sketch** button. Select the **btnSend** button from the **Objects and Timeline** panel:

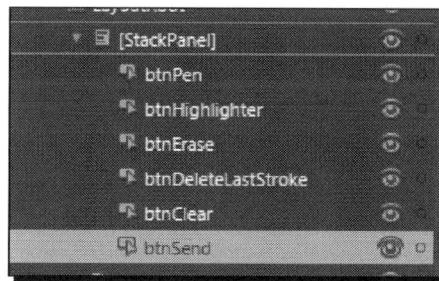

33. Set the **Visibility** of the **btnSend** control to **Collapsed**:

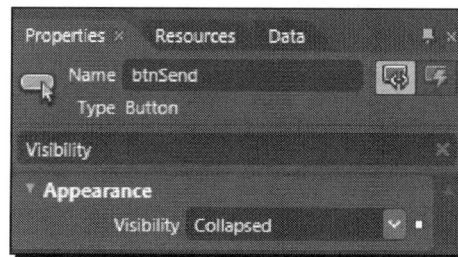

Be sure to save your work throughout the development process, you would not want to lose all this effort!

What just happened?

We modified an existing control and added several input controls in order to collect some information from a potential customer. We learned how to add columns to a `Grid` and used Blend to create an event handler for our submit button.

By using Blend, we are able to set up our input controls very quickly and have visual feedback of our progress the entire time. Hand coding of all this XAML, while possible, is just not what most developers are going to want to spend their time doing, not when there is code to write!

Validating data

With Silverlight, **data validation** has been fully implemented, allowing controls to be bound to data objects and those data objects to handle the validation of data and provide feedback to the controls via the **Visual State Machine**.

The Visual State Machine is a feature of Silverlight used to render to views of a control based on its state. For instance, the mouse over state of a button can actually change the color of the button, show or hide parts of the control, and so on.

Controls that participate in data validation contain a **ValidationStates** group that includes a **Valid**, **InvalidUnfocused**, and **InvalidFocused** states. We can implement custom styles for these states to provide visual feedback to the user.

Data object

In order to take advantage of the data validation in Silverlight, we need to create a data object or client side business object that can handle the validation of data.

Time for action – creating a data object

We are going to create a data object that we will bind to our input form to provide validation. Silverlight can bind to any properties of an object, but for validation we need to do two way binding, for which we need both a **get** and a **set** accessor for each of our properties. In order to use two way binding, we will need to implement the `INotifyPropertyChanged` interface that defines a `PropertyChanged` event that Silverlight will use to update the binding when a property changes.

1. Firstly, we will need to switch over to Visual Studio and add a new class named `CustomerInfo` to the Silverlight project:

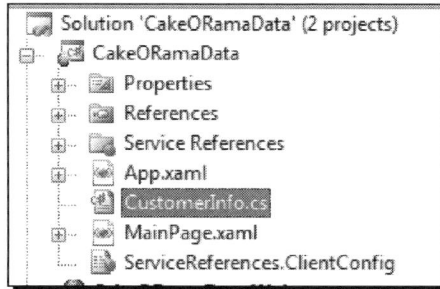

2. Replace the body of the `CustomerInfo.cs` file with the following code:

```
using System;
using System.ComponentModel;

namespace CakeORamaData
{
  public class CustomerInfo : INotifyPropertyChanged
  {
    public event PropertyChangedEventHandler PropertyChanged =
delegate { };

    private string _cutomerName = null;
    public string CustomerName
    {
      get { return _cutomerName; }
      set
      {
        if (value == _cutomerName)
          return;

        _cutomerName = value;

        OnPropertyChanged("CustomerName");
      }
    }

    private string _phoneNumber = null;
    public string PhoneNumber
    {
      get { return _phoneNumber; }
      set
```

```
    {
      if (value == _phoneNumber)
        return;

      _phoneNumber = value;

      OnPropertyChanged("PhoneNumber");
    }
  }

  private string _email = null;
  public string Email
  {
    get { return _email; }
    set
    {
      if (value == _email)
        return;

      _email = value;

      OnPropertyChanged("Email");
    }
  }

  private DateTime _eventDate = DateTime.Now.AddDays(7);
  public DateTime EventDate
  {
    get { return _eventDate; }
    set
    {
      if (value == _eventDate)
        return;

      _eventDate = value;

      OnPropertyChanged("EventDate");
    }
  }

  private void OnPropertyChanged(string propertyName)
  {
    PropertyChanged(this, new PropertyChangedEventArgs
    (propertyName));
  }
  }
}
```

> **Code Snippets**
>
> Code snippets are a convenient way to stub out repetitive code and increase productivity, by removing the need to type a bunch of the same syntax over and over.

The following is a code snippet used to create properties that execute the `OnPropertyChanged` method and can be very useful when implementing properties on a class that implements the `INotifyPropertyChanged` interface.

To use the snippet, save the file as `propnotify.snippet` to your hard drive.

In Visual Studio go to **Tools | Code Snippets Manager** (*Ctrl + K, Ctrl + B*) and click the **Import** button. Find the `propnotify.snippet` file and click **Open**, this will add the snippet.

To use the snippet in code, simply type **propnotify** and hit the *Tab* key; a property will be stubbed out allowing you to change the name and type of the property.

```xml
<?xml version="1.0" encoding="utf-8" ?>
<CodeSnippets  xmlns="http://schemas.microsoft.com/
VisualStudio/2005/CodeSnippet">
    <CodeSnippet Format="1.0.0">
        <Header>
            <Title>propnotify</Title>
            <Shortcut>propnotify</Shortcut>
            <Description>Code snippet for a property that raises
             the PropertyChanged event in a class.</Description>
            <Author>Cameron Albert</Author>
            <SnippetTypes>
                <SnippetType>Expansion</SnippetType>
            </SnippetTypes>
        </Header>
        <Snippet>
            <Declarations>
                <Literal>
                    <ID>type</ID>
                    <ToolTip>Property type</ToolTip>
                    <Default>int</Default>
                </Literal>
                <Literal>
                    <ID>property</ID>
                    <ToolTip>Property name</ToolTip>
```

```xml
                              <Default>MyProperty</Default>
                    </Literal>
                    <Literal>
                         <ID>field</ID>
                         <ToolTip>Private field</ToolTip>
                         <Default>_myProperty</Default>
                    </Literal>
                    <Literal>
                         <ID>defaultValue</ID>
                         <ToolTip>Default Value</ToolTip>
                         <Default>null</Default>
                    </Literal>
               </Declarations>
               <Code Language="csharp">
                    <![CDATA[private $type$ $field$ = $defaultValue$;
       public $type$ $property$
           {
             get { return $field$; }
             set
             {
                 if (value == $field$)
                     return;

                 $field$ = value;

                 OnPropertyChanged("$property$");
             }
          }
             $end$]]>
             </Code>
          </Snippet>
       </CodeSnippet>
</CodeSnippets>
```

What just happened?

We created a data object or client-side business object that we can use to bind to our input controls.

We implemented the INotifyPropertyChanged interface, so that our data object can raise the PropertyChanged event whenever the value of one of its properties is changed. We also defined a default delegate value for the PropertyChanged event to prevent us from having to do a null check when raising the event. Not to mention we have a nice snippet for stubbing out properties that raise the PropertyChanged event.

Now we will be able to bind this object to Silverlight input controls and the controls can cause the object values to be updated so that we can provide data validation from within our data object, rather than having to include validation logic in our user interface code.

Data binding

Binding data is one of the most powerful features of .NET Windows and ASP.NET programming, and Silverlight was not left out. Silverlight provides a `Binding` class due to which any property of an object can be bound to any **DependencyProperty** of a control.

Because Silverlight controls are defined in XAML, the `Binding` class can also be defined in XAML using a **Binding Expression**, which is just a XAML way of declaring a `Binding` class.

Time for action – binding our data object to our controls

We are going to bind our `CustomerInfo` object to our data entry form, using Blend. Be sure to build the solution before switching back over to Blend.

> **1.** With `MainPage.xaml` open in Blend, select the **LayoutRoot** control. In the **Properties** panel enter **DataContext** in the search field and click the **New** button:

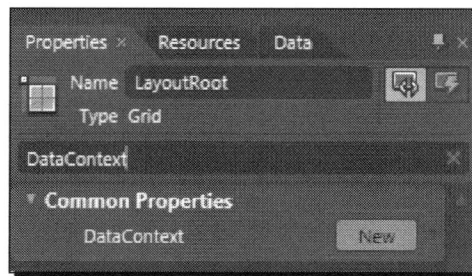

> **2.** In the dialog that opens, select the `CustomerInfo` class and click **OK**:

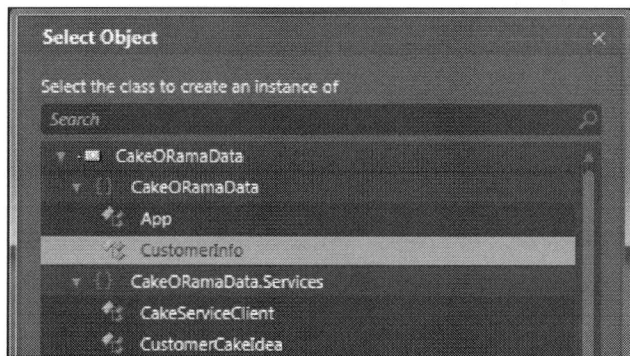

3. Blend will set the **DataContext** of the **LayoutRoot** to an instance of
a `CustomerInfo` class:

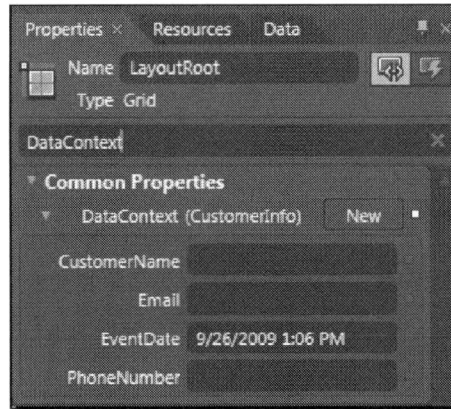

4. Blend inserts a namespace to our class; set the `Grid.DataContext` in the XAML
of `MainPage.xaml`:

```
xmlns:local="clr-namespace:CakeORamaData"
```

```
<Grid.DataContext>
  <local:CustomerInfo/>
</Grid.DataContext>
```

5. Now we will bind the value of **CustomerName** to our **customerName** textbox.
Select the **customerName** textbox and then on the **Properties** panel enter **Text** in
the search field. Click on the **Advanced property options** icon, which will open
a context menu for choosing an option:

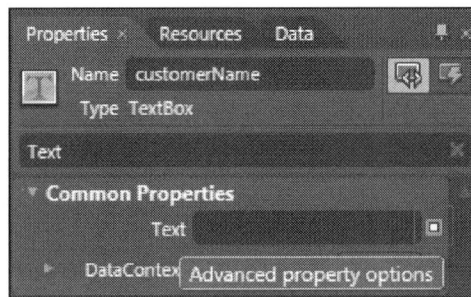

6. Click on the **Data Binding** option to open the **Create Data Binding** dialog:

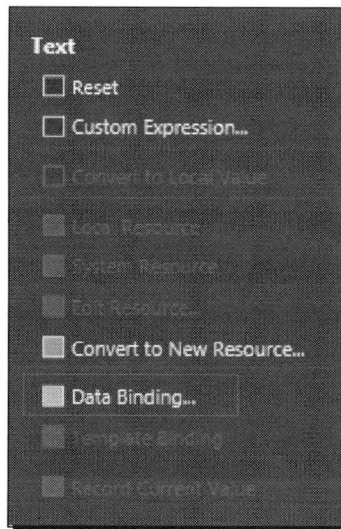

7. In the **Create Data Binding** dialog (on the **Explicit Data Context** tab), click the arrow next to the **CustomerInfo** entry in the **Fields** list and select **CustomerName**:

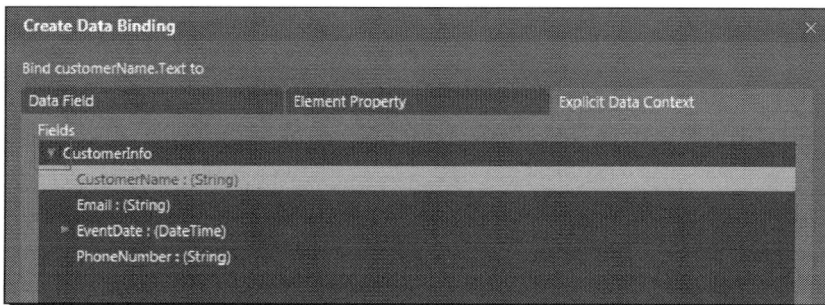

8. At the bottom of the **Create Data Binding** dialog, click on the **Show advanced properties** arrow to expand the dialog and display additional binding options:

9. Ensure that **TwoWay** is selected in the **Binding direction** option and that **Update source when** is set to **Explicit**. This creates a two-way binding, meaning that when the value of the `Text` property of the textbox changes the underlying property, bound to `Text` will also be updated. In our case the **customerName** property of the `CustomerInfo` class:

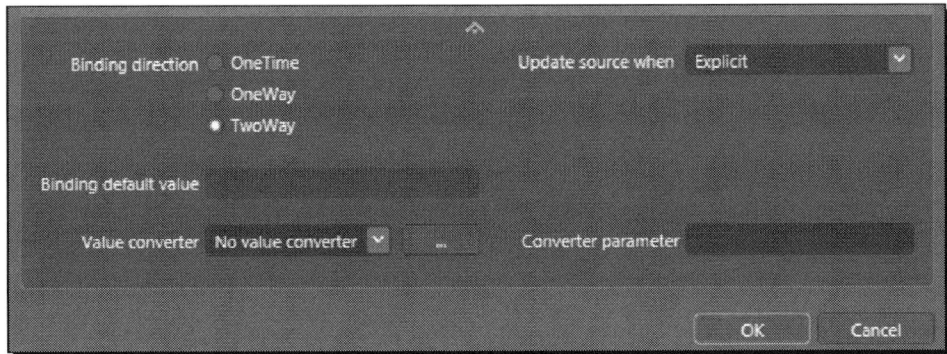

10. Click **OK** to close the dialog; we can now see that Blend indicates that this property is bound by the yellow border around the property input field:

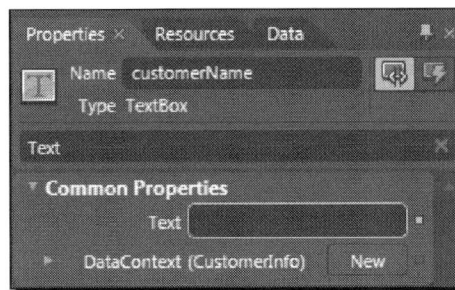

11. Repeat this process for both the **phoneNumber** and **emailAddress** textbox controls, to bind the `Text` property to the **PhoneNumber** and **Email** properties of the `CustomerInfo` class. You will see that Blend has modified our XAML using the Binding Expression:

```
<TextBox x:Name="customerName" Margin="94,8,8,0" Text="{Binding
CustomerName, Mode=TwoWay, UpdateSourceTrigger=Explicit}"
TextWrapping="Wrap" VerticalAlignment="Top" Grid.Column="1" Grid.
Row="1" MaxLength="40"/>
```

12. In the **Binding Expression** code the `Binding` is using the **CustomerName** property as the binding **Path**. The **Path (Path=CustomerName)** attribute can be omitted since the `Binding` class constructor accepts the path as an argument.

13. The **UpdateSourceTrigger** is set to **Explicit**, which causes any changes in the underlying data object to force a re-bind of the control.

14. For the **eventDate** control, enter **SelectedDate** into the **Properties** panel search field and following the same process of data binding, select the **EventDate** property of the `CustomerInfo` class. Remember to ensure that **TwoWay/Explict** binding is selected in the advanced options:

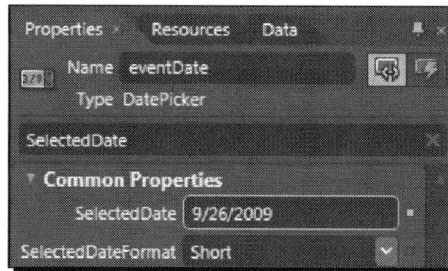

What just happened?

We utilized Silverlight data binding to bind our input controls to properties of our `CustomerInfo` class. In the process, we setup the binding to be two way, allowing the controls to set the property values of the `CustomerInfo` class, thus removing the need to add a bunch of text changed event handlers to manually do it ourselves, saving us more time in development.

We also had a chance to see how much time using Blend can save and how easy it is to add data bindings to controls. We saw the **Binding Expression** syntax used to define a `Binding` in XAML and also how to setup a `Binding` so that changes to the underlying object cause the control to re-bind the value.

Validation

Before we submit information to the server using our WCF service, we need to validate the data input from the user and provide feedback to the user if invalid information is supplied.

Silverlight can report a validation error in one of three scenarios:

- Exceptions thrown from the binding type converter
- Exceptions thrown from the binding object's set accessor
- Exceptions thrown from one of the validation attributes found in the `DataAnnotations` assembly

We will focus on the `set` accessor method as this provides the simplest way to get our data validated.

Time for action – validating data input

We will make use of some additional properties of `Binding` to allow the controls to display the validation states. Blend does not provide a visual way for us to add these additional properties so we have to do it manually in XAML.

1. Switch to the XAML view of the `MainPage.xaml` in Blend and scroll down to where our textbox controls are located.

2. Within the `Binding Expression` (between the { and } of the `Binding`), add the following two attributes to each one of the bindings on our input controls:

```
{Binding CustomerName, Mode=TwoWay, UpdateSourceTrigger=Explicit,
NotifyOnValidationError=True, ValidatesOnExceptions=True }
```

3. The `NotifyOnValidationError` and `ValidatesOnException` will both cause the control to display an error message if a validation or exception error occurs when the value of the bound property changes.

4. Now we need to modify our data object to provide validation in the `set` accessor of each property. Change the `CustomerInfo.cs` file to implement our property validation:

```
using System;
using System.ComponentModel;
using System.Text.RegularExpressions;

namespace CakeORamaData
{
  public class CustomerInfo : INotifyPropertyChanged
  {
    private static Regex RegexPhoneNumber = new Regex(@"((\(\
d{3}\) ?)|(\d{3}-))?\d{3}-\d{4}", RegexOptions.Multiline);
    private static Regex RegexEmail = new Regex(@"^([\w\-
\.]+)@((\[([0-9]{1,3}\.){3}[0-9]{1,3}\])|(([\w\-]+\.)+)([a-zA-
Z]{2,4}))$", RegexOptions.Multiline | RegexOptions.IgnoreCase);

    public event PropertyChangedEventHandler PropertyChanged =
delegate { };

    private string _cutomerName = null;
    public string CustomerName
    {
      get { return _cutomerName; }
      set
      {
```

```
      if (value == _cutomerName)
        return;

      if (String.IsNullOrEmpty(value))
        throw new ArgumentException("Customer Name is
        required.");

      if (value.Length < 3 || value.Length > 40)
        throw new ArgumentException("Customer Name must be at
         least 3 characters and not more than 40 characters
         in length.");

    _cutomerName = value;

    OnPropertyChanged("CustomerName");
  }
}

private string _phoneNumber = null;
public string PhoneNumber
{
  get { return _phoneNumber; }
  set
  {
    if (value == _phoneNumber)
      return;

    if (String.IsNullOrEmpty(value))
      throw new ArgumentException("Phone Number is
      required.");

    if (!RegexPhoneNumber.IsMatch(value))
      throw new ArgumentException("A valid phone number in the
      format (XXX) XXX-XXXX or XXX-XXX-XXXX is required.");

    _phoneNumber = value;

    OnPropertyChanged("PhoneNumber");
  }
}

private string _email = null;
public string Email
{
  get { return _email; }
```

```csharp
    set
    {
      if (value == _email)
        return;

      if (String.IsNullOrEmpty(value))
        throw new ArgumentException("Email Address is
        required.");

      if (!RegexEmail.IsMatch(value))
        throw new ArgumentException("A valid email address is
        required.");

      _email = value;

      OnPropertyChanged("Email");
    }
  }

  private DateTime _eventDate = DateTime.Now.AddDays(7);
  public DateTime EventDate
  {
    get { return _eventDate; }
    set
    {
      if (value == _eventDate)
        return;

      _eventDate = value;

      OnPropertyChanged("EventDate");
    }
  }

  private void OnPropertyChanged(string propertyName)
  {
    PropertyChanged(this, new PropertyChangedEventArgs
    (propertyName));
  }
 }
}
```

5. Open the `MainPage.xaml.cs` file and in the constructor add the following code to set the `LayoutRoot.DataContext` with a new instance of `CustomerInfo`:

```
public MainPage()
{
  this.Loaded += new RoutedEventHandler(MainPage_Loaded);
  InitializeComponent();
}

private void MainPage_Loaded(object sender, RoutedEventArgs e)
{
  LayoutRoot.DataContext = new CustomerInfo();
}
```

6. Also within the `MainPage.xaml` file in the `submitButton_Click` event handler, we will add code to force validation of our data object:

```
private void submitButton_Click(object sender, System.Windows.
RoutedEventArgs e)
{
  var bindingExpression = customerName.GetBindingExpression(TextBo
x.TextProperty);
  bindingExpression.UpdateSource();

  bindingExpression = phoneNumber.GetBindingExpression(TextBox.
TextProperty);
  bindingExpression.UpdateSource();

  bindingExpression = emailAddress.GetBindingExpression(TextBox.
TextProperty);
  bindingExpression.UpdateSource();
}
```

7. In Visual Studio, choose **Debug | Start without Debugging** from the file menu. We are not going to debug because our properties throw exceptions and we just want to see the result. Just click the **Submit** button and all the textbox controls will highlight with red borders:

8. If you hover over the small arrow in the top-right corner of the textbox you will see the error message from the data object:

What just happened?

We implemented simple data validation in our objects and let the built in Silverlight binding process handle the rest by including some additional attributes in the Binding Expression. We implemented the INotifyPropertyChanged interface in our data object so that the data will be re-bound whenever the values are changed. We also made use of regular expressions to ensure that the phone number and email address are in a valid format.

Data submission

Data collected from users does not provide a benefit unless the user can submit it and we can store the information for later retrieval. The ability to analyze and report on the data is how businesses acquire and maintain clients and customers, which is where the profits are derived from.

Time for action – submitting data to the server

Now that we have setup a form for data input and validated the data, we can now submit the data to the server using our WCF service. We need to submit the information to the server in order for the sales staff of Cake O Rama to be able to review and contact the customer.

1. Switch back over to Visual Studio, open the MainPage.xaml.cs file and then add the following to the using statements:

```
using CakeORamaData.Services;
```

2. At the bottom of this file add the ConvertStrokesToStrokeInfoArray method. This method will convert the Silverlight Stroke objects from the inkPresenter to StrokeInfo objects as defined by our WCF service:

```
private ObservableCollection<StrokeInfo>
ConvertStrokesToStrokeInfoArray()
{
```

```
var strokeCollection = new ObservableCollection<StrokeInfo>();

foreach (Stroke stroke in this.inkPresenter.Strokes)
{
  var strokeInfo = new StrokeInfo
  {
    Width = stroke.DrawingAttributes.Width,
    Height = stroke.DrawingAttributes.Height,
    Color = new byte[]
      {
        stroke.DrawingAttributes.Color.A,
        stroke.DrawingAttributes.Color.R,
        stroke.DrawingAttributes.Color.G,
        stroke.DrawingAttributes.Color.B
      },
    OutlineColor = new byte[]
      {
        stroke.DrawingAttributes.OutlineColor.A,
        stroke.DrawingAttributes.OutlineColor.R,
        stroke.DrawingAttributes.OutlineColor.G,
        stroke.DrawingAttributes.OutlineColor.B
      }
  };
  strokeCollection.Add(strokeInfo);

  var pointCollection = new ObservableCollection
    <StylusPointInfo>();
  strokeInfo.Points = pointCollection;
  foreach (StylusPoint point in stroke.StylusPoints)
  {
    var pointInfo = new StylusPointInfo
    {
      X = point.X,
      Y = point.Y
    };
    pointCollection.Add(pointInfo);
  }
}
return strokeCollection;
}
```

> Note here that when we added a reference to the WCF service, our
> `StrokeInfo[]` array on the `CustomerCakeIdea` object was converted to
> a `System.Collections.ObjectModel.ObservableCollection<S`
> `trokeInfo>` by Silverlight.

3. Go to the `submitButton_Click` method and modify it to resemble the
   following code:

```
private void submitButton_Click(object sender, System.Windows.
RoutedEventArgs e)
{
  var bindingExpression = customerName.GetBindingExpression(TextBo
x.TextProperty);
  bindingExpression.UpdateSource();

  bindingExpression = phoneNumber.GetBindingExpression(TextBox.
TextProperty);
  bindingExpression.UpdateSource();

  bindingExpression = emailAddress.GetBindingExpression(TextBox.
TextProperty);
  bindingExpression.UpdateSource();

  if (!Validation.GetHasError(customerName)
    && !Validation.GetHasError(phoneNumber)
    && !Validation.GetHasError(emailAddress))
  {
    var info = LayoutRoot.DataContext as CustomerInfo;

    var idea = new CustomerCakeIdea
    {
      CustomerName = info.CustomerName,
      PhoneNumber = info.PhoneNumber,
      Email = info.Email,
      EventDate = info.EventDate,
      Strokes = ConvertStrokesToStrokeInfoArray()
    };

    var client = new CakeServiceClient();
    client.SubmitCakeIdeaCompleted += new EventHandler
     <AsyncCompletedEventArgs>(OnCakeIdeaSubmissionComplete);
     client.SubmitCakeIdeaAsync(idea);
  }
}
```

4. Add the following method to handle the `SubmitCakeIdeaCompleted` event to display a `MessageBox` once the submission is complete:

```
private void OnCakeIdeaSubmissionComplete(object sender,
AsyncCompletedEventArgs e)
{
    MessageBox.Show("Sketch has been submitted.");
}
```

Now we will test out our cake idea submission form and process. Build and run the solution in Visual Studio and when the Silverlight application loads in the browser input some information and draw a cake sketch:

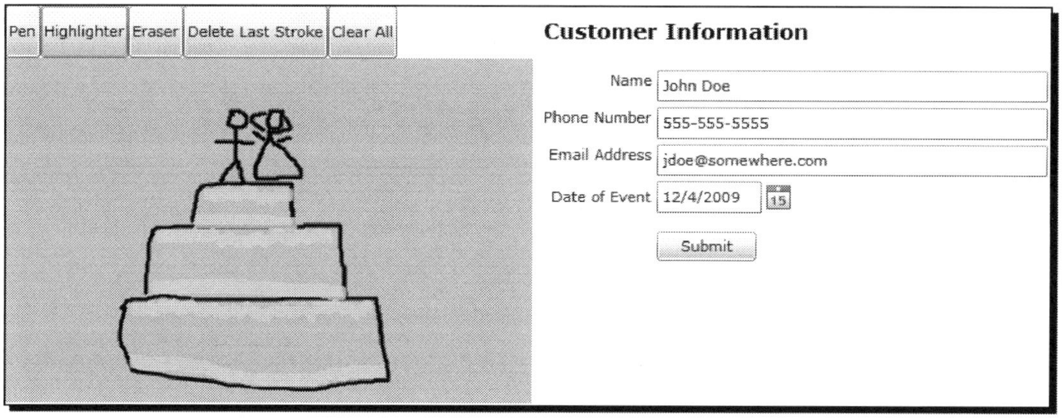

5. When we submit the information to the server, we will get a `MessageBox` telling us that we submitted the information, as shown in the next screenshot:

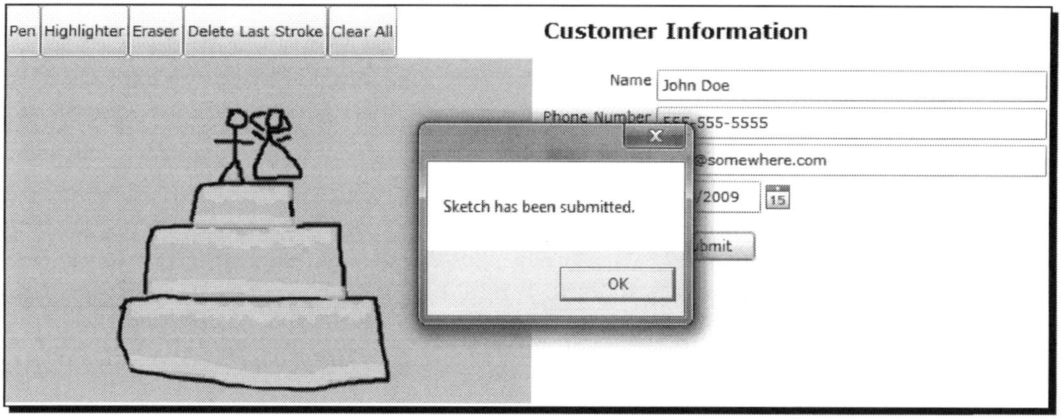

6. Open **Windows Explorer** and navigate to the path that we setup in the WCF service for storing the customer XML files, and open the newly submitted file. We should now have the data from the cake sketch and customer information in our XML file.

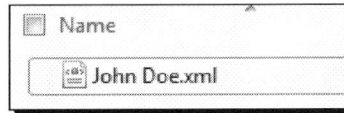

If we open the XML file, we should see the saved customer and ink stroke information:

```xml
<?xml version="1.0" encoding="utf-8"?>
<customer name="John Doe" phone="555-555-5555" email="jdoe@
somewhere.com">
  <eventDate>2009-10-04T16:03:41.0966771-04:00</eventDate>
  <strokes>
    <stroke width="3" height="3">
      <color a="255" r="0" g="0" b="0" />
      <outlineColor a="0" r="0" g="0" b="0" />
      <points>
        <point x="92" y="189" />
        <point x="91" y="192" />
        <point x="90" y="197" />
        <point x="89" y="199" />
        <point x="88" y="208" />
        <point x="88" y="210" />
        <point x="88" y="212" />
        <point x="88" y="213" />
      </points>
    </strokes>
  </customer>
```

What just happened?

We placed code in the `MainPage.xaml.cs` file to ensure that all of our text input controls did not have any validation errors, by making use of the `Validation` class.

We made use of the `CustomerCakeIdea` business object to store the customer input and ink stroke data and sent that information to the server via the WCF service, where we saved the information to an XML file for later use by the sales staff. We used an anonymous delegate to handle the asynchronous response from the WCF service and utilized a messagebox to inform the user of the successful submission.

Summary

In this chapter, we covered the process of collecting and handling data input from a customer and saving that input on the server. We also looked at how to bind data to control properties and how to provide simple data validation using the built in visual states provided in the textbox control. We discussed the following:

- How to create a Windows Communication Foundation service
- How to mark a business object for serialization in WCF
- How to create an input form in Silverlight
- How to create a data object for use with binding
- How to bind data from a data object to Silverlight controls
- How to provide input validation using the built-in validation states
- How to consume a WCF in Silverlight and process an asynchronous request

In the next chapter, we will learn how to leverage the WCF RIA services to build a common middle tier, access saved data using RIA services, add Silverlight support to a SharePoint site, and access SharePoint data from Silverlight.

6

Back Office Applications

Data storage is always a major concern with business applications, after all, what good is collecting data if you cannot access it and consume it for reporting, sales forecasts, and so on.

Silverlight opens up some new avenues for data communication and storage by utilizing Windows Communication Foundation services, WCF Rich Internet Application Services, or SharePoint Services to transmit and store data.

In this chapter, we shall:

- ◆ Leverage the WCF RIA Services to build a common middle tier
- ◆ Access the data we saved from the previous chapter using RIA Services
- ◆ Add Silverlight support to a SharePoint site
- ◆ Access SharePoint data from Silverlight

WCF Rich Internet Application (RIA) Services

The Silverlight framework is termed a **Rich Internet Application** or **RIA** for short. Microsoft has provided a pattern that can be used in connection with ASP.NET to provide a common middle tier. Complex business applications typically make use of data and business layers along with service layers to pass data across tiers. These layers or tiers can become complex over time, and WCF RIA Services provides a pattern for utilizing best practices in web and service development to provide maintainable and extendable application logic.

By providing a common middle tier and separating presentation logic from business logic we can ensure that both our website and our Silverlight application will be accessing and using our data in the same manner. Typical applications require developers to either duplicate application logic on both the client and server or use the linking feature of Visual Studio to share files between projects.

For instance, if we were to create a database table to hold customers and a customer data object in our web application project we would also need to re-create that same file in our Silverlight application. If we were sharing the files using the `Add as Link` feature, we might also need to make the customer class partial and split up some of the logic to handle both server and client side requirements. On the server, our customer class might include a property that accesses data from the database or **Data Access Layer (DAL)**. We could not include that property on the client, since the DAL does not exist on the client. In this scenario we would have to spilt the customer file into both a client and server version.

WCF RIA Services bridges this gap and creates the client code automatically, ignoring the properties that we do not want included via simple attributes.

The below diagram outlines the role of RIA Services in a Silverlight/Web Application scenario:

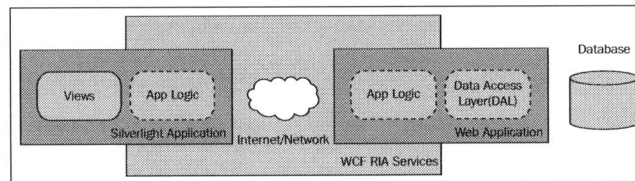

WCF RIA Services is designed to work with various data storage mechanisms, from relational databases to **Plain Old CLR Objects (POCO)**.

Time for action – creating a RIA Services application

We are going to create a WCF RIA Services application to read the customer information and sketch details we setup in the last chapter.

1. We need to download the free WCF RIA Services package in order to get started. The official Silverlight website will always contain the latest downloads for all Silverlight related tools. Visit `http://silverlight.net/riaservices/` and click on the **Download WCF RIA Services** link.

> * WCF RIA Services
> Microsoft WCF RIA Services simplifies the traditional n-tier application pattern by bringing together the ASP.NET and Silverlight platforms. The RIA Services provides a pattern to write application logic that runs on the mid-tier and controls access to data for queries, changes and custom operations. It also provides end-to-end support for common tasks such as data validation, authentication and roles by integrating with Silverlight components on the client and ASP.NET on the mid-tier.

2. Install **WCF RIA Services**:

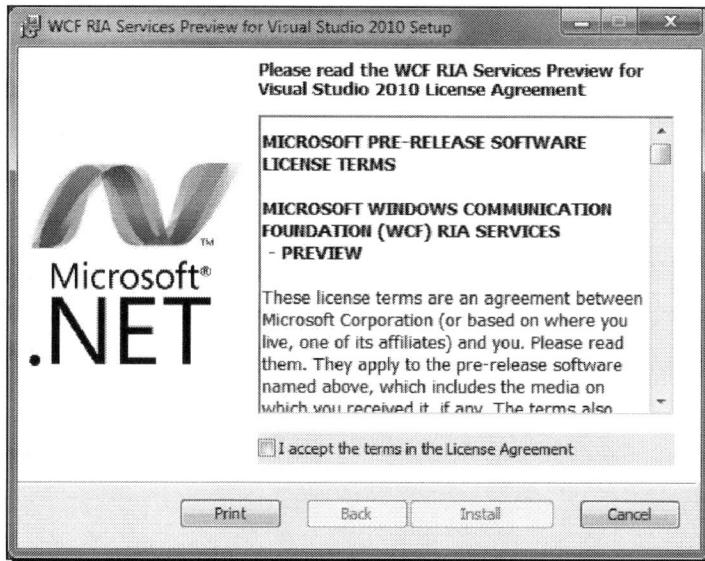

3. Start Visual Studio and on the **File** menu, choose **New**, and then **Project**. In the **New Project Dialog,** select **Silverlight Business Application** and name the project **CakeORamaApp** and click **OK**.

The **Silverlight Business Application** template will add a Silverlight project and an ASP.NET project. The default installation requires SQL Server Express and Visual Studio to be installed on the same machine.

The **Silverlight Business Application** template generates code and XAML files for a basic business application. The **XAML** files that are created and placed into the **Views** folder include **Home**, **About**, **ErrorWindow**, **LoginForm**, **LoginRegistrationWindow**, **LoginStatus**, and **RegistrationForm**. In addition, code files are placed in the **Models**, **Helpers**, and **Controls** folders, along with some resource files.

A file called `Styles.xaml` is placed in the **Assets** folder to hold the styles for the application, as shown in the following screenshot:

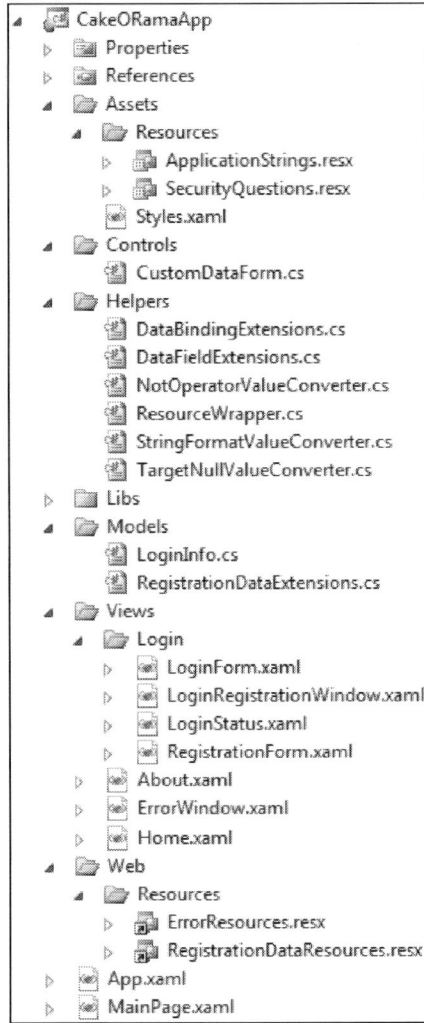

```
CakeORamaApp
  Properties
  References
  Assets
    Resources
      ApplicationStrings.resx
      SecurityQuestions.resx
      Styles.xaml
  Controls
    CustomDataForm.cs
  Helpers
    DataBindingExtensions.cs
    DataFieldExtensions.cs
    NotOperatorValueConverter.cs
    ResourceWrapper.cs
    StringFormatValueConverter.cs
    TargetNullValueConverter.cs
  Libs
  Models
    LoginInfo.cs
    RegistrationDataExtensions.cs
  Views
    Login
      LoginForm.xaml
      LoginRegistrationWindow.xaml
      LoginStatus.xaml
      RegistrationForm.xaml
    About.xaml
    ErrorWindow.xaml
    Home.xaml
  Web
    Resources
      ErrorResources.resx
      RegistrationDataResources.resx
  App.xaml
  MainPage.xaml
```

If SQL Server Express is installed, a default membership database will be created the first time you register a user.

4. Run the application to see the default layout and pages:

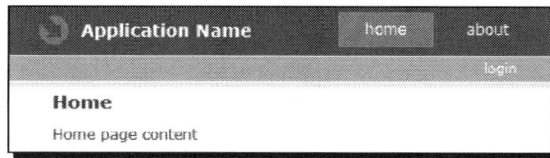

5. Open the **Assets|Resources|ApplicationStrings.resx** file and change the **ApplicationName** value to **Cake O Rama**:

Name	▲	Value
AboutPageTitle		About
ActivityLoadingUser		Initializing Application....
ActivityLoggingIn		Logging in...
ActivityRegisteringUser		Submitting Registration...
AlreadyRegisteredLabel		Already registered?
ApplicationName		Cake O Rama

6. We will add a new page to our application that will enable us to view information submitted by customers. To do this, we need to right-click on the **Views** folder in the Silverlight **CakeORamaApp** project in **Solution Explorer,** and choose **Add**, then **New Item**. In the **Add New Item** dialog box select the **Silverlight Page**. Name the page Submissions.xaml and click **Add**.

7. A **Silverlight Page** is part of the **Silverlight Navigation Framework**, which allows us to provide a frame in which to display pages much like an iframe in HTML.

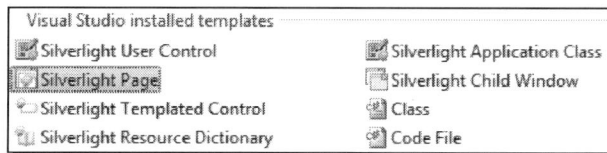

8. Open the MainPage.xaml file and find the following code segment:

```
<Rectangle
  x:Name="Divider1"
  Style="{StaticResource DividerStyle}"/>
<HyperlinkButton
  x:Name="Link2"
  Style="{StaticResource LinkStyle}"
  NavigateUri="/About"
  TargetName="ContentFrame"
  Content="{Binding Path=ApplicationStrings.AboutPageTitle,
Source={StaticResource ResourceWrapper}}"/>
```

9. We will add a navigation link to our page by adding the following code just below the previous code segment:

```
<Rectangle
  x:Name="Divider2"
  Style="{StaticResource DividerStyle}"/>
<HyperlinkButton
  x:Name="Link3"
  Style="{StaticResource LinkStyle}"
  NavigateUri="/Submissions"
  TargetName="ContentFrame"
  Content="submissions"/>
```

10. If we build and run our solution, we should see a new navigation button called **submissions**.

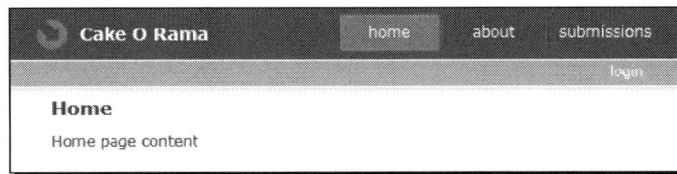

11. Right-click on the `Submissions.xaml` file and choose **Open in Expression Blend**:

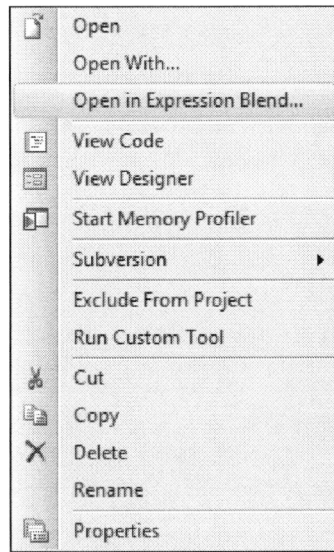

12. We are going to create a page that can display a list of the customer submissions, and when an item is selected, it can display the details of each submission. For that, we will use a grid divided into two columns. The left column will be our list and the right column will display the selected item details. Open the `Submissions.xaml` page and add a column to the default **LayoutRoot** grid.

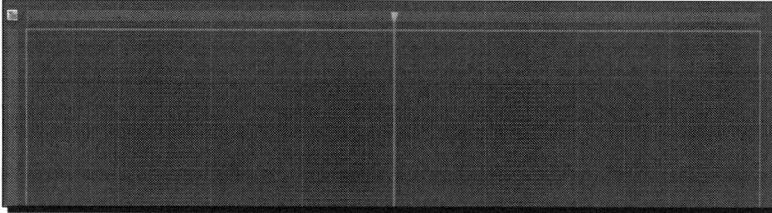

13. Click on the **Button** icon in the toolbox and hold the left button down. When the menu appears displaying other controls, select the **ListBox** control:

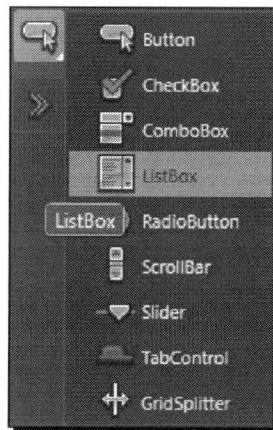

14. Double click on the **ListBox** icon in the toolbar to add a new listbox to our page, into the left column of our grid automatically. If we wanted to move it into a different column, we can simply drag it into the column or row of the grid:

15. Name the listbox **SubmissionList**, right-click on the new listbox control, choose **AutoSize** and then **Fill**; this makes the listbox fill the entire column and row. This is equivalent to setting the `HorizontalAlignment` and `VerticalAlignment` to `Stretch`:

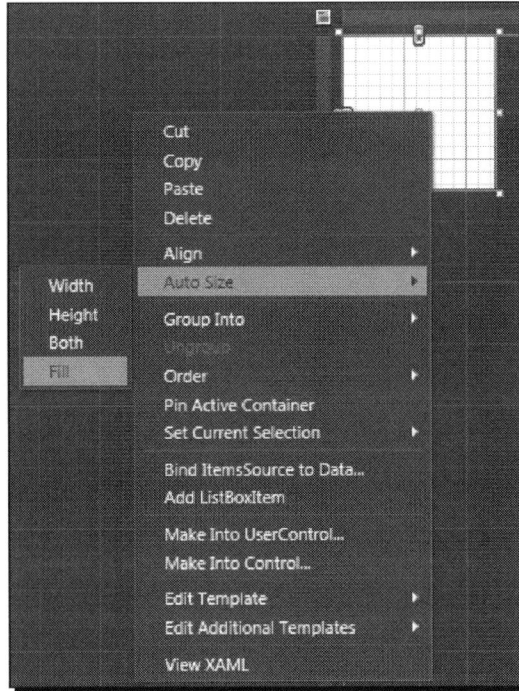

16. Change the **Background** of the `SubmissionList` to the following gradient with a left color value of #FF0D293F and a right color value of #FF284053:

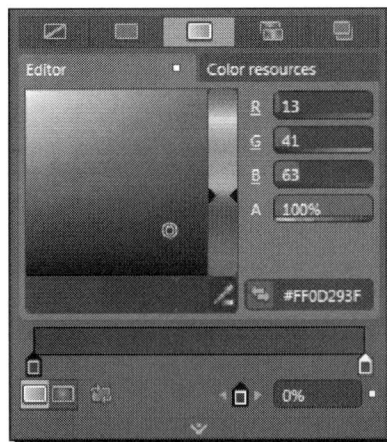

17. Change the **Foreground** of the `SubmissionList` to #FFFFFFFF.

18. Because we will be viewing the information that was submitted by customers and it includes an ink sketch, we need to add an `InkPresenter` control to the right column. Click on the **Assets** button and type **ink** into the search field. Select the **InkPresenter** control and then double-click on the **InkPresenter** in the toolbar to add a new instance to our page. Name the `InkPresenter` **SketchInk**, change the **Background** to #FFFFFFFF and position it into the left column of the grid as follows:

> Be sure that the **LayoutRoot** is selected in the **Objects and Timeline** panel before double-clicking on controls on the toolbar as Blend will add the new control as a child of the selected control.

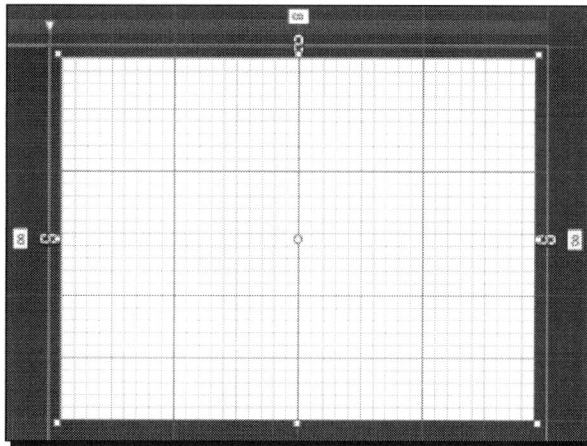

19. Change the properties of the `SketchInk` control to the following:

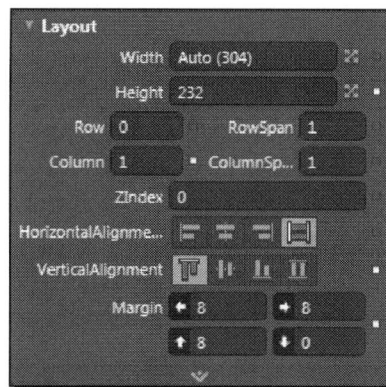

20. Add the following series of `TextBlock` controls below the `SketchInk` control and change the **Text** properties to reflect the labels:

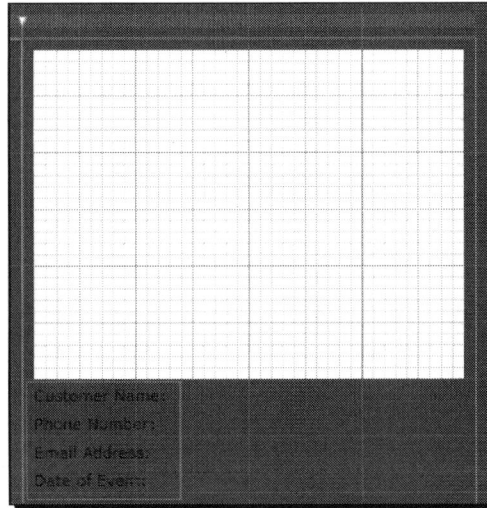

[☑ *notes...*   Remember that in Blend *Alt + Click* and *Drag* will make a copy
                   of the selected control.   ]

21. There is no need to worry about the black text, our page background is white, so it will look fine when the application is running.

22. Now we will add a series of labels that will display the results of the selected item. Add four more `TextBlock` controls and name them **Customer Name, Phone Number, Email Address,** and **Date of Event**. Change the color of the **Text** to `#FF136EDA` and position the controls as follows:

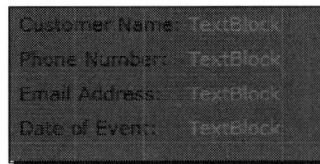

23. Save your work, switch back over to Visual Studio and press **Yes to All** on the dialog box that pops up in Visual Studio. In **Solution Explorer,** right-click on the **Services** folder of the **CakeORamaApp.Web** project and choose **Add, New Item**. In the **Add New Item** dialog box select **Domain Service Class** from the **Web Categories** and name it **CustomerSubmissionService**.

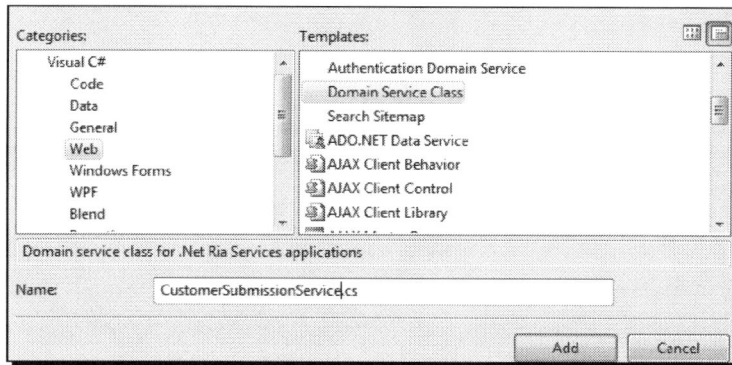

24. On the **Add New Domain Service** class dialog ensure the following options are selected and click **OK**:

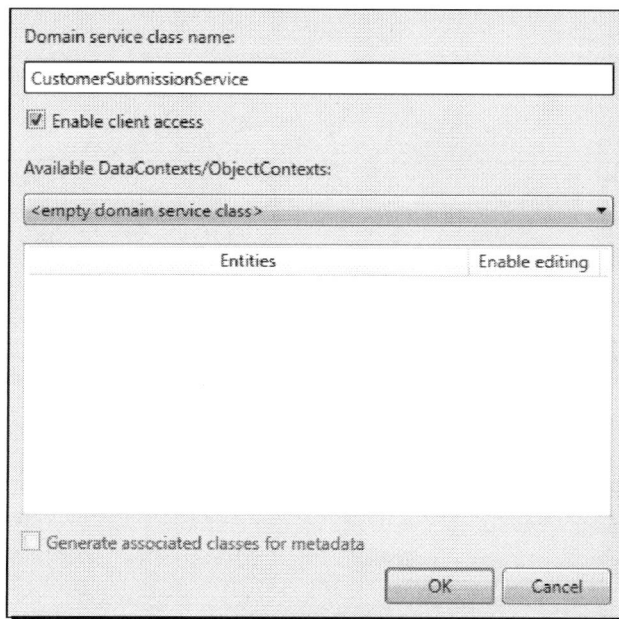

> RIA Services and ADO.NET Entity Framework work very well together when data is stored in a SQL Server database. Since our data was stored in an XML file we will not need the Entity Framework. We will cover RIA Services and the Entity Framework in the next chapter.

25. Add a new class to the **Services** folder of the **CakeORama.Web** project called **CustomerSubmission**.

26. Replace the code in the `CustomerSubmission.cs` file with the following:

```
using System;
using System.ComponentModel.DataAnnotations;

namespace CakeORamaApp.Web.Services
{
  public class CustomerSubmission
  {
    [Key]
    public string CustomerName { get; set; }
    public string PhoneNumber { get; set; }
    public string Email { get; set; }
    public DateTime EventDate { get; set; }
    public string Strokes { get; set; }
  }
}
```

27. The `CustomerSubmission` class will serve as our domain object that we can use to communicate between Silverlight and our ASP.NET application.

28. The `Strokes` property is a string that contains the XML for the strokes and points. We use a string because RIA Services can handle primitive types much easier than complex types when using POCO.

29. Open the `CustomerSubmissionService.cs` file and replace the code with the following:

```
namespace CakeORamaApp.Web
{
  using System;
  using System.Collections.Generic;
  using System.IO;
  using System.Web.DomainServices;
  using System.Web.Ria;
  using System.Xml.Linq;

  [EnableClientAccess()]
  public class CustomerSubmissionService : DomainService
  {
    private static string SubmissionDirectory =
      @"C:\Projects\CakeORama\Customer\Data\";

    public IEnumerable<CustomerSubmission> GetSubmissions()
    {
      var submissions = new List<CustomerSubmission>();
      var files = Directory.GetFiles(SubmissionDirectory);
      foreach (var file in files)
```

```
{
    var submission = new CustomerSubmission();
    submissions.Add(submission);

    // Customer
    var customerRoot = XElement.Load(file);
    submission.CustomerName = customerRoot.Attribute("name").
    Value;
    submission.Email = customerRoot.Attribute("email").Value;
    submission.PhoneNumber = customerRoot.Attribute("phone").
    Value;
    submission.EventDate = DateTime.Parse(customerRoot.
    Element("eventDate").Value);
    submission.Strokes = customerRoot.Element("strokes").
    ToString();
  }
  return submissions;
}
}
}
```

30. What we are doing here is reading the XML files that we saved from the previous chapter containing the data submitted by the customer and loading the data into a list of our `CustomerSubmission` objects.

31. Next we'll build the solution; this will cause Visual Studio to generate client code and add a **Generated_Code** folder to the Silverlight project. Visual Studio generates the code required to access data from the server, hiding the underlying WCF implementation, and generating the proxy classes. Using RIA Services we do not need to implement a separate WCF service or deal with data class duplication, saving us time and effort with building and testing a WCF service and related wire-up code. The folder is initially hidden but can be viewed by enabling the **Show All Files** option in **Solution Explorer**.

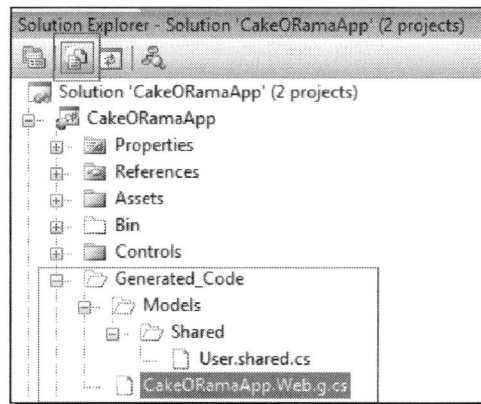

32. Open the `Submissions.xaml.cs` file and replace the existing code with the following code:

```
using System.Windows.Controls;
using System.Windows.Navigation;

using CakeORamaApp.Web.Services;

namespace CakeORamaApp.Views
{
  public partial class Submissions : Page
  {
    public Submissions()
    {
      InitializeComponent();
    }

    // Executes when the user navigates to this page.
    protected override void OnNavigatedTo(NavigationEventArgs e)
    {
      var context = new CustomerSubmissionContext();
  context.Load<CustomerSubmission>(context.GetSubmissionsQuery());
      SubmissionList.ItemsSource = context.CustomerSubmissions;
    }

  }
}
```

33. Build and run the solution, navigate to the **Submissions** page, and we can see that our customers are being loaded in the listbox.

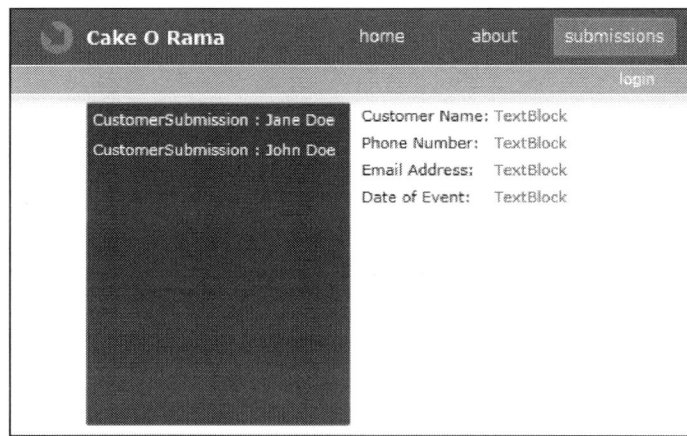

34. Switch back over to Blend and open the `Submissions.xaml` page. Add an event handler to the **SubmissionList** listbox for the **SelectionChanged** event.

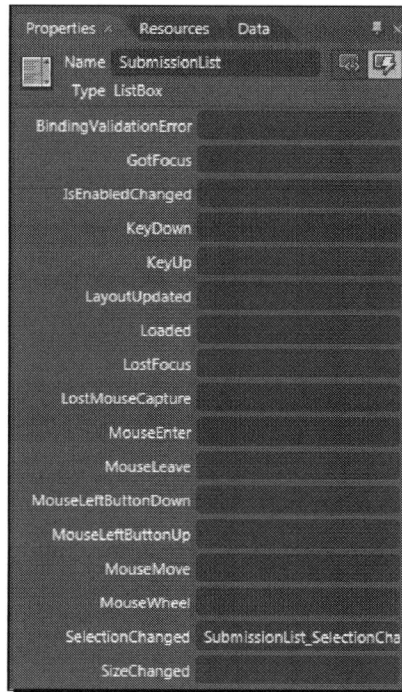

35. Switch back over to Visual Studio, press **Yes to All** on the dialog box that is displayed and add a reference to `System.Xml.Linq` in the **CakeORama.App** Silverlight project:

36. Replace the `using` section at the top of the `Submissions.xaml.cs` file with the following:

```
using System;
using System.Windows.Controls;
using System.Windows.Ink;
using System.Windows.Input;
using System.Windows.Media;
using System.Windows.Navigation;
using System.Xml.Linq;
using CakeORamaApp.Web.Services;
```

37. Replace the `SubmissionList_SelectionChanged` event handler of the `Submissions.xaml.cs` file with the following code:

```
private void SubmissionList_SelectionChanged(object sender,
System.Windows.Controls.SelectionChangedEventArgs e)
{
  if (e.AddedItems.Count == 0) return;

  var submission = e.AddedItems[0] as CustomerSubmission;
  if (submission == null) return;

  CustomerName.Text = submission.CustomerName;
  PhoneNumber.Text = submission.PhoneNumber;
  EmailAddress.Text = submission.Email;
  DateOfEvent.Text = submission.EventDate.ToShortDateString();

  var strokes = new StrokeCollection();

  var xml = XElement.Parse(submission.Strokes);
  foreach (var strokeElement in xml.Elements("stroke"))
  {
    var stroke = new Stroke();
    strokes.Add(stroke);

    stroke.DrawingAttributes.Width = Double.Parse(strokeElement.
     Attribute("width").Value);
    stroke.DrawingAttributes.Height = Double.Parse(strokeElement.
     Attribute("height").Value);

    var colorElement = strokeElement.Element("color");
    stroke.DrawingAttributes.Color = Color.FromArgb(
      Byte.Parse(colorElement.Attribute("a").Value),
      Byte.Parse(colorElement.Attribute("r").Value),
      Byte.Parse(colorElement.Attribute("g").Value),
      Byte.Parse(colorElement.Attribute("b").Value));
```

```
var outlineColorElement = strokeElement.
Element("outlineColor");
stroke.DrawingAttributes.OutlineColor = Color.FromArgb(
  Byte.Parse(outlineColorElement.Attribute("a").Value),
  Byte.Parse(outlineColorElement.Attribute("r").Value),
  Byte.Parse(outlineColorElement.Attribute("g").Value),
  Byte.Parse(outlineColorElement.Attribute("b").Value));

var points = new StylusPointCollection();
stroke.StylusPoints = points;

foreach (var pointElement in strokeElement.Element("points").
Elements("point"))
{
  points.Add(new StylusPoint(Double.Parse(pointElement.
  Attribute("x").Value),
    Double.Parse(pointElement.Attribute("y").Value)));
}

}
SketchInk.Strokes = strokes;}
```

38. Build and run the solution, we should now see the cake sketch that was submitted when we click on a customer record in the listbox:

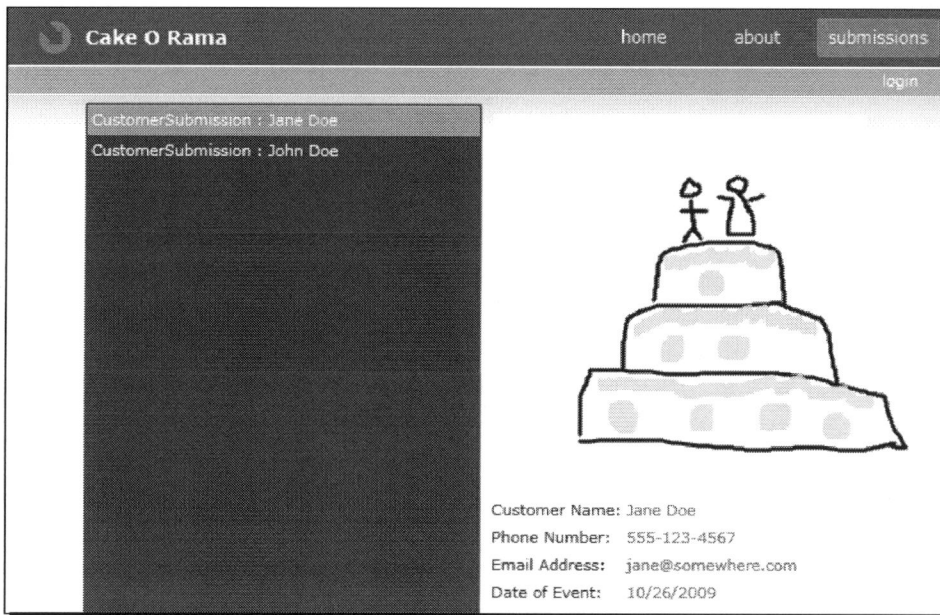

What just happened?

We utilized the WCF RIA Services framework to create a common middle tier that is shared between Silverlight and ASP.NET. We loaded the XML that we had saved from the previous chapter, so that the customer service representatives from Cake O Rama can view the information submitted by customers.

We got to see how easy it was to setup RIA Services and how our business objects on the server can be auto generated on the client, removing the tedious step of duplicating objects in ASP.NET and Silverlight.

Because we used the Silverlight Business Application template, we got the added benefit of a stubbed out customer service application complete with user authentication.

Have a go hero – styling the listbox

When we bound the `CustomerSubmission` data to our `ListBox` we used the default view, which just renders the object name and the property marked with the `[Key]` attribute. While this is fine for testing we should provide a cleaner look to the list.

1. Start Expression Blend with the **CakeORama** solution and open the `Sumissions.xaml` file. Click on the **SubmissionsList** control in the **Objects and Timeline** panel, then click on the breadcrumb at the top of the artboard, just under the **File Name** tab and create a new `DataTemplate` for the generated items:

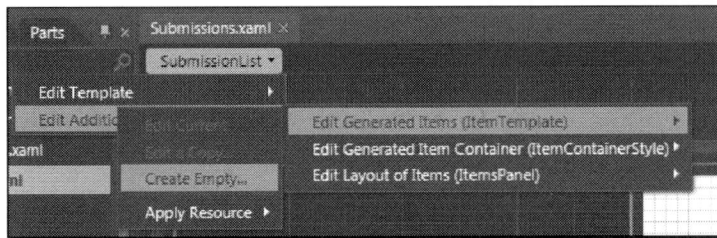

2. Name the template **SubmissionListItemTemplate** and save it locally:

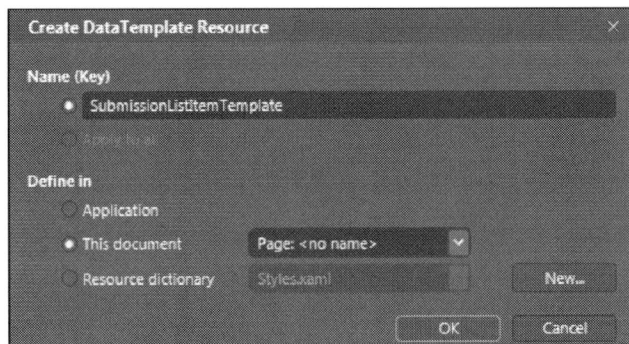

3. Add a textblock to the grid of the template, set the font size to **10pt** and change the **Foreground** to #FFFFFFFF:

4. Set the **Databinding** of the **Text** property of the textblock to **CustomerName**, so that this property will bind to the CustomerName property of the CustomerSubmission object:

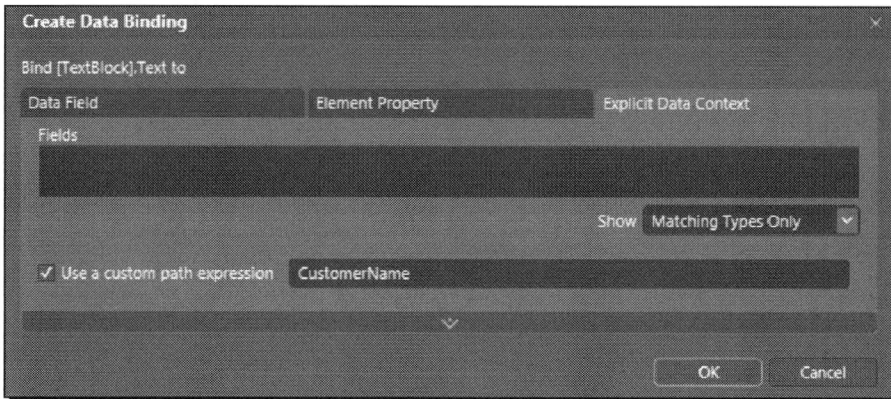

5. Save the Submissions.xaml page, build and run the solution, and our list should now display the value of the CustomerName field that we configured in the data binding options:

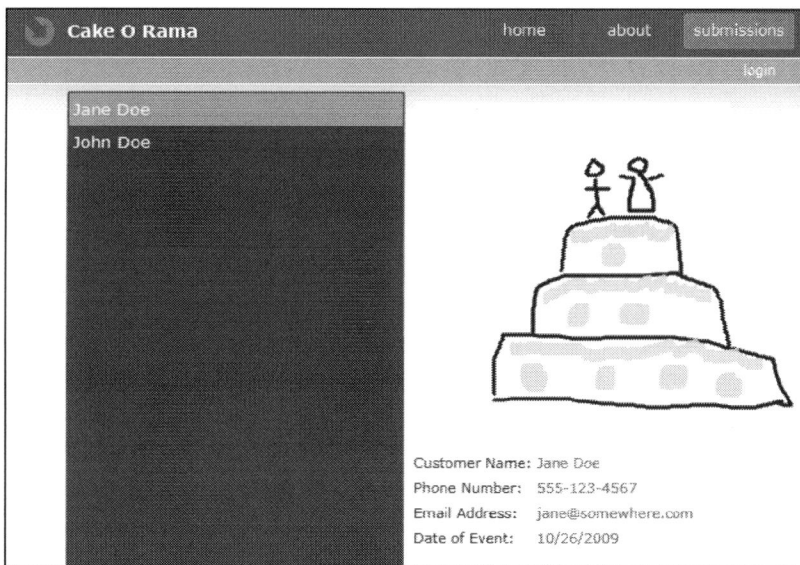

SharePoint

Microsoft Office SharePoint is a collaboration tool useful for content management, search and information sharing within or across organizations. With the list management and document storage capabilities, SharePoint can provide a central portal for employees of an organization, allowing for one location in which to keep important company information, client lists, and sales data.

We can utilize Silverlight in our SharePoint applications to spice them up and for improving the user experience. We can also consume SharePoint data from within our Silverlight applications, making SharePoint another data source from which to gather and display information.

Time for action – hosting a Silverlight application in SharePoint

We will setup a Silverlight application that we can host from within SharePoint.

1. Firstly, download and install the Visual Studio 2008 extensions for Windows SharePoint Services 3.0 from `http://www.microsoft.com/downloads/details.aspx?FamilyID=FB9D4B85-DA2A-432E-91FB-D505199C49F6&displaylang=en`.

File Name:	File Size	
VSeWSS 1 3 Mar 2009 CTP Release Notes.rtf	236 KB	Download
VSeWSSv13_AMD64_Build-433.exe	12.2 MB	Download
VSeWSSv13_x86_Build-433.exe	12.2 MB	Download

> We need to install this on a machine that has Windows SharePoint Services 3.0 installed. An evaluation Virtual PC download pre-installed with SharePoint, Visual Studio 2008 and the Visual Studio 2008 extensions for Windows SharePoint Services is available at `http://www.microsoft.com/downloads/details.aspx?FamilyID=FB9D4B85-DA2A-432E-91FB-D505199C49F6&displaylang=en`.

2. Start Visual Studio, choose **New Project** and under the **SharePoint** category choose **WebPart**.

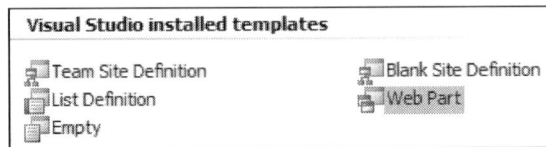

Visual Studio installed templates	
Team Site Definition	Blank Site Definition
List Definition	Web Part
Empty	

3. We are going to create a **Web Part** that can host a Silverlight application. Replace the code in the `WebPart1.cs` file with the following (from the code provided at: `http://thebreakpoint.spaces.live.com/blog/cns!25ED1118FDA97850!219.entry`):

```
using System;
using System.ComponentModel;
using System.Runtime.InteropServices;
using System.Web.UI;
using System.Web.UI.WebControls.WebParts;
using System.Xml.Serialization;

namespace SilverlightWebPart
{
    [Guid("a23c42db-353d-4692-95c1-4e45de6de30c")]
    [ToolboxData("<{0}:SilverlightWebPart runat=server></{0}:
    SilverlightWebPart>")]
    [XmlRoot(Namespace = "SilverlightWebPart")]
    public class WebPart1 : System.Web.UI.WebControls.WebParts.
    WebPart
    {
        #region Constructor

        public WebPart1()
        {
            // Initialize the properties with default values...
            XAPURL = "";
            SLHeight = 300;
            SLWidth = 300;
        }

        #endregion
        #region Properties

        // This property will be used to store the
        // Silverlight application url
        [WebBrowsable(true)]
        [Personalizable(PersonalizationScope.Shared)]
        [WebDisplayName(".Xap Url")]
        [WebDescription("The Url of the Silverlight Application
         you want to show in this web part.")]
        [Category("Silverlight")]
        public string XAPURL { get; set; }
```

```csharp
// This property must be used to indicate the Height
// of the Silverlight application - it will be used
// in the object tag
[WebBrowsable(true)]
[Personalizable(PersonalizationScope.Shared)]
[WebDisplayName("Silverlight object Height")]
[WebDescription("Height of the Silverligth object.")]
[Category("Silverlight")]
[DefaultValue(300)]
public int SLHeight { get; set; }

// This property must be used to indicate the Width
// of the Silverlight application - it will be used
// in the object tag
[WebBrowsable(true)]
[Personalizable(PersonalizationScope.Shared)]
[WebDisplayName("Silverlight object Width")]
[WebDescription("Width of the Silverlight object.")]
[Category("Silverlight")]
[DefaultValue(300)]
public int SLWidth { get; set; }

#endregion

#region Methods

protected override void CreateChildControls()
{

    base.CreateChildControls();
}

protected override void Render(HtmlTextWriter writer)
{

    base.Render(writer);

    // Here, the object tag is rendered using the width
    // and height
    // of the control, and the .xap url used as parameter
    // of the object
    // tag...

// <object>
```

```
writer.AddAttribute(HtmlTextWriterAttribute.Id,
"Silverlight3WebPartPlugin");
writer.AddAttribute(HtmlTextWriterAttribute.Width, this.
SLWidth.ToString());
writer.AddAttribute(HtmlTextWriterAttribute.Headers, this.
SLHeight.ToString());
writer.AddAttribute("data",
"data:application/x-silverlight-2");
writer.AddAttribute("type", "application/x-silverlight-2");
writer.RenderBeginTag(HtmlTextWriterTag.Object);

// <param/>
writer.AddAttribute(HtmlTextWriterAttribute.Name, "source");
writer.AddAttribute(HtmlTextWriterAttribute.Value,
this.XAPURL);
writer.RenderBeginTag(HtmlTextWriterTag.Param);
writer.RenderEndTag();

// <a>
writer.AddAttribute(HtmlTextWriterAttribute.Href,
"http://go.microsoft.com/fwlink/?LinkID=149156");
writer.AddAttribute(HtmlTextWriterAttribute.Style,
"text-decoration: none;");
writer.RenderBeginTag(HtmlTextWriterTag.A);

// <img/>
writer.AddAttribute(HtmlTextWriterAttribute.Src,
"http://go.microsoft.com/fwlink/?LinkId=108181");
writer.AddAttribute(HtmlTextWriterAttribute.Alt,
"Get Microsoft Silverlight");
writer.AddAttribute(HtmlTextWriterAttribute.Style,
"border-style: none");
writer.RenderBeginTag(HtmlTextWriterTag.Img);
writer.RenderEndTag();

// </a>
writer.RenderEndTag();

// </object>
writer.RenderEndTag();            }

    #endregion

    }
}
```

4. Build and run the application. (If using the SharePoint VPC, Visual Studio is already setup to configure and install the **WebPart** into our SharePoint site). When the WSS site loads, choose **Edit Page** from the **Site Action** menu:

5. Click the **Add a Web Part** link in the center window panel:

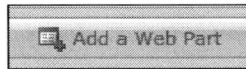

6. We can see our web part in the available web parts. Select the **WebPart1** and click the **Add** button.

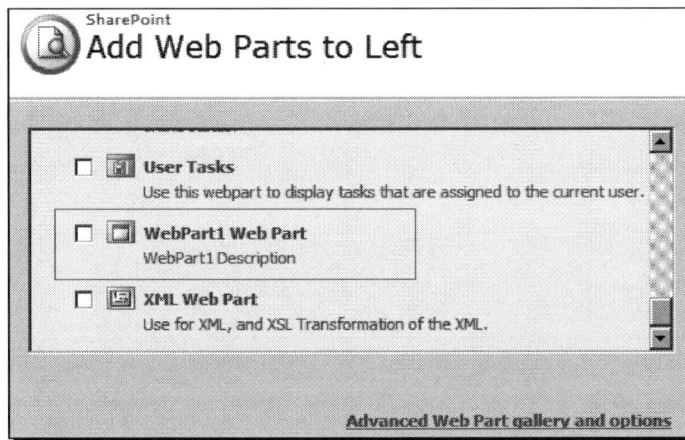

7. This installs the **WebPart** on the home page of the SharePoint application.

8. Now we will add a new **list** to SharePoint, that we will be able to access from within Silverlight. Choose **Create** from the **Site Actions** menu:

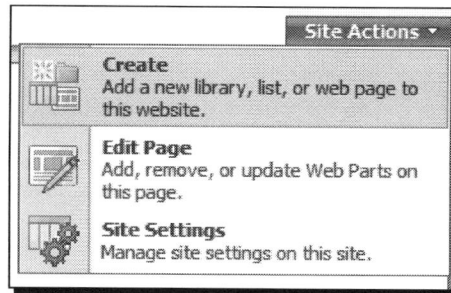

9. Click on the **Custom List** link in the **Custom Lists** category:

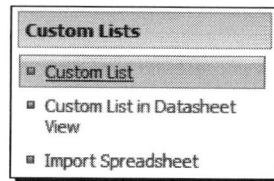

10. Name the list **Sales Associates** and click the **Create** button:

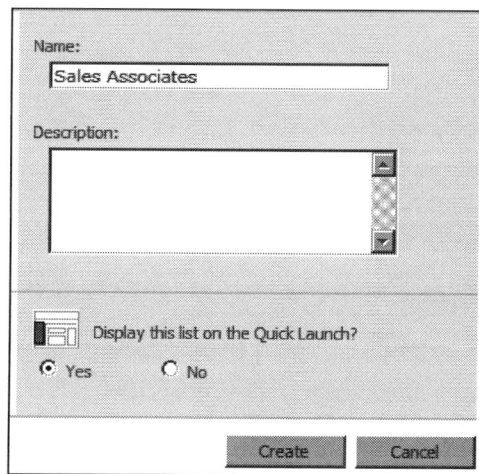

11. Select **New|New Item** from the menu:

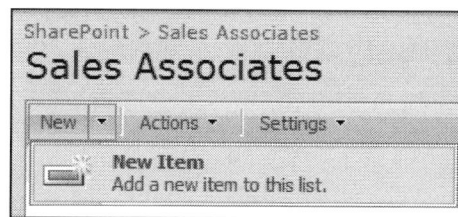

12. Add some **Sales Associates**:

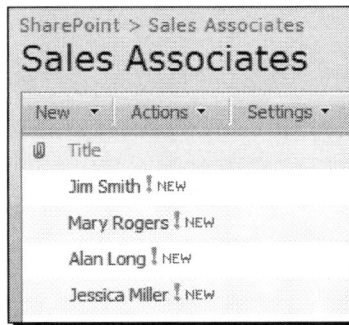

13. Now we need to go back to Visual Studio and choose **File|New|Project** and select **Silverlight Application**. Name the project `SharePointApp` and click **OK**.

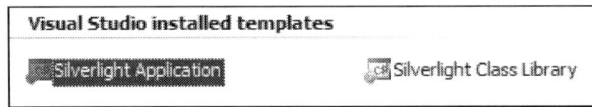

14. Add the following code to the `grid` of the `MainPage.xaml` file:

```
<ListBox x:Name="SalesAssociates"></ListBox>
```

15. SharePoint provides web services for accessing data, and we can take advantage of these services in Silverlight by adding a **Service Reference** to the **SharePoint Lists Service** named **ListService**.

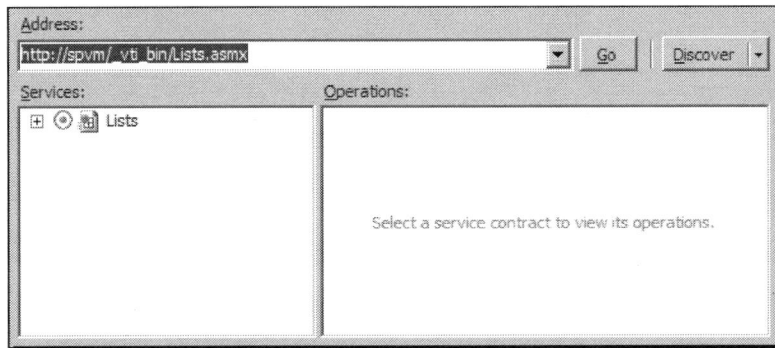

16. Because we are going to access a web service from a Silverlight application we need to include a client access policy file in the SharePoint server root (`C:\Inetpub\wwwroot\wss\VirtualDirectories\80`).

17. Open Windows Explorer and create a new file in the SharePoint root called
`clientaccesspolicy.xml`. Copy the following code into it, save, and close it:

```
<?xml version="1.0" encoding="utf-8" ?>
<access-policy>
  <cross-domain-access>
    <policy>
      <allow-from http-request-headers="*">
        <domain uri="*"/>
      </allow-from>
      <grant-to>
        <resource include-subpaths="true" path="/"/>
      </grant-to>
    </policy>
  </cross-domain-access>
</access-policy>
```

> A `Client Access Policy` file allows Silverlight applications to communicate across different domains from the domain in which the Silverlight client is actually loaded. This file provides restrictions and rights to the Silverlight runtime. Silverlight supports both the Silverlight client access policy file and the Flash cross domain policy file.

18. Add a `using` statement to the **Using** section of the `MainPage.xaml.cs` file:

```
using SharePointApp.ListService;
```

19. Insert the following code into the `MainPage_Loaded` event handler:

```
var service = new ListsSoapClient();
service.GetListItemsCompleted += new EventHandler<GetListItemsComp
letedEventArgs>(service_GetListItemsCompleted);
service.GetListItemsAsync("Sales Associates", null, null, null,
null, null, null);
```

20. Add the following event handler to bind the list results to the
`SalesAssociates` listbox:

```
void service_GetListItemsCompleted(object sender,
GetListItemsCompletedEventArgs e)
{
    var list = new List<object>();
    foreach (var node in e.Result.Elements().FirstOrDefault().
Elements())
    {
        list.Add(new { Title = node.Attribute("ows_Title").Value
});
    }
    SalesAssociates.ItemsSource = list;
}
```

21. We should see our results if we build and run the Silverlight application:

```
{ Title = Jim Smith }
{ Title = Mary Rogers }
{ Title = Alan Long }
{ Title = Jessica Miller }
```

22. We can also style the listbox by adding a `DataTemplate` or custom style for the list items.

23. Now that we have a working Silverlight application, we can copy it into a document library in SharePoint and utilize the Silverlight **Web Part** that we created earlier to load the Silverlight application into our SharePoint home page. Open the SharePoint website and go to the **Shared Documents** library:

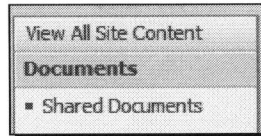

```
View All Site Content
Documents
  ▪ Shared Documents
```

24. Choose the **Upload** option and upload the XAP file from the `SharePointApp.Web/ClientBin` folder and click **OK**:

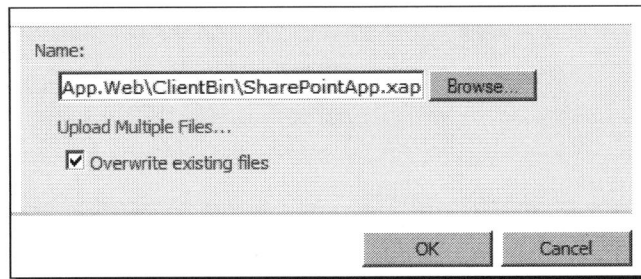

Name:

| App.Web\ClientBin\SharePointApp.xap | Browse... |

Upload Multiple Files...

☑ Overwrite existing files

| OK | Cancel |

25. We should now have our XAP file stored in **Shared Documents**:

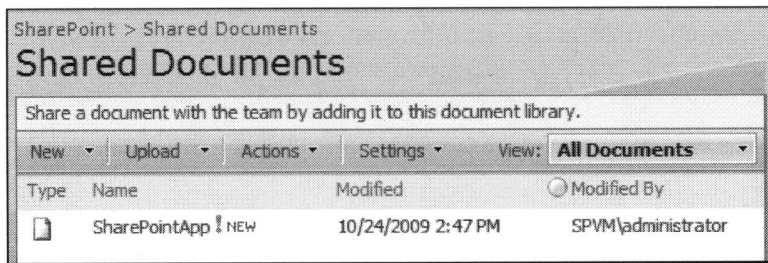

SharePoint > Shared Documents

Shared Documents

Share a document with the team by adding it to this document library.

| New ▾ | Upload ▾ | Actions ▾ | Settings ▾ | View: | All Documents ▾ |

Type	Name	Modified	○ Modified By
☐	SharePointApp ! NEW	10/24/2009 2:47 PM	SPVM\administrator

26. Return to the SharePoint home page (where we added our custom **Web Part**) and click on the arrow next to the **Web Part**:

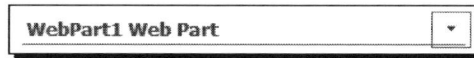

> WebPart1 Web Part   ▾

27. Choose **Modify Shared Web Part** to enter the **Web Part** editing mode:

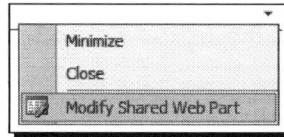

> ▾
> Minimize
> Close
> 📝 Modify Shared Web Part

28. Change the name of the **WebPart** panel, under the **Appearance** section, to **Sales Associates**:

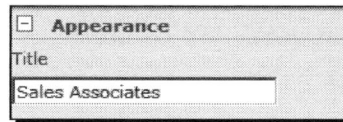

> ⊟ **Appearance**
> Title
> Sales Associates

29. Set the URL to the XAP file under the Silverlight section to: `http://spvm/Shared%20Documents/SharePointApp.xap` and click **OK**:

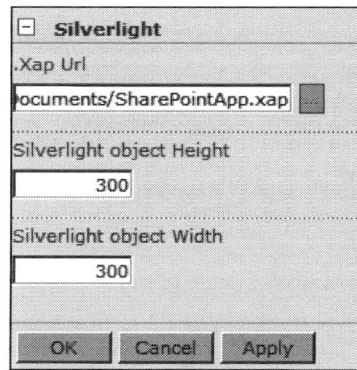

> ⊟ **Silverlight**
> .Xap Url
> ocuments/SharePointApp.xap ▢
> Silverlight object Height
> 300
> Silverlight object Width
> 300
> OK   Cancel   Apply

30. We should now have our Silverlight application, hosted within our SharePoint website and displaying information from our **Sales Associates** SharePoint list.

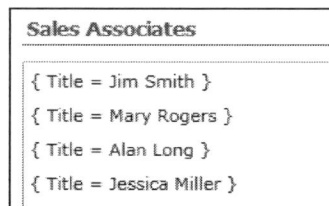

> Sales Associates
> { Title = Jim Smith }
> { Title = Mary Rogers }
> { Title = Alan Long }
> { Title = Jessica Miller }

What just happened?

We created a SharePoint `Web Part` to host a Silverlight Application and created a Silverlight Application to access list data stored within SharePoint.

We also got a look at including a `clientaccesspolicy.xml` file in SharePoint to allow Silverlight to access data via a SharePoint web service.

While developing completely in SharePoint can be complex, we can see that adding some basic Silverlight goodness is a fairly straight forward process, and opens up SharePoint to the Silverlight user experience.

Summary

In this chapter, we learned how to create a WCF RIA Services project for sharing a common middle tier between ASP.NET and Silverlight. We also implemented Silverlight in a SharePoint environment. In this chapter we discussed the following:

- ◆ How to create a WCF RIA Services Silverlight and ASP.NET application
- ◆ How WCF RIA Services works in both Silverlight and ASP.NET
- ◆ How to create a SharePoint WebPart for hosting a Silverlight application
- ◆ How to consume a SharePoint web service from Silverlight

In the next chapter, we will create a customer service application utilizing the Entity Framework and WCF RIA Services to allow customer service representatives the ability to manage customer and order information through a Silverlight frontend.

7
Customer Service Application

Organizations that sell products and deal with the public most often have some type of customer service department. Whether it is the owner fielding calls, or a full blown department having an application to easily view and edit customer information, it can save a lot of time and money for the business.

In the previous chapters we collected information from potential customers and started building an internal application for viewing the customer submissions. We will take this a step further by providing some additional functionality to allow us to edit and save customer information that can later be used to generate various reports.

In this chapter, we shall:

- ◆ Expand our customer service application to save to a database
- ◆ Make use of the Entity Framework, LINQ to SQL and WCF RIA Services
- ◆ Provide an easy to use interface for customer service associates

Customer data

We have collected some information from potential customers through our public Silverlight application that allowed the customer to draw a basic sketch of the type of cake they wanted and to include some information about themselves and the date of their event.

Because the cake sketch is drawn by the customer, we need to follow up with that customer to find out more information about the cake and the event. Before we get started with building the screens for customer service to be able to include this information, we need to work out a data model that can store this additional information. We are going to use SQL Server to store customer information and will make use of the Entity Framework to access the information.

One thing to consider when developing our model is that we already have some information that was submitted by the customer. We will leave this information in the XML file and once a customer service representative has opened and edited the information, we will remove the XML file and save the information to the database. This way we can keep potential customers out of the same pool of information as the verified customers.

We also want to keep in mind that we could have repeat customers, so we need to keep customer information separate from event and order information.

Time for action – creating the data model

We will create a data model that can support customers who may or may not order cakes for multiple events. We will also setup support for maintaining records of cakes that were ordered and the details of the cakes ordered, including images of the finished cakes.

1. Start SQL Server Management Studio or SQL Server Management Studio Express and connect to your local computer or development database server. (If SQL Server is installed, the local computer is your computer name or **local**; if using SQL Server Express it will be the local computer name plus SQLEXPRESS: computername\SQLEXPRESS).

> You can also connect to a database from within Visual Studio to add or edit tables, stored procedures and views. To connect to a database from within Visual Studio you use the Server Explorer and create a new database connection.

2. Right-click on the **Databases** node and choose **New Database...**:

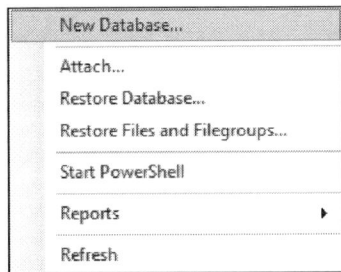

New Database...	
Attach...	
Restore Database...	
Restore Files and Filegroups...	
Start PowerShell	
Reports	▶
Refresh	

3. Name the database **CakeORama** and click **OK**:

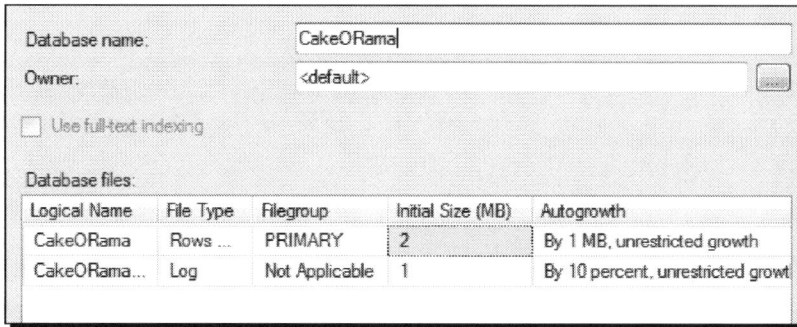

Logical Name	File Type	Filegroup	Initial Size (MB)	Autogrowth
CakeORama	Rows ...	PRIMARY	2	By 1 MB, unrestricted growth
CakeORama...	Log	Not Applicable	1	By 10 percent, unrestricted growt

Database name: CakeORama

Owner: <default>

☐ Use full-text indexing

Database files:

4. We will create a database diagram to make it easier to setup our tables. Expand the **CakeORama** database, right-click on the **Database Diagrams** and choose **New Database Diagram**:

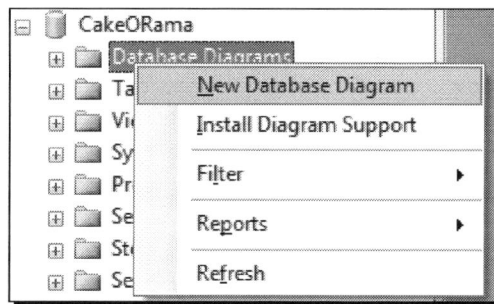

CakeORama
- Database Diagrams
  - New Database Diagram
  - Install Diagram Support
  - Filter ▸
  - Reports ▸
  - Refresh

5. If you get a prompt asking you if you want to create the support objects choose **Yes**:

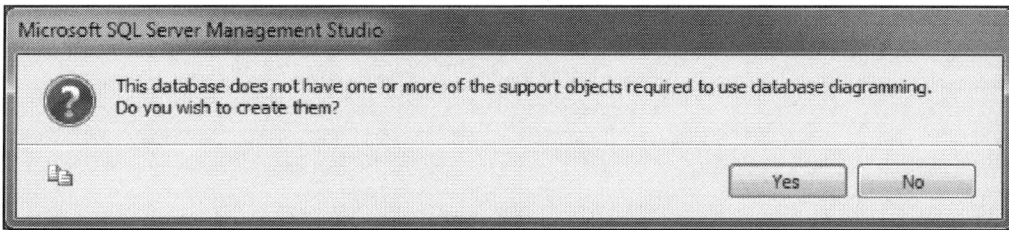

Microsoft SQL Server Management Studio

This database does not have one or more of the support objects required to use database diagramming. Do you wish to create them?

Yes   No

6. When the new diagram is created you are presented with the **Add Table** dialog, just close this dialog as we do not have any tables yet to add:

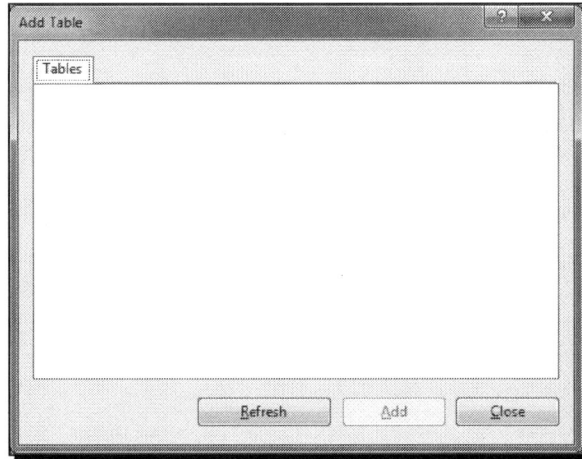

7. Right-click on the surface of the diagram and choose **New Table...**:

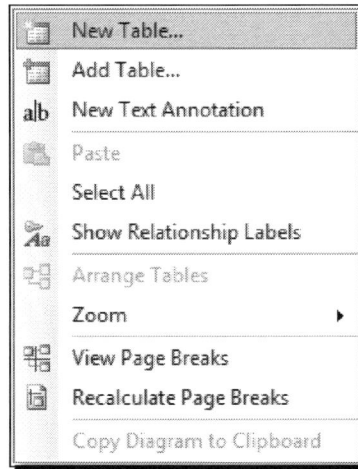

8. Name the new table **Customers** and click **OK**:

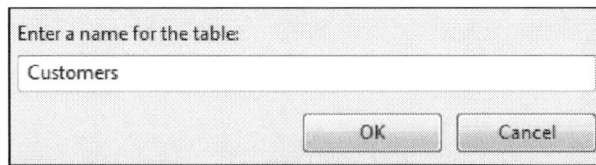

9. Layout the **Customers** table as follows, the **CustomerId** field is the Primary Key and is also an Identity column:

Customers		
Column Name	Data Type	Allow Nulls
🔑 CustomerId	int	☐
CustomerName	nvarchar(80)	☐
PhoneNumber	nvarchar(20)	☐
EmailAddress	nvarchar(255)	☐
		☐

10. Add another table named **Events** and add the following columns where the **EventId** column is the Primary Key and also an Identity column:

Events		
Column Name	Data Type	Allow Nulls
🔑 EventId	int	☐
CustomerId	int	☐
EventDate	datetime	☐
Comments	nvarchar(MAX)	☑
CustomerSketch	xml	☐
		☐

11. Create a foreign key relationship between the **Customers** and **Events** table on the **CustomerId** column:

Relationship name:

FK_Events_Customers

Primary key table:	Foreign key table:
Customers ▾	Events
CustomerId	CustomerId ▾

12. Our table structure should look like the following:

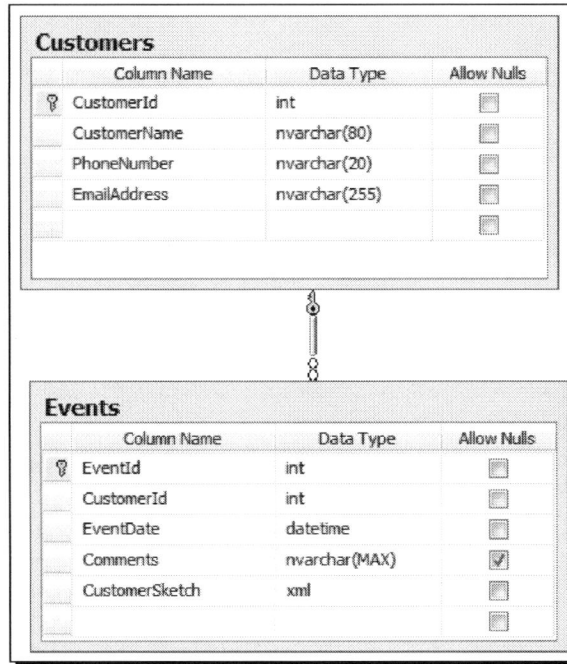

13. Be sure to save your work. If you get an error while saving, that states the **Prevent saving changes that require table re-creation** option is set, you can enable saving changes by going to **Tools|Options|Designers|Table|Database Designers** and un-checking the **Prevent saving changes that require table re-creation** option:

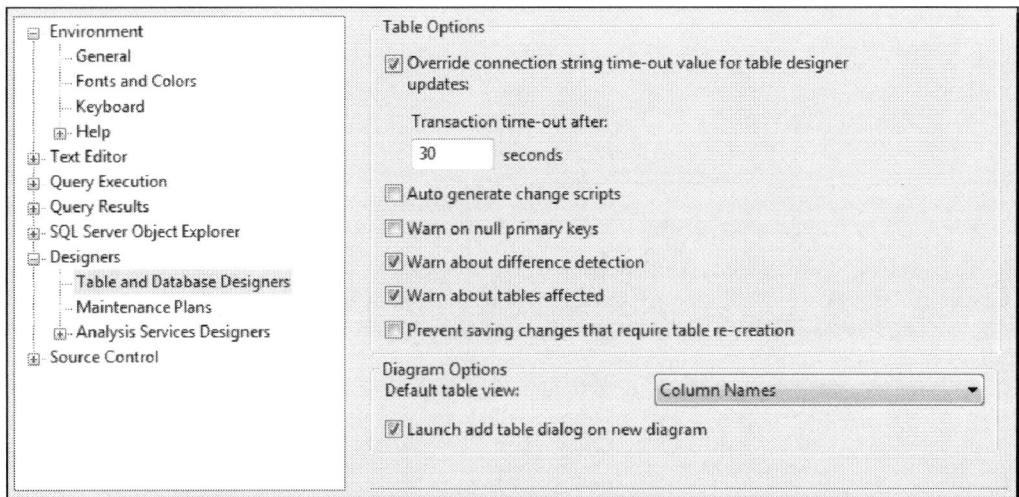

14. Since we added `CustomerSketch` as an XML column we need to also setup the indexes. Select the `CustomerSketch` column of the `Events` table and click on the **Manage XML Indexes** icon:

15. Click the **Add** button on the **XML Indexes** dialog box and add the following Primary XML Index:

⊟ **(General)**	
Columns	CustomerSketch
Is Primary	Yes
Primary Reference Name	
Type	XML
⊞ **Database Designer**	
⊟ **Identity**	
(Name)	XML_IX_Events
Description	

16. While the XML Indexes dialog is still open, add a Secondary XML Index for the **Path**:

⊟ **(General)**	
Columns	CustomerSketch
Is Primary	No
Primary Reference Name	XML_IX_Events
Secondary Type	Path
Type	XML
⊞ **Database Designer**	
⊟ **Identity**	
(Name)	XML_IX_Events_Path
Description	

17. Add another XML Index for **Value** and close the XML Indexes dialog:

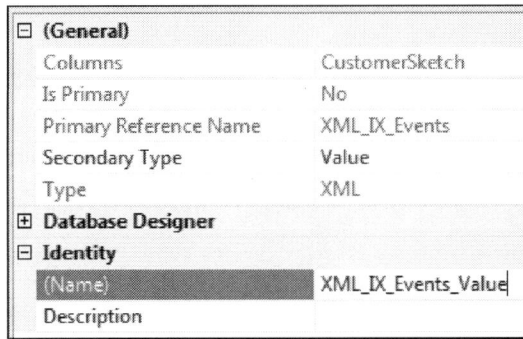

⊟ **(General)**	
Columns	CustomerSketch
Is Primary	No
Primary Reference Name	XML_IX_Events
Secondary Type	Value
Type	XML
⊞ **Database Designer**	
⊟ **Identity**	
(Name)	XML_IX_Events_Value
Description	

> For more information on XML indexes in SQL Server, what they mean and when and how to use them, see the following link: `http://msdn.microsoft.com/en-us/library/ms191497.aspx`.

18. Add a table called **Orders** to the diagram, creating an **OrderId** Primary Key/Identity column and the following additional columns:

Orders

	Column Name	Data Type	Allow Nulls
🔑	OrderId	int	☐
	EventId	int	☐
	OrderDate	datetime	☐
	Cost	money	☐
	OrderDetails	nvarchar(MAX)	☐
	FinalImage	image	☑
	IsPaid	bit	☐
	Status	int	☐
			☐

19. Create a foreign key relationship between the **Orders** and **Events** table on the **EventId** column:

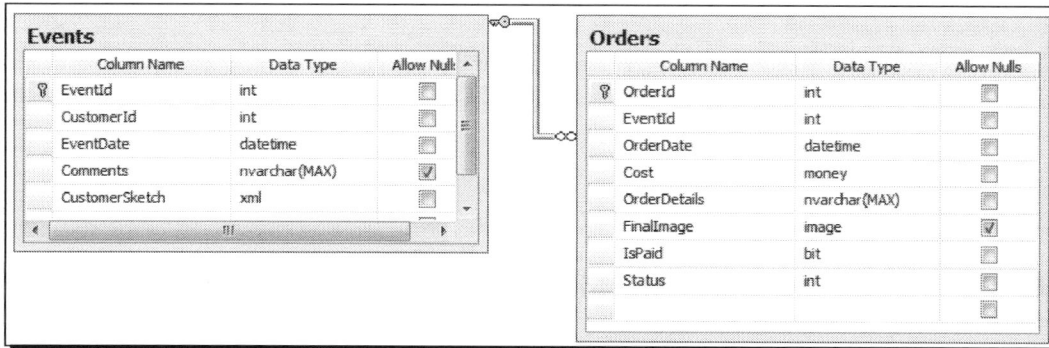

What just happened?

We created a simple data model in SQL Server to house our customer, event, and order information.

We setup the `Events` table to store the event information, including any special comments about the event and the original customer sketch. We also created a relationship to the `Customers` table, so that a customer record can have multiple events.

We set up the `Orders` table to store the final cake image and added an `OrderDetails` column, so that our customer service representative can write out the complete cake order details. We also created a relationship to the `Events` table, so that an event could have multiple cake orders such as a wedding where a bride and groom's cake might be created.

ADO.NET Entity Framework and WCF RIA Services

A common practice when developing data driven business applications is to create a set of classes that reflect the data stored in the database. Most often, developers will create classes that map to each table within a database to keep things as transparent as possible when dealing with large amounts of data.

Microsoft released a lightweight mapping framework called LINQ to SQL, which is basically a one-to-one mapping of .NET classes with database tables. The framework provides mappings to the database tables allowing **Language Integrated Queries (LINQ)** against the .NET classes, which actually query the database and return strongly typed objects that represent the data.

The ADO.NET Entity Framework takes some queues from LINQ to SQL but provides a much more flexible model for mapping tables and data, allowing for multiple table mappings and alternate data sources.

Both LINQ to SQL and the ADO.NET Entity Framework remove a lot of the redundant coding required to perform the **Creation, Retrieval, Updating, and Deletion (CRUD)** of database data and can speed up development of data driven applications in the process.

The WCF RIA Services framework can also take advantage of the Entity Framework classes and will provide a common middle tier for our ASP.NET and Silverlight application we created in Chapter 6.

Time for action – creating the Entity Framework

We will take advantage of the Entity Framework for our Silverlight customer service application and also utilize WCF RIA Services to create domain services and auto-generate client data classes.

We will create our Entity Framework classes from the SQL database that we created in the previous section.

1. Start Visual Studio and open the **CakeORamaApp** solution we created in the previous chapter.

2. Right-click on the **CakeORamaApp.Web** project and choose **Add|New Item**.

3. In the **Add New Item** dialog box, select the **Data** from the **Categories** pane, select the **ADO.NET Entity Data Model** and click **Add**:

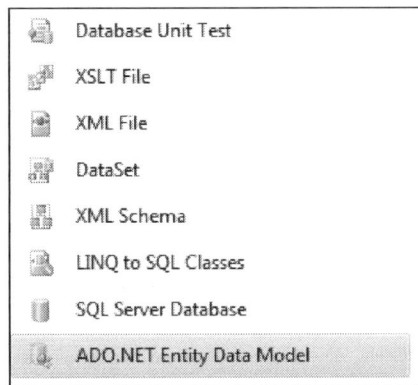

	Database Unit Test
	XSLT File
	XML File
	DataSet
	XML Schema
	LINQ to SQL Classes
	SQL Server Database
	ADO.NET Entity Data Model

4. Name the model **CakeORama** and click on the **Add** button.

5. On the screen that follows ensure that **Generate from database** is selected and click **Next**:

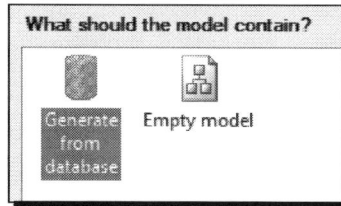

6. On the next screen, choose the **New Connection** button to setup a connection to our new database:

7. Enter the name of your local database server, select the **CakeORama** database and click **OK**:

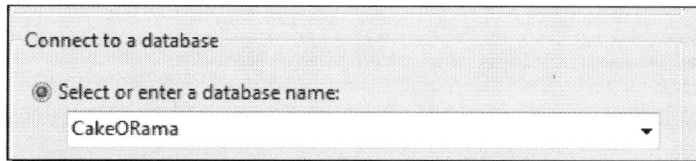

8. When the **New Connection** dialog closes, enter the following options on **Entity Data Model Wizard** and click **Next**:

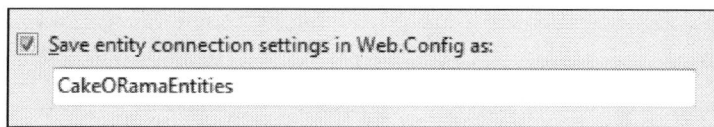

9. On the **Choose Your Database Objects** screen select all of the tables we created in the previous section, ensure that the two checkboxes are checked, change the namespace to **CakeORamaApp**, and click the **Finish** button:

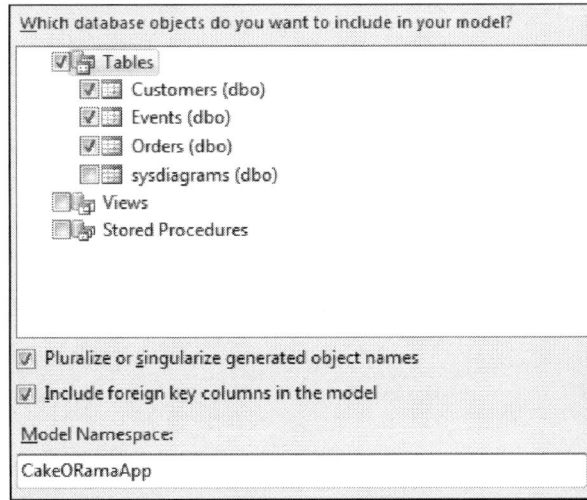

10. Visual Studio will add a new connection string to our `web.config` file and open the data model displaying our entity classes:

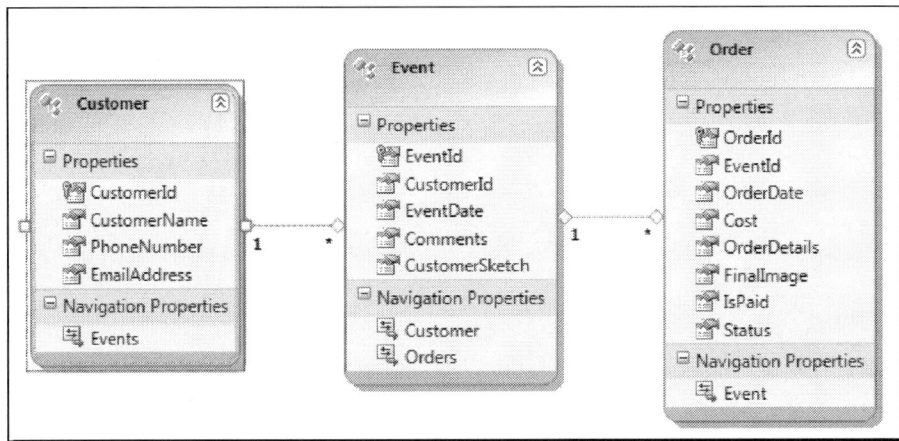

11. The **Mapping Details** and **Model Browser** panels that were also opened with the data model provide the ability to modify the entity details. Build the solution to allow Visual Studio to auto generate the entity classes and associated context objects.

12. We are going to use RIA Services so we need to add a Domain Service object in order to query data from our Silverlight application. Right-click on the **Services** folder in the **CakeORamaApp.Web** project and choose **Add|New Item**. Select **Web** from the **Categories** pane, then choose the **Domain Service Class** from the **Templates** pane, name the service **CustomerService** and click **Add**:

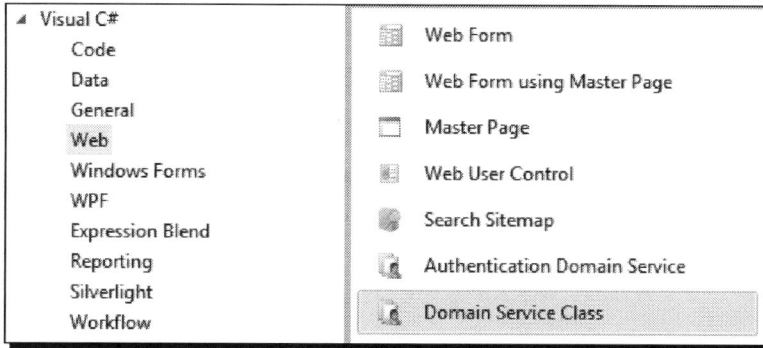

13. On the next screen, select the following information to generate client side classes for the domain service; check **Enable editing** and **Generate associated classes for metadata**, and click **OK**:

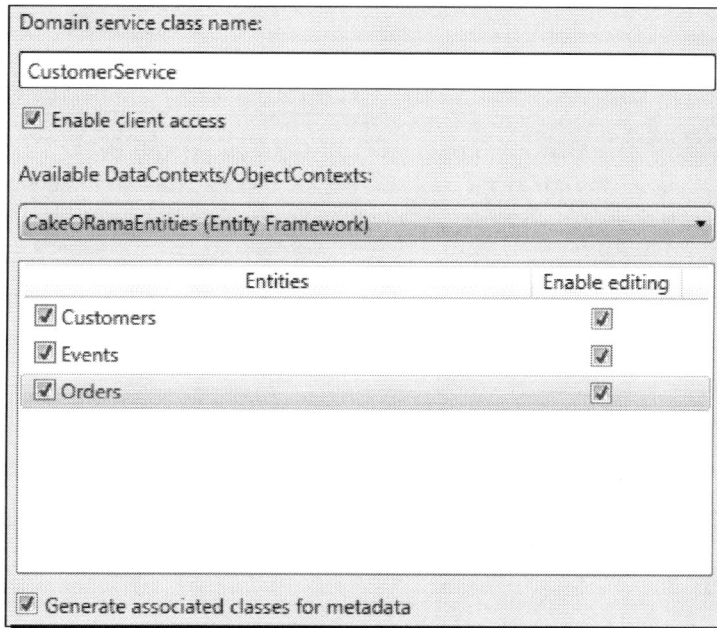

14. Visual Studio generated some basic methods for retrieving, inserting, updating and deleting our records.

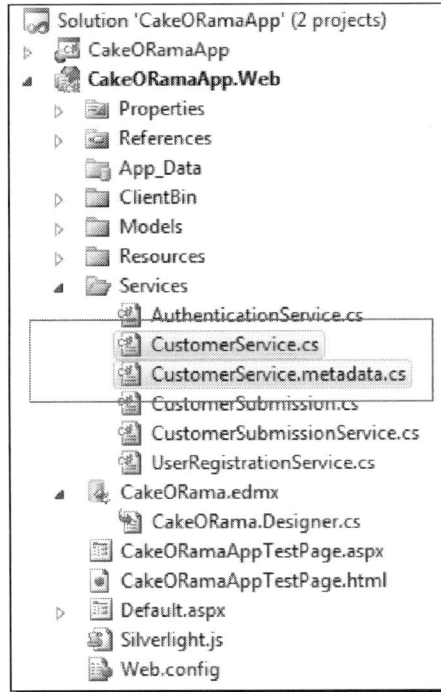

What just happened?

We created entity classes based on our database model using the ADO.NET Entity Framework. Visual Studio auto generated the classes based on the tables which eliminated the need for us to create a bunch of redundant code.

We created a RIA Domain Service for each of our entities allowing us to perform the standard database CRUD operations using our entity classes for transporting data.

We can see that Visual Studio generated entity classes for each of our database tables and for our Domain Service that uses our entity classes. Because we used RIA Services and the ADO.NET Entity Framework we can focus on providing a better user experience instead of spending our time setting up a data layer.

If we take a look at the `Customer` class that was generated, in the `CakeORama.Designer.cs` file, we can see a bunch of attributes and other code used to relate this class to the `Customers` table in our database. Visual Studio even created a property for a collection of `Events` related to a `Customer` record:

```
[XmlIgnoreAttribute()]
[SoapIgnoreAttribute()]
[DataMemberAttribute()]
[EdmRelationshipNavigationPropertyAttribute("CakeORamaApp", "FK_
Events_Customers", "Events")]
public EntityCollection<Event> Events
{
    get
    {
        return ((IEntityWithRelationships)this).RelationshipManager.
GetRelatedCollection<Event>("CakeORamaApp.FK_Events_Customers",
"Events");
    }
    set
    {
        if ((value != null))
        {
            ((IEntityWithRelationships)this).RelationshipManager.
InitializeRelatedCollection<Event>("CakeORamaApp.FK_Events_Customers",
"Events", value);
        }
    }
}
```

Likewise, our `CustomerService` Domain Service class handles our database CRUD operations:

```
public IQueryable<Customer> GetCustomers()
{
  return this.ObjectContext.Customers;
}

public void InsertCustomer(Customer customer)
{
  if ((customer.EntityState != EntityState.Added))
  {
    if ((customer.EntityState != EntityState.Detached))
    {
this.ObjectContext.ObjectStateManager.ChangeObjectState(customer,
EntityState.Added);
    }
```

```
      else
      {
        this.ObjectContext.AddToCustomers(customer);
      }
    }
  }

  public void UpdateCustomer(Customer currentCustomer)
  {
    if ((currentCustomer.EntityState == EntityState.Detached))
    {
      this.ObjectContext.AttachAsModified(currentCustomer, this.
ChangeSet.GetOriginal(currentCustomer));
    }
  }

  public void DeleteCustomer(Customer customer)
  {
    if ((customer.EntityState == EntityState.Detached))
    {
      this.ObjectContext.Attach(customer);
    }
    this.ObjectContext.DeleteObject(customer);
```

User experience

There is a movement in the software community user experience focused design and finding ways to simplify and improve the experience for users of software applications. When designing applications, it is important to always keep in mind the people who will be using the software and how we can make it as intuitive and easy to use as possible. After all, software should improve a process not over-complicate it.

Silverlight can greatly improve the user experience by providing great visuals for a fluid user interface, asynchronous background processing of web requests and the ability to use client memory to load and handle data. With these features we can build a customer service application that will give our users the best possible experience and help them do their jobs more effectively.

Time for action – saving customer information

In Chapter 5, we collected data from customers and created an application to view that customer information. We will now modify this project to allow us to save the customer information to our database and process orders for the customers.

What we want to be able to do here is allow our customer service representative to view a customer's submission, call or email the customer and then have the option to save the customer's information and process an order.

1. The first thing we need to do is install the **Silverlight Toolkit**, which can be found at: `http://www.codeplex.com/Silverlight`. The toolkit will give us some new data controls which we will be used to build our customer service application.

2. Start Expression Blend and open the **CakeORamaApp** solution.

3. Open the `Submissions.xaml` page and add a new textblock with the text value **Comments** and a textbox control named **Comments**:

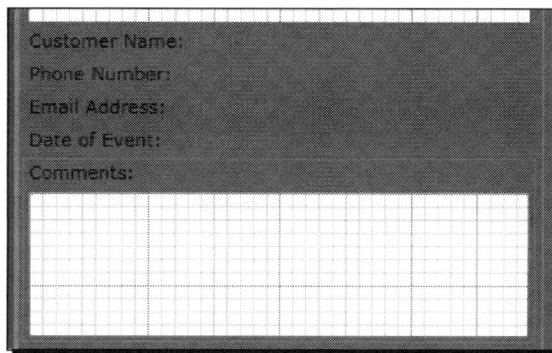

4. Next, we will add a button named `SaveButton` with a `Content` value **Save**. This button will enable just the customer and event information to be saved:

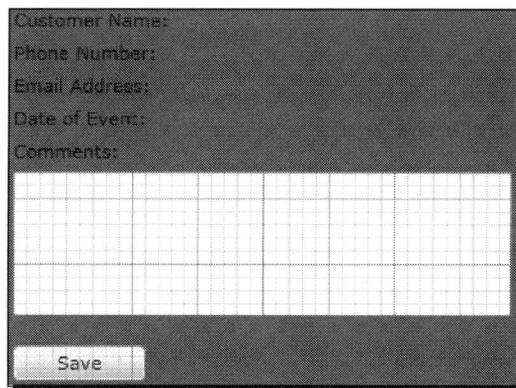

5. We will also add another button named OrderButton with a Content value of **Place Order**. This button will move us to another page (which we will create shortly) that will allow the customer service representative to enter order information for the customer. Set the **Width** of the OrderButton to **100**:

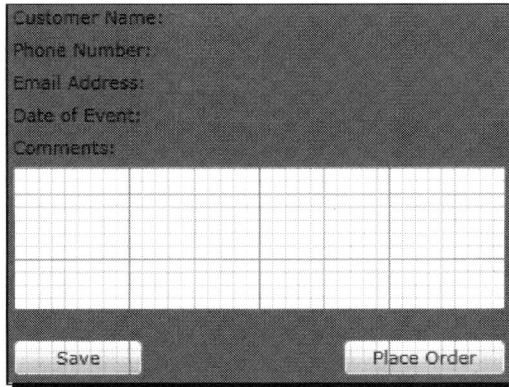

6. Add **Click** event handlers for both buttons:

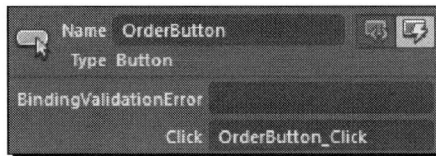

7. Switch over to Visual Studio and open the Submissions.xaml.cs file from the **CakeORamaApp** project.

8. In order to process the currently selected submission we need to add a new private variable to the Submissions class:

```
private CustomerSubmission _currentSubmission;
```

9. Modify the SubmissionList_SelectionChanged event handler to set the _currentSubmission value before setting the labels:

```
private void SubmissionList_SelectionChanged(object sender,
System.Windows.Controls.SelectionChangedEventArgs e)
{
  if (e.AddedItems.Count == 0) return;

  var submission = e.AddedItems[0] as CustomerSubmission;
  if (submission == null) return;

  _currentSubmission = submission;
```

10. Add the `System.Linq` namespace so that we can make use of LINQ to query our data objects:

```
using System.Linq;
```

11. We are going to want our application to have access to the current `Customer` instance and `CustomerContext` no matter what page we navigate to, so we need to create a static class that can contain our current `Customer` instance. Add a new class to the `CakeORamaApp` project called `AppState` and replace the default generated code with the following:

```
using System;
using CakeORamaApp.Web;
using CakeORamaApp.Web.Services;

namespace CakeORamaApp
{
  public static class AppState
  {
    public static CustomerContext CustomerContext { get; set; }
    public static Customer Customer { get; set; }
public static Event CurrentEvent { get; set; }
  }
}
```

12. Add the `CakeORamaApp.Web` namespace at the top of the file:

```
using CakeORamaApp.Web;
```

13. Replace the code in the `OnNavigatedTo` method of the `Submissions` class to the following:

```
if (AppState.CustomerContext == null)
{
  AppState.CustomerContext = new CustomerContext();
  AppState.CustomerContext.Load<Customer>
                  (AppState.CustomerContext.GetCustomersQuery());
  AppState.CustomerContext.Load<Event>
                  (AppState.CustomerContext.GetEventsQuery());
  AppState.CustomerContext.Load<Order>
                  (AppState.CustomerContext.GetOrdersQuery());
}
var context = new CustomerSubmissionContext();
context.Load<CustomerSubmission>(context.GetSubmissionsQuery());
SubmissionList.ItemsSource = context.CustomerSubmissions
```

14. We will create a method to handle saving the customer information that can be used by both the **Save** and **Order** buttons. Add the following private method to the `Submissions` class:

```
private void SaveCustomer(Action<System.Windows.Ria.
SubmitOperation> callbackAction)
{
  // Check to see if a customer record already exists.
  AppState.Customer = AppState.CustomerContext.Customers.Where(c
=> c.CustomerName == _currentSubmission.CustomerName
    && c.EmailAddress == _currentSubmission.Email).
FirstOrDefault();

  if (AppState.Customer == null)
  {
    AppState.Customer = new Customer();
    AppState.CustomerContext.Customers.Add(AppState.Customer);
  }
  // Set the customer data.
  AppState.Customer.CustomerName = _currentSubmission.
CustomerName;
  AppState.Customer.EmailAddress = _currentSubmission.Email;
  AppState.Customer.PhoneNumber = _currentSubmission.PhoneNumber;

  AppState.CurrentEvent = AppState.Customer.Events.Where(ev =>
ev.EventDate.Month == _currentSubmission.EventDate.Month
    && ev.EventDate.Day == _currentSubmission.EventDate.Day
    && ev.EventDate.Year == _currentSubmission.EventDate.Year).
FirstOrDefault();
  if (AppState.CurrentEvent == null)
  {
    AppState.CurrentEvent = new Event();
    AppState.Customer.Events.Add(AppState.CurrentEvent);
  }
  AppState.CurrentEvent.EventDate = _currentSubmission.EventDate;
  AppState.CurrentEvent.CustomerSketch = _currentSubmission.
Strokes;
  AppState.CurrentEvent.Comments = Comments.Text;

  AppState.CustomerContext.SubmitChanges(callbackAction, null);
}
```

15. We will handle the operation for the `SaveButton` by adding the following code to the `SaveButton_Click` event handler:

```
SaveCustomer(new Action<System.Windows.Ria.SubmitOperation>((o) =>
  {
    if (o.HasError)
       MessageBox.Show(String.Concat("Failed to save
customer information.\nError:", o.Error.Message), "Error",
MessageBoxButton.OK);
    else
       MessageBox.Show("Customer information saved successfully.",
"Save Customer Information", MessageBoxButton.OK);
  }));
```

> If you do not see the `CustomerContext` class you may need to build your solution as this causes Visual Studio to auto generate the Silverlight classes for the Domain Service.

16. Open the `CustomerService.cs` file in the `CakeORamaApp.Web` project under the **Services** folder and add the following method:

```
private void RemoveSubmission(Customer customer)
{
  var files = Directory.GetFiles(@"C:\Projects\CakeORama\Customer\
Data\", String.Concat(customer.CustomerName, ".xml"));
  foreach (var file in files)
  {
    var customerRoot = XElement.Load(file);
    var email = customerRoot.Attribute("email").Value;

    if (email == customer.EmailAddress)
    {
      File.Delete(file);
      break;
    }
  }
}
```

17. Modify the `InsertCustomer` method to remove the original customer submission XML file, once this customer record is saved:

```
public void InsertCustomer(Customer customer)
{
  if ((customer.EntityState != EntityState.Added))
  {
    if ((customer.EntityState != EntityState.Detached))
```

```
    {
      this.ObjectContext.ObjectStateManager.ChangeObjectState
                        (customer, EntityState.Added);
    }
    else
    {
      this.ObjectContext.AddToCustomers(customer);
    }
    RemoveSubmission(customer);
  }
}
```

18. Build and run the solution, then select a customer record, enter some comments, and click the **Save** button:

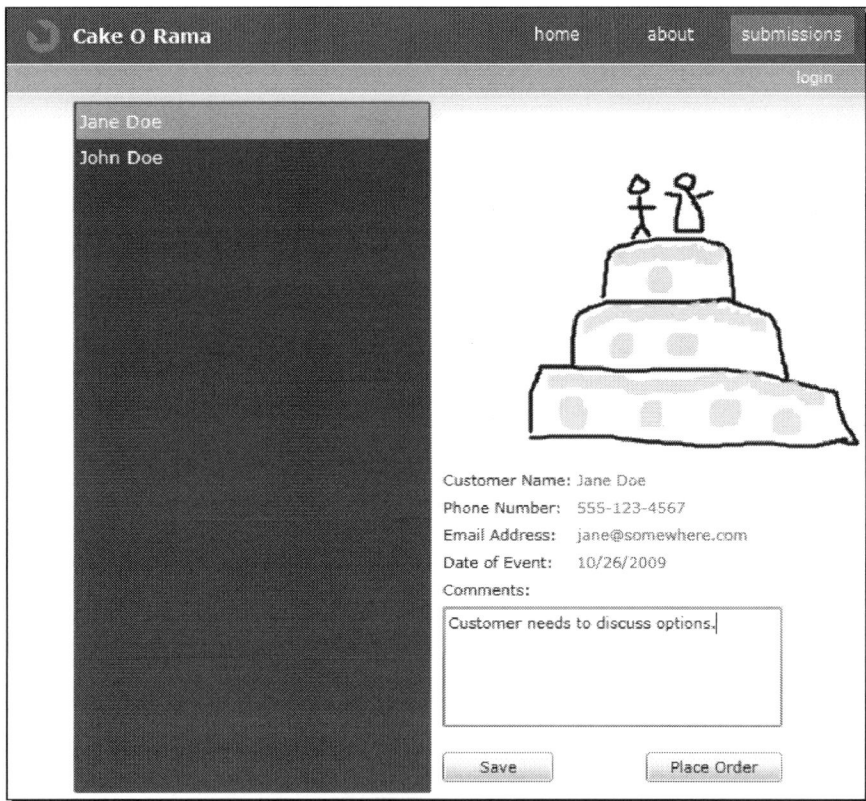

19. If we look in our `CakeORama` database we should see our saved data, with the proper relationship created between the `Events`, `Customers`, and `Orders` tables:

	CustomerId	CustomerName	PhoneNumber	EmailAddress
1	2	Jane Doe	555-123-4567	jane@somewhere.com

	EventId	CustomerId	EventDate	Comments	CustomerSketch
1	1	2	2009-10-26 16:23:31.467	Customer needs to discuss options.	<strokes><stroke width="3" height="3"><color a="...

20. We can also see that the customer submission XML file was removed if we use Windows Explorer to look in the `C:\Projects\CakeORama\Customer\Data` directory.

RIA Services/Entity errors

To catch any errors thrown by the RIA Services or Entity Framework while debugging, we can go to **Debug|Exceptions...** in Visual Studio and put check marks in the **Thrown** column for both the **Common Language Runtime Exceptions** and the **Managed Debugging Assistants** check boxes.

---

21. We need to add a new page to our project to handle accepting orders. In Visual Studio, add a new page to the **Views** folder of the `CakeORamaApp` project named `SubmitOrder.xaml`.

22. Switch over to Expression Blend and open the `SubmitOrder.xaml` page.

23. Click the **Assets** button on the toolbar:

24. In the **search** field, enter **dataform** and then select the **DataForm** control:

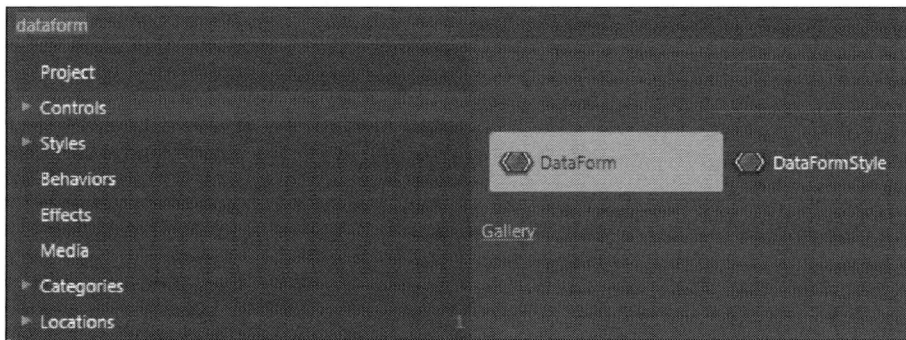

25. Double-click on the **DataForm** icon in the toolbox to add a new instance to the `SubmitOrder.xaml` page and name it **OrderDataForm**:

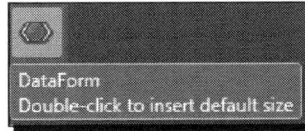

26. Set the dataform to occupy all of the available space by changing the **HorizontalAlignment** and **VerticalAlignment** properties:

27. Ensure that the **AutoGenerateFields** and the **AutoCommit** checkboxes are unchecked under the **Miscellaneous** category:

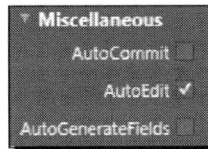

28. On the **OrderDataForm** breadcrumb, select **Edit Additional Templates|Edit EditTemplate|Create Empty...**:

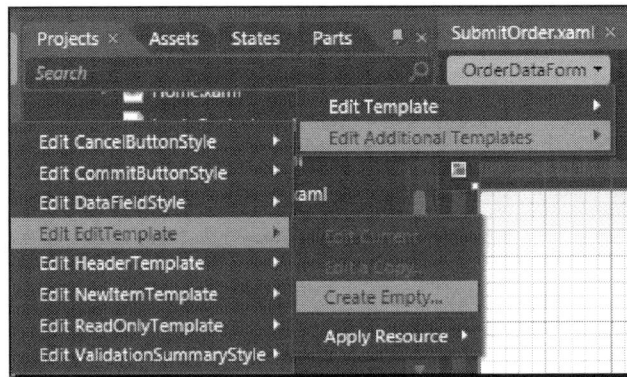

29. Name the template **OrderEditTemplate**, ensure that the **This document** option is selected and click **OK**:

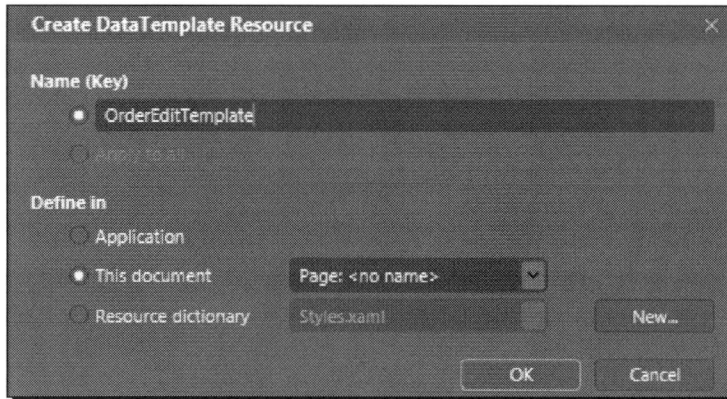

30. Right-click on the **Grid**, choose **Change Layout Type** and then **StackPanel** from the menu to change the default **Grid** panel in the template to a **StackPanel**:

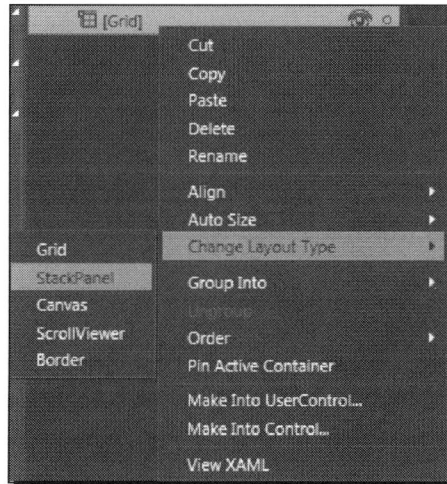

31. Click the **Assets** button on the toolbar, type **datafield** in the search box and select the **DataField** control:

32. Select the **StackPanel** control in the **Objects and Timeline** panel and then double-click the **DataField** toolbar icon to add a new instance of the datafield to the stackpanel.

33. Click the **Assets** button again, and then search for and select a **DatePicker** control:

34. Select the newly added **DataField** from the **Objects and Timeline** panel and then double-click the **DatePicker** icon on the toolbar to add a new instance to the **DataField**.

35. Click on the **Advanced property options** of the **SelectedDate** property of the **DatePicker**:

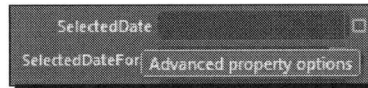

36. Choose **Data Binding...** from the options, set the following values on the **Create Data Binding** dialog box and click **OK**:

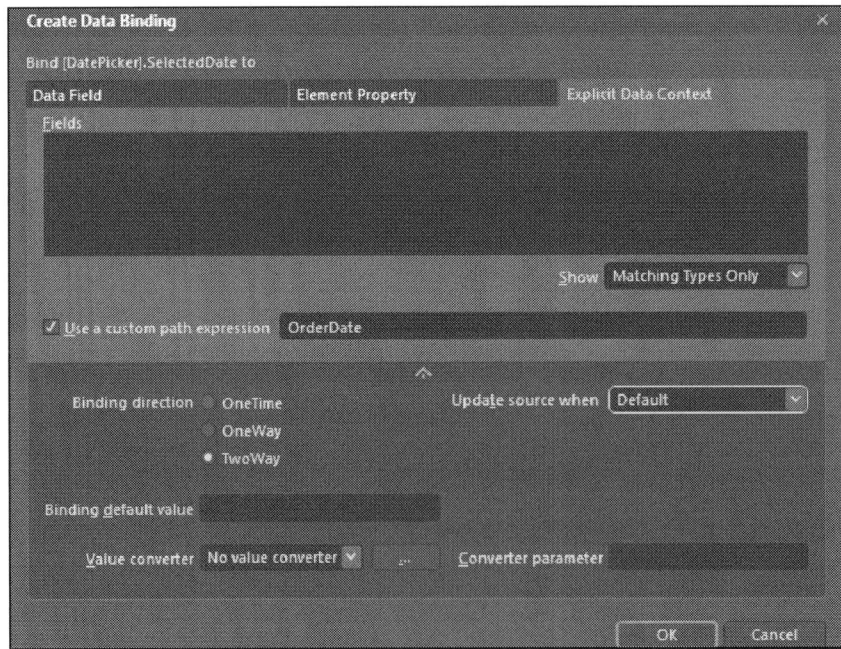

37. On the toolbar, left-click and hold the left mouse button on the **DatePicker** icon to re-select the **DateField**:

38. Select the **StackPanel** from the **Objects and Timeline** panel and double-click the **DataField** icon on the toolbar to add another **DataField** instance.

39. With the newly added **DataField** selected in the **Objects and Timeline** panel, left-click and hold the **Grid** icon on the toolbar and select the **ScrollViewer** control:

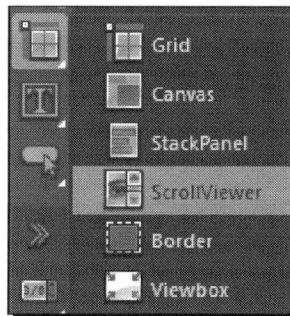

40. Set the **Height** of the ScrollViewer to 200.

41. Double-click the **TextBox** icon on the toolbar to add a new textbox to the ScrollViewer:

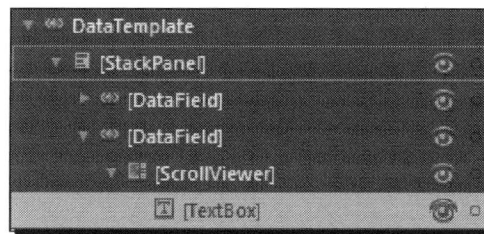

42. In the following screenshot, we **Create Data Binding** of the **TextBox**:

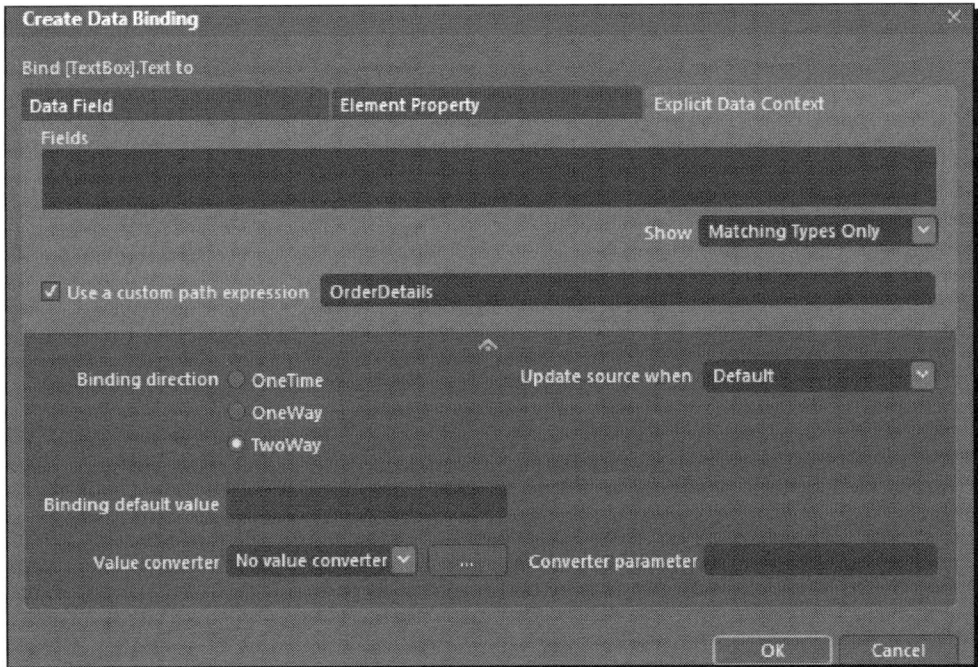

Create Data Binding   ✕

Bind [TextBox].Text to

Data Field	Element Property	Explicit Data Context

Fields

Show Matching Types Only ▾

☑ Use a custom path expression   OrderDetails

∧

Binding direction ○ OneTime   Update source when Default ▾
                   ○ OneWay
                   ● TwoWay

Binding default value

Value converter No value converter ▾   …   Converter parameter

OK   Cancel

43. Add a `DataField` to the `StackPanel`, add a `TextBlock` to the `DataField` and create a Data Binding path expression to **Cost**.

44. Add another `DataField` to the `StackPanel` then click on the **Button** icon on the toolbar, hold the left mouse button down and select the **CheckBox** control:

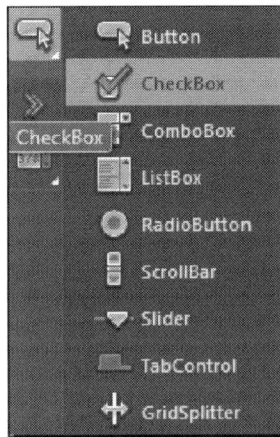

45. Double-click the **CheckBox** icon to add a new checkbox to the `DataField` and then create a Data Binding on the **IsChecked** property with a path expression of **IsPaid**.

46. We now have a custom data form:

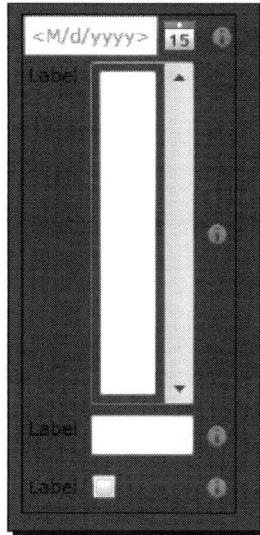

47. We need to customize the label text of our `DataFields` and although the `Label` property is visible in Blend, we cannot edit the value from the **Properties** panel. To edit the labels we will have to switch to XAML mode and hand edit them. Click on the XAML mode icon at the top right of the art board:

48. Add the `Label` property the first `DataField`, setting the value of the property to `Order Details`:

```
<dataFormToolkit:DataField Label="Order Date">
```

49. Set the other `Label` values as follows:

```
<dataFormToolkit:DataField Label="Order Details">
<dataFormToolkit:DataField Label="Cost">
<dataFormToolkit:DataField Label="Is Paid">
```

50. Now our data form looks a little better:

> This code creates a template for the `Edit` mode of the `DataForm` and by customizing the template we can remove unneeded fields such as the `EventId` and `OrderId` properties.

51. Add an event handler to the **EditEnded** event of the **OrderDataForm**:

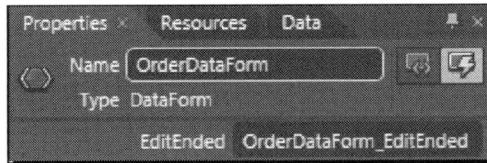

52. Save your work and switch back over to Visual Studio. Open the `Submissions.xaml.cs` file and add the following code to the `OrderButton_Click` event handler:

```
SaveCustomer(new Action<System.Windows.Ria.SubmitOperation>((o) =>
{
    if (o.HasError)
```

```
      MessageBox.Show(String.Concat("Failed to save customer
information.\nError:", o.Error.Message), "Error",
MessageBoxButton.OK);
    else
      this.NavigationService.Navigate(new Uri("/SubmitOrder.xaml",
UriKind.Relative));
}));
```

53. This code will navigate us to the `SubmitOrder.xaml` page as long as there were no errors while saving the customer information.

54. Add a new file to the `CakeORamaApp` project called `OrderStatus.cs` and replace the auto generated code with the following:

```
namespace CakeORamaApp
{
  public enum OrderStatus
  {
    New,
    Pending,
    Cancelled,
    Complete,
  }
}
```

55. Open the `SubmitOrder.xml.cs` file and add the following `using` statements to the top of the file:

```
using CakeORamaApp.Web;
using CakeORamaApp.Web.Services;
```

56. Insert the following code into the `OnNavigatedTo` method:

```
if (AppState.Customer == null || AppState.CurrentEvent == null)
{
  this.NavigationService.Navigate(new Uri("/Submissions", UriKind.
Relative));
  return;
}
var order = new Order
{
  EventId = AppState.CurrentEvent.EventId,
  OrderDate = DateTime.Now,
  Status = (int)OrderStatus.New
};
AppState.CurrentEvent.Orders.Add(order);

OrderDataForm.ItemsSource = AppState.CurrentEvent.Orders;
```

57. In the `OrderDataForm_EditEnded` event handler, insert the following code that will save the current changes and take our users back to the `Submissions.xaml` page, so they can process the next submission:

```
AppState.CustomerContext.SubmitChanges();
this.NavigationService.Navigate(new Uri("/Submissions", UriKind.
Relative));
```

58. Build and run the solution, navigate to the **Submissions** page, select one of the submissions, and click on the **Place Order** button. On the `SubmitOrder` page, enter some details about the **Order** and click on the **OK** button:

Order Date	11/2/2009
Order Details	Three layer chocolate cake with white icing, trimmed in pink roses.
Cost	500
Is Paid	☐

OK   Cancel

59. If we check our database we can see the order details for this customer:

	CustomerId	CustomerName	PhoneNumber	EmailAddress
1	6	Emily Harris	555-555-5555	emily@somewhere.com

	EventId	CustomerId	EventDate	Comments	CustomerSketch
1	5	6	2009-10-04 16:03:41.097	Customer wants a chocolate cake.	<strokes><stroke width="3" height="3"><color a="

	OrderId	EventId	OrderDate	Cost	OrderDetails	FinalImage	IsPaid	Status
1	1	5	2009-11-02 12:24:08.063	500.00	Three layer chocolate cake with white icing, trim...	NULL	0	0

What just happened?

We modified our existing submissions page to handle saving customer information to the database and processing an order for the customer. We made use of the `DataForm` class to simplify the data entry process and took advantage of RIA Services to persist our data to the server.

We also customized the `DataForm EditTemplate` to only display the fields that were relevant to our order entry.

Customer service

To provide the best possible customer service, our representatives should be able to look up customer information by name, phone, or email and be able to find customer details, including events and orders.

We will provide an interface that makes it easy for the customer service representative to quickly locate a customer and sort through their associated events and orders, checking the status of the orders and adding additional comments or corrections.

Using the ADO.NET Entity Framework allows us to load the entities into memory and then as changes are made to them they track their own modification state. Since the entities are tracking their own state, we can do **TwoWay** binding to control elements so that updates persist back to the entities and one save button can handle all of our entity changes.

Time for action – creating a customer lookup form

We saved customer information in the previous section through the submissions interface. However, for our customer service representatives to lookup customer information, we will need to provide a lookup feature and the ability to make changes to existing orders for the current customer.

We will make use of a variety of controls from `DatePicker` to `ListBox` to `Expander`, and perform TwoWay data binding of our `Customer` entity. Because of the relationship between `Customer` and `Event` entities and the relationship between `Event` and `Order` entities, we can make a drill down type of form using listboxes that implement custom `ItemTemplates`. To do this, we will need to complete the following steps:

1. Start Visual Studio, open the `CakeORamaApp` solution, right-click on the **CakeORamaApp** project and select **Add|New Item** and choose a **Silverlight Page** named `CustomerSearch.xaml`:

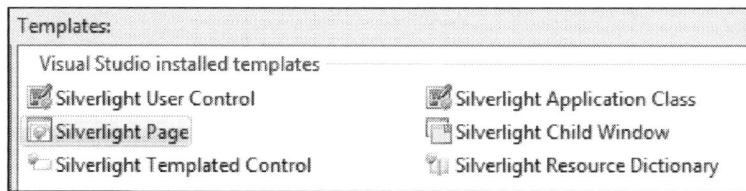

Templates:

Visual Studio installed templates

Silverlight User Control	Silverlight Application Class
Silverlight Page	Silverlight Child Window
Silverlight Templated Control	Silverlight Resource Dictionary

2. Drag the `CustomerSearch.xaml` file into the **Views** folder.

3. Open the `MainPage.xaml` file and add the following code just after the `submissions` navigation link:

```
<Rectangle x:Name="Divider3" Style="{StaticResource
DividerStyle}"/>


<HyperlinkButton x:Name="Link4" Style="{StaticResource LinkStyle}"
        NavigateUri="/CustomerSearch" TargetName="ContentFram
e" Content="find customers"/>
```

4. Open the `CustomerSearch.xaml` file for editing in Visual Studio and replace the contents of the file with the following XAML:

```
<navigation:Page x:Class="CakeORamaApp.CustomerSearch"
        xmlns="http://schemas.microsoft.com/winfx/2006/xaml/
presentation"
        xmlns:x="http://schemas.microsoft.com/winfx/2006/xaml"
        xmlns:d="http://schemas.microsoft.com/expression/
blend/2008"
        xmlns:mc="http://schemas.openxmlformats.org/markup-
compatibility/2006"
        mc:Ignorable="d"
        xmlns:navigation="clr-namespace:System.Windows.
Controls;assembly=System.Windows.Controls.Navigation"
        d:DesignWidth="640" d:DesignHeight="480"
        Title="CustomerSearch Page">
  <navigation:Page.Resources>
    <DataTemplate x:Key="CustomerListItemTemplate">
      <Grid>
        <TextBlock Text="{Binding CustomerName, Mode=OneWay}"
TextWrapping="Wrap" d:LayoutOverrides="Width, Height"/>
      </Grid>
    </DataTemplate>
  </navigation:Page.Resources>
    <Grid x:Name="LayoutRoot">
    <TextBlock HorizontalAlignment="Left"
VerticalAlignment="Top" Text="Find Customers" FontSize="21.333"
TextWrapping="Wrap" Foreground="#FF4583CD" FontWeight="Bold"/>
    <TextBlock x:Name="AlertLabel" VerticalAlignment="Top"
TextWrapping="Wrap" Margin="0,35,304,0" Foreground="#FFD81A1A"
FontWeight="Bold" FontSize="16"/>
    <TextBlock HorizontalAlignment="Left"
VerticalAlignment="Top" Text="Customer Name:" TextWrapping="Wrap"
Margin="0,64,0,0"/>
    <TextBlock HorizontalAlignment="Left" Margin="11,92,0,0"
VerticalAlignment="Top" Text="Email Address:"
TextWrapping="Wrap"/>
```

```xml
    <TextBlock HorizontalAlignment="Left" Margin="7,120,0,0"
VerticalAlignment="Top" Text="Phone Number:" TextWrapping="Wrap"/>
    <TextBox x:Name="CustomerName" VerticalAlignment="Top"
TextWrapping="Wrap" Margin="98,64,304,0" Width="238"/>
    <TextBox x:Name="EmailAddress" Margin="98,92,304,0"
VerticalAlignment="Top" TextWrapping="Wrap" Width="238"/>
    <TextBox x:Name="PhoneNumber" Margin="98,120,304,0"
VerticalAlignment="Top" TextWrapping="Wrap" Width="238"/>
    <Button x:Name="SearchButton" VerticalAlignment="Top"
Content="Search" Margin="261,160,304,0" Click="SearchButton_Click"
Width="75"/>
    <Border BorderBrush="Black" BorderThickness="1"
Margin="0,186,304,0" CornerRadius="4">
        <ListBox x:Name="CustomerList" Background="{x:Null}"
BorderBrush="{x:Null}" FontSize="14.667" ItemTemplate="{StaticRes
ource CustomerListItemTemplate}" SelectionChanged="CustomerList_
SelectionChanged"/>
    </Border>

    </Grid>
</navigation:Page>
```

5. Open the `CustomerSearch.xaml.cs` file and replace the contents with the following code:

```csharp
using System;
using System.Linq;
using System.Windows.Controls;
using System.Windows.Navigation;
using CakeORamaApp.Web;

namespace CakeORamaApp
{
  public partial class CustomerSearch : Page
  {
    public CustomerSearch()
    {
      InitializeComponent();
    }

    // Executes when the user navigates to this page.
    protected override void OnNavigatedTo(NavigationEventArgs e)
    {
      if (AppState.CustomerContext == null)
      {
        AppState.CustomerContext = new CustomerContext();
        AppState.CustomerContext.Load<Customer>(AppState.
CustomerContext.GetCustomersQuery());
```

```
        AppState.CustomerContext.Load<Event>(AppState.
CustomerContext.GetEventsQuery());
        AppState.CustomerContext.Load<Order>(AppState.
CustomerContext.GetOrdersQuery());
    }
  }

    private void SearchButton_Click(object sender, System.Windows.
RoutedEventArgs e)
    {
      var name = CustomerName.Text;
      var email = EmailAddress.Text;
      var phone = PhoneNumber.Text;

      var customers = AppState.CustomerContext.Customers.Where(c
=>
        (!String.IsNullOrEmpty(name) && c.CustomerName.ToLower().
Contains(name))
        || (!String.IsNullOrEmpty(email) && c.EmailAddress.
Equals(email))
        || (!String.IsNullOrEmpty(phone) && c.PhoneNumber.
Equals(phone)));
      if (customers.Count() == 0)
      {
        AlertLabel.Text = "No customer records found.";
        return;
      }

      CustomerList.ItemsSource = customers;
    }

    private void CustomerList_SelectionChanged(object sender,
System.Windows.Controls.SelectionChangedEventArgs e)
    {
      if (e.AddedItems.Count == 0)
        return;

      var customer = e.AddedItems[0] as Customer;
      if (customer == null)
        return;

      AppState.Customer = customer;

      this.NavigationService.Navigate(new Uri("/CustomerDetails",
UriKind.Relative));
    }
  }
}
```

6. Build and run the solution; click on the **Find Customers** link and we should be presented with the following form:

7. Add a new folder to the CakeORamaApp project called **Converters** and then add a new file called StatusListConverter.cs to the folder.

8. Replace the body of the StatusListConverter.cs file with the following:

```
using System;
using System.Collections.Generic;
using System.Reflection;
using System.Windows.Controls;
using System.Windows.Data;

namespace CakeORamaApp.Converters
{
  public class StatusListConverter : IValueConverter
  {
    #region IValueConverter Members

    public object Convert(object value, Type targetType, object
parameter, System.Globalization.CultureInfo culture)
    {
      if (value == null)
        return null;
```

```
        int result;
        Int32.TryParse(value.ToString(), out result);

        var items = new List<ComboBoxItem>();
        var fields = typeof(OrderStatus).GetFields(BindingFlags.
Public | BindingFlags.Static);
        foreach (var field in fields)
        {
            items.Add(new ComboBoxItem { Content = field.Name,
IsSelected = (result == (int)field.GetValue(null)) });
        }
        return items;
    }

    public object ConvertBack(object value, Type targetType,
object parameter, System.Globalization.CultureInfo culture)
    {
        if (value == null)
          return 0;

        var status = (OrderStatus)Enum.Parse(typeof(OrderStatus),
value.ToString(), true);
        return (int)status;
    }
    #endregion
  }
}
```

> We just setup a class that implemented IValueConverter,
> which provides us with a simple value to convert data bound
> values into other types.

9. Open the `Styles.xaml` file found in the **Assets** folder and add the following namespace to the top of the file:

```
xmlns:converters="clr-namespace:CakeORamaApp.Converters"
```

10. Add the following reference at the top of the **Resources** section:

```
<converters:StatusListConverter x:Key="StatusListConverter"/>
```

11. Add a new **Silverlight Page** called `CustomerDetails.xaml` to the `CakeORamaApp` project and drag the file into the **Views** folder.

12. Add a reference the `System.Windows.Controls.Toolkit` assembly to gain access to some additional Silverlight controls such as the `Extender` control.

13. Replace the body of the CustomerDetails.xaml file with the following code:

```
<navigation:Page
            xmlns="http://schemas.microsoft.com/winfx/2006/xaml/
presentation"
            xmlns:x="http://schemas.microsoft.com/winfx/2006/xaml"
            xmlns:d="http://schemas.microsoft.com/expression/
blend/2008"
            xmlns:mc="http://schemas.openxmlformats.org/markup-
compatibility/2006"
            mc:Ignorable="d"
            xmlns:controls="clr-namespace:System.Windows.
Controls;assembly=System.Windows.Controls"
        xmlns:navigation="clr-namespace:System.Windows.
Controls;assembly=System.Windows.Controls.Navigation"
            xmlns:dataFormToolkit="clr-namespace:System.
Windows.Controls;assembly=System.Windows.Controls.Data.
DataForm.Toolkit" xmlns:controlsToolkit="clr-namespace:System.
Windows.Controls;assembly=System.Windows.Controls.Toolkit" x:
Class="CakeORamaApp.CustomerDetails"
            d:DesignWidth="640" d:DesignHeight="480"
            Title="CustomerDetails Page">
  <navigation:Page.Resources>
    <DataTemplate x:Key="OrderItemTemplate">
      <StackPanel>
        <controlsToolkit:Expander d:LayoutOverrides="Width"
Header="{Binding OrderDate, Mode=TwoWay, UpdateSourceTrigger=Defau
lt}">
          <Grid>
            <TextBlock HorizontalAlignment="Left" Margin="0,8,0,0"
VerticalAlignment="Top" Text="Order Date:" TextWrapping="Wrap"/>
            <controls:DatePicker Height="26" Margin="70,8,0,0"
VerticalAlignment="Top" SelectedDate="{Binding OrderDate,
Mode=TwoWay, UpdateSourceTrigger=Default}" HorizontalAlignment="Le
ft" Width="124"/>
            <TextBlock HorizontalAlignment="Left"
 Margin="0,82,0,0" VerticalAlignment="Top" Text="Details:"
TextWrapping="Wrap"/>
            <ScrollViewer Margin="0,102,0,0" Height="100">
              <TextBox Text="{Binding OrderDetails, Mode=TwoWay,
UpdateSourceTrigger=Default}" TextWrapping="Wrap"/>
            </ScrollViewer>
            <TextBlock HorizontalAlignment="Left"
 Margin="0,49,0,0" VerticalAlignment="Top" Text="Status:"
TextWrapping="Wrap"/>
```

```xml
            <ComboBox HorizontalAlignment="Left"
 Margin="44,49,0,0" VerticalAlignment="Top" Width="150"
ItemsSource="{Binding Status, Mode=TwoWay, UpdateSourceTrigger=Def
ault, Converter={StaticResource StatusListConverter}}"/>
            <CheckBox Margin="213,49,175,0"
VerticalAlignment="Top" Content="Is Paid" IsChecked="{Binding
IsPaid, Mode=TwoWay, UpdateSourceTrigger=Default}" d:
LayoutOverrides="Width" HorizontalAlignment="Left"/>
            <TextBlock Margin="213,8,159,0"
VerticalAlignment="Top" Text="Cost:" TextWrapping="Wrap" Horizonta
lAlignment="Left"/>
            <TextBox HorizontalAlignment="Left" Margin="250,8,0,0"
VerticalAlignment="Top" Text="{Binding Cost, Mode=TwoWay, UpdateSo
urceTrigger=Default}" TextWrapping="Wrap" Width="104"/>
          </Grid>
        </controlsToolkit:Expander>
      </StackPanel>
    </DataTemplate>
    <DataTemplate x:Key="EventItemTemplate">
      <controlsToolkit:Expander Header="{Binding EventDate,
Mode=TwoWay}" d:DesignWidth="208" d:DesignHeight="288">
        <StackPanel Margin="0">
          <StackPanel Orientation="Horizontal">
            <TextBlock HorizontalAlignment="Right"
Margin="0,0,8,0" VerticalAlignment="Top" Text="Event Date:"
TextWrapping="Wrap"/>
            <controls:DatePicker Height="26" Margin="0"
VerticalAlignment="Top" SelectedDate="{Binding EventDate,
Mode=TwoWay, UpdateSourceTrigger=Default}" HorizontalAlignment="Ri
ght" Width="206"/>
          </StackPanel>
          <TextBlock HorizontalAlignment="Left" Margin="0"
VerticalAlignment="Top" Text="Comments:" TextWrapping="Wrap"/>
          <ScrollViewer Margin="0" Height="100" d:LayoutOver
rides="VerticalAlignment, Height" HorizontalAlignment="Left"
Width="206">
            <TextBox Text="{Binding Comments, Mode=TwoWay, UpdateS
ourceTrigger=Default}"/>
          </ScrollViewer>
          <controlsToolkit:Expander HorizontalAlignment="Stretch"
Header="ORDERS">
            <ListBox HorizontalAlignment="Stretch" VerticalAlign
ment="Stretch" ItemTemplate="{StaticResource OrderItemTemplate}"
ItemsSource="{Binding Orders}" Background="{x:Null}"
BorderBrush="{x:Null}"/>
          </controlsToolkit:Expander>
        </StackPanel>
```

```
        </controlsToolkit:Expander>
</DataTemplate>
<Style x:Key="EventListContainerStyle"
 TargetType="ListBoxItem">
  <Setter Property="Padding" Value="3"/>
  <Setter Property="HorizontalContentAlignment" Value="Left"/>
  <Setter Property="VerticalContentAlignment" Value="Top"/>
  <Setter Property="Background" Value="Transparent"/>
  <Setter Property="BorderThickness" Value="1"/>
  <Setter Property="TabNavigation" Value="Local"/>
  <Setter Property="Template">
    <Setter.Value>
      <ControlTemplate TargetType="ListBoxItem">
        <ScrollViewer Height="300">
          <Grid Background="{TemplateBinding Background}">
            <VisualStateManager.VisualStateGroups>
              <VisualStateGroup x:Name="CommonStates">
                <VisualState x:Name="Normal"/>
                <VisualState x:Name="MouseOver">
                  <Storyboard>
                    <DoubleAnimationUsingKeyFrames
                     Storyboard.TargetName="fillColor"
                     Storyboard.TargetProperty="Opacity">
                    <SplineDoubleKeyFrame KeyTime="0"
                                          Value=".35"/>
                    </DoubleAnimationUsingKeyFrames>
                  </Storyboard>
                </VisualState>
                <VisualState x:Name="Disabled">
                  <Storyboard>
                    <DoubleAnimationUsingKeyFrames
                     Storyboard.TargetName="contentPresenter"
                     Storyboard.TargetProperty="Opacity">
                    <SplineDoubleKeyFrame KeyTime="0"
                                          Value=".55"/>
                    </DoubleAnimationUsingKeyFrames>
                  </Storyboard>
                </VisualState>
              </VisualStateGroup>
              <VisualStateGroup x:Name="SelectionStates">
                <VisualState x:Name="Unselected"/>
                <VisualState x:Name="Selected">
                  <Storyboard>
```

```
      <DoubleAnimationUsingKeyFrames
        Storyboard.TargetName="fillColor2"
        Storyboard.TargetProperty="Opacity">
      <SplineDoubleKeyFrame KeyTime="0"
                            Value=".75"/>
      </DoubleAnimationUsingKeyFrames>
      </Storyboard>
  </VisualState>
  </VisualStateGroup>
  <VisualStateGroup x:Name="FocusStates">
    <VisualState x:Name="Focused">
      <Storyboard>
        <ObjectAnimationUsingKeyFrames
        Duration="0"
        Storyboard.TargetName=
          "FocusVisualElement"
        Storyboard.TargetProperty="Visibility">
          <DiscreteObjectKeyFrame KeyTime="0">
          <DiscreteObjectKeyFrame.Value>
            <Visibility>Visible</Visibility>
          </DiscreteObjectKeyFrame.Value>
          </DiscreteObjectKeyFrame>
        </ObjectAnimationUsingKeyFrames>
      </Storyboard>
    </VisualState>
    <VisualState x:Name="Unfocused"/>
  </VisualStateGroup>
  </VisualStateManager.VisualStateGroups>
  <Rectangle x:Name="fillColor"
   Fill="#FFBADDE9"
   RadiusX="1" RadiusY="1"
   IsHitTestVisible="False" Opacity="0"/>
  <Rectangle x:Name="fillColor2"
       Fill="#FFBADDE9"
   RadiusX="1" RadiusY="1"
   IsHitTestVisible="False" Opacity="0"/>
  <ContentPresenter x:Name="contentPresenter"
   HorizontalAlignment="{TemplateBinding
   HorizontalContentAlignment}"
   Margin="{TemplateBinding Padding}"
   Content="{TemplateBinding Content}"
   ContentTemplate="{TemplateBinding
   ContentTemplate}"/>
  <Rectangle x:Name="FocusVisualElement"
   Stroke="#FF6DBDD1" StrokeThickness="1"
   RadiusX="1" RadiusY="1"
   Visibility="Collapsed"/>
```

```
            </Grid>
          </ScrollViewer>
        </ControlTemplate>
      </Setter.Value>
    </Setter>
  </Style>
</navigation:Page.Resources>
<Grid>
  <TextBlock HorizontalAlignment="Left" Text="Customer Details"
TextWrapping="Wrap" Foreground="#FF4583CD" FontWeight="Bold"
FontSize="18" VerticalAlignment="Top" d:LayoutOverrides="Horizonta
lAlignment"/>
  <TextBlock HorizontalAlignment="Left" Margin="0,30,0,0"
VerticalAlignment="Top" Text="Customer Name:"
TextWrapping="Wrap"/>
  <TextBlock HorizontalAlignment="Left" Margin="7,58,0,0"
VerticalAlignment="Top" Text="Phone Number:" TextWrapping="Wrap"/>
  <TextBlock HorizontalAlignment="Left" Margin="11,86,0,0"
VerticalAlignment="Top" Text="Email Address:"
TextWrapping="Wrap"/>
  <TextBox HorizontalAlignment="Left" Margin="98,30,0,0"
VerticalAlignment="Top" Width="222" Text="{Binding CustomerName,
Mode=TwoWay, UpdateSourceTrigger=Default}" TextWrapping="Wrap"/>
  <TextBox HorizontalAlignment="Left" Margin="98,58,0,0"
VerticalAlignment="Top" Width="222" Text="{Binding PhoneNumber,
Mode=TwoWay, UpdateSourceTrigger=Default}" TextWrapping="Wrap"/>
  <TextBox HorizontalAlignment="Left" Margin="98,86,0,0"
VerticalAlignment="Top" Width="222" Text="{Binding EmailAddress,
Mode=TwoWay, UpdateSourceTrigger=Default}" TextWrapping="Wrap"/>
  <ListBox x:Name="EventsList" Background="{x:
Null}" Margin="0,149,0,8" ItemTemplate="{StaticResource
EventItemTemplate}" ItemsSource="{Binding Events, Mode=OneWay,
UpdateSourceTrigger=Default}" ItemContainerStyle="{StaticResource
EventListContainerStyle}"/>
  <TextBlock HorizontalAlignment="Left" Margin="0,128,0,0"
VerticalAlignment="Top" Text="EVENTS" TextWrapping="Wrap"
FontWeight="Bold" FontSize="12"/>
  <Button Margin="350,86,0,0" x:Name="SaveButton" Content="Save
Customer Details" Click="SaveButton_Click" HorizontalAlignment="Le
ft" VerticalAlignment="Top" Width="140" Height="28"/>
  </Grid>
</navigation:Page>
```

14. Replace the code in the `CustomerDetails.xaml.cs` file with the following code to bind the currently selected `Customer` instance and handle saving the modified entities:

```
using System;
using System.Windows;
using System.Windows.Controls;
using System.Windows.Navigation;
using CakeORamaApp.Web;
using CakeORamaApp.Web.Services;

namespace CakeORamaApp
{
  public partial class CustomerDetails : Page
  {
    public CustomerDetails()
    {
      InitializeComponent();
    }

    // Executes when the user navigates to this page.
    protected override void OnNavigatedTo(NavigationEventArgs e)
    {
      if (AppState.CustomerContext == null)
      {
      AppState.CustomerContext = new CustomerContext();
        AppState.CustomerContext.Load<Customer>(AppState.
        CustomerContext.GetCustomersQuery());
        AppState.CustomerContext.Load<Event>(AppState.
        CustomerContext.GetEventsQuery());
        AppState.CustomerContext.Load<Order>(AppState.
        CustomerContext.GetOrdersQuery());
      }

      this.DataContext = AppState.Customer;
    }

    private void SaveButton_Click(object sender,
    RoutedEventArgs e)
    {
      AppState.CustomerContext.SubmitChanges(new Action<System.
      Windows.Ria.SubmitOperation>((o) =>
        {
          if (o.HasError)
```

```
            MessageBox.Show(String.Concat("Failed to save
customer information.\nError:", o.Error.Message), "Error",
MessageBoxButton.OK);
            else
            MessageBox.Show("Customer information saved
successfully.", "Save Customer Information", MessageBoxButton.OK);
            }), null);
        }
    }
}
```

15. If we build and run the solution, we can make changes to our customer information that will be persisted to the database. Try performing a search for one of our existing customers and make a change to the phone number of the customer. Click on the **Save Customer Details** button when you are finished:

16. If we go back to the **Find Customers** page and perform the search again, we can see that our entity record has persisted to the database:

> **Customer Details**
>
> Customer Name: Emily Harris
>
> Phone Number: 555-555-1224
>
> Email Address: emily@somewhere.com

What just happened?

We created a complex form containing several listbox controls with custom `ItemTemplate` definitions that made use of `Expander` controls to present the information to the user in a way that allowed them to view segments of the information at a time, reducing screen clutter.

We used TwoWay data binding to ensure that information that was changed on screen would persist to our entity classes. We created a custom `IValueConverter` class to convert the `Status` integer value of the `Order` class to a list of the `OrderStatus` values.

Along the way we made good use of the ADO.NET Entity Framework and RIA Services to utilize a common middle tier that retrieves and persists data to a SQL Server database.

Have a go hero – adding data validation to our customer details form

Now that we have created a form for entering and saving customer details, we should provide some validation of the data utilizing some of the methods we learned in Chapter 5.

We will make use of the `Validation` attributes and the metadata class created with our RIA Services Domain Service to provide basic data validation for our objects now.

1. Start Visual Studio and open the `CakeORamaApp` solution. In the **CakeORamaApp. Web** project, open the `CustomerService.metadata.cs` file under the **Services** folder.

2. Modify the `Customer` class to include the following attributes:

```
[MetadataTypeAttribute(typeof(Customer.CustomerMetadata))]
public partial class Customer
{
  internal sealed class CustomerMetadata
  {
    // Metadata classes are not meant to be instantiated.
    private CustomerMetadata()
```

```
    {
    }

    public int CustomerId;

    [Required(ErrorMessage="Customer name is required.")]
    public string CustomerName;

    [Required(ErrorMessage = "Email address is required.")]
    [RegularExpression(@"^([\w\-\.]+)@((\[([0-9]{1,3}\.){3}[0-
9]{1,3}\])|(([\w\-]+\.)+)([a-zA-Z]{2,4}))$",
    ErrorMessage = "A valid email address must be in the format
user@domain.com.")]
    public string EmailAddress;

    public EntityState EntityState;

    public EntityCollection<Event> Events;

    [Required(ErrorMessage = "Phone number is required.")]
    [RegularExpression(@"((\(\d{3}\) ?)|(\d{3}-))?\d{3}-\d{4}",
    ErrorMessage = "A valid phone number must be in the format
(XXX) XXX-XXXX or XXX-XXX-XXXX.")]
    public string PhoneNumber;
  }
}
```

> These attributes are used by the **Validation Engine** to validate the values of the properties.

3. Open the CustomerDetails.xaml file and modify the Customer field XAML as follows (adding x:Name values to each control and adding the NotifyOnValidationError=True and ValidatesOnExceptions=True to the binding):

```
<TextBox x:Name="CustomerNameTextBox" HorizontalAlignment="L
eft" Margin="98,30,0,0" VerticalAlignment="Top" Width="222"
Text="{Binding CustomerName, Mode=TwoWay, UpdateSourceTrigger=Def
ault, NotifyOnValidationError=True, ValidatesOnExceptions=True }"
TextWrapping="Wrap"/>
<TextBox x:Name="PhoneNumberTextBox" HorizontalAlignment="L
eft" Margin="98,58,0,0" VerticalAlignment="Top" Width="222"
Text="{Binding PhoneNumber, Mode=TwoWay, UpdateSourceTrigger=Defa
ult, NotifyOnValidationError=True, ValidatesOnExceptions=True }"
TextWrapping="Wrap"/>
```

```
<TextBox x:Name="EmailAddressTextBox" HorizontalAlignment="L
eft" Margin="98,86,0,0" VerticalAlignment="Top" Width="222"
Text="{Binding EmailAddress, Mode=TwoWay, UpdateSourceTrigger=Def
ault, NotifyOnValidationError=True, ValidatesOnExceptions=True }"
TextWrapping="Wrap"/>
```

4. Modify the `SaveButton_Click` method of the `CustomerDetails.xaml.cs` file as follows to perform a validation check before submitting the values:

```
private void SaveButton_Click(object sender, RoutedEventArgs e)
{
  if (Validation.GetHasError(CustomerNameTextBox)
    || Validation.GetHasError(PhoneNumberTextBox)
    || Validation.GetHasError(EmailAddressTextBox))
  {
    // Do not submit changes...
    return;
  }
  AppState.CustomerContext.SubmitChanges(new Action<System.
Windows.Ria.Data.SubmitOperation>((o) =>
    {
      if (o.HasError)
        MessageBox.Show(String.Concat("Failed to save
customer information.\nError:", o.Error.Message), "Error",
MessageBoxButton.OK);
      else
        MessageBox.Show("Customer information saved
successfully.", "Save Customer Information", MessageBoxButton.OK);
    }), null);
}
```

5. Run the solution without debugging (*Ctrl + F5*); otherwise Visual Studio will break on the validation exceptions. On the home page, choose **Find Customers** and enter information regarding one of the customers that we have already added. Click the **Search** button to find the customer details and click on the customer in the list to load the details:

6. Remove two of the digits from the phone number and click on the **Save Customer Details** button. We can see that Silverlight has highlighted the invalid control. As with all Silverlight controls, the validation messages are completely customizable using styles. If we hover the mouse over the control, Silverlight displays a Tooltip containing the validation message corresponding to the `Validation` attribute that failed during the validation of the `PhoneNumber` property of the `Customer` class:

Customer Details

Customer Name: | Emily Harris

Phone Number: | 555-555-12 | A valid phone number must be in the format (XXX) XXX-XXXX or XXX-XXX-XXXX.

Email Address: | emily@somewhere.com | Save Customer Details

> Silverlight also provides a `ValidationSummary` control that works much like the ASP.NET `ValidationSummary` in that error messages are displayed in one place, rather than next to each control. This can be easier for users to understand in some scenarios as all of the errors are grouped into one place and the controls that caused the errors are highlighted.

Summary

In this chapter we looked at taking a customer service application from data modelling through to user interface design. We looked at how we can make use of the ADO.NET Entity Framework and RIA Services to create common data objects that can be persisted to a data store. We delved into more complex user interfaces, utilizing custom `DataTemplates`, and performing TwoWay data binding. In this chapter we specifically discussed the following:

- How to create a basic database model
- How to create an ADO.NET Entity Framework model
- How to create a Domain Service form and Entity model
- How to utilize WCF RIA Services with our Entity model
- How to use the `DataForm` control
- How to build a more complex business application
- How to use custom `DataTemplates` to define a custom look to listbox controls

In the next chapter, we will make use of data visualizations to create a management dashboard complete with graphs containing metrics about our customers and orders.

8
Executive Dashboard Application

Executives and other business decision makers rely on collected data to drive their business forward. In Silverlight, we can provide visualizations of data to make the decision makers jobs a bit easier. After all, looking at data on a graph can provide a better understanding of the information than just plain spreadsheets or grid data.

By providing data in an intuitive way, we can better serve the needs of the business. And by providing an application to allow executives to visualize collected data, we can better assist the growth and success of the business.

In this chapter, we shall:

- ◆ Add data visualization to our existing application
- ◆ Create an executive dashboard to view collected data
- ◆ Make use of the Silverlight Toolkit for data visualization

Data visualization

The **Silverlight Toolkit** provides controls for data visualization, namely `Chart` and `DataGrid` controls. With these controls, we can display data in a variety of ways, providing views of the data that make sense to decision makers.

We will make use of these data visualization controls to display information about our customers and their orders. This information can help the sales staff determine what types of cakes are selling and what time of year they sell the most.

Time for action – creating the Executive Dashboard

We will create our dashboard as a page in the customer service application that we created in Chapter 7. By doing this, we can take advantage of the data classes that we already built, and thereby reduce the amount of code required to get our dashboard up and running.

1. Download and install the Silverlight Toolkit from CodePlex:
   `http://www.codeplex.com/Silverlight.`

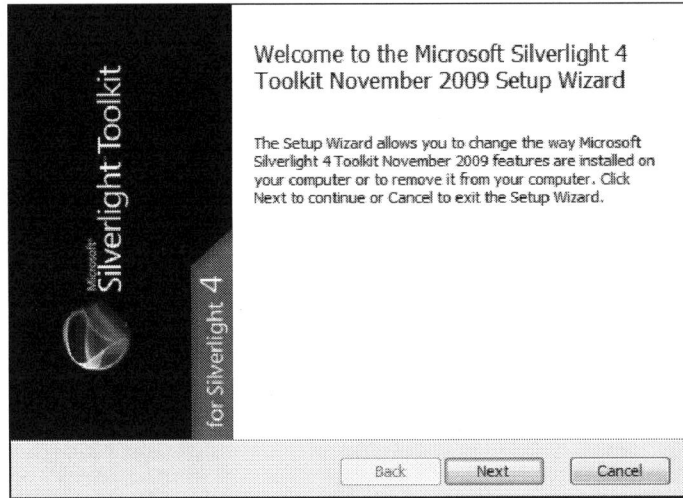

2. Start Visual Studio and open the **CakeORamaApp** solution.

3. Right click on the **Views** folder of the **CakeORamaApp** project, choose **Add New Item**, and add a new **Silverlight Page** named `Dashboard.xaml`:

4. Open the `MainPage.xaml` file and insert the following code right after the **Find Customers** link in the navigation:

```
<Rectangle
    x:Name="Divider4"
    Style="{StaticResource DividerStyle}"/>
<HyperlinkButton
```

```
x:Name="Link5"
Style="{StaticResource LinkStyle}"
NavigateUri="/Dashboard"
TargetName="ContentFrame"
Content="dashboard"/>
```

5. Switch over to Expression Blend and open the `Dashboard.xaml` file.

6. Add a `TextBlock` to the top of the page to serve as our heading. Set the `Text` property to **Executive Dashboard** and the `FontSize` to **16pt**:

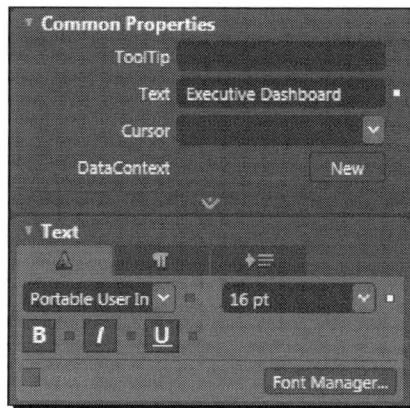

7. Position the `TextBlock` at the top-left corner of the page:

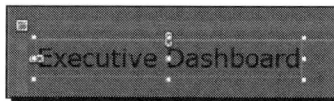

8. Click on the **Assets** icon in the toolbox:

9. In the search field, type **chart** and then select the **Chart** control:

10. Double-click the **Chart** icon to add a new chart control to the page:

11. Position the chart just under the page title:

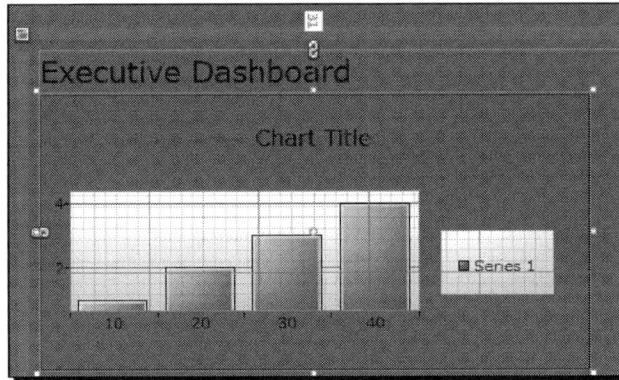

12. Name the chart **SalesDataChart** and set the following chart properties:

13. Expand the **SalesDataChart** in the **Objects and Timeline** panel and select the **[ColumnSeries]** node:

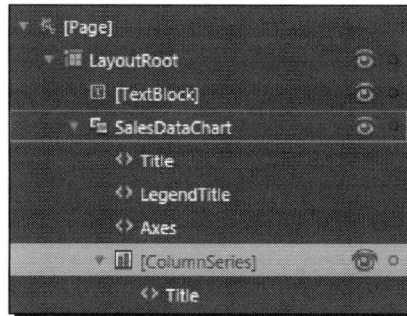

14. Change the **Title** of the series to **Sales**:

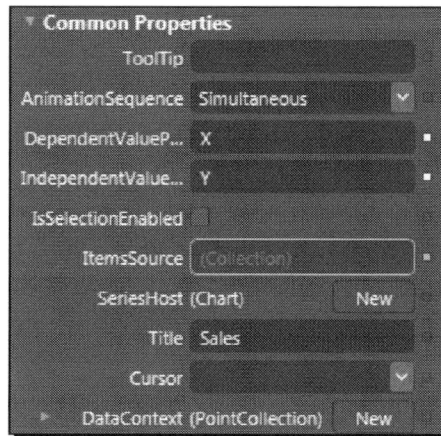

We can see that the **ItemsSource** is highlighted by a yellow border, indicating that it has a data binding. The default chart implementation includes a binding to a collection of points in order to provide a visual of the chart at design time. We can ignore this for now as we are going to change this later on.

15. Change the **DependentValuePath** and **IndependentValuePath** to the following as we are going to create a custom class for binding to the chart:

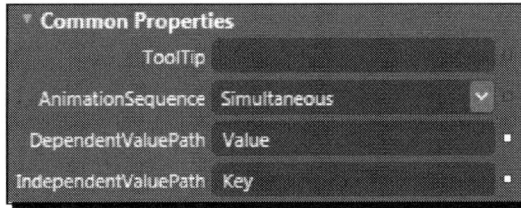

16. Save your work, close the `Dashboard.xaml` file, and switch back over to Visual Studio.

17. Open the `Dashboard.xaml` file and remove the following XAML from the `DataContext` of the chart. Having this data defined in the XAML will interfere with the binding of our sales information:

```
<chartingToolkit:Chart.DataContext>
        <PointCollection>
            <Point>1,10</Point>
            <Point>2,20</Point>
            <Point>3,30</Point>
            <Point>4,40</Point>
        </PointCollection>
</chartingToolkit:Chart.DataContext>
```

18. Open the `Dashboard.xaml.cs` file and replace the `OnNavigatedTo` method handler with the following code:

```
protected override void OnNavigatedTo(NavigationEventArgs e)
{
    if (AppState.CustomerContext == null)
    {
        AppState.CustomerContext = new CustomerContext();
        AppState.CustomerContext.Load<Customer>(AppState.
CustomerContext.GetCustomersQuery());
        AppState.CustomerContext.Load<Event>(AppState.CustomerContext.
GetEventsQuery());
        AppState.CustomerContext.Load<Order>(AppState.CustomerContext.
GetOrdersQuery(),
            new Action<System.Windows.Ria.LoadOperation<Order>>((op) =>
```

```
    {
      this.Dispatcher.BeginInvoke(() =>
        {
          // Orders finished loading, bind to the sales data
          //chart control.
          var orders = op.Entities.Where
          (o => o.OrderDate.Year == DateTime.Now.Year);

          var salesData = new Dictionary<string, double>();
          for (int i = 1; i <= 12; i++)
          {
            salesData.Add(CultureInfo.CurrentUICulture.
            DateTimeFormat.GetAbbreviatedMonthName(i),
              (double)orders.Where
              (o => o.OrderDate.Month == i).Sum(o => o.Cost));
          }

          SalesDataChart.DataContext = salesData;
        });
    }), null);
  }
}
```

[The `salesData` dictionary which we created above represents the `IndependentValuePath` (months) and `DependentValuePath` (cost) of the columns in the chart.]

19. Build and run the solution, then choose the **dashboard** link and we should see the following screen (or similar depending on the amount of data in the `Orders` table):

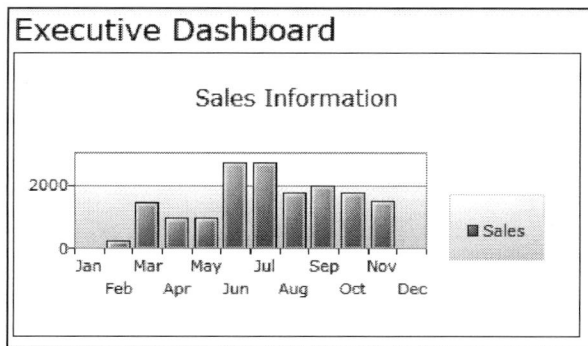

20. Switch back to Blend and open the `Dashboard.xaml` file.

21. Add another chart next to the **Sales Information** chart and name it **SalesPieChart**:

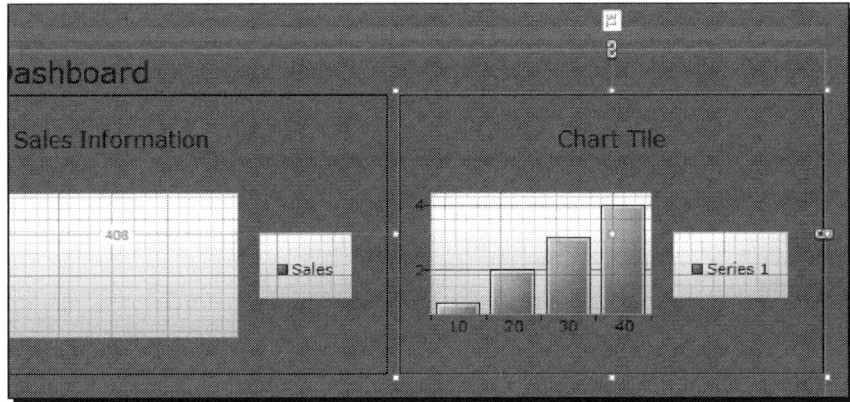

22. Set the **Properties** of the **SalesPieChart** to the following:

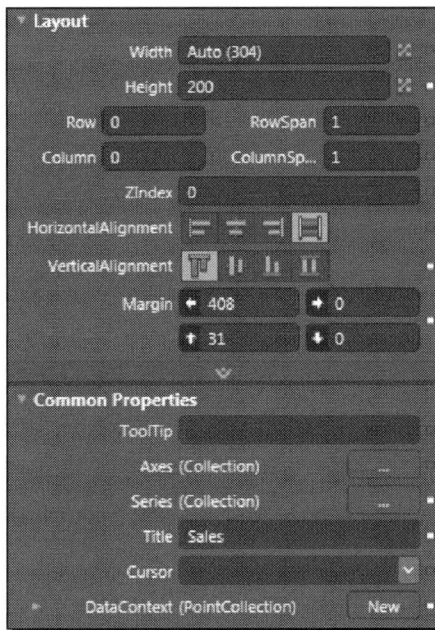

23. Click on the **Advanced property options** button next to the **DataContext** property:

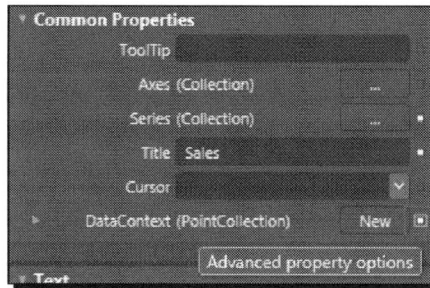

24. Choose the **Reset** option to clear the **DataContext** for this chart since we will be binding a custom object:

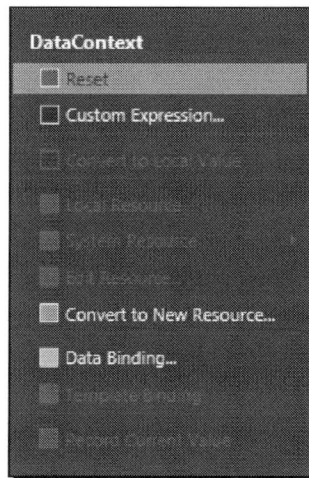

25. Click on the button next to the **Series (Collection)** labeled **Edit items in this collection**:

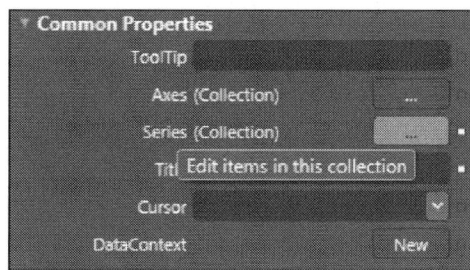

26. When the **ISeries Collection Editor** dialog opens, delete the current entry:

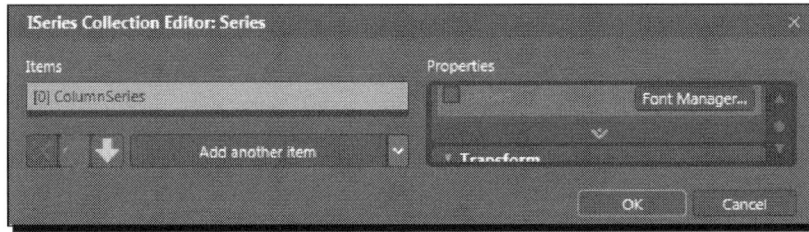

27. From the **Add another item** dropdown list, select the **PieSeries:**

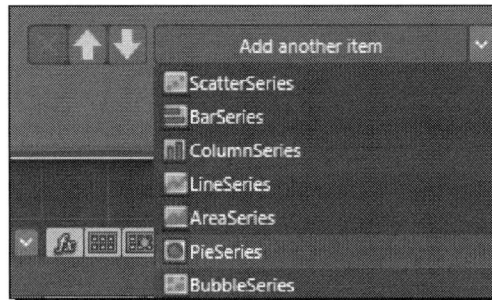

28. Set the **DependentValuePath** and the **IndependentValuePath** to the following and click the **OK** button to close the **ISeries Collection Editor** dialog:

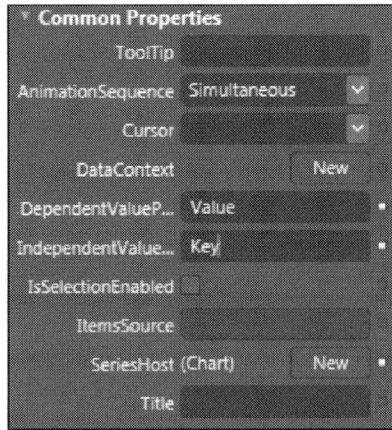

29. Switch to **XAML** view:

30. Edit the XAML for the **SalesPieChart** to set the binding for our `PieSeries`:

```
<chartingToolkit:PieSeries ItemsSource="{Binding}" DependentValueP
ath="Value" IndependentValuePath="Key"/>
```

> Using `{Binding}` without any arguments will cause the series to bind to the default `DataContext` value of the chart.

31. Save and close the `Dashboard.xaml` file, build the solution from within Blend and switch back over to Visual Studio.

32. Open the `Dashboard.xaml.cs` file and change the code in the `OnNavigatedTo` method to bind to the pie chart, as well as the column chart:

```
SalesDataChart.DataContext = salesData;
SalesPieChart.DataContext = salesData;
```

33. Build and run the application to see both our column and pie charts in action:

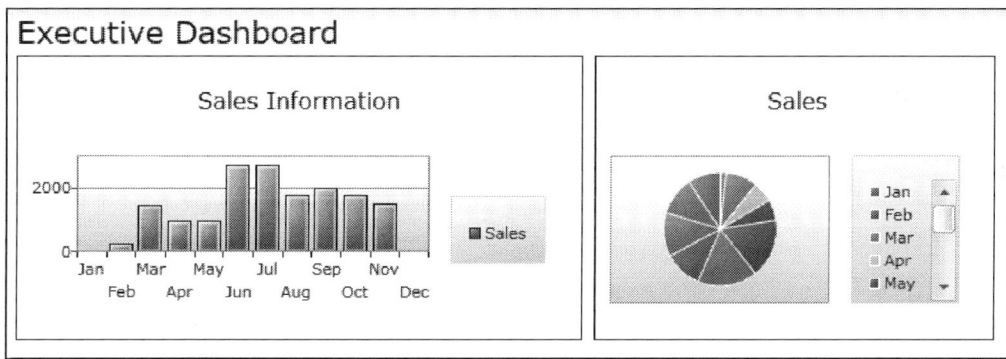

What just happened?

We added charting controls to display sales data to help our sales staff view the months of the year in which they have the most sales. We got to work with two charts, one displaying columns and the other displaying a pie chart. We learned how easy it was to bind our existing data to these charts using some basic LINQ queries to organize and group the data.

Have a go hero – adding more sales data

We can make our `SalesDataChart` more informative by adding an additional year of sales information. By doing this, we can allow the sales staff to compare the previous year to the current year, to ensure that sales are increasing.

1. Start Visual Studio, open the **CakeORamaApp** solution and then open the `Dashboard.xaml` file.

2. Modify the `SalesChartData` control XAML to the following to add an additional `ColumnSeries`:

```
<chartingToolkit:Chart x:Name="SalesDataChart" Title="Sales
Information" Margin="0,31,0,0" HorizontalAlignment="Left"
VerticalAlignment="Top" Width="400" Height="200">
  <chartingToolkit:ColumnSeries ItemsSource="{Binding [0]}" Dep
endentValuePath="Value" IndependentValuePath="Key" Title="Last
Year"/>
  <chartingToolkit:ColumnSeries ItemsSource="{Binding [1]}" Depe
ndentValuePath="Value" IndependentValuePath="Key" Title="Current
Year"/>
</chartingToolkit:Chart>
```

> Notice that we changed the `Binding` of the `ColumnSeries` controls to be index values. We will be binding an array to this chart and Silverlight's binding is smart enough to treat these as indexer values on the `DataContext` object.

3. Save the `Dashboard.xaml` file and then open the `Dashboard.xaml.cs` file.

4. In the `OnNavigatedTo` method, modify the code to the following to allow for the prior year's sales data:

```
protected override void OnNavigatedTo(NavigationEventArgs e)
{
  if (AppState.CustomerContext == null)
  {
    AppState.CustomerContext = new CustomerContext();
    AppState.CustomerContext.Load<Customer>
      (AppState.CustomerContext.GetCustomersQuery());
  AppState.CustomerContext.Load<Event>
      (AppState.CustomerContext.GetEventsQuery());
  AppState.CustomerContext.Load<Order>
      (AppState.CustomerContext.GetOrdersQuery(),
        new Action<System.Windows.Ria.LoadOperation<Order>>((op) =>
        {
```

```
      this.Dispatcher.BeginInvoke(() =>
      {
        var currentYear = DateTime.Now.Year;
        var pastYear = DateTime.Now.AddYears(-1).Year;

        // Orders finished loading, bind to the sales data chart
control.
        var orders = op.Entities.Where(o => o.OrderDate.Year ==
currentYear
            || o.OrderDate.Year == pastYear);

        var salesDataCurrentYear = new Dictionary<string,
double>();
        var salesDataPastYear = new Dictionary<string,
double>();
        for (int i = 1; i <= 12; i++)
        {
  salesDataCurrentYear.Add(CultureInfo.CurrentUICulture.
                    DateTimeFormat.GetAbbreviatedMonthName(i),
            (double)orders.Where(o => o.OrderDate.Month == i &&
o.OrderDate.Year == currentYear).Sum(o => o.Cost));
                                  salesDataPastYear.
Add(CultureInfo.CurrentUICulture.DateTimeFormat.GetAbbreviatedMont
hName(i),
            (double)orders.Where(o => o.OrderDate.Month == i &&
o.OrderDate.Year == pastYear).Sum(o => o.Cost));
        }

        SalesDataChart.DataContext = new List<Dictionary<string,
double>>
        {
          salesDataPastYear,
          salesDataCurrentYear
        };

        SalesPieChart.DataContext = salesDataCurrentYear;
      });
    }), null);
  }
}
```

5. Build and run the solution to see our past and current year's sales information:

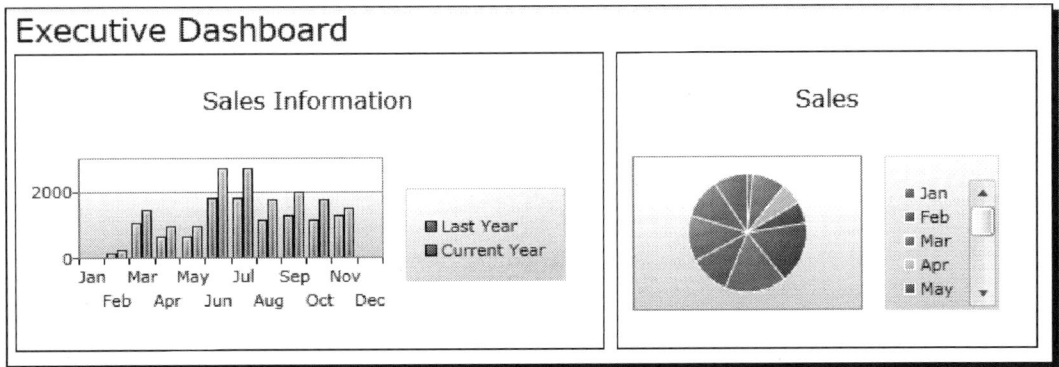

Spreadsheet data

While data visualization is more visually appealing, sometimes having access to the raw data is required in the decision making process. Silverlight includes a **DataGrid** control that allows us to present grid data in a format to which spreadsheet users are accustomed.

Spreadsheets, (while not the best looking applications) do provide value to end users as the data is laid out in rows and is easily comparable and organized.

Time for action – extending the Executive Dashboard

We will add grid functionality to our dashboard and present all of the collected data to our end users. To do this we will make use of the **Silverlight Toolkit DataGrid**.

1. Start Expression Blend and open the **CakeORamaApp** solution.

2. Open the Dashboard.xaml file in the art board.

3. Click on the **Assets** icon in the toolbox, type **data** into the search field, and select the **DataGrid** control:

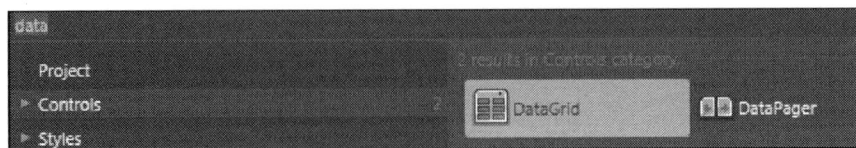

4. Name the `DataGrid` **OrdersGrid** and set the following **Properties**:

5. Save and close the `Dashboard.xaml` file in Blend. Switch over to Visual Studio and open the `Dashboard.xaml.cs` file.

6. Modify the code in the `OnNavigatedTo` method to the following:

```
SalesPieChart.DataContext = salesDataCurrentYear;
OrdersGrid.ItemsSource = orders.OrderByDescending(o =>
o.OrderDate);
```

7. Build and run the solution to see our grid being filled with **Order** data:

Cost	EventId	Events	FinalImage	IsPaid	OrderDate	OrderDetails
1000.0000	7	Event : 7			11/22/2009 5:34:23 PM	
500.0000	5	Event : 5			11/2/2009 5:24:08 PM	Three layer chocolate cake with wh
250.0000	2	Event : 2			10/22/2009 6:03:24 PM	
300.0000	2	Event : 2			10/22/2009 6:03:00 PM	
300.0000	2	Event : 2			10/22/2009 6:03:00 PM	

> The Silverlight DataGrid provides the ability to filter, group, and sort the results. To accomplish this we have to bind it to an instance of `ICollectionView`, which defines the methods for these operations.

8. We can also edit the values of the DataGrid by default, but to ensure that the edits are committed correctly we need to implement the `IEditableObject` interface on the bound data objects.

9. To add paging support, our data source simply needs to implement the `IPagedCollectionView` interface and we can even use a `DataPager` control to aid in the visuals of paging data.

10. We can customize our grid by editing the templates and columns of the grid. Switch over to Visual Studio, right click on the **CakeORamaApp**, add a new folder called `Converters` then add a new class named `DateConverter.cs` to it.

11. Replace the contents of the `DateConverter.cs` file with the following code:

```csharp
using System;
using System.Windows.Data;

namespace CakeORamaApp.Converters
{
  public class DateConverter : IValueConverter
  {
    #region IValueConverter Members
    public object Convert(object value, Type targetType, object
parameter, System.Globalization.CultureInfo culture)
    {
      if (value != null)
      {
        DateTime dt;
        if (DateTime.TryParse(value.ToString(), out dt))
        {
          if (parameter == null)
            return dt.ToShortDateString();
          else
            return dt.ToString(parameter.ToString());
        }
      }
      return null;
    }
    public object ConvertBack(object value, Type targetType,
object parameter, System.Globalization.CultureInfo culture)
    {
      return null;
    }
    #endregion
  }
}
```

> We will use the `ConverterParameter` in the `DateConverter` to provide the format string for the date conversion. The `ConverterParameter` is a value that we can bind to in XAML to provide additional conversion information in our value converters.

12. Add another class to the `Converters` folder called `CurrencyConverter.cs` and replace the contents of the file with the following code:

```
using System;
using System.Globalization;
using System.Windows.Data;

namespace CakeORamaApp.Converters
{
  public class CurrencyConverter : IValueConverter
  {
    #region IValueConverter Members
    public object Convert(object value, Type targetType, object
parameter, System.Globalization.CultureInfo culture)
    {
      if (value == null) return null;
      double result;
      if (Double.TryParse(value.ToString(), NumberStyles.Currency,
null, out result))
      {
        return result.ToString("C");
      }
      return null;
    }
    public object ConvertBack(object value, Type targetType,
object parameter, System.Globalization.CultureInfo culture)
    {
      return null;
    }
    #endregion
  }
}
```

13. Build the solution and switch back over to Blend.

14. Open the `Dashboard.xaml` file and click on the **OrdersGrid** in the **Objects and Timeline** panel:

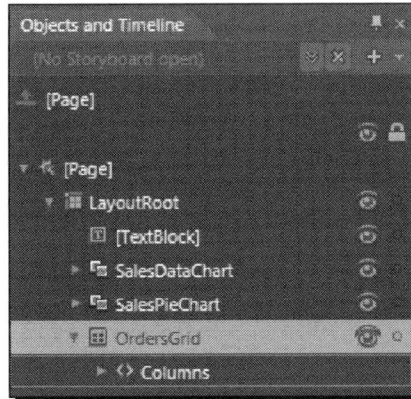

15. Uncheck the **AutoGenerateColumns** checkbox, we will add the columns that we want manually:

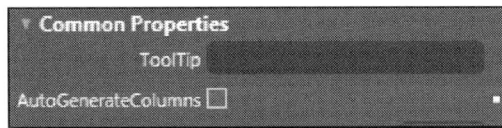

16. Click the **Edit items in this collection** button for the **Columns**:

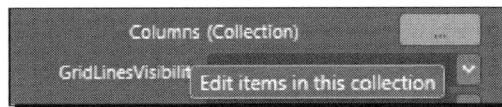

17. In the **DataGridColumn Collection Editor** dialog, click the **Add another item** button:

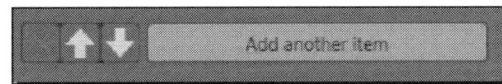

18. In the **Select Object** dialog box that is opened, select **DataGridTextColumn** and click **OK**:

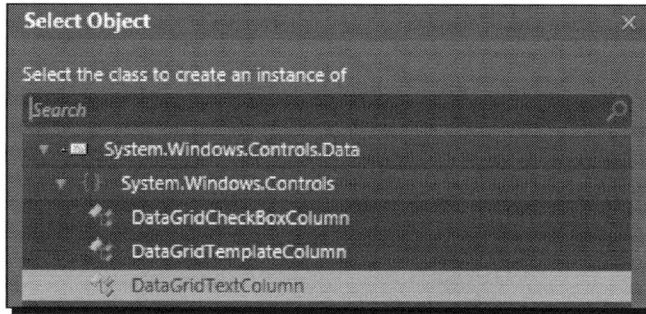

19. In the **Column Properties,** set the following values:

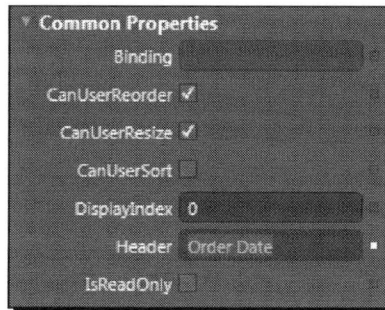

20. Click on the **Advanced property options** for the **Binding** property:

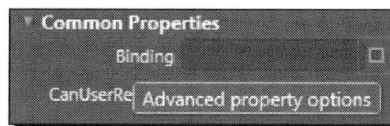

21. Select **Data Binding...** from the options presented:

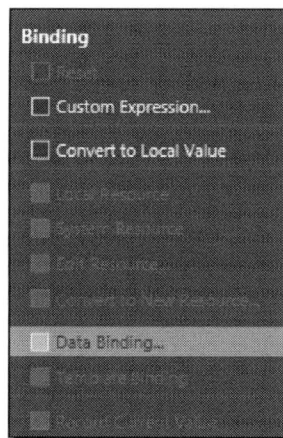

22. In the **Create Data Binding** dialog, select the **Explicit Data Context** tab, check the **Use a custom path expression** checkbox and enter **OrderDate** as the value:

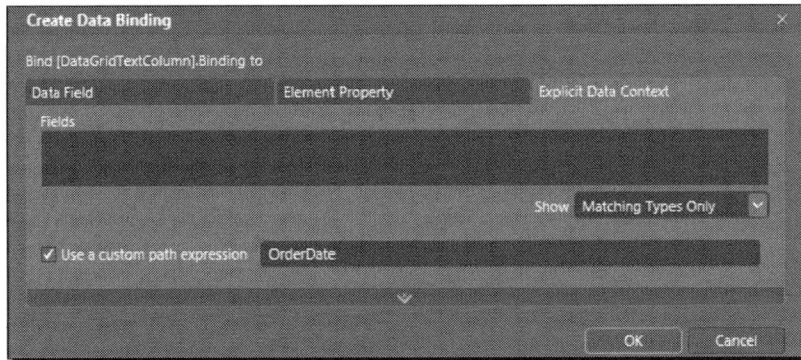

23. Click on the **Show advanced properties** arrow to expand the dialog:

24. Click on the button next to the **Value converter** drop down as displayed:

25. In the **Add Value Converter** dialog box that opens, select the **DateConverter** and click **OK**:

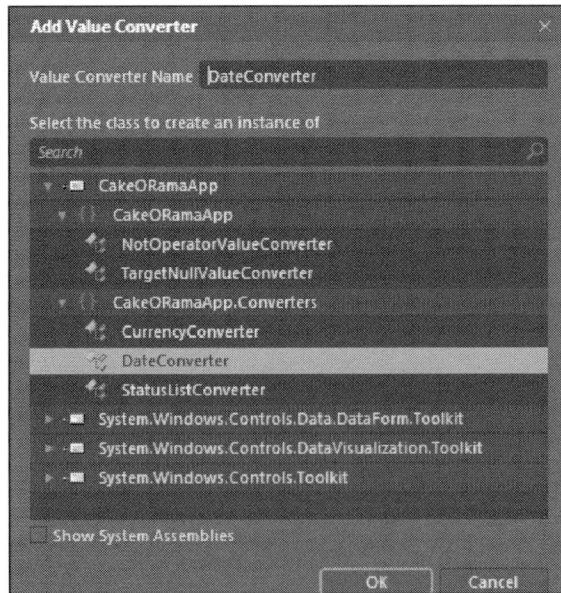

26. Enter **D** into the **Converter parameter** field and click **OK**. This is the date format that we will use to format our date value:

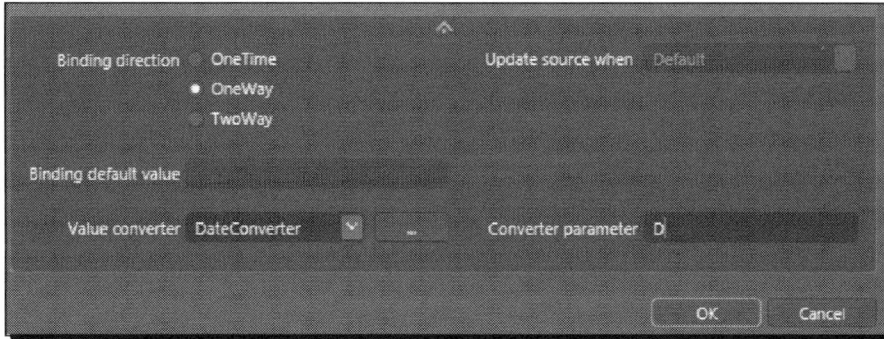

27. Add another `DataGridTextColumn`, set the **Header** to **Cost** and configure the binding to make use of the **CurrencyConverter** class:

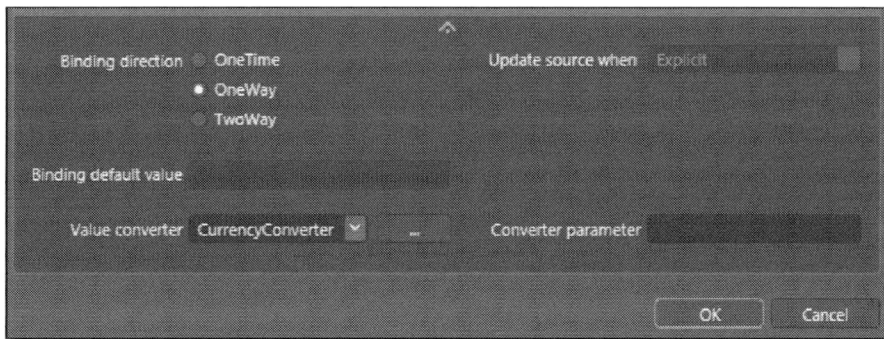

28. Add another column, this time choose the **DataGridCheckBoxColumn**:

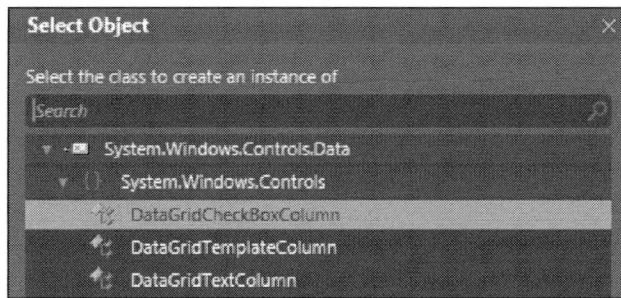

29. Enter **Paid** for the **Header** and set the binding path expression to **IsPaid**:

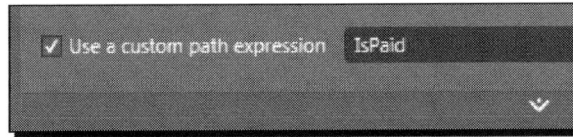

30. Add one more **DataGridTextColumn** with a **Header** value of **Details** and set the binding path expression to **OrderDetails**:

31. Build and run the solution to see our custom columns and how the value converters we created have altered the way the data is displayed:

Order Date	Cost	Paid	Details
Sunday, November 22, 2009	$1,000.00	☐	
Monday, November 02, 2009	$500.00	☐	Three layer chocolate cake with white icing, trimmed in pink roses.
Thursday, October 22, 2009	$250.00	☐	
Thursday, October 22, 2009	$300.00	☐	

We can copy and paste the grid data into Excel or use the sample provided by Brad Abrams at: `http://blogs.msdn.com/brada/archive/2009/07/14/business-apps-example-for-silverlight-3-rtm-and-net-ria-services-july-update-part-4-seo-export-to-excel-and-out-of-browser.aspx`.

What just happened?

We extended the Executive Dashboard by adding a DataGrid from the Silverlight Toolkit. We also created two value converter classes that implement the `IValueConverter` interface and provide a way to alter bound data during the binding process to provide formatting or other actions to the data.

We customized the DataGrid by adding our own custom columns to just show the relevant data, rather than including key properties and such.

Have a go hero – adding paging to our grid

In most business scenarios, we will be dealing with large amounts of data and having the ability to view that data several rows at a time, rather than all at once can be beneficial to the user.

We are going to add paging to our grid using the `DataPager` control. When a `DataPager` control is bound to the same data source as the `DataGrid`, the `DataPager` will be paged as we page through the data in the `DataPager` control.

1. Start Expression Blend and open the **CakeORamaApp** solution.

2. We need to add some additional test data, so that we have data to page through. We can either do that through some SQL scripts or use our application to add orders.

3. Open the `Dashboard.xaml` file, click on the **Assets** icon in the toolbox, add a `DataPager` control, name the control `OrdersPager`, set the **PageSize** to `10`, and position it below the grid as follows:

Order Date	Cost	Paid	Details

4. Build the solution, switch over to Visual Studio, and open the `Dashboard.xaml.cs` file. We will bind the `DataPager` in code, since that is where we handled the binding of the `DataGrid`.

5. Add a reference to the `System.Windows.Data` assembly, which can be found in the `C:\Program Files\Microsoft SDKs\Silverlight\v4.0\Libraries\Client` folder.

6. Add the following using statement to the top of the file:

```
using System.Windows.Data;
```

7. Modify the `OnNavigatedTo` method, where the `OrdersGrid` is bound, to the following:

```
var view = new PagedCollectionView(orders.OrderByDescending(o =>
o.OrderDate));

OrdersPager.Source = view;

OrdersGrid.ItemsSource = view;
```

8. Build and run the solution to see paging in action:

Summary

In this chapter we covered building a dashboard application to provide sales information to our sales staff and company executives. We made use of the data visualization components to add charts and spreadsheet grids to our application. We specifically discussed the following:

- How to add different charting controls to our application
- How to bind data to charting controls
- How to make use of LINQ to provide custom queries for data binding
- How to implement `IValueConverter` to provide custom formatting of bound data
- How to implement a `DataGrid` with custom columns and paging

In the next chapter, we will explore building an application for delivery personnel; making use of live mapping.

9
Delivery Application

The rise of mobile devices with built-in cellular internet connections means that your applications can go places too. The new craze in laptop computers has been the 'netbook' form factor. Netbooks are small, inexpensive, and very often include an 'air card', which connects the computer to the internet using a mobile phone network. Some telecom providers give netbooks away in exchange for signing a service contract.

Cake-O-Rama needs to deliver their cakes to the right places on time and track where the cakes are being delivered. They would also like to capture signatures, just like many parcel delivery services.

As in any delivery service, time lost getting directions or stuck in traffic is money lost. In this chapter, we're going to imagine that Cake-O-Rama has outfitted its delivery staff with netbook computers to be more productive. To these ends, we are going to create a signature capture control and a complete mapping solution.

In this chapter, we shall:

- Create a custom control
- Create a custom map
- Add GPS unit style driving route calculation function to our map
- Incorporate traffic data and route around traffic

Creating a signature capture control

Cake-O-Rama would like to go paperless. This includes delivery sign off sheets, where the customer signs off on receipt of the cake. The inspiration for this idea comes from the electronic signature devices at many retails stores. You have most certainly seen them. They have an area that accepts a signature and buttons to clear the signature field and to accept the signature. If you play with them enough, you'll notice that the accept button doesn't work if there is no signature. We're going to build a similar mechanism for Cake-O-Rama and learn about creating a "lookless" custom control in the process.

You may have heard the term "lookless" when Silverlight controls are talked about. Certainly, these controls have a look, so what could this term mean. The term "lookless" refers to the fact that while the control has a default look, the control's properties, events and logic are not tied to the control's appearance. For example, all three of the following radically different looking items are all **Button** controls.

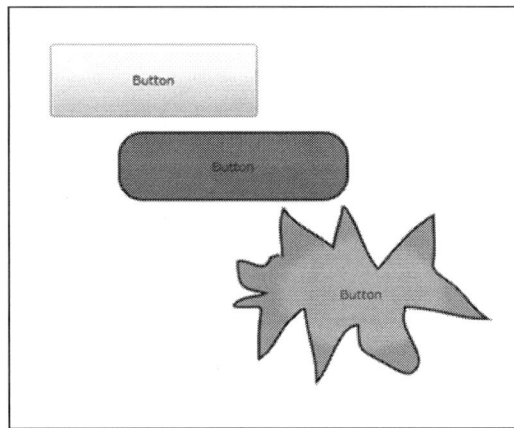

If you look at the XAML for the buttons, you'll see that the only real difference between them is the `Style` resource that they use:

```
<Button Height="64" HorizontalAlignment="Left" Margin="126,47,0,0"
VerticalAlignment="Top" Width="183" Content="Button"/>

<Button Height="61" Margin="186,124,251,0" Style="{StaticResource
PinkButtonStyle}" VerticalAlignment="Top" Content="Button"/>

<Button Margin="287,189,128,135" Style="{StaticResource
WackyButtonStyle}" Content="Button"/>
```

The first button does not have a `Style` attribute. The second and third buttons refer to `Style` resources that change the way the control looks. This should remind you of the work we did in Chapter 2, when we created the navigation control for the website. You may be wondering: if the first button doesn't define a `Style` attribute, then how does it know what to look like? The answer lies in how the control was designed. The control has a default style definition that the Silverlight runtime applies in the absence of any `Style` attribute entries.

Creating our own lookless control

In order to create a lookless control that can be completely customized like the `Button` control, we'll need to create a custom control. We have explored creating composite controls before. In a composite control, however, the control's look is fixed and cannot be overridden with a Style attribute.

Time for action – creating a custom control

The best way to create a custom control is to create a **Silverlight Class Library** project type. Although we can add a custom control to any Silverlight project, this approach affords us extra flexibility. A `Silverlight Class Library` project compiles of a DLL file, which we can re-use across different solutions. Let's create our control now.

1. Create a new Silverlight application in Visual Studio and name it **SignatureControl**. Be sure to use the Silverlight Application template that we've been using throughout most of this book.

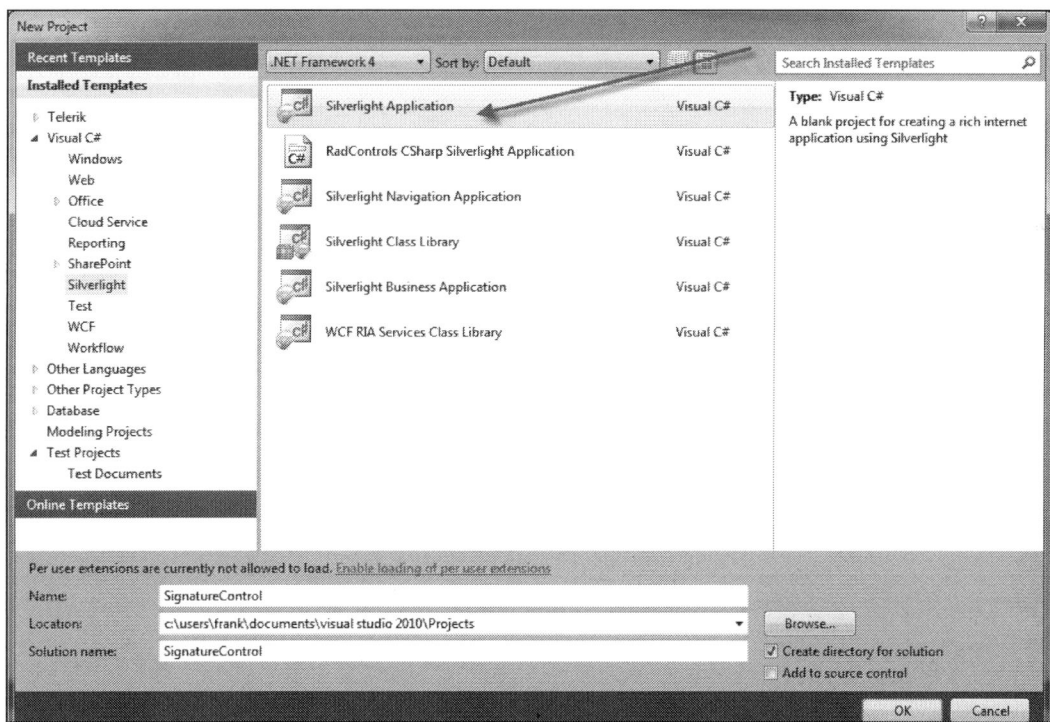

2. In **Solution Explorer**, you'll see the usual two projects: one for the Silverlight application and a web project named **SignatureControl.web** that hosts the **SignatureControl** Silverlight application.

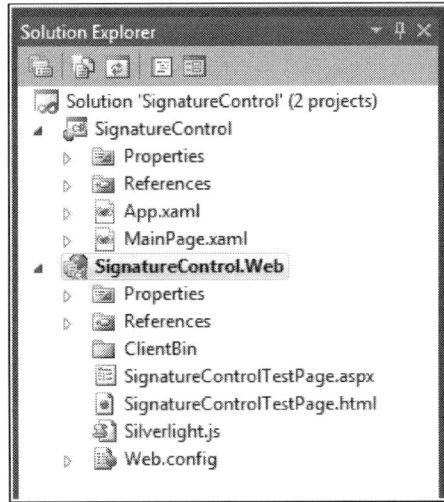

3. From Visual Studio's menu bar, choose **Add|New Project** from the **File** menu:

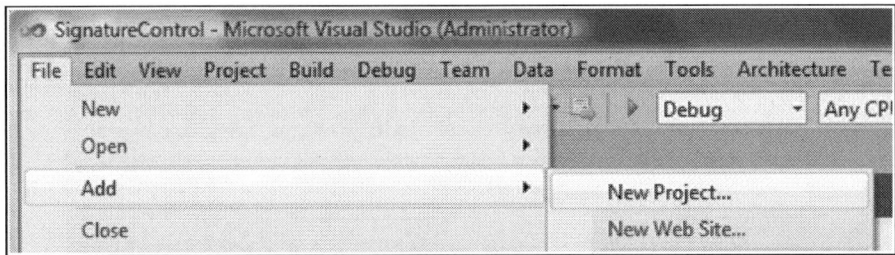

4. In the dialog box that comes up, choose the **Silverlight Class Library** project template and in the **Name** textbox type **CakeORamaControlLibrary**:

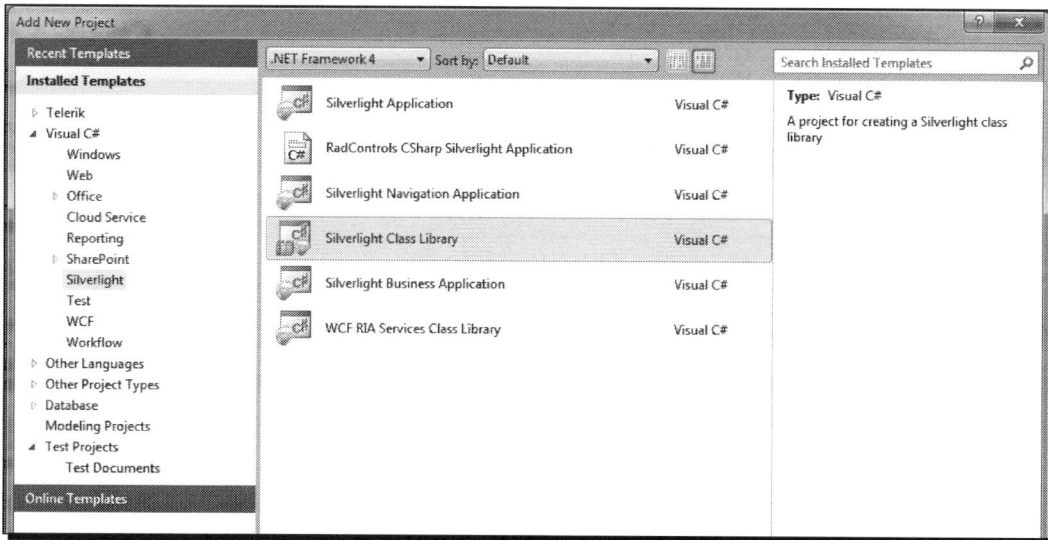

5. Click **OK**. You now have three projects in your solution.

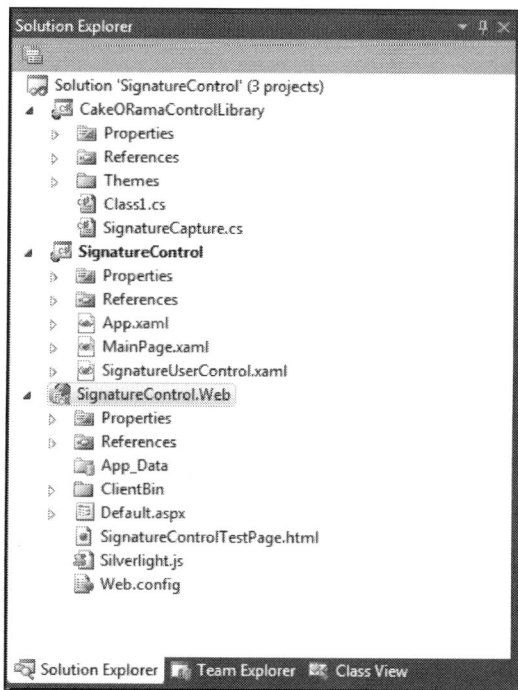

6. Right-click on the **CakeOramaControlLibrary** and choose **Add|New Item...** from the context menu:

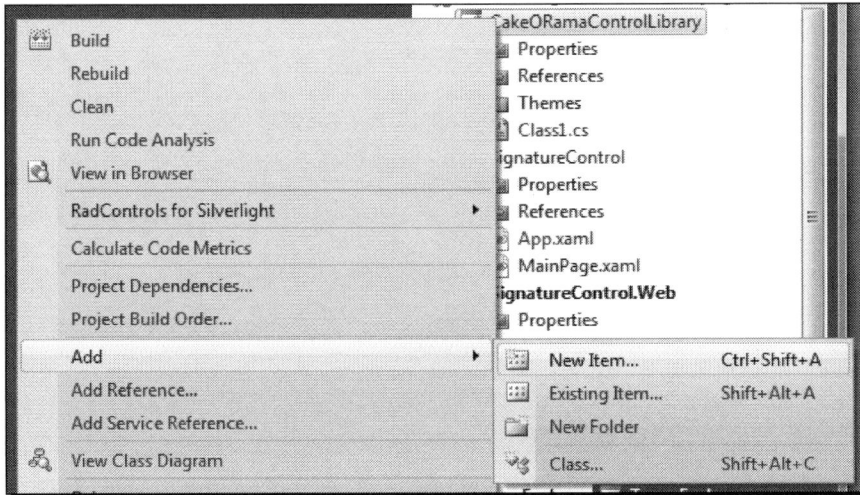

7. Choose **Silverlight Templated Control** and enter `SignatureControl.cs` in the **Name** textbox and then click **Add**.

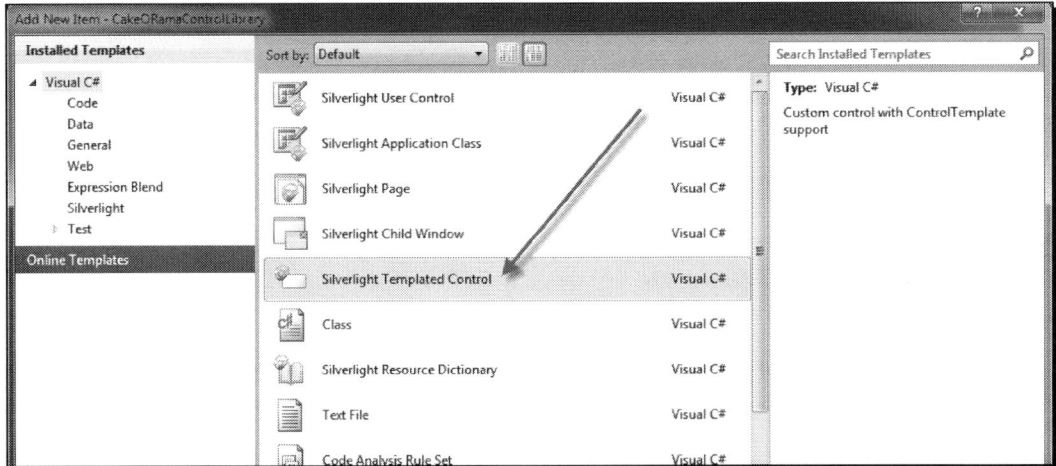

8. You'll notice now that there is a new folder named **Themes** in your project along with a file called `Generic.xaml`:

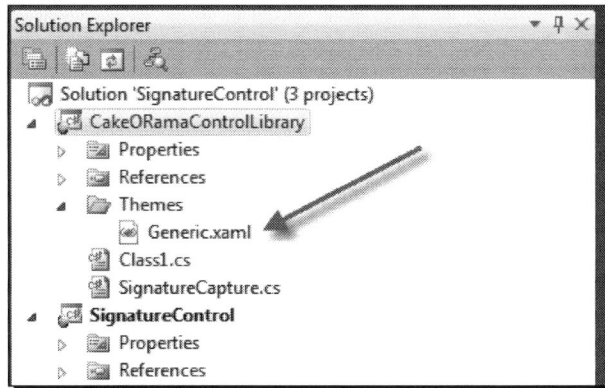

9. If you open up the `Generic.xaml` file, you'll see that it is a resource dictionary and that the template had already filled a `Style` with a `TargetType` of `local:SignatureControl`.

10. If you look in the `SignatureControl.cs` file, you'll see the following line of code inside the constructor method. It loads a default style for the control type.

```
this.DefaultStyleKey = typeof(SignatureControl);
```

What just happened?

We just created a lookless control. Granted, it doesn't do anything at the moment as we've not added any custom code. However, this is a good time to point out a few things about how custom controls work. First of all, you'll notice that the `SignatureControl` has no XAML file. Unlike composite controls, which contain both a XAML file and a code-behind file, custom controls only consist of a code behind file. The default look for the control is defined in the `Generic.xaml` file, which is defined automatically as:

```
<Style TargetType="local:SignatureControl">
  <Setter Property="Template">
    <Setter.Value>
      <ControlTemplate TargetType="local: SignatureControl">
        <Border Background="{TemplateBinding Background}"
            BorderBrush="{TemplateBinding BorderBrush}"
            BorderThickness="{TemplateBinding BorderThickness}">
        </Border>
      </ControlTemplate>
    </Setter.Value>
  </Setter>
</Style>
```

This is simply what the template in Visual Studio put in for us. We'll improve upon it in the next section. The important thing to note is that both `Style` and `TargetType` of `ControlTemplate` are set to point to `SignatureControl`.

The link between the code behind file and the template defined in the `Generic.xaml` resource dictionary is here in our control's default constructor:

```
public SignatureControl()
{
  this.DefaultStyleKey = typeof(SignatureControl);
}
```

The highlighted line of code above tells the Silverlight runtime to look for a `Style` definition that should apply to our control. This is where the look for the lookless control gets defined. Remember, our control really only consists of a code behind file. It has no look, but the control does know how to find a way to draw itself in the absence of any other Style or `ControlTemplate` directives.

Improving the default template

To create a signature control that actually can take in a signature, we'll need to add some code and refine our default template to include an `InkPresenter` control. Additionally, we'll also add some code to make the `InkPresenter` interactive.

Time for action – putting the control together

We have the basis for creating our first lookless control, but we need to add an `InkPresenter` control and wire up the events like we did in Chapter 4. Let's do that now by completing the following steps:

1. Replace the `Style` definition in the `Generic.xaml` file that Visual Studio created for us, with the following code:

```
<Style TargetType="local:SignatureControl" >
  <Setter Property="Template">
    <Setter.Value>
      <ControlTemplate TargetType="local:SignatureControl">
        <Grid>
          <InkPresenter x:Name="inkPresenter"
                        Strokes="{TemplateBinding Strokes}"
                        Background="{TemplateBinding
                                          Background}"/>
        </Grid>
```

```
          </ControlTemplate>
        </Setter.Value>
      </Setter>
  </Style>
```

2. Add a reference to the `System.Windows.Ink` namespace by adding this line to the top of the `SignatureControl.cs` file:

```
using System.Windows.Ink;
```

3. Add the following code to the `SignatureControl.cs` file. Don't worry if it doesn't all make sense yet. We're going to pick it apart in a moment.

```
private InkPresenter _inkPresenter = null;
private Stroke _stroke;

public event EventHandler MinimumStrokeCountReached;

public StrokeCollection Strokes
{
    get
    {
return GetValue(StrokesProperty) as StrokeCollection;
    }
    set
    {
SetValue(StrokesProperty, value);
    }
}

public static readonly DependencyProperty StrokesProperty =
      DependencyProperty.Register("Strokes", typeof(StrokeCollecti
on), typeof(SignatureControl),
new PropertyMetadata(new StrokeCollection(), new PropertyChangedCa
llback((o, a) =>
{
    SignatureControl source = (SignatureControl)o;
    source.UpdateStrokes();
}
    )));

public static readonly DependencyProperty
DrawingAttributesProperty =
```

```
        DependencyProperty.Register("DrawingAttributes", typeof(Drawin
gAttributes), typeof(SignatureControl),
        new PropertyMetadata(new DrawingAttributes(), new PropertyChan
gedCallback((o, a) =>
{
    SignatureControl source = (SignatureControl)o;
    source.UpdateDrawingAttributes();
}
)));

public DrawingAttributes DrawingAttributes
{
    get
    {
return GetValue(DrawingAttributesProperty) as DrawingAttributes;
    }
    set
    {
SetValue(DrawingAttributesProperty, value);
    }
}

public static readonly DependencyProperty StrokeMinimumProperty =
        DependencyProperty.Register("StrokeMinimum", typeof(int), type
of(SignatureControl),
        new PropertyMetadata(0, new PropertyChangedCallback((o,a) =>
{
    SignatureControl source = (SignatureControl)o;
}
)));


public int StrokeMinimum
{
    get
    {
return (int)GetValue(StrokeMinimumProperty);
    }
    set
    {
```

```
SetValue(StrokeMinimumProperty, value);
    }
}

public override void OnApplyTemplate()
{
    FindInkPresenterControl();

    InitializeInkPresenter();

    UpdateStrokes();

    base.OnApplyTemplate();
}

private void FindInkPresenterControl()
{
    _inkPresenter = this.GetTemplateChild("inkPresenter") as
InkPresenter;
}

protected void UpdateStrokes()
{
    if (_inkPresenter != null)
    {
_inkPresenter.Strokes = Strokes;
    }
}

private void UpdateDrawingAttributes()
{

}

private void InitializeInkPresenter()
{
    if (this._inkPresenter != null)
    {
this._inkPresenter.MouseLeftButtonDown += new
MouseButtonEventHandler(_inkPresenter_MouseLeftButtonDown);
```

```
this._inkPresenter.MouseMove += new MouseEventHandler(_
inkPresenter_MouseMove);
this._inkPresenter.MouseLeftButtonUp += new
MouseButtonEventHandler(_inkPresenter_MouseLeftButtonUp);

    }
}

private void _inkPresenter_MouseLeftButtonUp(object sender,
MouseButtonEventArgs e)
{

    if (this._stroke != null)
    {
this._stroke.StylusPoints.Add(e.StylusDevice.
GetStylusPoints(this._inkPresenter));
    }

    this._inkPresenter.ReleaseMouseCapture();

    CheckStrokeCount();

    this._stroke = null;
}

private void _inkPresenter_MouseMove(object sender, MouseEventArgs
e)
{

    if (this._stroke != null)
    {
this._stroke.StylusPoints.Add(e.StylusDevice.
GetStylusPoints(this._inkPresenter));
    }

}

private void _inkPresenter_MouseLeftButtonDown(object sender,
MouseButtonEventArgs e)
{
```

```
        this._stroke = new Stroke();
        this._inkPresenter.Strokes.Add(this._stroke);

        this._inkPresenter.CaptureMouse();

        this._stroke.DrawingAttributes = this.DrawingAttributes;

    }

    private void CheckStrokeCount()
    {
        if (this._inkPresenter.Strokes.Count >= this.StrokeMinimum)
        {
if (MinimumStrokeCountReached != null)
{
        // Raise event
        MinimumStrokeCountReached(this, new EventArgs());
}
        }
    }
```

4. Now build the solution by choosing **Build Solution** from the **Build** menu or by pressing *Ctrl + Shift + B.*

5. Next, we'll add a reference to the **CakeORamaControlLibrary** project.. Right click on the **References** folder in the SignatureControl project and click on **Add Reference...**

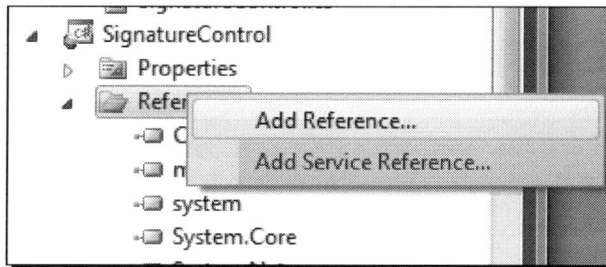

6. In the **Add References** dialog box, click on the **Projects** tab and select **CakeORamaControlLibrary** and click **OK**.

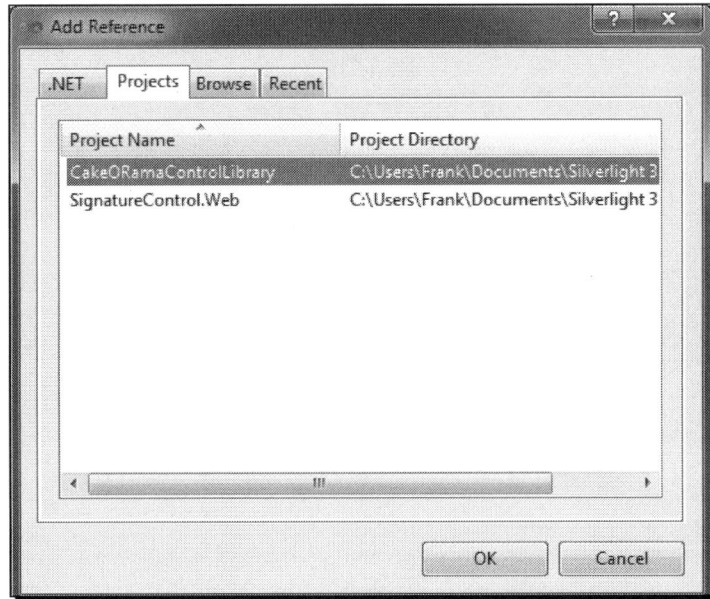

7. Go to the `MainPage.xaml` file in the **SignatureControl Silverlight** application project and add an XML namespace reference to the file:

```
xmlns:cakeorama="clr-namespace:CakeORamaControlLibrary;assembly=Ca
keORamaControlLibrary"
```

8. Inside the `Grid` element, add the following XAML to insert a `SignatureControl`:

```
<cakeorama:SignatureControl Background="LightBlue"
StrokeMinimum="2" Height="109" Width="384" />
```

9. Now your screen should look like the following:

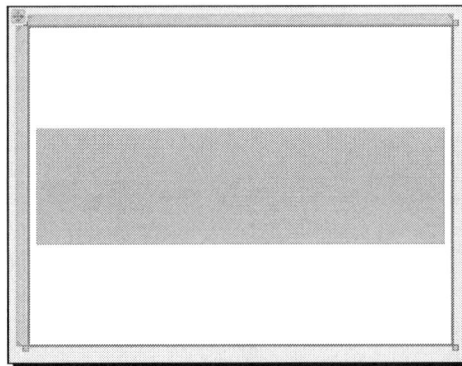

10. Run the solution now by choosing **Start Debugging** from the **Debug** menu or pressing *F5*. When the application loads, draw in the light blue box. You could even sign your name:

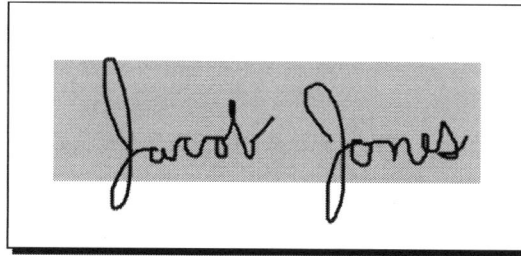

11. Close the browser window to end the debugging session.

What just happened?

There was a lot of code we just typed and a few concepts thrown all in the same mix. So let's go through them one by one.

Dependency properties

The most alarming bits of code were the ones that registered dependency properties. It's something unique to Silverlight and WPF, so unless you've worked with these technologies already, the code to register a dependency property can look a little daunting.

```
public static readonly DependencyProperty StrokeMinimumProperty =
    DependencyProperty.Register("StrokeMinimum", typeof(int), typeof(S
ignatureControl),
    new PropertyMetadata(0, new PropertyChangedCallback((o,a) =>
{
    SignatureControl source = (SignatureControl)o;
}
)));
```

You'll see that with the help of Intellisense, the purpose of each parameter of the `DependencyProperty.Register` method.

```
///
/// </summary>
public static readonly DependencyProperty StrokesProperty =
    DependencyProperty.Register("Strokes", typeof(StrokeCollection), typeof(SignatureCapture),
```

> DependencyProperty DependencyProperty.Register(string name, **Type propertyType**, Type ownerType, PropertyMetadata typeMetadata)
> Registers a dependency property with the specified property name, property type, owner type, and property metadata for the property.
> **propertyType:** *The type of the property.*

```
            source.UpdateStrokes();
```

The `DependencyProperty.Register` method takes in a series of meta data about this `DependencyProperty`: its name, the type the property contains, the type of control to which it belongs, and any additional metadata, including defining a method for when the property changes.

By convention, the dependency property always ends in `Property`. Also, the name value assigned to the dependency property is always the same as the property it acts as the representative for. For example, `StrokeMinimumProperty` has a name registered to it of `StrokeMinimum` and the regular property for the class is also `StrokeMinimum`. The regular property acts as a wrapper for its related dependency property as follows:

```
public int StrokeMinimum
{
    get
    {
return (int)GetValue(StrokeMinimumProperty);
    }
    set
    {
SetValue(StrokeMinimumProperty, value);
    }
}
```

The more you use it, the more it will make sense. Trust me.

The OnApplyTemplate method

The real magic of lookless controls happens here in the `OnApplyTemplate` method. This method gets called when a template is applied. A template is applied when a `ControlTemplate` is applied to the control:

```
public override void OnApplyTemplate()
{
    FindInkPresenterControl();

    InitializeInkPresenter();

    UpdateStrokes();

    base.OnApplyTemplate();
}
```

The OnApplyTemplate method is where you'll want to put any kind of initialization logic. We did just that by making calls to several methods. The FindInkPresenterControl method, which looks for a child item in the template named InkPresenter and assigns a reference to the _inkPresenter member. The _inkPresenter member has class wide scope and this is what we used throughout the control.

```
private void FindInkPresenterControl()
{
    _inkPresenter = this.GetTemplateChild("inkPresenter") as
InkPresenter;
}
```

Using _inkPresenter as a reference to the InkPresenter control, we attached event handlers to respond to the user's actions and collect ink. Much of this code should look familiar as it is very similar to the sketching application that we made in Chapter 2.

```
private void InitializeInkPresenter()
{
    if (this._inkPresenter != null)
    {
this._inkPresenter.MouseLeftButtonDown += new
MouseButtonEventHandler(_inkPresenter_MouseLeftButtonDown);
    this._inkPresenter.MouseMove += new MouseEventHandler(_inkPresenter_
MouseMove);
    this._inkPresenter.MouseLeftButtonUp += new MouseButtonEventHandler(_
inkPresenter_MouseLeftButtonUp);
    }
}
```

TemplateBinding

Sharp-eyed readers may have noticed a new binding syntax keyword: TemplateBinding in the Style inside the Generic.xaml file:

```
<InkPresenter
  x:Name="inkPresenter"
  Strokes="{TemplateBinding Strokes}"
  Background="{TemplateBinding Background}">
</InkPresenter>
```

The XAML above binds property values in the control template to exposed properties of the SignatureControl class. This means we can link properties of the control class to the presentation layer. If you remember that we assigned the color LightBlue to the background of the SignatureControl in the XAML file:

```
<cakeorama:SignatureControl Background="LightBlue" StrokeMinimum="2"
Height="109" Width="384" />
```

The `TemplateBinding` markup extension makes the connection between properties in the control template to the value of an exposed property on the control. In case you're wondering, we never defined the `Background` property explicitly. We inherited it from the `Control` base class.

You may be thinking that this is an awful lot of trouble to do something that would be really easy with a composite control. You're right, but there's a considerable upside. Let's see what that is.

Implementing the custom control

Now that we have a custom lookless control, let's see how flexible its visual appearance can be. We'll use Blend to edit a copy of our control's template.

Time for action – putting our lookless control to the test

Let's open up our control solution in Blend to see how flexible our control really is.

1. Open up the **SignatureControl** solution in Expression Blend.

2. Open up the `MainPage.xaml` file and right-click on the **SignatureControl.**

3. Choose **Edit Template|Edit a Copy.**

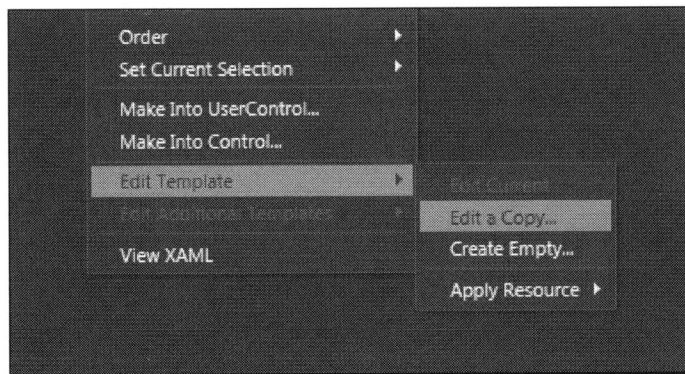

4. Change the `Background` property to a green gradient (or whatever you like). This is what my control looks like:

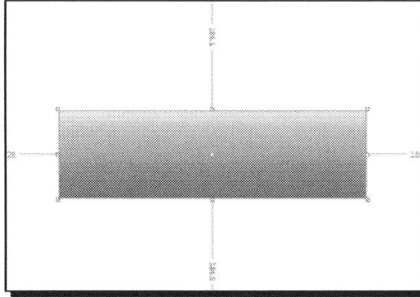

5. Run the solution and write a signature in the box and you'll see the control has the same function but a different look.

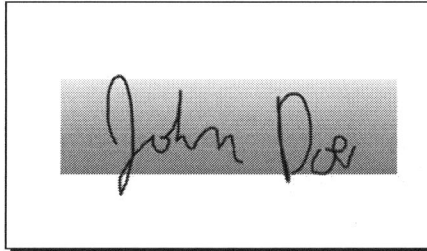

6. Close the browser window to end the debugging session.

What just happened?

We used Blend's control template editing capabilities to really show off the flexibility that our lookless control provides. Just like the Button controls we saw at the beginning of the chapter, we can create radically different looking styles for the same control just like we did with the Button control.

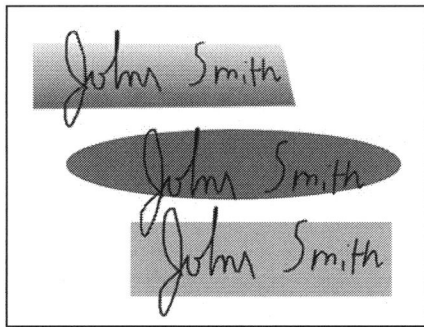

The XAML mark up only differs in which style we reference:

```
<cakeorama:SignatureControl Height="109" Width="384"
Margin="183,0,73,50" VerticalAlignment="Bottom" />
<cakeorama: SignatureControl Height="109" Width="384"
Margin="42,51,214,0" VerticalAlignment="Top"
Style="{StaticResource RedOvalStyle}" >
<cakeorama: SignatureControl Margin="102,186,73,193"
Style="{StaticResource YellowStyle}"/>
```

We're not quite done yet. Let's finish this control so that it behaves like the signature capture devices at stores.

Time for action – finishing the control

Like most signature capture devices you'd find in stores, they won't let you accept a signature unless you've written something in the space provided. We already have the functionality to do this in the control, but we've not used it yet. Let's wire up the `MinimumStrokeCountReached` event now. The `MinimumStrokeCountReached` method fires when the number of strokes on the `InkPresenter` meets or exceeds the number defined in the `StrokeMinimum` property.

1. Open the **SignatureControl** solution in Visual Studio.

2. In the `MainPage.xaml` file, insert the following XAML:
   ```
   <Grid x:Name="LayoutRoot" Background="LightBlue">
   <cakes:SignatureControl
   x:Name="signature"
         StrokeMinimum="2"
   MinimumStrokeCountReached="signature_MinimumStrokeCountReached"
         Margin="10,85,10,98">
   <cakes:SignatureControl.Background>
       <LinearGradientBrush EndPoint="0.5,1" StartPoint="0.5,0">
         <GradientStop Color="#FFFDE7E4" Offset="1"/>
         <GradientStop Color="#FFFBCCC6" Offset="0.741"/>
         <GradientStop Color="#FFF88679"/>
       </LinearGradientBrush>
     </cakes:SignatureControl.Background>
   </cakes:SignatureControl>
   <Button x:Name="btnClear" Click="btnClear_Click"
   Content="Clear" Width="100" Height="55" HorizontalAlignmen
   t="Right" Margin="0,0,8,28" VerticalAlignment="Bottom" d:
   LayoutOverrides="Width, Height" />
   <TextBlock HorizontalAlignment="Left" VerticalAlignment="Top"
   Text="Please Sign Below:" TextWrapping="Wrap" FontSize="32"
   ```

```
Margin="8,34,0,0"/>
<Button x:Name="btnOK" Click="btnClear_Click"
Content="Accept" Width="100" Height="55" HorizontalAlignme
nt="Left" Margin="10,0,0,28" VerticalAlignment="Bottom" d:
LayoutOverrides="Width, Height" IsEnabled="False" />
</Grid>
```

3. In the `MainPage.xaml.cs` file, add the following code:

```
private void btnClear_Click(object sender, System.Windows.
RoutedEventArgs e)
{
    signature.Strokes.Clear();

    btnOK.IsEnabled = false;

}
private void btnOK_Click(object sender, System.Windows.
RoutedEventArgs e)
{
    // Accept Signature
}
private void signature_MinimumStrokeCountReached(object sender,
EventArgs e)
{
    this.btnOK.IsEnabled = true;
}
```

4. Run the solution by choosing **Start Debugging** from the **Debug** menu or by pressing *F5*.

5. You'll notice that the **Accept** button is not enabled until there are at least two strokes in the signature box. With one stroke, you should see the following:

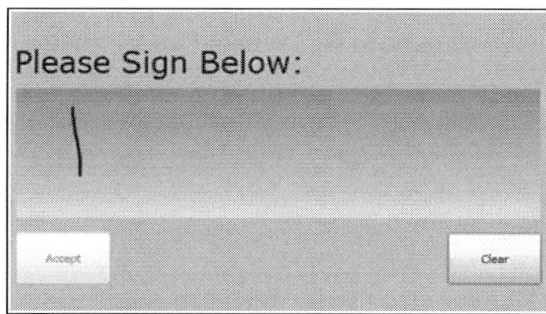

6. And with the second stroke, the **Accept** button is enabled.

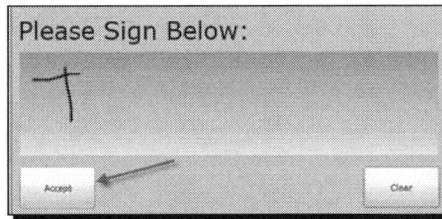

7. Close the browser window to stop debugging.

What just happened?

Not only did we create a custom control that's lookless, but we created a smart signature control that fires an event when the user draws enough strokes to make a signature (or at least a plausible signature). Best of all, we made the minimum number of strokes a property. That means the control can be used in more places and more situations.

The goal to strive for in control development is maximum reusability, whether you plan to sell controls or re-use them across multiple projects.

Mapping application

Many businesses deal with location-based data, whether store locations, regional sales data, or routing deliveries. Time is money and time lost in traffic is money lost. It would be helpful to find delivery locations, get traffic directions, and, if possible, avoid as many traffic jams as possible.

We explored latitude and longitude coordinates briefly in Chapter 2 when we built the store location map. However, in that application, we simply provided the latitude and longitude (also known as latlong) coordinates for each of Cake-o-Rama's locations. In the real world, it is not plausible to have someone go to each location with a GPS device or use mapping software to determine the latlong coordinates of a particular address. Therefore, we need a method to convert street addresses to latitude and longitude. That process is called **Geocoding**.

Geocoding

Geocoding is the process of converting an address, place name, or postal code to a set of latitude and longitude coordinates. Manually geocoding an address would require a lot of effort in creating a catalog of latitude and longitude coordinates and how they relate to postal addresses. Fortunately for us, there exists a plethora of geocoding services on the internet. All we have to do is to connect to them.

All geocoding services use latitude and longitude coordinates. It really doesn't matter which service we use. In the samples in this chapter, we're going to use the **Bing Maps API**. The Bing Maps API provides a series of geocoding services and we're going to use that API to really enhance our delivery application. In Chapter 4, we created an application key to interact with the Bing Maps Silverlight control, which we'll use now to interact with the Bing Maps API.

Time for action – Geocoding addresses to work

As mentioned previously, hardly anyone will know their latlong offhand. In order to work with the map control, we'll need a way to convert street addresses to latitude and longitude coordinates. The Bing Maps API provides a geocoding service for just this purpose. However, to access the geocoding API, we'll need to authenticate the geocoding service with the credentials we just created.

1. Open up Visual Studio and create a new Silverlight project and name it **DeliveryApplication**.

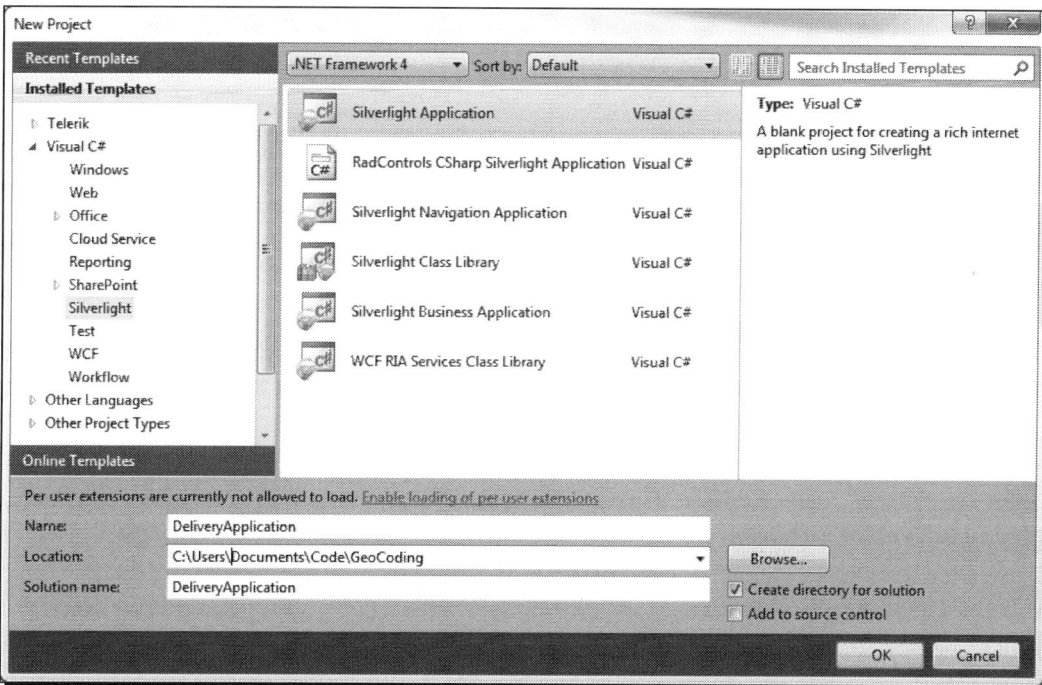

2. In order to use the Bing Silverlight Maps control, we'll need to add references to appropriate DLLs, just as we did in chapter 4. To do this, right click on the references folder in the **DeliveryApplication** project and choose **Add Reference...**

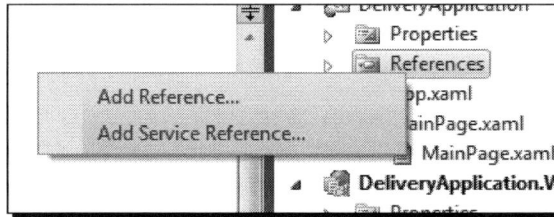

3. In the **Add Reference** dialog box, click on the **Browse** tab and browse to the directory where you installed the Bing Maps Silverlight control. Select both the `Microsoft.Maps.MapControl.dll` and `Microsoft.Maps.MapControl.Common.dll` files. Click **OK.**

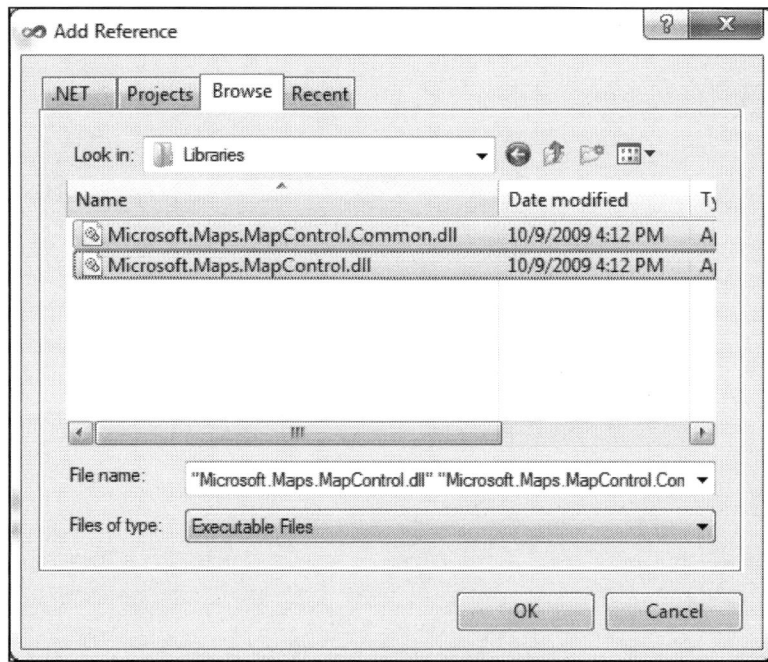

4. Next, we need to add the reference to the Bing Maps API web services. To do this, right-click on the `References` folder once again. This time however, click on **Add Service Reference...**

5. In the **Add Service Reference** dialog box, enter: `http://dev.virtualearth.`
`net/webservices/v1/geocodeservice/GeocodeService.svc` into the
Address textbox and click the **Go** button. Type **PlatformServices** into the
Namespace textbox and click **OK**.

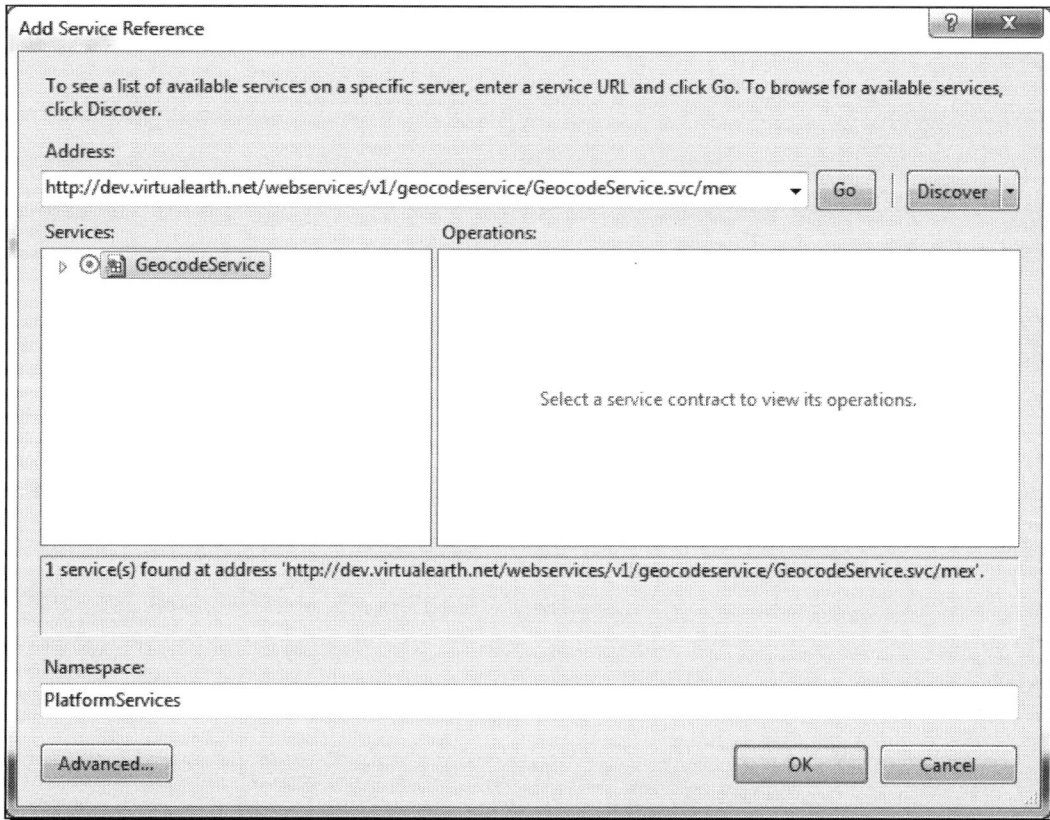

6. Next, we'll need to add our Bing Maps Account key as an application wide resource
in the `App.xaml` file. Modify the `App.xaml` file to the following. Make sure you
replace `[Bing Maps Account Key]` with your individual key:

```
<Application xmlns="http://schemas.microsoft.com/winfx/2006/xaml/
presentation"
            xmlns:x="http://schemas.microsoft.com/winfx/2006/
xaml"
            x:Class="DeliveryApplication.App"
            xmlns:sys="clr-namespace:System;assembly=mscorlib"
            >
    <Application.Resources>
```

```
        <sys:String x:Key="MyCredentials">[Bing Maps Account
Key]</sys:String>
    </Application.Resources>
</Application>
```

7. Edit the `MainPage.xaml` file, so that it contains the following XAML. Note how we reference the Bing Maps API key stored as a resource in the `App.xaml` file.

```
<UserControl x:Class="DeliveryApplication.MainPage"
    xmlns="http://schemas.microsoft.com/winfx/2006/xaml/
presentation"
    xmlns:x="http://schemas.microsoft.com/winfx/2006/xaml"
    xmlns:d="http://schemas.microsoft.com/expression/blend/2008"
    xmlns:mc="http://schemas.openxmlformats.org/markup-
compatibility/2006"
    mc:Ignorable="d"
    xmlns:m="clr-namespace:Microsoft.Maps.MapControl;assembly=Micr
osoft.Maps.MapControl"
    d:DesignHeight="300" d:DesignWidth="400">

    <Grid x:Name="LayoutRoot" Background="White">
        <Grid.ColumnDefinitions>
            <ColumnDefinition Width="271*" />
            <ColumnDefinition Width="100*" />
        </Grid.ColumnDefinitions>
        <Grid.RowDefinitions>
            <RowDefinition Height="255*" />
            <RowDefinition Height="45*" />
        </Grid.RowDefinitions>
        <m:Map x:Name="map"
            Center="39.04801,-76.84817"
            ZoomLevel="10"
            Grid.Row="0"
            Grid.ColumnSpan="2"
            >
            <m:Map.CredentialsProvider>
              <m:ApplicationIdCredentialsProvider
                  ApplicationId="{StaticResource MyCredentials}"
/>
            </m:Map.CredentialsProvider>
        </m:Map>
        <TextBox x:Name="txbAddress"
            Grid.Row="1"
            Grid.Column="0"
            Margin="10" />
        <Button x:Name="btnGeoCode"
```

```
                        Content="GeoCode"
                        Grid.Row="1"
                        Grid.Column="1"
                        Margin="5"
                        Click="btnGeoCode_Click" />

        </Grid>
</UserControl>
```

8. Next, we'll need to add some code in the `MainPage.xaml.cs` file. First, we'll add the click event handler for the **btnGeoCode** button. Note how we once again use the Bing Maps key stored in the `App.xaml` as our credentials to access the Bing API services.

```
private void btnGeoCode_Click(object sender, RoutedEventArgs e)
{

    PlatformServices.GeocodeServiceClient geocodeClient =
new PlatformServices.GeocodeServiceClient("CustomBinding_
IGeocodeService");

    PlatformServices.GeocodeRequest request = new
PlatformServices.GeocodeRequest();
    request.Query = txbAddress.Text;

    request.Credentials = new Credentials();
    request.Credentials.ApplicationId = App.Current.Resources["MyC
redentials"] as string;

    geocodeClient.GeocodeCompleted += new EventHandler<PlatformSer
vices.GeocodeCompletedEventArgs>(client_GeocodeCompleted);
    geocodeClient.GeocodeAsync(request);
}
```

9. In the above code, we make an asynchronous call to the Geocode service and assign an event handler for the `GeocodeCompleted` event. Let's add the following code:

```
private void client_GeocodeCompleted(object sender,
PlatformServices.GeocodeCompletedEventArgs e)
{
    PlatformServices.GeocodeResponse response = e.Result;
    if (response.Results.Count > 0)
    {
        PlatformServices.GeocodeResult result = response.Results.
First();
        if (result.Locations.Count > 0)
        {
```

```
        Pushpin pushpin = new Pushpin();

        Location location = new Location(result.Locations.
First().Latitude, result.Locations.First().Longitude);

        pushpin.Location = location;

        map.Children.Add(pushpin);

        map.SetView(result.BestView);

    }
  }
}
```

10. Run the solution by choosing **Start Debugging** from the **Debug** menu or by pressing *F5*.

11. Enter **12012 Sunset Hills Rd. Reston, VA 20191** into the textbox and click **GeoCode** and you'll see a pushpin marking the address.

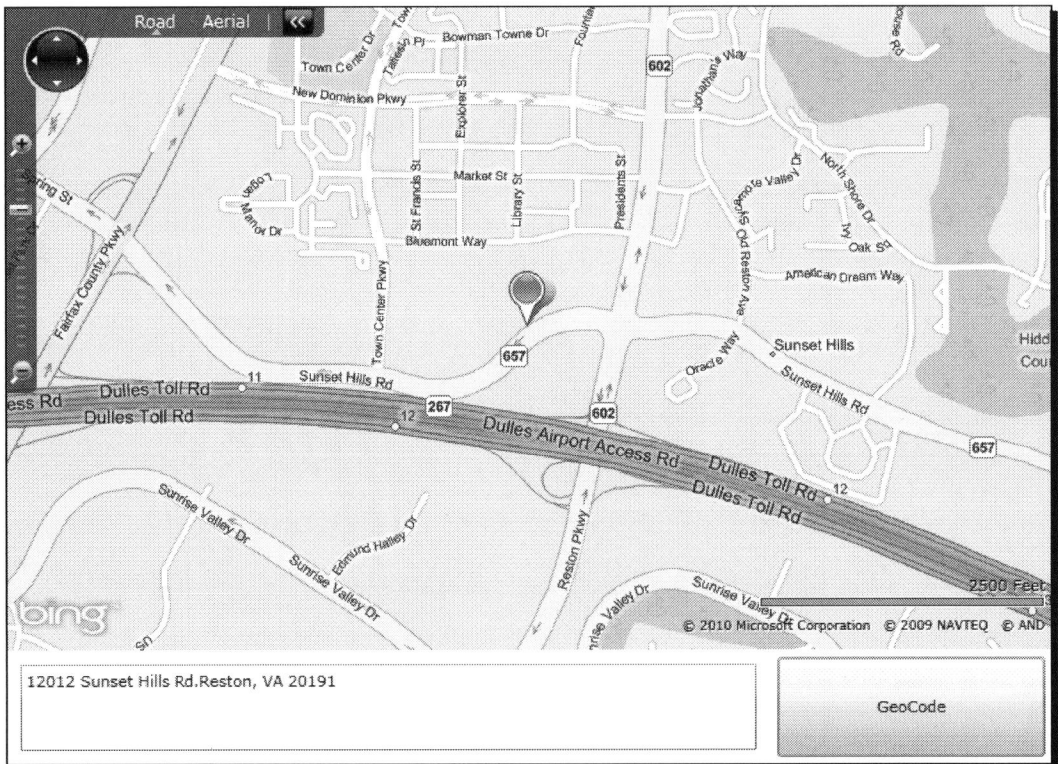

12. Now, enter **Washington Monument** into the textbox and click **Geocode,** then click on **Aerial** to switch to aerial view. You'll see the Washington Monument in the map control.

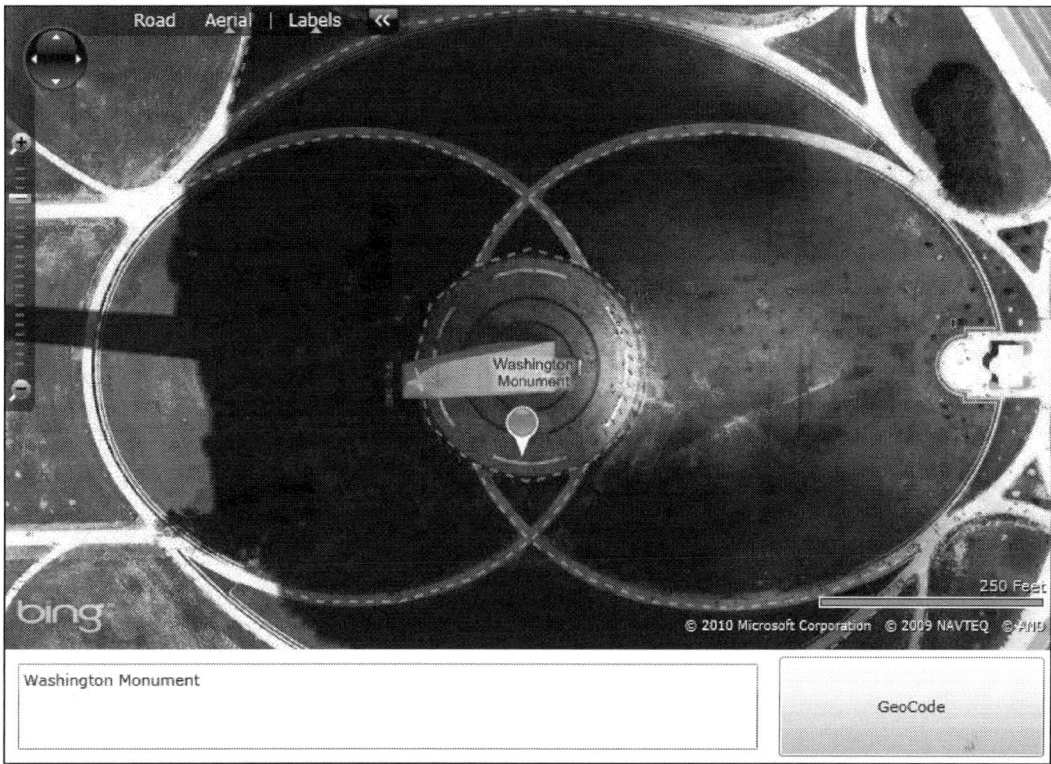

13. Have fun and experiment. The geocoding API will find zip codes, town names and landmarks from around the world. When you're done, close the browser window to end the debugging session.

What just happened?

We just created a Silverlight application that uses the Bing API geocoding service to place pushpins on the map in the corresponding location. You may have noticed that some addresses are a little off. This isn't an error in our code. If you've ever used a GPS navigation system and noticed that some addresses are slightly off the mark, then you'll be aware that geocoding is not an exact science. Some of the information linking addresses to latlongs has a degree of inaccuracy, so keep this in mind.

Let's take a closer look at the call to the Bing API web service. We start off the process in the btnGeoCode_Click method, where we create a `GeocodeServiceClient` object to communicate with the geocoding service. The geocode service requires a `GeocodeRequest` object. We set the `Query` property to the contents of the `txbAddress` textbox. We then add our Bing Maps key to the request's `Credentials.ApplicationId` property to gain access to the service. Once that's all done, we pass the request object to the `GeocodeAsync` method.

```
PlatformServices.GeocodeServiceClient geocodeClient = new
PlatformServices.GeocodeServiceClient("CustomBinding_
IGeocodeService");

PlatformServices.GeocodeRequest request = new PlatformServices.
GeocodeRequest();

request.Query = txbAddress.Text;

request.Credentials = new Credentials();

request.Credentials.ApplicationId = App.Current.Resources["MyCredentia
ls"] as string;

geocodeClient.GeocodeCompleted += new EventHandler<PlatformServices.
GeocodeCompletedEventArgs>(client_GeocodeCompleted);

geocodeClient.GeocodeAsync(request);
}
```

Like any service request in Silverlight, this request runs asynchronously. When the request comes back, the `client_GeocodeCompleted` event fires. That's where we take the first element in the `GeocodeResponse.Results` array and assign it to the `result` variable.

```
PlatformServices.GeocodeResult result = response.Results.First();
```

GeocodeResult contains an array of `Location` objects. Most of the time, we are only interested in the top result which is the first element of the array. Using LINQ, we get the latitude and longitude of the first result and create a new `Location` object. We take that location and assign it to a `Pushpin` object. Here is that code:

```
Location location = new Location(result.Locations.First().Latitude,
result.Locations.First().Longitude);

pushpin.Location = location;
```

Naturally, we'll need to add the `Pushpin` to the `map` control's `Children` collection in order for it to appear on our map:

```
map.Children.Add(pushpin);
```

Once that's done, we'll set the view of the map so that it focuses in on the geocoded location. `GeocodeResult` has a property which represents the best view for a given geocoded result. It's essentially a rectangle defined by a series of latitude and longitudes. The Bing Maps Silverlight control will automatically center and zoom in on that rectangle. The code to make that happen is one line:

```
map.SetView(result.BestView);
```

Wasn't that simple? The best part is that we get all the intelligence behind converting place names to a location included with the geocoding service. We didn't have to add any code to make that work. Now that we can convert addresses, place names and zip codes and then place markers onto the map that correspond with their latitude and longitude coordinates, we will want to go one more step by including route planning into our application.

Route planning

Those of you familiar with a GPS navigation system may already have some experience with route planning. You enter a starting point, then a destination, and the device calculates a route that connects the two points. Some GPS units even allow you to set preferences, such as avoiding toll roads or routing around traffic. Fortunately for us, the Bing Maps API provides services that rival any commercially available GPS unit. That means our applications can be as smart as those devices. We just have to code it.

Time for action – adding routing to our application

In order to add route planning to our application, we'll need to connect to Bing's route service. Bing's route service uses the same authentication scheme as the geocoding service. To support routing, we'll need to track the locations that we geocode. We'll also need to add UI elements to support multiple waypoints and route calculation. At the end of this exercise, we'll end up with something like this:

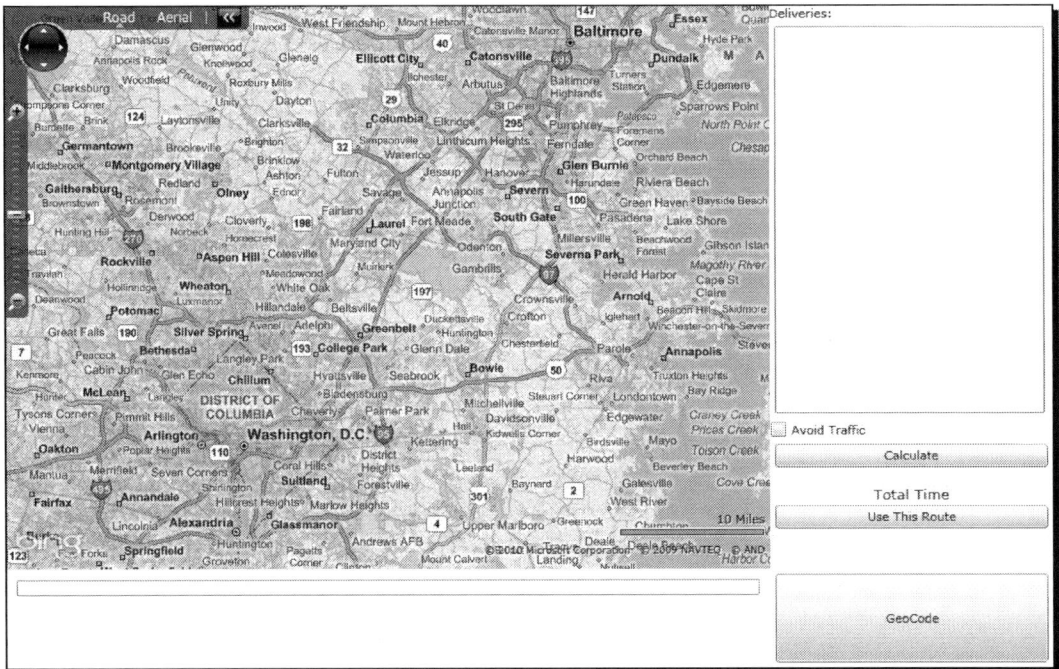

To get started, you will need to complete the following steps:

1. Open up the **DeliveryApplication** solution in Visual Studio.

2. Let's start off by connecting to the route service to our project. Right-click on the **DeliveryApplication** Silverlight project and choose **Add Service Reference...**

3. In the **Add Service Reference** dialog, enter: `http://dev.virtualearth.net/webservices/v1/routeservice/routeservice.svc` into the **Address** textbox and click **Go**. Type `RouteService` into the **Namespace** textbox and click **OK**.

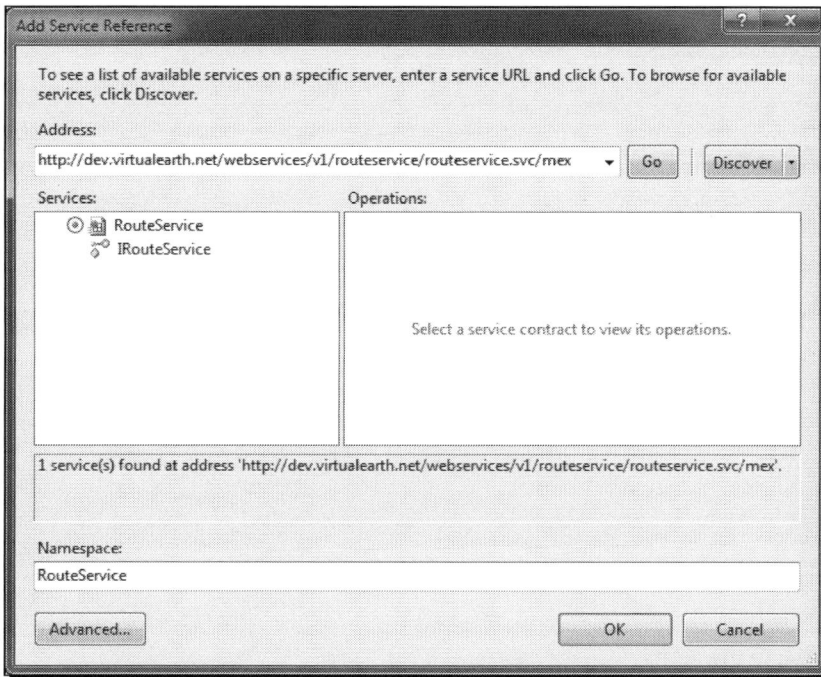

4. Next, we'll want to create a class to store delivery locations. Let's add a class file named `DeliveryLocation`. Right-click on the **DeliveryApplication** project in the **Solution Explorer** tab. Choose **Add|New Item...** from the context menu.

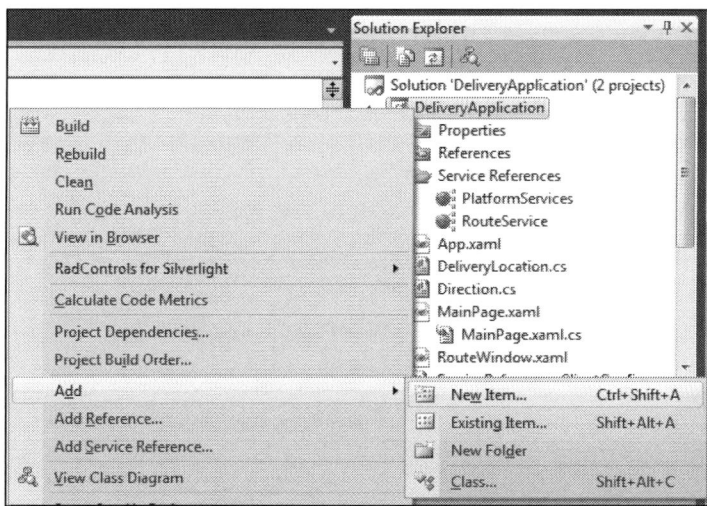

5. In the **Add New Item** dialog box, choose **Class**. Enter `DeliveryLocation.cs` in the **Name** textbox. Click **OK** to add the class.

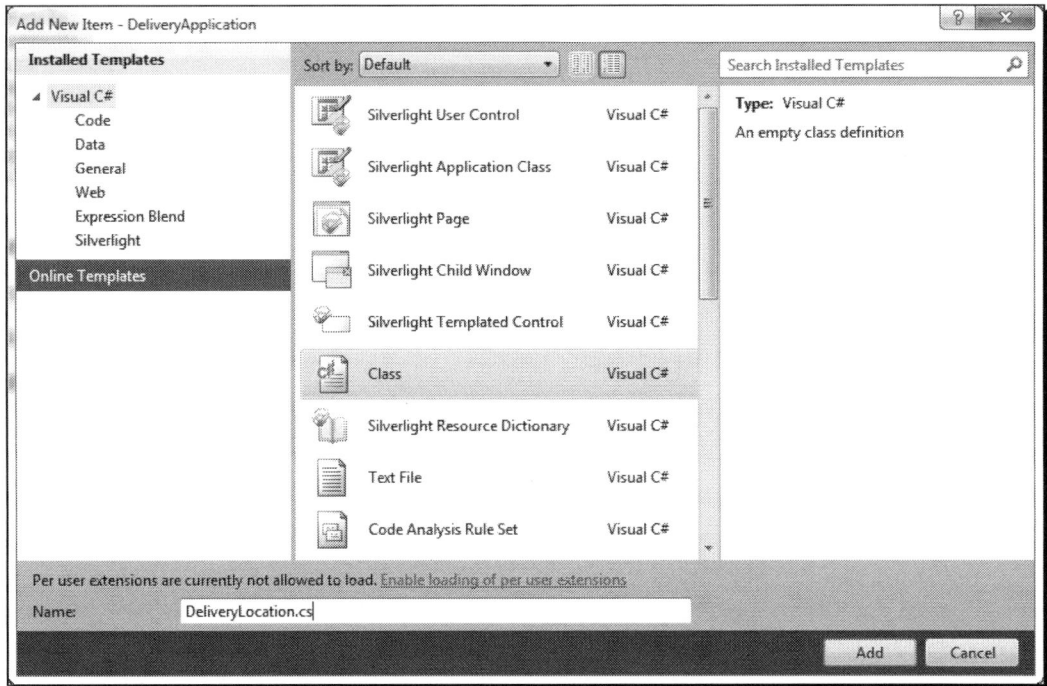

6. Edit the contents of the `DeliveryApplication.cs` file so that it contains the following code:

```
using Microsoft.Maps.MapControl;

namespace DeliveryApplication
{
    public class DeliveryLocation
    {
        public Location Location { get; set; }

        public string Address { get; set; }
    }
}
```

7. Now, let's update the UI. Edit the `MainPage.xaml` file so that it contains the following code:

```
<UserControl x:Class="DeliveryApplication.MainPage"
    xmlns="http://schemas.microsoft.com/winfx/2006/xaml/
presentation"
    xmlns:x="http://schemas.microsoft.com/winfx/2006/xaml"
    xmlns:d="http://schemas.microsoft.com/expression/blend/2008"
    xmlns:mc="http://schemas.openxmlformats.org/markup-
compatibility/2006"
    mc:Ignorable="d"
    xmlns:m="clr-namespace:Microsoft.Maps.MapControl;assembly=Micr
osoft.Maps.MapControl"
    Loaded="UserControl_Loaded"
    d:DesignHeight="768" d:DesignWidth="1024" >
    <Grid x:Name="LayoutRoot" Background="White">
        <Grid.ColumnDefinitions>
            <ColumnDefinition Width="271*" />
            <ColumnDefinition Width="100*" />
        </Grid.ColumnDefinitions>
        <Grid.RowDefinitions>
            <RowDefinition Height="188*" />
            <RowDefinition Height="67*" />
            <RowDefinition Height="45*" />
        </Grid.RowDefinitions>
        <m:Map x:Name="map"
              Center="39.04801,-76.84817"
              ZoomLevel="10" Grid.RowSpan="2">
            <m:Map.CredentialsProvider>
              <m:ApplicationIdCredentialsProvider
                ApplicationId="{StaticResource MyCredentials}"
/>
            </m:Map.CredentialsProvider>
            <m:MapLayer x:Name="routeLayer" />
        </m:Map>
        <TextBox x:Name="txbAddress"
                Grid.Row="2" Margin="10,10,10,68" />
        <Button x:Name="btnGeoCode"
                Content="GeoCode"
                Grid.Row="2"
                Grid.Column="1"
                Margin="5"
                Click="btnGeoCode_Click" />
        <TextBlock HorizontalAlignment="Left"
                VerticalAlignment="Top"
```

```
                        Text="Deliveries:"
                        TextWrapping="Wrap"
                        Grid.Column="1"/>
        <ListBox x:Name="lbxDestinations"
                    Margin="5,20,8,7"
                    Grid.Column="1"
                    Grid.RowSpan="1">
            <ListBox.ItemTemplate>
                <DataTemplate>
                    <StackPanel>
                        <TextBlock Text="{Binding Address}"
TextWrapping="Wrap"></TextBlock>
                            <StackPanel Orientation="Horizontal">
                                <Button Content="Up"
                                        Tag="{Binding}"
                                        Click="UpButton_Click" />
                                <Button Content="Down"
                                        Tag="{Binding}"
                                        Click="DownButton_Click" />
                                <Button Content="Remove"
                                        Tag="{Binding}"
                                        Click="RemoveButton_Click" />
                            </StackPanel>
                    </StackPanel>
                </DataTemplate>
            </ListBox.ItemTemplate>
        </ListBox>
        <StackPanel Grid.Column="1"
                    Grid.Row="1"
                    Orientation="Vertical"
                    d:LayoutOverrides="Height">
            <CheckBox x:Name="cbxTraffic"
        Content="Avoid Traffic" />
            <Button x:Name="btnCalculateRoute"
        Click="btnCalculateRoute_Click"
        Height="22"
        Content="Calculate" Margin="5,5,5,0"
            />
            <TextBlock x:Name="txbTotalTime"
                        Text="Total Time"
                        Margin="5,15,5,0"
                        TextWrapping="Wrap"
                        FontSize="13.333"
                        HorizontalAlignment="Center"
```

```
                    Width="70"/>
          <Button x:Name="btnUseRoute"
                    Click="btnUseRoute_Click"
                    Content="Use This Route"
                    Margin="5,0"/>
      </StackPanel>
    </Grid>
</UserControl>
```

8. Next, let's modify the code-behind file `MainPage.xaml.cs`. First, add the following `using` statements.

```
using Microsoft.Maps.MapControl;
using System.Collections.ObjectModel;
```

9. Add the two following private members to the class:

```
private ObservableCollection<DeliveryLocation> _locations = new
ObservableCollection<DeliveryLocation>();
private RouteService.RouteResponse _currentRoute;
```

10. Let's add some code to perform some geocoding. Let's add the event handler for the **GeoCode** button and the completed event handler for the web service call.

```
private void btnGeoCode_Click(object sender, RoutedEventArgs e)
{
    routeLayer.Children.Clear();

    PlatformServices.GeocodeServiceClient geocodeClient =
new PlatformServices.GeocodeServiceClient("CustomBinding_
IGeocodeService");

    PlatformServices.GeocodeRequest request = new
PlatformServices.GeocodeRequest();
    request.Culture = map.Culture;
    request.Query = txbAddress.Text;

    request.Credentials = new Credentials();
    request.Credentials.ApplicationId = App.Current.Resources["MyC
redentials"] as string;

    geocodeClient.GeocodeCompleted += new EventHandler<PlatformSer
vices.GeocodeCompletedEventArgs>(client_GeocodeCompleted);
    geocodeClient.GeocodeAsync(request);
}
```

```csharp
private void client_GeocodeCompleted(object sender,
PlatformServices.GeocodeCompletedEventArgs e)
{
    PlatformServices.GeocodeResponse response = e.Result;
    if (response.Results.Count > 0)
    {
        PlatformServices.GeocodeResult result = response.Results.
First();
        if (result.Locations.Count > 0)
        {
            Pushpin pushpin = new Pushpin();

            Location location = new Location(result.Locations.
First().Latitude, result.Locations.First().Longitude);

            pushpin.Location = location;
            map.Children.Add(pushpin);
            map.SetView(result.BestView);

            DeliveryLocation dl = new DeliveryLocation() { Address
= this.txbAddress.Text, Location = location };

            pushpin.Tag = dl;
            this._locations.Add(dl);
        }
    }
}
```

11. Now let's add the event handlers for the **Up**, **Down**, and **Remove** buttons.

```csharp
private void UpButton_Click(object sender, RoutedEventArgs e)
{
    Button btnSender = sender as Button;
    DeliveryLocation dl = btnSender.Tag as DeliveryLocation;

    MoveLocationUp(dl);
}
private void DownButton_Click(object sender, RoutedEventArgs e)
{
    Button btnSender = sender as Button;
    DeliveryLocation dl = btnSender.Tag as DeliveryLocation;

    MoveLocationDown(dl);
}
private void RemoveButton_Click(object sender, RoutedEventArgs e)
{
```

```
    Button btnSender = sender as Button;
    DeliveryLocation dl = btnSender.Tag as DeliveryLocation;

    ClearRoute();

    // Remove from collection
    this._locations.Remove(dl);

    // Find the marker
    var pushpinsToDelete = map.Children.OfType<Pushpin>().Where(x
=> x.Location == dl.Location);

    // Delete the marker
    pushpinsToDelete.ToList().ForEach(x => map.Children.
Remove(x));
}
```

12. Now, we'll add the supporting code for the above event handlers.

```
    private void MoveLocationUp(DeliveryLocation dl)
    {
        MoveLocation(dl, -1);
    }

    private void MoveLocationDown(DeliveryLocation dl)
    {
        MoveLocation(dl, 1);
    }
    private void MoveLocation(DeliveryLocation dl, int direction)
    {
        ClearRoute();

        if (this._locations.Count > 1)
        {
            int origIndex = this._locations.IndexOf(dl);
            this._locations.Remove(dl);
            this._locations.Insert(origIndex + direction, dl);
        }
    }
    private void ClearRoute()
    {
        this._currentRoute = null;
        routeLayer.Children.Clear();
        this.txbTotalTime.Text = "";
    }
```

13. Then we'll add the event handler for the **Calculate Route** button and the code responsible for making the call to the **Route** service and drawing the route on the map.

```
private void btnCalculateRoute_Click(object sender,
RoutedEventArgs e)
{
    routeLayer.Children.Clear();

    RouteService.RouteServiceClient routeServiceClient = new
RouteService.RouteServiceClient("CustomBinding_IRouteService");

    routeServiceClient.CalculateRouteCompleted += new EventHandler
<RouteService.CalculateRouteCompletedEventArgs>(routeServiceClient
_CalculateRouteCompleted);

    RouteService.RouteRequest routeRequest = new RouteService.
RouteRequest();
    routeRequest.Culture = map.Culture;
    routeRequest.Credentials = new Credentials();
    routeRequest.Credentials.ApplicationId = App.Current.Resources
["MyCredentials"] as string;

    routeRequest.Options = new RouteService.RouteOptions();
    routeRequest.Options.RoutePathType = RouteService.
RoutePathType.Points;

    routeRequest.ExecutionOptions = new RouteService.
ExecutionOptions();
    routeRequest.ExecutionOptions.SuppressFaults = true;

    if (this.cbxTraffic.IsChecked.Value)
    {
        routeRequest.Options.TrafficUsage = RouteService.
TrafficUsage.TrafficBasedRouteAndTime;
    }
    else
    {
        routeRequest.Options.TrafficUsage = RouteService.
TrafficUsage.None;
    }

    // Set the waypoints of the route to be calculated using the
Geocode Service results stored in the geocodeResults variable.
    routeRequest.Waypoints = new System.Collections.ObjectModel.
ObservableCollection<RouteService.Waypoint>();
```

```
    this._locations.ToList().ForEach(x => routeRequest.Waypoints.
Add(GeocodeResultToWaypoint(x)));

    // Make the CalculateRoute asnychronous request.
    routeServiceClient.CalculateRouteAsync(routeRequest);
}
private void routeServiceClient_CalculateRouteCompleted(object
sender, RouteService.CalculateRouteCompletedEventArgs e)
{
    if (e.Error == null)
    {
        long timeInSeconds = e.Result.Result.Summary.
TimeInSeconds;

        TimeSpan t = new TimeSpan(0, 0, int.Parse(timeInSeconds.
ToString()));

        this.txbTotalTime.Text = string.Format("Driving Time:
{0}", t.ToString());

        DrawRoute(e);

        this._currentRoute = e.Result;
    }
}


private RouteService.Waypoint GeocodeResultToWaypoint(DeliveryLoca
tion deliveryLocation)
{
    RouteService.Waypoint waypoint = new RouteService.Waypoint();
    waypoint.Description = deliveryLocation.Address;
    waypoint.Location = new Location();
    waypoint.Location.Latitude = deliveryLocation.Location.
Latitude;
    waypoint.Location.Longitude = deliveryLocation.Location.
Longitude;
    return waypoint;
}
private void DrawRoute(DeliveryApplication.RouteService.
CalculateRouteCompletedEventArgs e)
{
    if (e.Result.Result.Legs.Count > 0)
    {
        // Set properties of the route line you want to draw.
        Color routeColor = Colors.Blue;
```

```
          SolidColorBrush routeBrush = new SolidColorBrush(routeColo
r);

          MapPolyline routeLine = new MapPolyline();
          routeLine.Locations = new LocationCollection();
          routeLine.Stroke = routeBrush;
          routeLine.Opacity = 0.65;
          routeLine.StrokeThickness = 5.0;

          double distance = e.Result.Result.Summary.Distance;
          long seconds = e.Result.Result.Summary.TimeInSeconds;

          TimeSpan time = new TimeSpan(0, 0, int.Parse(seconds.
ToString()));

          // Retrieve the route points that define the shape of the
route.
          foreach (Location p in e.Result.Result.RoutePath.Points)
          {
              routeLine.Locations.Add(new Location(p.Latitude,
p.Longitude));
          }

          //routeLayer.AddChild(routeLine);

          routeLayer.Children.Add(routeLine);

          // Figure the rectangle which encompasses the route. This
is used later to set the map view.
          LocationRect rect = new LocationRect(routeLine.
Locations[0], routeLine.Locations[routeLine.Locations.Count - 1]);

          map.SetView(rect);
      }
}
```

14. In the `UserControl_Loaded` event handler, set the `ItemsSource` of the `lbxDestinations` listbox control to `_locations`:

```
private void UserControl_Loaded(object sender, RoutedEventArgs e)
{
   this.lbxDestinations.ItemsSource = this._locations;
}
```

15. Run the solution by choosing **Start Debugging** from the **Debug** menu or by pressing *F5*.

16. In the textbox type **Rockville, MD** and click the **GeoCode** button.

17. Once the marker for Rockville has been added, type in **Tysons Corner, VA** and click the **GeoCode** button so that you'll have two markers on the map.

18. Click on **Calculate** to calculate the route and you'll see the following:

19. Notice that the **Driving Time** textbox displays the estimated time it would take to drive the route.

20. Check the **Avoid Traffic** checkbox and click **Get Route** once again.

21. Depending on when you get the route and the traffic conditions between Rockville, MD and Tysons Corner, VA, the route will change. Here's a sample of what the route looks like when there's a severe traffic incident on the connector road between I-270 South and I-495 West.

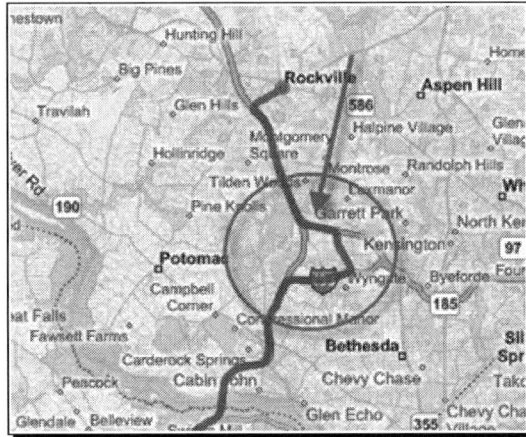

22. For fun, let's add another location that's really far away from the DC area. The folks on the Silverlight team in Redmond deserve a cake. Let's type in **1 Microsoft Way, Redmond, WA** , click **GeoCode**, and then click **Get Route**. Immediately, you'll notice that it will take considerably longer to get the result back.

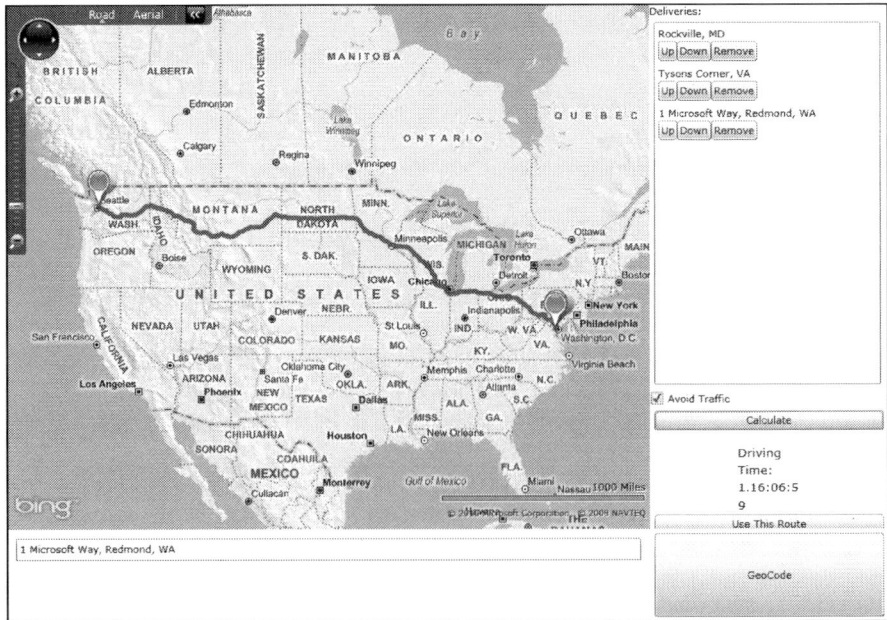

23. Go ahead, have fun and play with the routing service by adding different way points. Add as many delivery stops as you like and use the **Up**, **Down**, and **Remove** buttons to change the delivery route.

24. Try running the same route with the **Avoid Traffic** option checked and then cleared. Note the differences which are most obvious during peak traffic times.

25. When you have finished, close the browser window to end the debugging session.

What just happened?

We connected to a route calculation service provided by the Bing Maps API. This routing service returns a custom driving route based on the parameters we send to it. Let's take a closer look at the code we added, particularly the modification we made to the map control.

```
<m:MapLayer x:Name="routeLayer" />
```

That line of XAML adds a `MapLayer` named `routeLayer` to the map control. Maps can have any number of layers. In previous work with adding elements to the map control, we simply added to the control's `Children` collection. Using layers gives us an extra level of control over how to display data on a map. The visibility of `MapLayer` can be turned on and off independent of other `MapLayer` elements or other elements in the `Children` collection of a map. In fact, the line of code below, the first line of code in the `btnGetRoute_Click` method, clears all the elements in the `Children` collection of the `routeLayer`.

```
routeLayer.Children.Clear();
```

When the user adds additional delivery stops or turns traffic avoidance on or off and then clicks on **Get Route**, the route is re-drawn. We can clear the layer so as not to confuse the user with the new route being drawn on top of the old one. Since the location markers are not part of the `routeLayer`, they are not touched.

The routing service's `CalculateRoute` method accepts one parameter: a `RouteRequest` object. The line of code below creates a `RouteRequest` object named `routeRequest`:

```
RouteService.RouteRequest routeRequest = new RouteService.
RouteRequest();
```

As before, we assign the credentials to our request object:

```
routeRequest.Credentials = new Credentials();
routeRequest.Credentials.ApplicationId =  App.Current.Resources["MyCre
dentials"] as string;
```

The routing service supports a number of configuration options. These options are represented by the `RouteOptions` object set, the `Options` property of the `RouteRequest` object to a new instance of a `RouteOptions` object. We then set `RoutePathType` to `Points`:

```
routeRequest.Options = new RouteService.RouteOptions();
routeRequest.Options.RoutePathType = RouteService.RoutePathType.
Points;
```

The user interface has the option to avoid traffic when we calculate a route. The following code uses the `cbxTraffic` checkbox's `IsChecked` property to set the `TrafficUsage` property to the appropriate value:

```
if (this.cbxTraffic.IsChecked.Value)
{
  routeRequest.Options.TrafficUsage = RouteService.TrafficUsage.
TrafficBasedRouteAndTime;
}
else
{
routeRequest.Options.TrafficUsage = RouteService.TrafficUsage.None;
}
```

Now that all the options in our `RouteRequest` object have been set, it's time to add the waypoints we have selected. The code below sets the `Waypoints` property to an `ObservableCollection` of `WayPoints` and uses LINQ to parse through all the elements in the `_deliveryStops` and pass it to the `GeocodeResultToWaypoint` method.

```
    routeRequest.Waypoints = new System.Collections.ObjectModel.Observ
ableCollection<RouteService.Waypoint>();

    this._deliveryStops.ToList().ForEach(x => routeRequest.Waypoints.
Add(GeocodeResultToWaypoint(x)));
```

The `GeocodeResultToWaypoint` method below converts a `DeliveryStop` object to a `Waypoint` object that the routing service uses:

```
private RouteService.Waypoint GeocodeResultToWaypoint(DeliveryStop
deliveryStop)
{
    RouteService.Waypoint waypoint = new RouteService.Waypoint();
    waypoint.Description = deliveryStop.Address;
    waypoint.Location = new RouteService.Location();
    waypoint.Location.Latitude = deliveryStop.Location.Latitude;
    waypoint.Location.Longitude = deliveryStop.Location.Longitude;
    return waypoint;
}
```

With the all the options set, it's time to call the routing service's `CalculateRoute` method and pass the `RouteRequest` object we just set up:

```
client.CalculateRouteAsync(routeRequest);
```

When the web service returns, first we get the estimated time it will take to drive the route. This information is stored as seconds. The following code takes the result, converts it into something more meaningful and shows it on the user interface.

```
long timeInSeconds = e.Result.Result.Summary.TimeInSeconds;
TimeSpan t = new TimeSpan(0, 0, int.Parse(timeInSeconds.ToString()));
this.txbTime.Text = string.Format("Driving Time: {0}", t.ToString());
```

Next, there is the call to the `DrawRoute` method. This is the method where we will actually draw onto the `MapLayer`:

```
DrawRoute(e);
```

The `DrawRoute` method creates a `MapPolyline` object named `routeLine` and sets its display properties as follows:

```
MapPolyline routeLine = new MapPolyline();
routeLine.Locations = new LocationCollection();
routeLine.Stroke = routeBrush;
routeLine.Opacity = 0.65;
routeLine.StrokeThickness = 5.0;
```

The `MapPolyLine` takes a series of latlong points and renders them on the map as a line. The code below iterates through the results from the routing service and adds them to the `MapPolyline`:

```
foreach (RouteService.Location p in e.Result.Result.RoutePath.Points)
{
    routeLine.Locations.Add(new Location(p.Latitude, p.Longitude));
}
```

Once complete, the following code adds the `routeLine` to the `routeLayer`:

```
routeLayer.AddChild(routeLine);
```

You may have noticed that the map automatically centers on the route. The code below gets the bounding rectangle of the `routeLine` and sets the map's `View` property accordingly.

```
LocationRect rect = new LocationRect(routeLine.Locations[0],
routeLine.Locations[routeLine.Locations.Count - 1]);

// Set the map view using the rectangle which bounds the rendered //
route.
map.View = map.GetViewFromBoundingRectangle(rect);
```

The routing service returns a great deal of information. The best way to see everything is to use Visual Studio's debugging tools. If you place a breakpoint in the `DrawRoute` method, use the **QuickWatch** feature of Visual Studio to examine the results more closely by examining the `e.Result.Result` object.

> QuickWatch is a debugging tool in Visual Studio that lets you examine objects in memory more closely.

To activate QuickWatch and get a closer look at the result set, set a breakpoint at the `DrawRoute` method and right-click on `e.Result.Result`. Choose **Expression: 'e.Result. Result'|QuickWatch...** from the context menu as shown in the following screenshot:

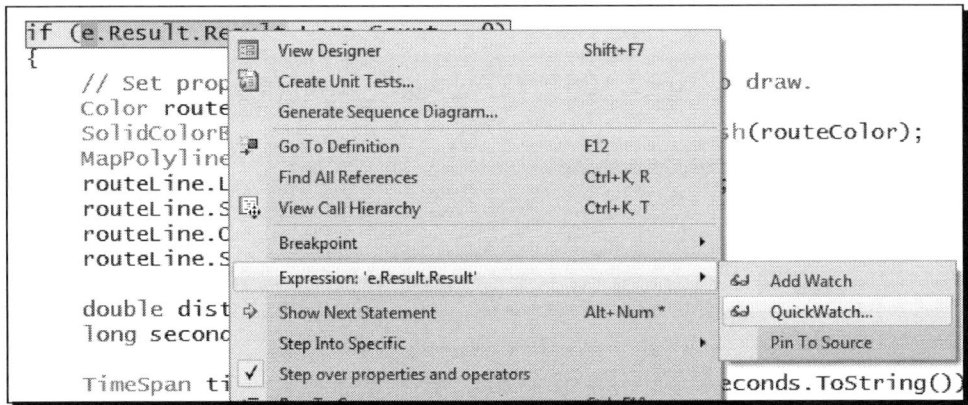

The QuickWatch dialog box will display a tree view of all the values in **e.Result.Result.** Feel free to explore all the data it contains to see just how rich the Bing Maps API is.

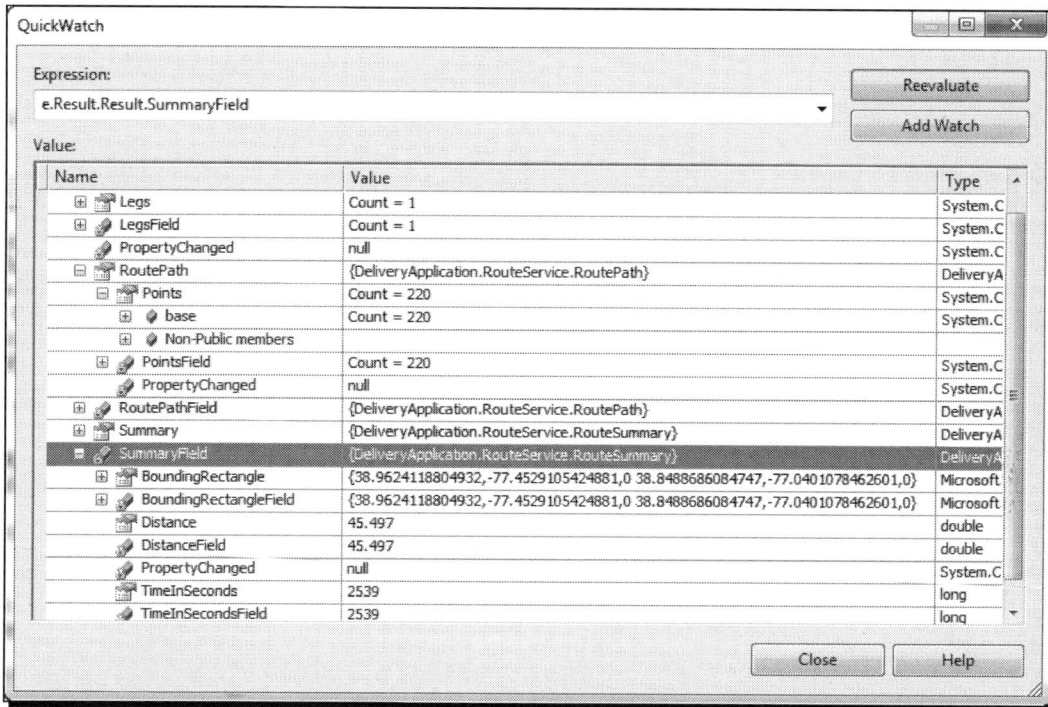

Name	Value	Type
⊞ Legs	Count = 1	System.C
⊞ LegsField	Count = 1	System.C
PropertyChanged	null	System.C
⊟ RoutePath	{DeliveryApplication.RouteService.RoutePath}	DeliveryA
⊟ Points	Count = 220	System.C
⊞ base	Count = 220	System.C
⊞ Non-Public members		
⊞ PointsField	Count = 220	System.C
PropertyChanged	null	System.C
⊞ RoutePathField	{DeliveryApplication.RouteService.RoutePath}	DeliveryA
⊞ Summary	{DeliveryApplication.RouteService.RouteSummary}	DeliveryA
⊟ SummaryField	{DeliveryApplication.RouteService.RouteSummary}	DeliveryA
⊞ BoundingRectangle	{38.9624118804932,-77.4529105424881,0 38.8488686084747,-77.0401078462601,0}	Microsoft
⊞ BoundingRectangleField	{38.9624118804932,-77.4529105424881,0 38.8488686084747,-77.0401078462601,0}	Microsoft
Distance	45.497	double
DistanceField	45.497	double
PropertyChanged	null	System.C
TimeInSeconds	2539	long
TimeInSecondsField	2539	long

Bing Maps API has rich functionality which can be explored and examined further by referring to the following links:

♦ http://www.viawindowslive.com/VirtualEarth.aspx

♦ http://msdn.microsoft.com/en-us/library/dd877956.aspx

Summary

In this chapter, we explored two elements that would be useful to delivery personnel: signature capture and route planning. When building the signature capture control, we used a custom control rather than a user control. Custom controls can be a template and formatted in any number of ways. Finally, we took the map control to the next level of utility by connecting it to a power API exposed by a service.

In this chapter we specifically discussed the following:

- How to create a custom, lookless control
- How to create our own DependencyProperties
- How to use the TemplateBinding syntax
- How to sign up for Bing Maps API developer account
- How to retrieve an authentication token from the Bing Maps API servers
- How to use Geocode locations using the Bing Maps API
- How to get a driving route from the Bing Maps API
- How to draw a line on the map that corresponds to a driving route

In the next chapter, we will discuss how to architect loosely coupled Silverlight applications so that they are more scalable and extensible.

10
Where to Go From Here

Throughout this book, we have learned a lot about Silverlight development. From the basics of XAML to building a location aware application, we have covered a lot of ground. Now at this point in our journey, let's take a look ahead to see where we can go from here.

In this chapter, we shall:

◆ Taking Silverlight out of the browser

◆ Going offline with Silverlight

◆ Understanding Windows Presentation Foundation

◆ Examining the future of Silverlight

More Silverlight features

Making a Silverlight application mobile involves more than just installing it on a mobile computer. There are several factors to consider when making an application mobile. While your code will run on a netbook just as it would on a standard laptop or desktop computer, creating a well crafted mobile solution requires special planning.

First and foremost is network availability. Even the best implemented mobile telephone network has holes in its coverage areas. Realistically speaking, a connected application is actually an occasionally connected application. This especially applies to your application once it is taken outside of the confines of an office environment. Therefore, any well conceived solution must take into account offline use.

Checking network connectivity

Most web based applications would fail if the user lost network connectivity. Most HTML based solutions require interaction between the server and the client to process data or maintain their state. Since Silverlight runs entirely on the local machine, it can continue to operate and use local resources even if the network is unavailable.

However, you probably would want to know if the network was unreachable before making any calls to a network-based resource. Sure, we could make the call and wait for a timeout error and handle the error accordingly. However, that approach forces the user to wait for a response that will never come and the resulting error message may not be relevant—a timeout error only proves that a given resource could not be reached in a certain amount of time. Ideally, we should check if there is a network connection before attempting to use a network resource. If we had that information, we could design the interface to prevent the user from making network calls while the connection was unavailable.

Fortunately, checking network availability can be accomplished with just one line of code. The `NetworkInterface` class in the `System.Net.NetworkInformation` namespace has a method that returns **true** if the network is available and **false** if it is not. To test network availability, the code is as simple as:

```
bool networkAvail = NetworkInterface.GetIsNetworkAvailable();
```

You can check for network availability at startup or prior to making a web service call. However, a more useful approach would be subscribing to the `NetworkAddressChanged` event. This event fires when the network address changes and when you lose and regain network connectivity. To subscribe to this event, just add this line of code to your application:

```
NetworkChange.NetworkAddressChanged += new NetworkAddressChangedEventH
andler(NetworkChange_NetworkAddressChanged);
```

> The `GetIsNetworkAvailable` method only tells you if you have a connection to a network, not if you can reach a particular URL or web service.

Checking for a network connection makes your Silverlight application more robust and more able to work in occasionally connected scenarios. Let's see how to put together a Silverlight application that knows when it's connected to the network and when it's not.

Time for action – detecting network connectivity

Let's see how to use the `GetIsNetworkAvailable` method and the
`NetworkAddressChanged` event together in making a more connection savvy solution.

1. Create a new Silverlight application in Visual Studio and name it **OfflineTestApp**.

2. Add the following XAML code to the `Grid` named `LayoutRoot` in the
`MainPage.xaml` file:

```
<Ellipse  x:Name="ellipseIndicator"
 Height="82"
 HorizontalAlignment="Center"
 Stroke="Black"
 Fill="Gray"
 StrokeThickness="1"
 VerticalAlignment="Top"
 Width="86" />
```

3. In the `MainPage.xaml.cs` file, add this line of code to the `MainPage` constructor
method, right after the `InitializeComponent` method call:

```
NetworkChange.NetworkAddressChanged += new NetworkAddressChangedEv
entHandler(NetworkChange_NetworkAddressChanged);
```

4. Add the following event handler method to the `MainPage.xaml` file:

```
private void NetworkChange_NetworkAddressChanged(object sender,
EventArgs e)
{
    if (NetworkInterface.GetIsNetworkAvailable())
    {
this.ellipseIndicator.Fill = new SolidColorBrush(Colors.Green);
    }
    else
    {
this.ellipseIndicator.Fill = new SolidColorBrush(Colors.Red);
    }
}
```

5. Run the solution by pressing *F5* or choosing **Start Debugging** from the **Debug** menu.
We will see a gray circle:

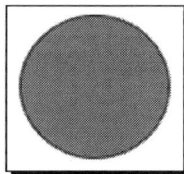

6. Here's the fun part; disconnect from the network by either removing the Ethernet cable or disabling your wireless adapter. The circle turned red:

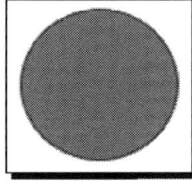

7. Reconnect to the network by either plugging the Ethernet cable back in or re-enabling the wireless adapter. The circle will turn green:

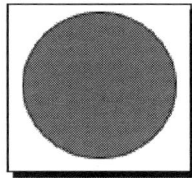

8. Close the browser window to stop debugging the application.

What just happened?

We just created a simple network connectivity tester by clubbing the `GetIsNetworkAvailable` method and the `NetworkAddressChanged` event. The `NetworkChange_NetworkAddressChanged` event handler changes the fill color of the ellipse named `ellipseIndicator` whenever the network address changes as it does when it loses connectivity. Based on the value returned by the `GetIsNetworkAvailable`, we turn the ellipse red or green.

So why was the ellipse gray when the application first started? Simple, the `NetworkAddressChanged` event hadn't fired yet and we didn't change the ellipse's color from the default defined in the XAML. This is an important point to make: the `NetworkAddressChanged` event only fires when the address changes. If we rely only on code called by this method to set our initial state, we could be in for a rude surprise. We can fix that by refactoring the code a little bit.

Have a go hero – refactoring the code

Let's go back to the **OfflineTestApp** solution we just created and modify the code so it is a little more scalable.

1. Add the following method to the `MainPage.xaml.cs` file:

```
private void UpdateIndicator()
{
    if (NetworkInterface.GetIsNetworkAvailable())
    {
this.ellipseIndicator.Fill = new SolidColorBrush(Colors.Green);
    }
    else
    {
this.ellipseIndicator.Fill = new SolidColorBrush(Colors.Red);
    }
}
```

2. Replace all the code in the `NetworkChange_NetworkAddressChanged` event handler with the following line:

```
UpdateIndicator();
```

3. Add the same line to the constructor method:

```
UpdateIndicator();
```

4. For reference, the `MainPage.xaml.cs` file should look like this:

```
public MainPage()
{
    InitializeComponent();
    NetworkChange.NetworkAddressChanged += new NetworkAddressChang
edEventHandler(NetworkChange_NetworkAddressChanged);
    UpdateIndicator();
}
private void NetworkChange_NetworkAddressChanged(object sender,
EventArgs e)
{
    UpdateIndicator();
}
private void UpdateIndicator()
{
    if (NetworkInterface.GetIsNetworkAvailable())
```

```
        {
this.ellipseIndicator.Fill = new SolidColorBrush(Colors.Green);
        }
        else
        {
this.ellipseIndicator.Fill = new SolidColorBrush(Colors.Red);
        }
    }
```

5. Run the solution, and depending on your network connection, you will either see a green circle or a red circle.

Executing outside the browser

Making a Silverlight application more sensitive to changes in network connectivity is only the first step to creating a more robust solution. If a Silverlight application is hosted in a browser window and the user refreshes the page, one of two things will happen. Either the page will be cached locally and your application's state will reset or the user will see an error screen such as the next one:

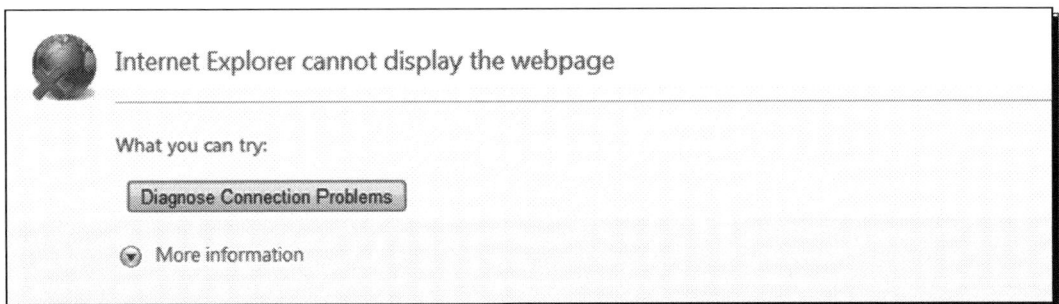

Neither one of these scenarios is appealing; either way, the data that your user was working with could be lost. While a smart application developer would preserve the state and handle an accidental refresh gracefully, there could still be further complications. The better solution for applications designed to be used on the go would be to take the browser entirely out of the equation. Yes, you read that right.

We want to remove a web-based application from the confines of the browser. Silverlight supports the notion of running out-of-the-browser, where end users can choose to detach a Silverlight application from its hosting page and install it on the local desktop machine. Once on the desktop, end users can start the application regardless of their network connection status. End users will even have the option to create shortcuts to the application on the desktop and, if they are running Windows, add a shortcut in the **Start** menu as well.

Enabling out of browser support

In order for a Silverlight application to run locally, you must enable out of browser support in your Silverlight project. In the Silverlight project properties window, you will need to make sure the checkbox for **Enable running application out of the browser** is checked. The **Out-of-Browser Settings...** button opens up a settings window that lets us further customize our application's installation.

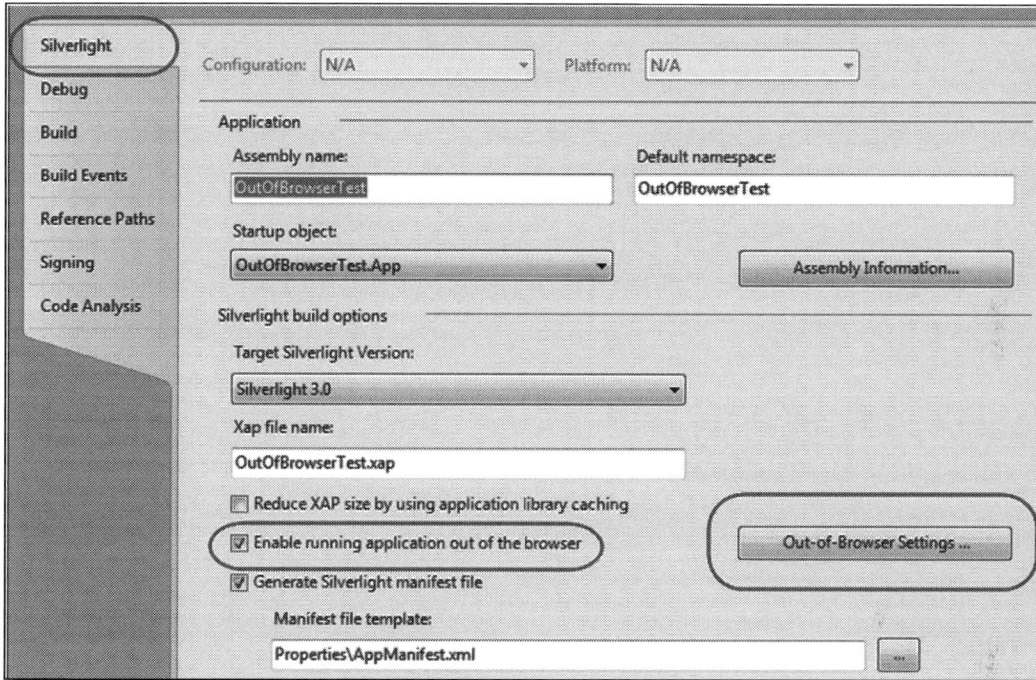

Let's explore building an out-of-browser solution.

Time for action – creating an out-of-browser solution

Adding out-of-browser support to a Silverlight application is quite easy, as shown below:

1. Create a new Silverlight application in Visual Studio and name it **OutOfBrowserTestApp**.

2. Add the following XAML code to the Grid named LayoutRoot in the MainPage.xaml file:

```
<Button x:Name="btnInstallLocally"
Content="Install Locally"
        Click="btnInstallLocally_Click"
```

```
            Height="23"
            Width="109"
            HorizontalAlignment="Left"
            Margin="12,30,0,0"
            VerticalAlignment="Top"
/>
```

3. In the `MainPage.xaml.cs` file, add the following code:

```
private void btnInstallLocally_Click(object sender,
RoutedEventArgs e)
{
    Application.Current.Install();
}
```

4. Your `MainPage.xaml` should look like this in design view:

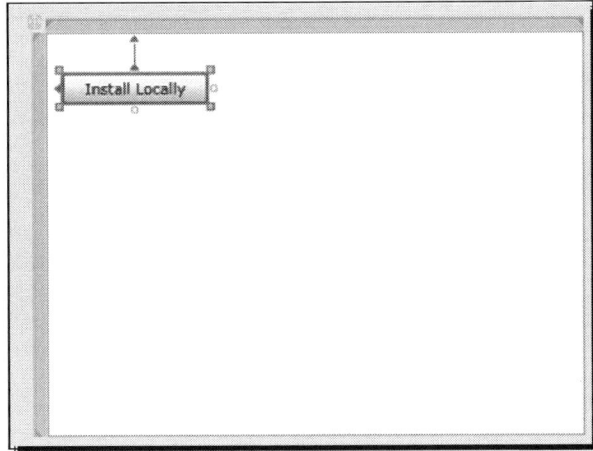

5. Next, we will enable out of browser support in the project settings. To do this, right mouse click on the Silverlight project in **Solution Explorer**:

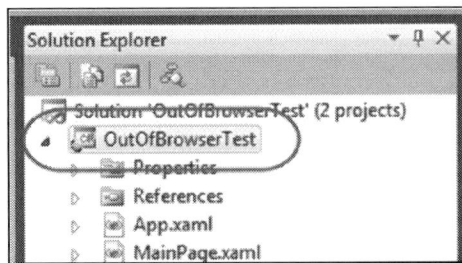

6. This brings up the project settings window. Click on the **Silverlight** tab to edit the Silverlight specific settings for this project:

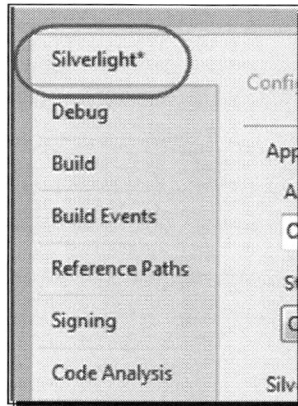

7. Make sure that the checkbox for **Enable running application out of browser** is checked:

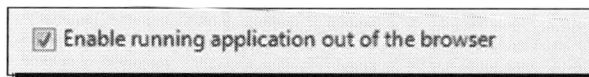

8. Click on the **Out-of-Browser Settings** button:

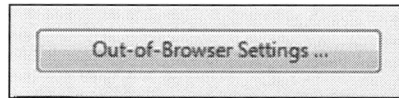

9. Customize the text in the **Window Title**, **Shortcut Name**, and **Application Description** fields:

Out-of-Browser Settings

Window Title

OutOfBrowserTest Application

Width   Height

Shortcut name

OutOfBrowserTest Application

Application description

OutOfBrowserTest Application on your desktop; at home, at work or on the go.

16 x 16 Icon

...

32 x 32 Icon

...

48 x 48 Icon

...

128 x 128 Icon

...

Use GPU Acceleration

Show install menu

OK   Cancel

10. Click the **OK** button.

11. Run the solution by pressing *F5* or choosing **Start Debugging** from the **Debug** menu.

12. Click on the **Install Locally** button and we can see the install dialog appear:

13. Check the checkbox next to **Desktop** and click on **OK**.

14. The application now appears in a separate window detached from the browser:

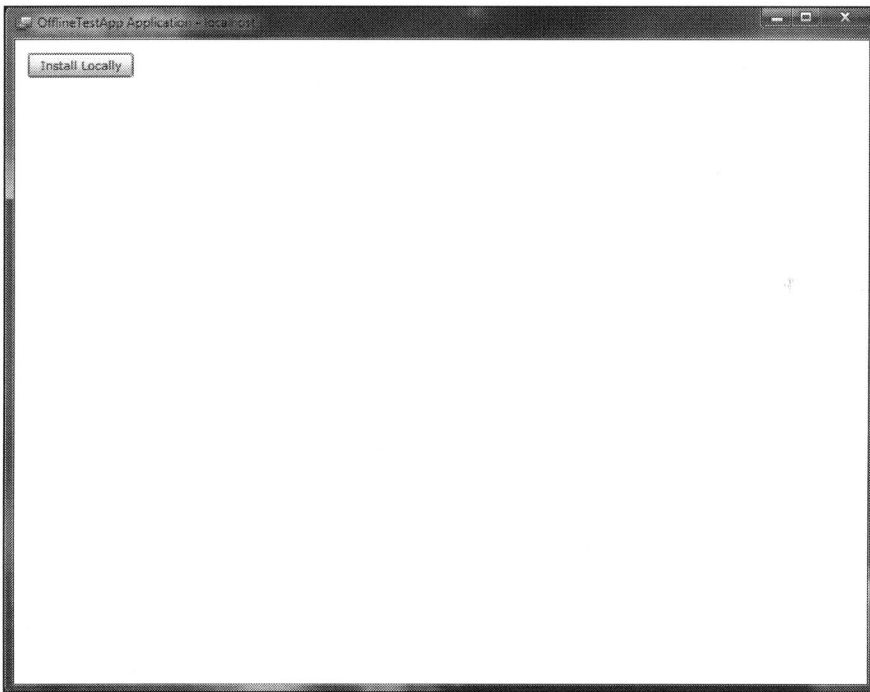

15. Notice that the application hosted in the browser is still running in a background window. Click on that window to activate it.

16. Click on the **Install Locally** button once again.

17. You will see Visual Studio reporting that an exception has been thrown with an error message of **Application is already installed**.

```
blic partial class MainPage : UserControl

    public MainPage()
    {
        InitializeComponent();
    }

    private void btnInstallLocally_Click(object sender, Rou
    {
        Application.Current.Install();
    }
```

InvalidOperationException was u

Application is already installed.

18. Choose **Stop Debugging** from the **Debug** menu to stop the debugger.

What just happened?

We modified the Silverlight application to support running out of the browser and customized our install experience. We changed the name of our application, some of its metadata and provided a UI-based method of installing the application. Remember, not all users will be tech savvy enough to right-click click on your application to look for the install context menu. Giving them a choice to install the application through the interface is a good habit.

When we tried to install an already installed application, we saw that the Silverlight runtime will throw an exception. This is important to note that we cannot install the same application twice. To avoid throwing an exception at run time, we can check the `Application.Current.InstallState` property to see if our application is already installed. In fact, let's do that now.

Time for action – checking the InstallState property

We are going to check to see if our application is already installed before installing it. If it is, we will alert the user by showing a messagebox. Otherwise, we will install it.

1. Open the **OutOfBrowserTestApp** solution we just created in Visual Studio.

2. Open up the `MainPage.xaml.cs` file and modify the `btnInstallLocally_Click` method, so that it contains the following code:

```
private void btnInstallLocally_Click(object sender,
RoutedEventArgs e)
{
```

```
        if (Application.Current.InstallState == InstallState.
Installed)
        {
MessageBox.Show("Application already installed");
        }
        else
        {
Application.Current.Install();
        }
    }
```

3. Run the solution by pressing *F5* or choosing **Debug Solution** from the **Debug** menu.

4. Click on the **Install Locally** button. We will see a dialog box telling us that the application is already installed:

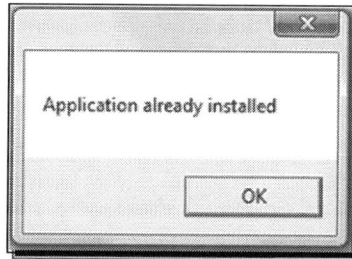

5. Close the browser window to stop debugging the solution.

What just happened?

We added some logic to our Silverlight application to see if it has already been installed by looking at the `Application.Current.InstallState` property. The `Application.Current.InstallState` property is an enumeration of `InstallState`, which defines four states: `NotInstalled`, `Installed`, `Installing`, and `InstallFailed`.

When the `Application.Current.InstallState` property changes, the `Application.Current.InstallStateChanged` event is fired.

The ability to run Silverlight outside of a browser radically changes the landscape of client application development technologies. However, there are very good reasons to use **Windows Presentation Foundation (WPF)**, the big brother of Silverlight.

Installing a Silverlight application locally

Installing a Silverlight application locally is easy: you simply right click on the Silverlight application and choose **Install [application name] Application onto this computer...** from the context menu as follows:

Silverlight
Install OfflineTestApp Application onto this computer...

This brings up the **Install application** dialog, which on Windows looks like the following:

Clicking **OK** installs the program locally (even if the user does not have administrator rights).

Alternatively, we can write code to install the application within our own user interface. For example, we could add an **Install Locally** button. The `Click` event handler for that button would only have to contain the following line of code:

```
Application.Current.Install();
```

Deployment concerns

Allowing end users (even ones without administrative rights) to install their own applications may sound like a nightmare scenario to many network administrators. However, these fears are unfounded. Silverlight applications running out-of-browser are subject to the same security restrictions as those running inside of a browser. Updating an installed Silverlight application is easy as well. Your application can either provide a **Check for Updates** button or perform the update check automatically and notify the user that an update is available. The following code demonstrates checking for updates to the Silverlight XAP:

```
App.Current.CheckAndDownloadUpdateCompleted += new CheckAndDownloadUpd
ateCompletedEventHandler(App_CheckAndDownloadUpdateCompleted);
App.Current.CheckAndDownloadUpdateAsync();
```

The `CheckAndDownloadUpdateAsync` method causes Silverlight to check the original XAP URI using an HTTP GET to see if it has been updated from the current version. If an update does exist, the HTTP response from the update check contains the updated bits. The `CheckAndDownloadUpdateCompleted` event is raised once the response is received and the code in the event handler notifies the user of the update:

```
void App_CheckAndDownloadUpdateCompleted(object sender,
CheckAndDownloadUpdateCompletedEventArgs e)
{
  if (e.UpdateAvailable)
  {
    MessageBox.Show("An application update has been downloaded. " +
       "Restart the application to run the new version.");
  }
  else if (e.Error != null &&
    e.Error is PlatformNotSupportedException)
  {
    MessageBox.Show("An application update is available, " +
       "but it requires a new version of Silverlight. " +
       "Visit the application home page to upgrade.");
  }
  else
  {
    MessageBox.Show("There is no update available.");
  }
}
```

Uninstalling a Silverlight application

To uninstall a Silverlight application, you can right-click on the application and choose **Remove this application...** from the context menu.

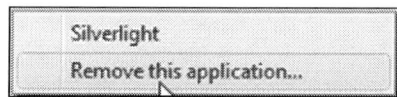

On the following dialog box, users are asked to confirm whether or not to permanently remove the application. To cancel the uninstall process, click **No**. To confirm the remove operation, click **Yes**.

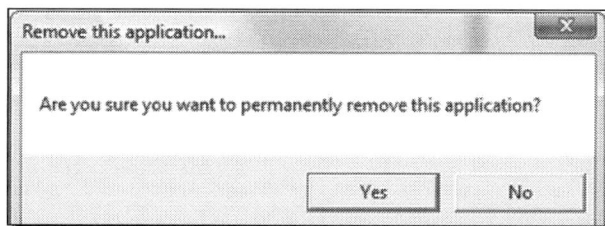

Beyond Silverlight

As fully featured and robust as Silverlight is, it still has its limitations. Remember that Silverlight is web-centric and cross-platform. That means that all your code will run in a sandboxed environment with limited privileges. Even in elevated trust, Silverlight still does NOT have full access to a user's file system, which may be required of an intranet business application. Silverlight out of browser applications that run with elevated trust can only access the **MY** folders of a user's computer on Windows and equivalent folders on a Mac. However, Silverlight applications deployed to Windows can make use of COM Interop, which can provide additional access to resources on the client computer. For scenarios requiring direct access to the resources on a user's machine, WPF provides an excellent choice for Windows development.

Windows Presentation Foundation (WPF)

Silverlight has its origins in WPF, due to which many of the same concepts apply to WPF as well. A quick glance at the features of WPF will reveal some familiar names: XAML, Storyboards and Dependency Properties. Developers familiar with Silverlight already have a working knowledge of WPF.

Silverlight and WPF do have some differences, however. Most of these differences stem from WPF having been designed for Windows desktop application development. As a desktop application, a WPF solution will have more access to the local resources on a user's computer.

Some features that WPF has that are missing from Silverlight, (apart from full local resource access) are attached events, which work in much the same way as attached properties. Triggers which can be used to execute code or change states based on events and the `IMultiValueConverter` interface which allows for multiple data bound value conversions where the `IValueConverter` interface only allows for one value conversion.

When to use WPF

WPF has access to the whole .NET Framework and all the resources on a user's machine. However, due to security concerns, Silverlight runs in a 'sandbox' mode, meaning that the Silverlight runtime has certain security restrictions.

Some scenarios where WPF might win over Silverlight would be an application that must read and write files to the local user's hard drive in locations other than the folders available under the profile (**My Documents**, **My Pictures**, and so on) or an application that must interface with hardware such as scanners, cameras, or industrial hardware. If the application needs to be platform independent or available to users outside of the company network, then Silverlight is the obvious choice with a service oriented approach utilizing WCF and RIA services.

Time for action – creating a WPF application

Let's take a look at a WPF application and see how it compares to Silverlight. Most of what we will see in WPF will be familiar after what we have learned with Silverlight.

1. Start Visual Studio and create a new **WPF Application** called **WPFTest**:

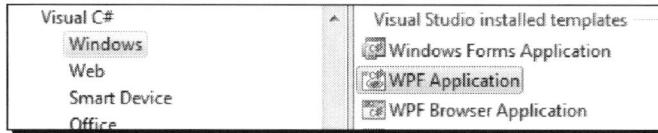

2. Open the `Window1.xaml` file and we can see that the root node of the XAML document is a window, rather than a usercontrol or a page:

```
<Window x:Class="WPFTest.Window1"
    xmlns="http://schemas.microsoft.com/winfx/2006/xaml/
presentation"
    xmlns:x="http://schemas.microsoft.com/winfx/2006/xaml"
    Title="Window1" Height="300" Width="300">
    <Grid>
    </Grid>
</Window>
```

3. Other than the root node, the rest of the XAML is familiar; in fact, if we add a button we can see that the code looks exactly the same:

```
<Button x:Name="myButton" Width="75" Height="24" Content="My
Button"/>
```

4. Build and run the solution and we can see that WPF starts in a regular window rather than requiring a browser for initial launch:

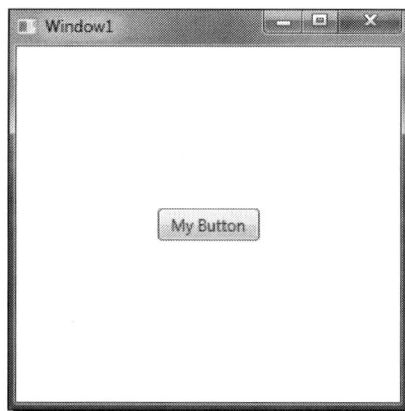

> Some things to note are that while the XAML is similar, WPF has full access to the entire .NET Framework, rather than the subset provided by Silverlight and that WPF is Windows centric and will not run on the Mac OS.

Future of Silverlight

As Rich Internet Applications mature, expect to see more and more desktop-like features being added; we can already see this happening with the addition of printing support in Silverlight, out-of-browser support for disconnected applications, and extended local storage access for trusted applications. With the addition of COM support in Silverlight 4 the step is even closer in a Windows development environment. The rise of cloud computing and cloud-based services will change the landscape of desktop applications as well.

As we move into the future of Silverlight, we will most likely see the merging of Silverlight and WPF into one platform. The ability to share our Silverlight and regular .NET libraries is already a step in that direction.

Summary

In this chapter, we learned how to enable out-of-browser support in Silverlight and how to check for network connectivity to allow our application to be network aware. We created a WPF application and compared Silverlight to WPF. We examined some scenarios where WPF might be more appropriate than Silverlight for business intranet development and took a glimpse into the future of Silverlight and Rich Internet Applications in general.

Through the course of this book we have learned the basics required to build business applications using Silverlight and while every business solution differs, they all deal with data; collecting it, presenting it, and reporting on it in some fashion. We have learned the basic skills to start implementing our next project in Silverlight. We have also gained enough knowledge to be able to present Silverlight as a viable and useful development option to decision makers during the planning of the next project.

Index

DataFields, label text customizing 277
event handler, adding 278
InsertCustomer method, modifying 269
Label property, adding 277
method, creating 268, 269
page, adding 271
RIA Services/Entity errors 271
Silverlight Toolkit, installing 265
System.Linq namespace, adding 267

V

Validation attributes 294
video
adding, to Silverlight project 87-90
encoding 101
VideoBrush
creating 91
using 91
video formats 101
Viewbox container 29
Visibility property 95
Visual State Manager
used, to add visual cues 52-54
VisualTree 46
Volume property 98

W

Waypoint object 368
Waypoints property 368
WCF
Silverlight-enabled service, creating 177-185
wsHttpBinding 181

WCF RIA Services
about 219
and ADO.NET Entity Framework 257-236
installing 221
listbox, styling 236, 237
role in Silverlight 220
WCF Rich Internet Application Services. *See*
       WCF RIA Services
WebGet attribute 176
website
enhancing, Silverlight used 27
Windows Communication Foundation. *See* **WCF**
Windows Forms developers 8
Windows Presentation Foundation. *See* **WPF**
WPF 8
about 388
application, creating 389, 390
uses 388
WPF developers 8
WrapPanel container 29
wsHttpBinding 181

X

XAML 10, 11, 46, 50

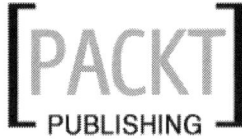

Thank you for buying
Microsoft Silverlight 4 Business
Application Development: Beginners Guide

About Packt Publishing

Packt, pronounced 'packed', published its first book "*Mastering phpMyAdmin for Effective MySQL Management*" in April 2004 and subsequently continued to specialize in publishing highly focused books on specific technologies and solutions.

Our books and publications share the experiences of your fellow IT professionals in adapting and customizing today's systems, applications, and frameworks. Our solution based books give you the knowledge and power to customize the software and technologies you're using to get the job done. Packt books are more specific and less general than the IT books you have seen in the past. Our unique business model allows us to bring you more focused information, giving you more of what you need to know, and less of what you don't.

Packt is a modern, yet unique publishing company, which focuses on producing quality, cutting-edge books for communities of developers, administrators, and newbies alike. For more information, please visit our website: www.packtpub.com.

Writing for Packt

We welcome all inquiries from people who are interested in authoring. Book proposals should be sent to author@packtpub.com. If your book idea is still at an early stage and you would like to discuss it first before writing a formal book proposal, contact us; one of our commissioning editors will get in touch with you.

We're not just looking for published authors; if you have strong technical skills but no writing experience, our experienced editors can help you develop a writing career, or simply get some additional reward for your expertise.

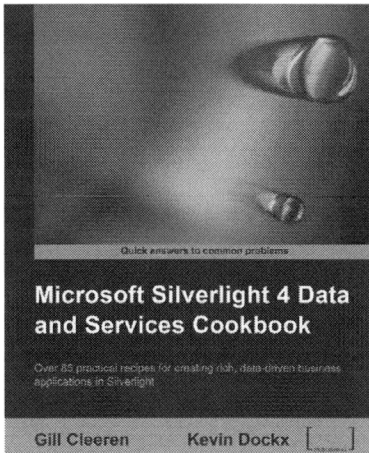

Microsoft Silverlight 4 Data and Services Cookbook

ISBN: 978-1-847199-84-3   Paperback: 385 pages

Over 85 practical recipes for creating rich, data-driven business applications in Silverlight

1. Design and develop rich data-driven business applications in Silverlight

2. Rapidly interact with and handle multiple sources of data and services within Silverlight business applications

3. Understand sophisticated data access techniques in your Silverlight business applications by binding data to Silverlight controls, validating data in Silverlight, getting data from services into Silverlight applications and much more!

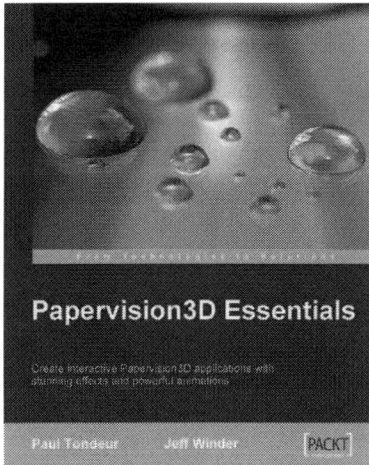

Papervision3D Essentials

ISBN: 978-1-847195-72-2   Paperback: 428 pages

Create interactive Papervision 3D applications with stunning effects and powerful animations

1. Build stunning, interactive Papervision3D applications from scratch

2. Export and import 3D models from Autodesk 3ds Max, SketchUp and Blender to Papervision3D

3. In-depth coverage of important 3D concepts with demo applications, screenshots and example code.

6950465R0

Made in the USA
Lexington, KY
05 October 2010